The South
and
Segregation

The South
and
Segregation

By Peter A. Carmichael

Public Affairs Press, Washington, D. C.

136978

To the memory of my father

ARCHIBALD ALEXANDER CARMICHAEL

PREFACE

What is called the South's side in this book is only by accident a position of the South. It might have been the North's side or the Orient's or that of any land or people, contrasted to a neighboring one. Nature is all the sides there are. An apologia for one of them is no more than an amplified display of it, not an argument or polemic.

One would be very shallow and hardly fitted to confront the world if he had not learned that nature is a hard master and takes pitiless toll of the heedless. If, having incurred the consequences of his ignorance, he pretended that they were no fault of his but were the machinations of other people, that would not be surprising to the informed. Something that would surprise would be the emergence from the informed themselves of a party in sympathy with such a character. If presently this party organized a faith dedicated to the supposition that nature is not nature and that a form of make-believe either rules or should rule over all, it would be time for serious minds to take heed. And if at length this corruption of thought had infected the legal system, eating into its heart, violent and dismaying symptoms could be expected.

All of this is what we see now in the race disturbances. It was precipitated by the Supreme Court's decision against school segregation ten years ago. Precipitated indeed, like a dropped bomb.

If we inquire how that happened, a tale all but incredible unfolds. The Constitution, it is alleged, gave warrant for it. The Constitution, we learn, grows, of itself; or it is something to be molded at the will of the Supreme Court. Moreover, the Court is at liberty to make what it will of the Constitution today, and the opposite tomorrow. If it chooses, it may go outside the law and pick out what it assumes to be evidence to justify its divagations, ignoring contrary evidence and incompetently employing what it selects. In this remarkable aberration it will be casuistically vindicated by law pedagogues in the foremost law schools, who have a copious vocabulary of deceit and who write as if, with them, sophistry and obeisance, not logical depth or critical power, were the wherewithal for comprehending the Constitution and for judging the Court's performance under its oath to support it.

In the presence of this sedition it is not easy for an attentive witness to maintain the attitude of detachment. That, in the circumstances, is rather like the cold indifference of persons today who look upon atrocious crime without turning a hand. Nevertheless, the intent of this book is non-polemical. The palpable realities need no glossing; they in themselves tell far beyond the capacity of partisanship, acrimony, or rage.

For publishing reasons it has been necessary to compress this record to a degree which is somewhat disturbing to its form and connections. Enough remains, however, for the general purpose of laying bare the course of what has happened; what is conclusive can hardly be made more conclusive, and what is already sordid can hardly be kept from becoming more sordid with elaboration. Some exhibits which might more appropriately have gone into the text have been crowded into footnotes.

The inclusion here of much matter taken from copyright sources is possible through the kindness of the authors and copyright-holders. Passages taken from the *American Sociological Review* and the *Antioch Review* are, by their length, conspicuous examples. Clarence O. Amonette, Esq., of Berkeley, California, has generously contributed information on constitutional questions through publications and correspondence, and many other individuals have favored me with other information. For all of this I am grateful.

Baton Rouge, Louisiana   PETER A. CARMICHAEL

CONTENTS

About the Author

Peter A. Carmichael has been a professor of philosophy at Louisiana State University for twenty-seven years. Previously he taught philosophy and psychology in colleges in Virginia, West Virginia, and South Carolina. He has been a contributor to philosophical, educational, and literary periodicals. Before becoming a teacher he was a newspaper writer on papers in Alabama, North Carolina, Virginia, and Maryland.

He has been an arbitrator of industrial disputes in the South during a period of more than twenty years.

He was educated at Johns Hopkins, Columbia, and the University of North Carolina.

Chapter 1

JUDICIAL OBLIQUITY

The dawn of a fairer day for the American Negro, the advent of an era heedless of racial distinctions, is officially with us. It was heralded in May, 1954 by the decision of the United States Supreme Court outlawing racial segregation in public schools. A year afterwards it was advanced by decrees specifying what must be done to enforce the decision. Since then integration has been fighting its way.

Equality, mutuality, good will, hopefully envisioned by integrationists, seldom arrive fighting their way. If fighting is not already outlived and superseded, eirenic visions are only imaginative, belied by the actualities. If fighting is the ultimate policy, held in abeyance pending a critical turn of events, talk about good will and its fruits is as idle as it is deceitful.

In the decade since the Court's decision, we have seen a fighting policy in execution. Communities hitherto peaceful have been torn by dissension and some have been swiftly occupied by military forces with displays of might reminiscent of Nazi invasions, to the dismay of the enlightened world. Criminal violence both upon and by the Negro is frequent. In a few places schools are closed because the courts forbid them to operate without integration, and integration is repugnant to the white residents.

Tension, uneasiness, and bitterness on this scale do not arise from nothing. Yet there is a disposition on the part of some—integrationists —to believe that all the trouble is factitious. They suppose that racial segregation has no natural cause or justification. They think that perversity in the white man explains it.

Respect for facts, enlightened by a disposition of reasonableness (without which it is useless to argue anything), can hardly fail to recognize that the country acted precipitately or prematurely on segregation, or that the Supreme Court did so. For suddenly there was a reversal of law, tradition, and custom, not as the outcome of natural processes of orientation and development, nor by way of legislation, but by the mandate of a court. This, to those it affected most, was revolutionary. It meant, to them, not only the disruption of social codes and practices, founded, as we shall see, on natural origins and dispositions, natural affinities and aversions; worse than that—worse

1

to the sentiments of loyalty and confidence—it meant betrayal of the Constitution and subversion of the judicial office. The charge nowadays that the South is defying the law by not integrating its schools is hardly noticed in the South, much of which is convinced that the Supreme Court defied the law itself, that its decision is thoroughly unconstitutional, and that a genuine respect for law justifies, even dictates, resort to every remaining legal safeguard before submitting to the Court's mandate.

In the mandate there is a patent ground for question. The mandate calls for piecemeal integration, a little here, more there, without a stated term for its full accomplishment anywhere. Thus in one community or school there may be prompt action, in another practically none. Yet this is ostensibly a matter of constitutional right, the right of equal protection of the laws. The Court turns it into unequal protection.

Moreover, the Court had repeatedly affirmed the constitutionality of school segregation before the 1954 decision.[1] The same Congress that wrote the Fourteenth Amendment and submitted it to the states for ratification enacted a measure providing for school segregation in the District of Columbia, and segregation was perpetuated there by subsequent congressional acts.[2] That school segregation was lawful— duly approved by Congress and by states and sustained by the Supreme Court—is therefore beyond question. Accordingly, the 1954 decision must have been not just a judicial decision but a lawmaking act; either a modification of the Constitution or a radically new enactment for its enforcement. In the first instance it must have usurped the powers of the states, which alone can amend the Constitution; in the other, it must have usurped the powers of Congress, which alone, under the Constitution, can enact Federal laws. That the present Court, under these circumstances, should have incurred the censure and distrust now so familiar can hardly cause surprise.

If we look into details, the enormity of what has happened is astonishing. The Court declared in the leading segregation case, *Brown* v. *Board of Education of Topeka:* "Separate educational facilities are inherently unequal."[3] If we take this literally, it makes schooling practically impossible within the law. Separate schools, courses, teachers; separate textbooks, maps, yardsticks, though all of the same make or authorship, will be unequal and therefore unconstitutional. The separation *per se,* or *inherently,* makes them unequal. To be equal, they must merge.

Now this is a presumption against universal reason. It would practically destroy mathematics and all its applications in science and the world's work, by taking away the meaning of "equal," namely, "exactly as much as," "neither more nor less than." No separate things could be equal. The only thing that anything could equal would be itself.

The law, the courts, and the civilized world depend on the fixed, universal sense of "equal" in countless affairs. Let anyone try altering it, let him maintain that two magnitudes interchangeable without remainder are not equal, or that two magnitudes not so interchangeable are equal; that, for example, $1 + 1$ does not equal 2, or that $1 + .1$ does equal 2. The whole scale of the world will collapse around him. He is submitted to the reality denominated by the term, not vice versa. The Supreme Court is of course no exception. It is powerless to impose on "equal" any meaning contrary to the universal, axiomatic one —it is bound by oath to support the Constitution, which is to say adhere to the meaning of its terms.

In fact, graduates of Negro schools may and often do pass to colleges and universities on the same terms as graduates of white schools. So it is literally untrue, judging by education's own standards and practices, that *separate* means *inherently unequal*, in education; so far, then, as the Court's decision rests on that premise, it rests on falsity. Nothing in the decision or in the decrees for enforcing it arising from that ground, can be rationally defended since sheer falsity is not a demonstrative ground.

Did the Court mean only that separate facilities were inherently unequal when white pupils were in one set and Negro pupils in another? That is too absurd—axioms of thought are independent of race. Then was it in truth "equal" that the Court was talking about, and hence was the decision really a decision about equal protection of the laws? And if it was not (as seems obvious), was the Court outrageously distorting the term "equal" in order to read into the Constitution something foreign to it, such as compulsory integration?

The Court admits that facilities in some Negro schools were equal to those of white schools, but finds one thing lacking: white association. Without the presence of white pupils, the Negro pupils did not have, in the Court's judgment, as good opportunity as the white pupils; which means, the Court says, that they did not have equal facilities. But this must mean that white pupils are *facilities*—facilities, at the state's disposal, for the education of Negro pupils; and that the state cannot provide schools for Negroes without providing white pupils as facilities.

It may be doubted that anything so extraordinary and so repugnant to a free mind has ever before issued from an American court of justice. This one obliquity, unnoticed in the agitation that has followed the decision, is enough, I dare say, to drive impartial minds to distrust not only the Court but the press, pulpit, and other media through which the decision is constantly defended. It is no excuse that these agencies are, perhaps, unaware that they are defending such a perversity. Unless they know what they are about, they convict themselves of irresponsibility, to say the least.

A host of other obliquities is to be seen in this decision and the accompanying decision in *Bolling* v. *Sharpe*,[4] a case concerning segregation in the public schools of the District of Columbia. Witness:

Usurping legislative powers of Congress and the states. All legislative powers conferred by the Constitution are vested in Congress, and all other legislative powers are reserved to the states by the Constitution. Had the constitutionality of segregation laws never been judicially proven or acknowledged, it is conceivable that the Supreme Court might have constitutionally annulled them, under its assumed review power. But having been declared constitutional by the Court, segregation had in it the authority of the law of the land. Thereafter only a change in the law of the land could have made it unlawful. Law of course cannot change itself. The Supreme Court may officially declare it, but the officiality and finality of its act (like that of a jury's verdict or a voter's vote), as well as the univocal character of the law once declared, precludes a subsequent reversal by the Court of its declaration, or decision. Only a reversal of the law of the land can then warrant a reversal of the decision. But only the states and Congress can change the law of the land. In presuming to change—reverse—it in *Brown,* the Supreme Court usurped powers of the states and Congress, in violation of the Constitution.

Invoking an impossible educational standard. The Court takes for granted the idea that separate schools are unequal in respect of "qualities which are incapable of objective measurement."[5] But qualities which are incapable of objective measurement are of course incapable of being truly or substantially found to be either equal or unequal, and so must fall outside the equal-protection guarantee. They can only be liked, disliked, tolerated, not tolerated, and so on, according to personal disposition. The Constitution is impersonal.

Illogically reasoning that since (according to its ruling) a state cannot lawfully deny integrated public schooling, it cannot lawfully permit unintegrated schooling.[6] As well reason that since no state can lawfully forbid people to worship, none can lawfully permit them not to worship. This illogicality opens the way, of course illicitly, for the Court to prohibit segregation in private schools. Already, however,

it has recoiled from that, in the Girard College case.[7] Thus it is
nullifying its own ruling. To derive from the equal-protection clause
a prohibition upon the *permission* of segregated schools, there must
be in that clause some general provision inclusive of the prohibition,
since no particularization of it is found there. That, were it there,
would require that the prohibition apply to inequality wherever equal
protection applies, which is wherever state law applies. Now of course
state law applies in economic affairs—to ownership and income, for
example; hence the permission of economic inequality must be unconstitutional. Or if not, the Court's ruling on permission is grievously
mistaken. Little wonder then that the Girard College compromise
should have occurred, though it is tantamount to a reversal of the
ruling here.

Extending the decision beyond intrinsically imposed limits. The
grounds given by the Court for ordering integration are limited, applying only to pupils "of similar age and qualifications."[8] The decision
is not so limited, applying to all indifferently. In so far as it is thus
made to apply to pupils of different ages and qualifications, it is therefore groundless. And if age and qualifications are the real, lawful
determiners, the proposition "Separate educational facilities are inherently unequal" is clearly untenable, inasmuch as it precludes limitation by age, aptitude, or anything else.

Distorting the protection of law. The decision regards, primarily,
not the provisions of law but their (alleged) effects. It admits that
equal provisions had been made in some cases, but thinks the effects
were unequal—it asserts that segregation "generates [in Negro pupils]
a feeling of inferiority as to their status in the community."[9] The
Court's premise must then be that wherever inferiority feelings occur,
under the eye of the law, equal protection is denied. If so, then countless persons, in all walks, are denied equal protection—underlings of
all sorts, the penniless, friendless, homeless, rejected. Or if such cases
are not to be outlawed, then it is special privilege, hence discriminatory, and hence a violation itself of equal protection, to single out
Negro school pupils for consideration and advantage. It is a radical
departure to make the law's effects, whether proven or only putative,
a test of equal protection. It presumes that equal protection of the
laws means not equal public provisions equally applied, but equaliza-
ation of life, even down to the feelings of children of different races.
This is communism to the utmost degree.

On this conception law is turned upside down. Lawmaking is
virtually transferred from the lawmaker to some uncertain element of
the public, whose feeling of inferiority to some other element is now

to govern. Law, which is by nature regulative, not contingent or fortuitous, gives place to nihilism under this, since not even the wisest legislator can foretell whether some element will feel inferior to some other when a law applies to it.

Stultifying the law. If the measure of the law's protection is not in the provisions or apportionments the law makes, but in the effects of them; if what counts is not what the state provides but what the recipients make of it, then equal protection is stultified. For if the results to one person surpass those to another (which is practically certain to happen), then the other person has been denied equal protection, under the Court's standard. And if anyone develops a superiority feeling, it will mean unequal protection the same as if it were inferiority feeling, since *superior* and *inferior* alike signify *unequal.* In the event, which is very likely, that no reliable method of measuring the results is available, there is no way of determining whether equal protection has been denied, and the ground of the Court's decision vanishes. Thus equal protection, a constitutional right of all, is so transformed by the Court that it becomes practically impossible in education.

Depriving of constitutional rights. It is a right of every American, implicit in the prohibitions and reservations of the Bill of Rights, to refuse personal associations which he finds objectionable, and it is a prerogative of Congress and the states to protect this right by appropriate legislation. The right is extinguished when the Supreme Court coerces white pupils into association with Negroes or vice versa. When the Court makes white pupils *facilities to* Negroes, against their will, it is manifestly committing them to involuntary servitude in violation of the Thirteenth Amendment.

Misreading or neglecting to read "authorities." The decision is not founded on law, since there is no applicable law saying that separate schools are unequal (just the opposite, that they are equal, is declared in some Federal laws[10]). The Court went outside the law to "modern authority" in psychology and sociology for what it offers as grounds for the decision. But in fact the decision is by no means conclusively supported there. What the Court cites is a miscellany of studies and opinions, which, however, it certainly cannot have read with care and comprehension (not long before, it had acknowledged that it was not competent to pass judgment on such writings[11]); for it neglects to take account of abundant cautions in them that findings in this field are inconclusive and that the field is handicapped by admitted lack of demonstrative methods. Some of the citations are avowedly polemical and at least one is scornful of scientific objectivity (which alone could give the reliability the Court presumably thought it could count on here). Moreover, psychology and sociology themselves are without much scientific status, in spite of the fact that both have been distinguished by individuals of high attainments. One of the Court's citations is a collection of opinions solicited by a partisan society and consisting mainly of what, had their authors been subjected to cross-examination in court, would very probably have been dismissed as hearsay. One or two others are casual items of no bearing, or of only polemical bearing. Altogether, this is an exhibit which if offered to bona fide scientists as a piece of science, would undoubtedly be rejected.

Ignoring evidence. A court of justice is the highest reposal of a people's trust in law and government. When the Supreme Court turned from the law and ventured into fields which it had confessed itself incompetent to judge, and drew from them what it offers as support for the school decision, it brought discredit to the judicial office. Of course it can independently consult and utilize legally pertinent knowledge from outside the law; but only what is common knowledge, since judges are not competent in specialties beyond the pale of law. That its confession of incompetence was not an affectation of modesty is well evidenced by its performance on this venture. One of the requisites of creditable research, one that must be satisfied before a conclusion of any generality can be asserted, is comprehensiveness. The investigator, who must be qualified to recognize what is relevant, cannot shirk or slur over anything adverse to any thesis he may wish to advance. He must faithfully avoid one-sidedness. The Court's performance is a failure, even a grotesque failure, under both of these standards. An immense amount of relevant evidence exists, though one would never know this from the scanty, not wholly unbiased citations the Court gives. A great part of it, like much found in the citations themselves, is antithetical to the Court's "finding," but the Court either did not know that or else was content to disregard it. In a university or research institute of standing, a piece of work such as the Court did on the writings of "modern authority" it invokes would guarantee the failure and rejection of its author.

Misjudging a lower court's "finding." One of the school-segregation cases arose in Kansas, where a Federal district court held, or intimated, that segregation engenders a sense of inferiority—"is usually interpreted as denoting . . . inferiority"—in Negro pupils, and went on to say that this "affects the motivation . . . to learn," that it "has a tendency to retard [their] educational and mental development" and also "to deprive them of some of the benefits they would receive

in a racially integrated school system."[12] The Supreme Court calls
this a finding. That is a somewhat ambiguous term, but not as the
Court uses it here. Undoubtedly the Court means *finding of fact*. I
venture to say that any informed and thoughtful person who reads
the record of the case will be surprised to see that the evidence could
have been judged to establish such fact. There was no testimony that
the Negro children for whom the suit was brought had either unequal
provisions or inferiority feeling. Witnesses in their behalf were mostly
college and university teachers from outside—Missouri, Michigan,
Indiana, Ohio. None testified anything that could reasonably be
thought to prove that school segregation induces inferiority feeling
or retardation of learning. One of them, from Missouri, opined, "if
the colored children are denied the experience in school of associating
with white children . . . then the colored child's curriculum is being
greatly curtailed,"[13] though he admitted that the course of study in
the Negro schools directly concerned in the case was about equal to
that of the white schools (the court said it was equal). Another
witness, from Ohio, being asked whether he had made a survey to
determine what relation, if any, school segregation bore to the success
or failure of Negro graduates, replied that he had not. Asked whether
there was any scientific evidence to support an opinion of his that
part of a child's education is on the playground and that Negro pupils
are deprived if they are not free to play with white pupils, he replied
that such evidence would be hard to find.[14] An Indiana witness gave
the opinion that in segregated schools "you have a day-after-day
accumulation of attitudes that the Negro child is inferior because
segregation is differentiation and distinction,"[15] but he gave no supporting data. As persons versed in the criteria and procedures of
science are well aware, nothing could be concluded scientifically from
testimony such as this. But the district court, with nothing more
substantial to support it, ventured to declare categorically (though
with sophistical phraseology such as "is usually interpreted as" and
"has a tendency to") that segregation causes inferiority feeling in
Negro pupils and that that causes educational retardation. And the
Supreme Court took this as a *finding* of *fact!* In contrast to the
Kansas "finding," the following, which the Supreme Court, for reasons
not apparent, did not take to be a finding (or if it did, chose to disregard it), will doubtless be impressive to fair minds. It is from the
Virginia segregation case, which the Court lumped with the Kansas
and other cases.

"Eminent educators, anthropologists, psychologists and psychiatrists
appeared for the plaintiffs, unanimously expressed dispraise of segre-

gation in schools, and unequivocally testified the opinion that such separation distorted the child's natural attitude, throttled his mental development, especially the adolescent, and immeasurably abridged his educational opportunities. For the defendants equally distinguished and qualified educationists and leaders in the other fields emphatically vouched the view that, given equal physical facilities, offerings and instruction, the Negro would receive in a separate school the same educational opportunity as he would obtain in the classroom and on the campus of a mixed school. Each witness offered cogent and appealing grounds for his conclusion.

"On this fact issue the Court cannot say that the plaintiffs' evidence overbalances the defendants'."[16]

Textual carelessness. The Kansas court took occasion to refer to the renowned case of *Gong Lum* v. *Rice,* in which the Supreme Court, by a unanimous decision, upheld school segregation in Mississippi in 1927. Gong Lum, according to the Kansas court, was a Chinese pupil who wanted to attend a white school in Mississippi but was excluded and required to attend a Negro school. Not so. He was a grown man. The suit, though in his name, was in behalf of his daughter, who was the pupil concerned. A small matter, perhaps. Nevertheless, the Supreme Court, in referring to it, might be expected to be accurate. Instead, it, too, confused the Chinaman with his daughter.[17] Consider, too, this infelicitous period, from the Court's opinion in another of the segregation cases: "The 'equal protection of the laws' is a more explicit safeguard of prohibited unfairness than 'due process of law' . . ."[18] "Safeguard of prohibited unfairness"! Carelessness, crudity of thought and language hardly comport with the dignity and competence of a court of justice, least of all with the highest court in the land. They fit well, however, with the quality of thought and judgment evidenced by that court in the school-segregation cases, as will be seen in subsequent chapters.[19]

Sophistically distorting precedent. The Court says that in *Gong Lum* "the validity of the [separate-but-equal] doctrine itself was not challenged."[20] Compare the following from the *Gong Lum* opinion itself: "The case then reduces itself to the question whether a state can be said to afford to a child of Chinese ancestry born in this country, and a citizen of the United States, equal protection of the laws by giving him the opportunity for a common school education in a school which receives only colored children of the brown, yellow or black races."[21] Not the slightest factual difference, touching racial segregation, appears between the issue in this case and that in the Brown case. In each there were separate schools, white and colored; in each the petition was for admission of a colored person or persons to a white school. In *Gong Lum* the Supreme Court ruling was that segregation is not a denial of equal protection, so long as equal facilities are provided—a ruling which could only be the answer to such a question as, Does racial segregation *per se* in public schools constitute a denial of equal protection? But in *Brown* v. *Board of Education* the Court said: "We come then to the question presented: Does segregation of children in the public schools solely on the basis of race, even though the physical facilities and other 'tangible' factors may be equal, deprive the children of the minority group of equal educational opportunities?"[22] Here the Court resorts to two considerations which are absent from *Gong Lum:* (a) "intangibles," (b) minority group status. They are considerations which are also absent from the United States Constitution. Intangibles are not measurable and so are not capable of inclusion under *equal* protection; and the equal-protection guarantee is a guarantee to persons, not groups, whether minority or other.

With intangibles as a ground, not only is equal—demonstrably equal—protection put beyond realization, but law itself is eclipsed. The judges' temper, sentiment, volition determine. A decision is not then a judicial decision, not a resultant of law, fact, and logic. It is an expression of sympathy or antipathy, of mere personal disposition, like an expression of preference for, say, sweet over savory, or blue over red.[23] Equal protection is as different from this as a pair of laboratory balances is different from the sentiments of the person using them.

In *Gong Lum* the Court cited some fifteen decisions upholding racial segregation in schools and found the issue in it no different from the issue in them; and it unanimously concluded that segregation was within the discretion of states and not contrary to the Constitution. To say, as the Court now does in *Brown*, that the question of the legality of segregated schools was not judged in *Gong Lum,* is only to say that it was not judged in the manner that *Brown* was: not judged on the sophistical grounds that appeared only with the illicit mutation and expansion of the constitutional term "equal" wrought by the Court in *Brown*. Truly, in the previous cases it was hardly a matter of *judging* equality— of a *court* venturing to prescribe to *thought* the meaning of "equal," an enormity comparable to decreeing at an end the axiom, "Equals applied to equals give equals." Courts cannot judge axioms of thought. They necessarily presuppose them; otherwise they could reach no rational decisions. It is not in their purview to pronounce to the faculty of reason, telling it that separate things cannot be equal. To the contrary, they, like all rational minds, are bound to the very opposite of that, and are no more called to justify it than to justify two plus two equals four.[24]

Not truly adjudicating the issue. Just as the Court biased the evidence in its venture into psycho-sociological study, so it did the equal-protection question before it. If you can maneuver matters to a point where one thing is seen to be, or made to appear, inferior to another, of course you have inequality. But is it inequality such as the equal-protection guarantee prohibits? Is unequal feeling outlawed by that guarantee? If it is unlawful in Negro school children, can it be lawful in adult Negro school janitors, or in white ones, or in servants and toilers of any other description? How could the Court, without flagrant bias or betrayal of its trust, bring the law—literally subvert it—to the level of singling out one class for favor? How could it assume the principle of this decision—the outlawing of inferiority feeling under state sanctions—without applying it thereafter to all other classes? And if it did that, what would become of the Constitution and the institutions erected under its protection?

Forthwith abrogating the principle of its decision. After the school-segregation decision a suit was brought against Girard College in Philadelphia, a privately endowed, municipally directed school for white orphans, to compel it to open to Negroes. At length the school won the decision in the Pennsylvania Supreme Court. On appeal to the United States Supreme Court the decision was reversed and the case was remanded for further consideration. Then a lower court replaced the municipal directors of the school with a private board of trustees, which it appointed. This change leaving the school still segregated, was upheld by the Pennsylvania Supreme Court. Appealed to the United States Supreme Court, it was upheld there also.[25]

The Court has upheld "on its face" an Alabama pupil-placement law which establishes numerous criteria to guide school boards in deciding placements, such as: educational qualifications of the pupil, his home environment, health, morals, conduct, effect of his admission on himself and other pupils and on the curriculum, and effects on the community, such as ill will and economic retaliation.[26]

How are these decisions to be reconciled with the doctrine, "Separate educational facilities are inherently unequal"? In the Pennsylvania case the state is still a party, since one of its agencies appoints the trustees, who keep the school segregated in conformity with the will of its founder. Under the Alabama law a high degree of segregation is practically assured. Since the "inherently unequal" doctrine makes all school segregation through state action a violation of the equal-protection right, it is clear that the Court has abrogated its own doctrine. That means a double standard, hence discrimination against the appellees in the 1954 cases, and hence a violation, by the Court, of equal protection.

If there are conditions to equal protection, then it cannot be correctly represented in unconditional, absolute terms: nothing then can be *inherently* a case of unequal protection. To allow, as the Supreme Court now does, that a testator can will school segregation without violating the equal-protection right, is to acknowledge that that right is circumscribed, or conditioned, and hence that school segregation under state auspices is not unconditionally, *inherently,* a denial of the right.

Repudiating its predecessors. If *separate* necessarily means *unequal,* or if racially separate schools are as a matter of fact always unequal, within the meaning of "equal" in the equal-protection clause, then the authors and ratifiers of the clause must be presumed to have been cognizant of it. To suppose not would be a gross disrespect to their intelligence. To suppose they meant nothing determinate, or nothing that could be determined until psychologists and sociologists nearly a century later had spoken, would be an affront to our intelligence. Not to suppose that their official, repeated, and uncontested acts, as in legislating school segregation for the District of Columbia and for many states, conformed with the intent of the clause would be a gross presumption against their integrity. Not to suppose that the Supreme Court in judging school-segregation questions in the past was cognizant of the meaning and competent to declare it, is discrediting to the Court *per se.* Thus in repudiating its past acts the Court today discredits itself; and this not only justifies the partisan criticisms of the Court, now very familiar, but seriously damages its prestige in the eyes of the non-partisan. A corresponding loss in its capacity to preside over the administration of justice is involved, since without confidence in the organs of justice there is little confidence in the realization of justice itself.

Betraying the trust implicit in the judicial office. Justice, one of the fairest and loftiest objects of thought, is to a degree exemplified in the integrity of laws. Justice favors no system, monarchic, democratic, or other, as science favors no data, and art and philosophy no school. A law or system of law may reflect deep insight into our make and destiny or may be only an opportunistic compact of convenience. In any event it is the public policy, the aim and dedication of the state. Administration of it by courts presupposes in them absolute integrity: clear, discerning understanding to see what the law is; scrupulous respect for the law; constancy in applying it. Judges are minions of the law, as well as its ministers. They cannot modify the established meaning of constitutional terms on the ground that times have changed—*constitutional* times change only with constitutional amendment, with which the judges have nothing to do. In the school cases the Supreme Court boldly declared that it would not go back to 1868, when the equal-protection guarantee was incorporated in the Constitution, or to 1896, when segregation was expressly upheld by the Court. It would not abide by the meanings then established or wait for the proper authority, the states, to amend them by due constitutional procedure, if they so chose. Instead, it went outside the law, to controvertible, inconclusive, psycho-sociological writings as authority for its decision. A Cabinet officer or a general who took it upon himself to act in this manner would be cashiered; a President or Senator would be repudiated and perhaps impeached.

Degrading the judicial office. A supreme court of justice is not solely an organ for proving the claims of litigants, though it is chiefly that. In our system it is in practice the oracle and mainstay of the Constitution. Of those who execute the law, from the President and Cabinet down, it is customary to expect exemplary character and conduct. Even more is expected of the judiciary, and of the supreme bench especially. While most others are answerable politically, it, provided it maintains a decent respect for the morals of the day, is answerable not at all. Supreme, it is with us the ultimate of the law's light and integrity; not a means to an end, but the end; the unmoved mover, *integer vitae.* Men who cannot divest themselves of partisan dispositions, who cannot submit to fact, reason, and the law, cannot in truth qualify for the office, and if by chance they get in, not only is the office degraded but the majesty of law and with it the honor of those who have established and sustained it is betrayed. Judges can never dissemble nor repudiate their word through sophistry or otherwise, least of all through "reversal" of the law of the land, without betraying their office, their trust, and their country. A lying witness is discredited; a faithless judge, exposed, is more discredited; he betrays and dishonors not only his office but the state itself and integrity itself. If he is inflamed with zeal for or against a litigated cause, every degree of his heat counts not just against one party but against justice and the law. Jurors are disqualified for anything that intimates they are not neutral and detached. Suppose the justices of the Supreme Court had been answerable to the same requirements as ordinary jurors, how many of them, now that the obliquities of their

decision are apparent, would have qualified to sit in the school segregation cases?

Biasing the public judgment. Outside the bar, few persons take
the trouble of following the Supreme Court's decisions and tendencies, thanks to the general complacency and security of American life
and, heretofore, to our confidence in the Court. Regardless of his
reasons, anyone who demurs to a decision of much public concern is
likely to be suspected of defiance or disloyalty. When the import of
the school segregation decisions reached home, the white people it
affected most were profoundly disturbed, since it contradicted and
promised to nullify not only the law of centuries but the whole educational and social establishment fostered by the law. Between surrendering to this prospect and continuing in the habit of unwavering
trust in the Court, what could the South be expected to do? How little acquainted with the South those critics are who expected or rather
demanded integration forthwith may be seen in the fact that they
took integration to be only a matter of adjustment.[27] When the adjustment did not come, they could think of only one reason: defiance
of the Court, disrespect for law. No thought of inconstancy on the
Court's part, and of course no thought that the Court, resting on
what we have seen to be not law but demonstrable falsity, should
itself have nullified the law of the land and presumed to enact its
opposite. Not the Court, however, but the South received the blame,
and not simply blame but condemnation and excoriation. It was
"defiant" not only of the Court and the law but even of "morals."
Presently the South was in the position of one having no justification; everything it did or failed to do concerning integration was
condemned as violation of the law, though I believe no indictments
were returned, as would have been proper if violations had in fact
occurred. Having been betrayed by a decision founded on falsity,
the South was thereafter expected to ally itself with the betrayers
and faithfully uphold betrayal as the law of the land. You break the
rules and expect me not only to submit but to uphold you in your
perfidy, on pain of being made the culprit myself. Americans as well
as the Greeks, and in fact all ages, have words for this, but I will
leave them to the reader's meditation.[28]

Inducing false beliefs, false hopes, and lawbreaking. The school
decision led the uninformed and unreasoning among integrationists
to think that now everything was miraculously reversed not just in a
courtroom but in the facts of racial life: *Negro* was no more, all
racial lines were obliterated, the dream that black had turned to
white was now about to come true. If white people thought other-

wise, they might be officially lectured or stigmatized. Item: " . . . injustices flow from official and private racial discrimination. The troubles we see now, agitation and even bloodshed, will not compare to what we will see a decade from now unless real progress is made." —Attorney General Kennedy.[29]

Is it supposed that segregation arose from chance, accident, nothing, and hence that nothing—nothing more than words from Washington—should be needed to end it? But in that case why is it predicted that racial matters will get worse, notwithstanding the almost constant stream of words from Washington (including those of the Supreme Court)? From what should the worsening arise? It would be trifling to say from mere obstinacy—obstinacy about *nothing*. Effects do not rise higher than their source.

Here in a casual Washington aside is epitomized the whole affair of segregation. The uninformed and unperceiving, and those unwilling to see, completely misjudge the question. There are profound racial reasons for segregation, unknown to them yet deeply embedded in the South's history and in other history and showing in the North, even in two-year-old children. Abraham Lincoln, to whom the present tactics in Washington and the willful self-deception of integrationists in general would have been intolerable (since he was a thinking, forthright man), had no illusion about race. "Disgust" was his term for the feeling induced in white people by [also his term] "niggers."

The Washington-induced illusion that *Negro* is no more, at length makes bold to clash with the realities, and the spectacle that took place at Birmingham in 1963 is a result. That city, said the Associated Press on May 11, had been "kept virtually under siege since April 3"—under siege by organized bands of Negroes who marched in the streets for the purpose of gaining attention by defying the law, something which would quickly have got them jailed in, for example, Washington, D.C. In this they had the indulgence of Washington. Item: Washington sent agents to Birmingham to lobby for the Negroes (when Washington fears that it would be impolitic to send soldiers or marshals, it sends race lobbyists). Item: White people marched, or simply congregated, at Oxford, Mississippi a while before this, and Washington sent twenty-odd thousand soldiers and spent above five million dollars. Item: At Oxford, Washington caused the arrest of General Edwin A. Walker on a charge of inciting to riot, of which charge he was afterwards acquitted in a Federal court. Item: At Birmingham, systematic law-breaking—marching in the streets in defiance of a city ordinance—was directed by a Negro pastor, Martin Luther King, Jr., who not only was not touched by any Federal hand but was the beneficiary of solicitude on the part of the President.[30] Just before, this privileged favorite had announced his intention of violating the law. He said that if he thought a law was wrong, he was justified in violating it.[31] With the President's blessing, he no doubt felt confirmed in this pretense of superiority to the law. And if he had any doubts on points of law, he must have been entirely relieved when, at a lull in the subsequent violations, the Attorney General, volunteering his views, could find nothing to say against them except that "the timing" was questionable (because, possibly, impolitic) ![32]

Here was not merely a case of sympathy for the underdog. It was a case of Federal authority giving support to insurrection. To white people it would have been sternly said that they must rely on lawful, peaceful means to attain their aspirations. To Negroes it was said, silently but unmistakably, that lawbreaking is fair means to that end. This is a breakdown of government at Washington. The immediate motive for it is in the breakdown of respect for law, fact, and reason in the 1954 Supreme Court decision on school segregation.

Such is the insidiousness of this perfidy that, in the name of law, it assumes gospel character and the Court is exalted to the position of a supreme lawgiver. One may read: "The segregation cases reaffirm the fact that judges do make and unmake law," and we are invited to contemplate the Supreme Court "facing up to its lawmaking function."[33] Whence, we may ask, does the Supreme Court derive "its lawmaking function"? Not, of course, from the Constitution, which vests in Congress all the lawmaking power, and not from Congress, which has no authority to delegate such power. A writer in the *Yale Law Journal* remarks, "it is a 'childish fiction' that judges do not legislate."[34] Indeed. And an adult fiction that, in our system, they have any right to legislate. So their legislation must be *per se* invalid.[35] The pity is that writers in this department of learning are so obsequious towards the Court or so devoted to the integrationist cause, or they are so deficient in logical apprehension, that they see nothing questionable in such obliquity and suspect no danger to the integrity of government or the rights of citizens.

Congress is blamed for not legislating integration; and integrationist writers presume that the Supreme Court must be justified in legislating where Congress would not.[36] What is this but disrespect for law on their part? If things don't go to suit their side, are they justified in advocating usurpation of power, subversion of the Constitution, in order to bring them about? Perhaps no one would explicitly defend such a position, and perhaps those who are in it have closed their eyes to its full character. Critically regarded, it is not much different from the position, or the ethics, of the sophist or swindler, who, having got what he wanted, feelingly argues the lawfulness of sophistry and swindling, speciously disguised by him as the moving spirit of the age. In the case of the integration apologist the disguise is so heavy that perhaps few who wear it have yet seen through it. Consider: None of the obliquities of the Court's decision are acknowledged, though now they are obtrusively apparent; persons who object to them are accused of defying the Constitution, even though standing on constitutional grounds which the Court itself, till now, has stood on; nothing is admitted, less still is it sought out, towards explaining the position of the South; even the annulment of the constitutional right of trial by jury, "the only anchor," said Jefferson, "by which a government can be held to the principles of its constitution,"[37] is recurrently proposed in civil rights bills as a quick way of securing integration; the strategy of drowning out the opposition with allegation, vituperation, condemnation, behind which the integrationist's designs and concealments are kept from sight, is practiced—recalling the practice we attribute to Russia and Nazi Germany, of projecting vices of their own upon their intended victims by means of propaganda broadsides, in preparation for conquest of them.

It is not only deceivers and sycophants who fall to this lure. The late Justice Cardozo, a man of learning and highest judicial repute, remarked, ". . . courts sometimes exercise the privilege of overruling their own decisions."[38] Privilege? In constitutional questions this would mean the privilege of unmaking the duly determined law of the land. Surely there is a grave misconception here.[39]

The fact that the Court has to decide implies no privilege to go back and annul what it has already decided to be the law of the land (which only a constitutional amendment or act of Congress can then change, lawfully). Who but the lawbreaker would care to leave to the judges' "privilege" the fate of the already proven law? For the law-abiding conform with that law, under guidance, if need be, of legal counsel, who, too, has no choice but to conform.

One may divine, in this charged atmosphere, the presumption that the Supreme Court, to keep alive, actually could not be self-consistent: that would be "blindly or ambiguously adhering to outmoded precedent."[40] A further presumption is evident, expressible thus: Having made the precedent, the Court is free to unmake it. Evanescent jurisprudence, as this might be called, could learn a profitable lesson in the demi-legal quarter of private arbitration. For a generation or more the arbitration of issues between employers and unions and between employers themselves has gone on, and a large body of awards, prefixed by copious arbitral "opinions," exists.[41] Finely legalized contracts between employers and unions are found in all lines of industry. A typical provision is one forbidding arbitrators to add to, take from, or in any way modify the contract. Doubtless this did not come from nothing, but from a taste of arbitrator-made law. Today, if not always in the past, an arbitrator of standing would scorn to take liberties with a contract or to substitute his judgment for the discretion of either party. He does not aspire to remodel industry or to reform employers or unions. If he tried that, he would soon have no more cases. If he colored his awards with polemics or tried to justify them with sophisms, he would be laughed at, or worse. If he resorted to subterfuge, falsity, or irresponsibility to justify the arrogation to himself of powers over the parties or their contract, he would be deposed forthwith and perhaps he would also be prosecuted. His job is as cool and objective as an analytical chemist's. He is not deluded into thinking he can insinuate his predilections into his decisions under guise of adapting to the times. He does not forget that the parties are free and able to re-write their contract at pleasure, or that the one they have written is the only one before him. Obviously, judges who have forsaken the corresponding limitations of the Constitution, and the volunteer apologists who defend and applaud them for doing so, could find edification here.

If, truly, the Supreme Court makes law, then either it must follow it itself or else it is not really law. The first alternative precludes the privilege claimed by Justice Cardozo, while the second is a reduction to absurdity. A remarkable conception of law, coming from an eminent Supreme Court justice. It needs no arguing to see that this makes the Court an oligarchy. Justice Frankfurter said the Court's powers are "inherently oligarchic."[42] Justice Stone said "the only check upon our own [the Supreme Court judges'] exercise of power is our own sense of self-restraint."[43]

The same Justice Cardozo wrote: "[The judge's] duty to declare the law in accordance with reason and justice is seen to be a phase of his duty to declare it in accordance with custom. It is the customary morality of right-minded men and women which he is to enforce by his decree."[44] Reason and justice subordinated to custom? Who are the "right-minded"? How are their ways to be judicially ascertained, and by what warrant shall they be instituted over the law?

If we deliberately sought a standard for securing the maximum of disagreement among judges, and the maximum of uncertainty—virtual lawlessness—to all who come under their decrees, it would be hard to beat this. Custom having changed more or less in a given jurisdiction, the law, though unchanged on the books, is to be changed accordingly, by the judges; changed, moreover, to fit the supposed morality of "right-minded" people. As if these alone, in our system, are to be represented! As if the duly elected representatives of the public were elected for nothing! Since the "right-minded" are not identified (one might cynically suppose them to be Republicans), and since their "right-mindedness" is not defined, it is a fair surmise that the judge will take his own disposition as the standard of right-mindedness and custom, and forthwith legislate it to the people.

Thus we have the apotheosis of "judicial legislation," and the antithesis of the American system. A judge who presumes "to declare the law in accordance with custom" has signally failed to comprehend the judicial office. It cannot be *the law* that he would thus declare—that would be like declaring the truth or the Ten Commandments "in accordance with custom." Suppose the judges were to declare the law in accordance with itself, or with its duly ascertained intent; one result, undoubtedly, would be that the Supreme Court would not be in the seriously compromised position it is in now.

What state would have adopted the Constitution if given reason to believe that the absence of express, direct restraint on judicial power was, later on, to mean that the Court could by "judicial legislation" revise its provisions so as to make them mean the opposite of what they effectively, demonstrably, meant when adopted? Who would have been persuaded by the argument, the sophism, that the power to interpret, to expound and particularize, is the power to undo and reverse? Minds so tender as that would not, in the first place, have been equal to the feat of producing the Constitution. They have no kinship with those who, having fought down tyranny, took care to see that the government they established should leave no door open for the entrance of tyranny anew. If, however, posterity's respect for law, which is also respect for the terms in which law is formulated, is half-hearted or sinks to the level where judges and their apologists can successfully hold these terms to mean the opposite of what they meant when adopted, then anything goes.[45]

Do integrationists and Supreme Court apologists of today believe in the Constitution? Let us be precise. What a man believes in he holds, upholds, unequivocally. It has for him identity, character, constancy. The opposite, the equivocal, would be incompatible with honest devotion. One can believe in integration with all the earnestness and integrity of one who believes in segregation. But can one believe in the Constitution and at the same time countenance, let alone advocate or perpetrate, its reversal? Can he believe in it without scrupulously respecting its terms, duly proven and promulgated? Can he believe in it if he holds it to be too cumbrous, too slow and uncertain of amendment when he wants a change? Or when, to circumvent its amendment requirements, he resorts to the sophism that the Supreme Court's power to interpret and apply the Constitution involves power to revise it and make it mean the opposite of what it legally meant before?

Consider this, referring to the 1954 school cases in contrast to previous ones:

"These cases generally did not attack segregation in schools with any real moral conviction. Nor was the issue usually presented in the proper procedural manner. The cases were all argued and decided as if they were abstract legal problems, unrelated to real facts in life. The meaning of segregated education for the student, for the South, and for the nation as a whole was not presented to the Court."[46]

Is the merit of a litigated cause dependent on the moral conviction with which it is argued? Certainly it is not. Oratorical fervor, which is easily mistaken for conviction, is only an accident of proof. Moral conviction varies with peoples, traditions, and persons. The Constitution, faithfully construed, varies not at all. If it did vary, that would make it discriminatory and self-violative. The supposition that the tenor of the arguments determined the fate of early challenges of school segregation is unsupported here and is hardly reconcilable with the express judicial reasons underlying the decisions.

Is the law one thing in the abstract and another in its application, as surmised in this apology? Probably the same law affects everybody differently; for example, tax law, even when people's tax bills are the same. But this, it is obvious, in no way signifies variation in the law. The integration apologist seems not to understand that all law, natural as well as jural, is abstract and that application of it no more affects *it* than application of a yardstick affects the number system. He seems driven to complicating the simple and obvious in order to attain his goal.

Are litigants, not to say lawyers and judges, so imperceptive that, as intimated by the integration apologist, they cannot recognize and deal with the questions at issue? Or is it that the apologist, knowing that he cannot make two plus two something other than four, wants to change to a different procedure, one in which the "equals" sign is obscured or modified?[47]

What is back of the wave of books and articles deviously attempting to justify the school decision? If it was a bona fide judicial decision, what need has it of their backing? No reflective person who cared to go through a sampling of them would have much trouble finding probable answers to such questions. One thing is quickly apparent: the zeal of the authors for integration. It is not fact and reason that speak out, clear, unalloyed, and uncontrolled, but something else, as in, to take a moderate example: "Plaintiffs [in the school cases] . . . sought to influence the Supreme Court to create a new constitutional standard."[48]

The idea of the Court *creating* such a standard rather than judicially sounding the Constitution to see whether it is implicitly *given*, is, to these authors, in no way suspect but on the contrary proper and salutary. Of what would the Court "create" the standard? Of the arbitrary, irrational dictum that *separate* must mean *identical?* Of the manifest falsity that it is impossible for the state to provide equally for white and Negro? Of the repugnancy: White pupils are *facilities* for the education of Negro pupils? These indeed are the Court's apology for its decision; so the "new constitutional standard" must have come from them. The Court apologists, courtier-like, do not see or suspect them. "How judges can possibly interpret law and not make new law in the process is never explained,"[49] they say. Little wonder it is not explained, the question being a fiction; interpreting a document is not making it a new document, interpreting a will not making a new will, interpreting a law is not making a new law. But if one is so far wrong as to think it is making new law, probably he will surmise that the Supreme Court can "create a new constitutional standard." The courtier naturally and unquestioningly supposes his liege *sans peur et sans reproche.* Courtiers, however, are not jurisconsults.

Nor is it fact and reason alone, to say nothing of judicial polity, that shows through such an episode as: the Supreme Court hurrying up a corollary decision, years after, having it *telephoned* to the Federal circuit court at Omaha, which in turn projects it to posted agents in Little Rock—all this dispatch in one day—to frustrate the opening of non-integrated Little Rock schools.[50] The President stands by, ready to order paratroopers to the scene. The Secretary of Health, Education, and Welfare calls it "indefensible" that public schools in Arkansas and Virginia should be closed to prevent integration, though he does not put himself to the trouble of finding out the deeper reasons for the closings.[51] The Attorney General warns that if the South does not integrate, new factories will not be built there by Northern manufacturers, and the Federal Government will hold back its largess.[52] And so on. Consider the last. One might have thought that Congress, which votes the money, would have had the say, or surely not the Attorney General, about what is to be spent and where. Reasonableness, respect for facts, equanimity, one and all, pass into eclipse when exposed to the fire of integrationist zeal. Segregationists have been accused of everything, but have always had palpable facts to support them. These the integrationists find it expedient, if they notice them at all, to ignore.

Partisans cry out that such and such—some cause of theirs, like integration—must be a *natural* right, seeing, perhaps, that otherwise it cannot prevail. If it is not law, then by all that is holy it *ought* to be law. Impassioned as they are, they cannot see that what they are doing is but to mistake their will for the will of nature or, it may be, of God. Their adversaries become in their eyes instruments of Satan and must be conquered by whatever means it may require. Between dogma and law, zealotry and proof, a slogan and a fact, they seem to make no distinction. Suppose they calmed themselves long enough to investigate; in a great spokesman of the natural rights they invoke, Montesquieu, they would meet the rebuffs apparent in the following lines.

"Better is it to say that the government most conformable to nature is that which best agrees with the humor and disposition of the people in whose favor it is established. . . .

"Law in general is human reason, inasmuch as it governs all the inhabitants of the earth: the political and civil laws of each nation ought to be only the particular cases in which human reason is applied.

"They should be adapted in such a matter to the people for whom they are framed that it should be a great chance if those of one nation suit another. . . .

"They should be in relation to . . . the religion of the inhabitants, to their inclinations, riches, numbers, commerce, manners, and customs."[53]

Those who would coerce white people into association with Negroes, in the name of natural rights, must find little to please them here. Little, too, in the theory of John Locke, another great exemplar to our forefathers, holding that men are "by nature all free, equal, and independent;"[54] or in the Declaration of Independence idea of "unalienable rights." For such freedom and such rights include freedom of association: freedom to find your own and freedom from infringement of your own. It would be a strange evolution of principle to suppose that far-away colonists, in freeing themselves from monarchism and declaring natural rights as their justification, should by that same declaration commit themselves to a deeper bondage: that in throwing off political ties, they took on interracial ties; especially when the black race was in serfdom and hardly considered human. Such, however, is the power of racial zeal that it stifles reason or subordinates it to racial, in this case integrationist, ambition, the results being not always readily intelligible.

The passion for integration seems to burn strongest at a distance, and when supercharged with the inhumane presumption that people afar, under other conditions, are less virtuous than you, it may vitiate an entire polity. As a legal force, which it has now become under the aegis of the Supreme Court, this aggression operates with a fury reminiscent of the Ku Klux Klan. The Klan, in Reconstruction times, was a natural emergent, an instructive result of colliding racial forces. It claimed unwritten law as a justification. Its analogue in the integration movement today, a miscellaneous company of senators, pastors, editors, and free lancers, claim written law as theirs: law written by the Supreme Court in 1954. They continually refer to defiance of that law by segregationists but discreetly avoid notice of the fact that the Supreme Court has no authority to make law and that the 1954 school decision was itself a nullification—something more than defiance—of the duly declared law of the land.[55]

Judocracy, above laws and men, opens a new zone of government. In the name of interpreter of the Constitution, it transcends the constitutional bounds and assumes authority over them. It makes the Constitution say now this, now the opposite. Having by such means decreed integration, it devises a way to compel its adoption, thus usurping the enforcement power constitutionally vested in Congress. By this aggrandizement it has broken the barriers of our system of separate powers and checks and balances, and made room for an arch authority beyond their effective reach. Thus exalted, it reigns, answerable to no one, decreeing what it wills, like the fates of ancient myth.

If what the Court has done is legitimate, then the Constitution implies its own eclipse: implies that we can constitutionally have a supra-constitutional authority in and over our government. But that is a contradiction in terms. And the supposition that the Constitution or any part of it is eclipsed by the Supreme Court is repugnant to our system of government, as it doubtless is to the mind of the country. In fine, the Court's transcendent position is reduced to absurdity. This is further evidenced in particulars to be seen in the following pages.

[1] It is sometimes said by integrationists that the question decided in the 1954 case had not been decided before and that the Supreme Court did not, therefore, reverse precedent in the decision of that case. Though the question, Are racially segregated public schools unconstitutional? had not been litigated separately, it had come before the Court in conjunction with other questions and had been answered by the Court, always negatively. For example, in *Gong Lum* v. *Rice,* 275 U. S. 78, 85, a case concerning a Chinese schoolgirl in Mississippi, the Court said in 1927: "The question here is whether a Chinese citizen of the United States is denied equal protection of the laws when he is classed among the colored races and furnished facilities for education equal to that offered to all, whether white, brown, yellow, or black. Were this a new question, it would call for very full argument and consideration, but we think that it is the same question which has been many times decided to be within the constitutional power of the state legislatures to settle without intervention of the Federal courts under the Federal Constitution."

Notice that the question was twofold: (1) concerning racial classification, (2) whether a state denies equal protection when it separately furnishes colored pupils facilities for education equal to what it furnishes all others. Between (2) and the question in *Brown* v. *Board of Education* there was no constitutional difference; hence the supposition that *Brown* was without precedent is mistaken. Only by the enormity of counting white pupils as *facilities* for Negro pupils did the Court distinguish the Brown case from those before. Notice also that the question was "the same question which has been many times decided." Of course that was the school-segregation question, not the perhaps trivial question of the color classification of a Chinese. Those, therefore, who say that the school-segregation question *per se,* the question whether segregated schools were in themselves a denial of equal protection, had not been decided before 1954, contradict the Supreme Court itself.

Even when not directly at issue segregation in higher education had often been implicitly sustained by the Court. For example, in 1938 the Court, in *Missouri ex rel. Gaines* v. *Canada,* 305 U. S. 337, 344, while requiring admission of a Negro student to the University of Missouri's law school, did so on the ground that the state had not provided law training for Negroes "by furnishing equal facilities in separate schools, a method the validity of which has been sustained by our decisions." In 1948, four years before the Brown case reached the Court, it reaffirmed the Gaines ruling, in the case of a Negro student rejected by the law school of the University of Oklahoma, though still countenancing segregation on condition that the state provide for Negroes the opportunity for legal education "as soon as it does for applicants of any other group" (*Sipuel* v. *University of Oklahoma,* 332 U. S. 631, 633). Such rulings even though not in terms specifying segregation, strictly entail, or sustain it. A court decision, like any other decision or proposition, tacitly affirms, is inescapably committed to, the consequences it entails. Responsibility, liability, would vanish if this were not so and a great part of law and security would terminate.

Distortion, misapprehension, contradiction all confront the careful reader of integrationist legal opinion. Take this, by a New York University law professor, Mr. Bernard Schwartz, from a letter to the New York *Times,* March 26, 1959: "There was no express Supreme Court precedent upholding the constitutionality of segregation in education. *Plessy* v. *Ferguson* involved transportation: despite a widespread supposition to the contrary, the high court never sanctioned its doctrine in education." What could be more express and unequivocal than the *Gong Lum* opinion just quoted? In fact, *Plessy* v. *Ferguson,* 163 U. S. 537 (1896), invoked school segregation as support for segregation *per se.*

There is axiomatic warrant for the separate-but-equal principle declared in that celebrated case. For "equal," except in the trivial or technical case where anything is assumed equal to itself, or identical with itself, always presupposes "separate;" which is to say: unless separate, then not significantly equal. In other words, equal facilities are inherently separate—the antithesis of the Supreme Court doctrine in *Brown.* When it is said a half-century later that the separate-but-equal principle needs re-examination it is evidently presumed that "equal" has changed. That is greatly mistaken. For things to be equal today it is no more necessary that they be identical than it was in 1896. The uncompromised meaning of "equal" is axiomatic; so when the Supreme Court invoked "separate but equal" in its Plessy opinion it was doing nothing more than if it had invoked the multiplication table.

[2] Below, pp. 50, 52, 88. [3] 347 U. S. 483, 495. [4] 347 U. S. 497. [5] *Loc. cit.,* p. 493.

[6] Below, p. 90. [7] Below, p. 11. [8] *Brown* v. *Board of Education, loc. cit.,* p. 494.

[9] *Ibid.,* p. 495. [10] Below, p. 328.

[11] *Beauharnais* v. *Illinois,* 343 U. S. 250, 263 (1952).

[12] *Brown* v. *Board of Education, loc. cit.,* p. 494.

[13] *Brown* v. *Board of Education,* U. S. Supreme Court Transcript of Record, No. 1, p. 118.

[14] *Ibid.,* p. 159. [15] *Ibid.,* p. 176. [16] 103 F. Supp. 337, 338.

[17] *Brown* v. *Board of Education, loc. cit.,* p. 491.

[18] *Bolling* v. *Sharpe, loc. cit.,* p. 499.

[19] Nevertheless the Court could say, four years afterwards: "The basic decision in *Brown* was unanimously reached by this court only after the case had been briefed and twice argued and the issues had been given the most serious consideration." *Cooper* v. *Aaron,* 358 U. S. 1, 19. How "the most serious consideration" can be connected, by the highest tribunal in the country, with the grievous crudities of thought and utterance in its deliverances in the school cases of 1954 is difficult to comprehend. Incidentally, the substance of the Brown opinion is not much more than a restatement of parts of a brief by Attorney General James P. McGranery (*Brief for the United States as* amicus curiae, *October Term,* 1952, Nos. 8, 101, 191, 413, 448). In this is found:

" 'Separate but equal' is a contradiction in terms. Schools or other public facilities where persons are segregated by law, solely on the basis of race or color, cannot in any circumstances be regarded as equal." P. 17.

These are not statements of law or reason. The first is, manifestly, preposterous —under it, no two schools, citizens, or any other things, being separate, could be equal. The second is plainly an *ipse dixit.*

[20] *Brown* v. *Board of Education, loc. cit.,* p. 491.

21 275 U. S., 78, 85. 22 *Loc. cit.,* p. 493.

23 One of the justices (Mr. Douglas, with Justice Black concurring) puts it more strongly. Dissenting from the majority in a decision concerning Negro voting rights, he says: ". . . personal preference, not reason, seems to be controlling. . . . one who tries to rationalize the cases on cold logic or reason fails. The answer turns on the personal predilections of the judge; and the louder the denial the more evident it is that emotion rather than reason dictates the answer." *Hannah* v. *Larche,* 363 U. S. 420, 506.

24 Even mathematics, far excelling law in the rigor and ultimacy of its concepts, presupposes—does not assume provable—the authority of reason. (What indeed could prove it—what farther ground or authority?) For instance: ". . . the transitivity of identity" (as in: *a* is identical with *b, b* with *c,* hence *a* with *c)* is "one of the rules of logic which may be used in the proof of any arithmetical theorem; it is therefore, included among Peano's postulates [of arithmetic] no more than any other principle of logic."—C. G. Hempel, in *American Mathematical Monthly,* vol. 52, p. 547. Which is to say the postulates, or foundations, of reasoning are *used,* not proved—they would have to be used in the very attempt to prove them. The like applies to the concept "equal," over which, nevertheless, the Supreme Court presumes to rule.

But the same illogicality that supposes that the Supreme Court can overrule pure reason will say it is arbitrary and unwarrantable for the Court to take for granted the separate-but-equal "doctrine" of *Plessy* v. *Ferguson;* that unless separate-but-equal were duly litigated and decided, it could not properly be assumed, and would in any event be mere *obiter dictum.*

This goes on a supposition which is untenable. It supposes that nothing in law is settled or may be assumed unless it has been argued in court. Were that so, a party to a suit could not assume that one plus one equals two without a trial, and the court itself could not assume it until the lawyers had argued it. Which in turn, if it is really serious, must presume that knowledge, truth, reality show themselves only in the clash of litigants. Happily, this is not so. On the contrary, knowledge, truth, and reality owe little or nothing to the courtroom, which owes nearly everything to them. It is ignorance or dereliction to suppose that nothing of moment to a case can be assumed or acknowledged by a judge without first being litigated. Without assumptions, very numerous indeed, litigation itself could not get under way. The doctrine of judicial notice, applicable here and holding that common, non-technical knowledge is also judicial knowledge, or that what everybody knows the judges also know, of course covers many things. Among these will be something about the term "equal," for otherwise the judges could not even apportion time or place equally, fairly, to the litigants, let alone administer equal justice.

In *Gong Lum* and in *Plessy* the Court did not *decide* that separate is compatible with equal. It only took note of that fact. In a deeper sense it was only following an axiom of reason implicit in the concept "equal" and hence in the equal-protection clause itself. See above, n. 1.

25 357 U. S. 570; 358 U. S. 858. An account of these proceedings, in contrast to the Court's rejection of a plan of Little Rock, Arkansas, for transferring schools from public to private control—which the Court branded an "evasive scheme"—was given by David Lawrence in his newspaper column October 6 and 21, 1958.

26 *Shuttlesworth* v. *Birmingham Board of Education,* 358 U. S. 101; 162 F. Supp. 372, 382.

[27] For example, the Council of Methodist Bishops: "The decisions of the Supreme Court of the United States relative to segregation make necessary far reaching and often difficult community adjustments throughout the nation. We call upon our people to effect these adjustments in all good will, with brotherliness and patience." New York *Times,* November 14, 1958.

Simultaneously, the Roman Catholic Bishops of the United States, saying "the heart of the race question is moral and religious," and advocating social equality of the races, made this pronouncement: "If our attitude is governed by the great Christian law of love of neighbor and respect for his rights, then we can work out harmoniously the techniques for making legal, educational, economic and social adjustments." *Ibid.*

Ironically, the South is probably more religious than other sections. "The same could be said of Southerners as they entered World War II as when they embarked upon the Civil War: they were 'one of the few religious peoples left in the Western World'."—Francis B. Simkins: *The South Old and New,* New York, Alfred A. Knopf, 1948, p. 326.

Since religion is so various, it is idle to look to it for justification of integration (or segregation). To be religious one need not be "integrated," nor need one consort with strangers: the rich may rejoice and worship together, the poor, the white, the colored likewise. The supposition that religion must obliterate real class lines is groundless, though it strongly hints of socialism, communism, or theocracy. When a notorious political boss of Missouri died some years ago, with great odium upon him, his pastor took leave to say that he had been indeed a very religious man, having come to church every morning. The clerics, if their resolutions quoted here are fairly representative, are quite uninformed. Evidently they suppose that segregation is only an accident, which time and patience will suffice to overcome. If so, it behooves them to give more studious attention to the subject, for, as will be seen in subsequent chapters of this book, there are deep-lying natural reasons for segregation.

[28] Speeches, editorials, sermons rang with allegations that the South was nullifying the Constitution, that segregation denies the Negro his constitutional rights, that the issue was now raised: Is the South going to obey the laws? The sincerity of all this is highly questionable. It is well understood now that the school decision did not rest on existing law; to the contrary, it went against the law as repeatedly declared by the Supreme Court and lower courts, Federal and state—157 such cases, according to a count noted in the *Congressional Record* of March 12, 1956 by Senator Thurmond, of South Carolina. What lawbreaking there was, was obviously lawbreaking by the Court. What alone keeps the Court from having to answer for it is the remarkable doctrine (too remarkable to be openly avowed, yet manifest in what is avowed) that the power to interpret the Constitution, to ascertain and thereby conclusively determine its meanings, is also the power to deny meanings thus settled long since and to substitute their opposite, even at the cost of denying both fact and reason. Such, however, is the misconception, if not misrepresentation, of points of this kind in the integrationist press that people might be led to think the country had ratified compulsory integration; as when the New York *Times* called it "the will of the national majority" (January 30, 1959). In every test in Congress compulsory school integration had been rejected, and there had been no national vote on the subject, though Southern representatives had challenged

integrationists to put their case before the country in the form of an integration amendment to the Constitution.

29 *Time,* May 3, 1963, p. 22; *U. S. News and World Report,* May 6, 1963, p. 6.

30 New York *Times,* April 14, 1963.

31 I believe he has frequently said that anyone is justified in disobeying "unjust laws." In 1960 he drew criticism from the evangelist, Billy Graham, for thus defying law. United Press International, November 28, 1960.

32 Associated Press, May 10, 1963.

33 Alpheus T. Mason, *The Supreme Court from Taft to Warren,* Baton Rouge, Louisiana State University Press, 1958, pp. 191, 195.

34 Vol. 68, p. 221. He is alluding to a remark by the eminent English jurist, John Austin, who is criticizing Blackstone for upholding "the childish fiction employed by our judges, that judiciary or common law is not made by them . . ." *Lectures on Jurisprudence,* 5th ed. 2 vols., London, John Murray, 1885, vol. 2, p. 634. This is of little pertinency in our system, in which judges are constitutionally precluded from lawmaking.

35 Any "law" the Court might "make" would be *ex post facto,* and so a further violation of the Constitution (Art. I, Sec. 9 (3)). For it would presumably be made and applied in a case before the Court, hence after the fact; or, if not, then the Court would have to enact it prospectively and set an effective date. Would not the President have to sign the Court's "law" in that case? Need not Congress then close down? And the Constitution be closed out?

36 See, *e.g.,* Alpheus T. Mason, *op. cit.,* p. 191.

37 *Writings of Thomas Jefferson,* ed. H. A. Washington, Washington, D. C., Taylor and Maury, 1853, 9 vols., vol. 3, p. 71.

38 *The Nature of the Judicial Process,* New Haven, Yale University Press, 1921, p. 127.

39 Cp. Chief Justice Taft: ". . . constitutional principles must be applied as they are written. . . . They may not be remoulded by lawmakers or judges, to save exceptional cases of inconvenience, hardship, or injustice." *Tyson* v. *Banton,* 273 U. S. 418, 445.

Compare also Chief Justice Marshall: "Judicial power, as contradistinguished from the power of laws, has no existence. Courts are mere instruments of the law, and can will nothing . . . Judicial power is never exercised for the purpose of giving effect to the will of the judge; always for the purpose of giving effect to the will of the legislature . . ." *Osborn* v. *Bank of the United States,* 9 Wheaton 738, 866.

A term of law may reasonably be presumed to have only such meaning as the authors of the law expressly gave it or as it had or plausibly admitted of in the usage of their time (the practice today of prefacing legislative acts with definitions of their distinctive terms is a token of this). Any other meaning would be strictly illicit where lawmaking is expressly limited to the lawmaking branch, as it is in the Constitution.

Ordinarily the newness of an issue is altogether in the accidents, not the essence; it is superficial, not fundamental; relative to the run of previous cases, not to the fixity of the applicable law. The accidents, or adventitious elements, have no bearing on the type or species of case it is; and the law is of the type, or species. That the species is now for the first time exemplified by a case, is the novelty and is wholly accidental (immaterial).

The idea of gaps in the law encourages the pretensions of apologists for "judge-made law," and is associated with this confusion between the law and the accidents of a case. What is, or what would be, a gap in the law? Presumably it is the absence of law in some region of affairs of special concern. But absence of law is not a gap in law. The law like the land reaches so far and may embrace many odd points, isles, and shadowlands, but it no more contains gaps than nature contains them; and if it did, it would be only figuratively, and only the lawmaker could authoritatively designate them so. "Gap" is not the word; rather "boundary," "scope," "coverage." But "gap" nicely fits the judocratic purpose. It carries the idea of something needing to be filled, an idea which may be intensified into one of needing to be filled now, and hence calling for "judicial legislation." Why not *executive* legislation? It should be much faster. Perhaps the answer is that the stratagems and artifices of judocracy would have much less chance of succeeding there.

40 Alpheus T. Mason, *op. cit.*, p. 195.

41 In one series of these about forty volumes have been published: *Labor Arbitration Reports,* Bureau of National Affairs, Washington, D. C.

42 Carl Brent Swisher, *The Supreme Court in Modern Role.* New York, New York University Press, 1958, p. 171.

43 *Ibid.,* p 45. 44 *Op. cit.,* p. 106.

45 The late Judge Jerome Frank might be said to illustrate this nihilism in regarding "the uncertainty of law" as "not an unfortunate accident; it is of immense social value." Not surprisingly, he thought that the Supreme Court "exercises essentially political functions." A. T. Mason, *op. cit.,* pp. 192, 195. In this vein also runs the thought of a prominent political scholar, who speaks of "the difficult and in large measure unanswerable question to what extent the Supreme Court should be bound by its own precedents, thereby ensuring stability in the law and providing guidance for bench and bar and people." Carl Brent Swisher, *op. cit.,* p. 176.

With this compare: "One of the most fundamental social interests is that law shall be uniform and impartial. There must be nothing in its action that savors of prejudice or favor or even arbitrary whim or fitfulness."—Benjamin N. Cardozo, *op. cit.,* p. 112. Compare also: ". . . . it is not only important to find the right solutions of legal problems, but also to keep to solutions once obtained in order not to confuse the public and the legal profession. Indeed it has been said with some exaggeration that in law certainty is more important than justice." Sir Paul Vinogradoff, *Common-Sense in Law.* New York, Henry Holt & Co., 1914, pp. 176-177. Also Thomas Jefferson: "It is much more material that there should be a rule to go by than what that rule is . . ." *Constitution, Jefferson's Manual, and Rules of the House of Representatives,* 84th Congress, *House Document No.* 474, p. 117.

The idea that uncertainty in law is a public good is hardly an idea of *law.* Picture a state where rights were insecure, contracts and obligations undependable, sanctions indefinite and discriminatory, reliance, confidence, integrity lacking; it could hardly endure long enough to be a state.

Justice Thomas M. Cooley held: "What a court is to do . . . is to declare the law as written, leaving it to the people themselves to make such changes as new circumstances may require. The meaning of the Constitution is fixed when it is adopted, and it is not different at any subsequent time when a court has occasion to pass upon it." Quoted in *West Coast Hotel Company* v. *Parrish,* 300 U. S. 379, 404.

⁴⁶ Herbert Hill and Jack Greenberg, *Citizen's Guide to Desegregation,* Boston, Beacon Press, 1955, p. 52.

⁴⁷ Unless *separate* can be *equal,* how could the Court uphold or countenance it as in *Missouri ex rel. Gaines* v. *Canada, loc. cit.,* and again in *Sipuel* v. *University of Oklahoma, loc. cit.* (the latter only six years before the Brown decision)? In the former, "admissibility of laws separating the races in the enjoyment of privileges afforded by the state" is expressly recognized and *Sipuel* is a reaffirmation of *Gaines.* In *Brown* the Court cites these and others as precursors of its integration decision! *Loc. cit.,* p. 492. Even in *Sweatt* v. *Painter,* 339 U. S. 629 (1950), which it also cites and which required integration of the University of Texas law school on account of disparities between it and a separate Negro law school—disparities arising from a white-Negro population ratio of nearly six to one in favor of the white—even in that case segregation *per se* was not denied to be constitutional.

⁴⁸ Albert P. Blaustein and Clarence C. Ferguson, Jr., *Desegregation and the Law.* New Brunswick, Rutgers University Press, 1957, p. 133.

⁴⁹ *Ibid.,* p. 16. Cp.: "A judge, according to legal theorists, does not *make* but *finds* law, if not from precedent, then from principle revealed in precedent . . ." A. E. Teale, *Kantian Ethics,* London, Oxford University Press, 1951, p. 160. The controversy, if it might be so called, over the question of whether judges make the law or find it, is surely specious. For suppose there is no law, hence none to be found; then no legal answerability and of course nothing to adjudicate legally. To make explicit what is [found] implicit in law, to educe from it applicable rules, which a judge does, is only second-order making—a making directly applicable what has, by others, already been made law. It is no more making law than wearing a uniform is making a uniform. The emergence of the English common law from popular custom by way of judicial formulations in the distant past is not a parallel to the adjudication of constitutional questions with us today; and in any event the first provision of the Constitution, vesting all Federal lawmaking powers in Congress, precludes judicial lawmaking.

⁵⁰ See C. Vann Woodward in *Commentary,* November 1958, pp. 369f.

⁵¹ New York *Times,* December 2, 1958.

⁵² Associated Press, December 9, 1958.

⁵³ *On the Spirit of the Laws,* trans. Thomas Nugent, 2 vols., New York, Colonial Press, 1899, vol. 1, p. 6.

⁵⁴ *Two Treatises of Civil Government,* London, G. Routledge & Sons, 1884, ch. 8, sec. 95.

⁵⁵ Justice Cardozo observed: "Judges have, of course, the power though not the right . . . to travel beyond the walls of the interstices, the bounds set to judicial innovation by precedent and custom. None the less, by that abuse of power, they violate the law." *Op. cit.,* p. 129.

Justice Oliver Wendell Holmes said: "I have not adequately expressed the more than anxiety that I feel at the ever-increasing scope given to the Fourteenth Amendment in cutting down what I believe to be the constitutional rights of the States. As the decisions now stand, I hardly see any limit but the sky to the invalidating of those rights if they happen to strike a majority of this Court as for any reason undesirable. I cannot believe that the Amendment was intended to give us *carte blanche* to embody our economic or moral beliefs in its prohibitions." *Baldwin* v. *Missouri*, 281 U. S. 586, 595.

There is a type of mind, reflected in the "judge-made law" concept, which does not credit even the possibility of objective, impartial judgment where anything controversial is at stake. It supposes that the decision is only an expression of favor on the part of the judge; that what decides is always judicial bias one way or the other, no man being without that and no decision motivated, ultimately, by anything else: none the outcome of diagnosis, clarification, or untrammeled reason alone. Doubtless it is this parvanimity, this privation of understanding, that finds expression in the premise, now sometimes put forth in the intellectual mist at Washington, that the Supreme Court must have on it a Catholic and a Jew. Not yet an Irishman, a woman, a war veteran, it is true; but the way is prepared and the time is foreseeable when it will be "inherently unequal" for the Court not to include representatives of every massive and aggressive bloc interest.

CHAPTER 2

BROWN v. BOARD OF EDUCATION (I)

An open mind may conceive of numerous persuasive reasons against legalized racial segregation, such as: It is inhumane; it may be oppressive and humiliating; it stigmatizes; it is a burden upon conscience; it is a source of perpetual discord. These are, however, ethical and civic reasons, not necessarily of legal force. To find an indisputable bar to segregation in the United States Constitution is not easy, and the Supreme Court cannot be said to have demonstrated such a bar in the 1954 decisions. The Court did, it is true, find or hold that the equal-protection and due-process guarantees of the Constitution had been violated, but it did this not by strict judicial construction but by a peculiar extension of terms and by the assumption of a peculiar premise. The premise is found in the following paragraph of the Court's opinion in *Brown* v. *Board of Education of Topeka:*

"We conclude that in the field of public education the doctrine of 'separate but equal' has no place. Separate educational facilities are inherently unequal. Therefore, we hold that the plaintiffs and others similarly situated for whom the actions have been brought are, by reason of the segregation complained of, deprived of the equal protection of the laws guaranteed by the Fourteenth Amendment."[1]

If separate schools involve inequality before the law, of course there is no question, and consequently no defense for segregation by law. If they involve discriminatory treatment at the hands of the law, giving to one pupil a public benefit which is denied to another pupil of equal qualifications, again there is no defense or justification. Equal protection is manifestly incompatible with unequal provisions, unequal treatment, unequal action, touching those equally qualified.

The proposition, "Separate educational facilities are inherently unequal," may be construed in either of two senses: (1) axiomatically; (2) factually. Construed in sense (1), it will mean that, in principle and regardless of the facts, separation necessarily involves inequality; construed in sense (2), it will mean that separate educational facilities are, as a matter of fact, invariably unequal. Let us consider these constructions in turn.

(1) *Separation necessitates inequality?* This is at once seen to be untenable. If it were true, then two pennies, being separate, would be

unequal. Similarly, separate occurrences of a numeral or any other mathematical symbol, or of any word, would be unequal: 1 would not equal 1, x would not equal x, nor would "man" mean man or "Supreme Court" mean Supreme Court.

In the conduct of education the consequence would be frustration and breakdown. It would be illegitimate for a pupil transferred from School A to School B in the same city or in the same neighborhood to be put in the same grade, since the grades as well as the schools, being separate, would be unequal. In a public college it would be illegitimate for a student in Section A of a course to receive the same credit as one in Section B of that course since sections are separate and so must be unequal; and it would be out of the question for such a college to allow credit on equal terms for courses passed at another college. The establishment of separate schools at all, with the same grades and curricula, would be illegitimate even where there was no segregation, and also where there was only one race. School authorities would be guilty of denying equal protection of the law to the pupils, and hence guilty of nullifying a provision of the Constitution. In view of these consequences the public school authorities would doubtless be justified in expecting the Court to direct them how to operate the schools; for instance, how to serve the borough of Manhattan with just one first grade, or a school district in Texas with just one first grade.

All this is too preposterous, and the Court must be presumed to have meant nothing of the kind. It must have meant only that *racially* separate schools are unequal—inherently so. But then the inequality will be simply, "inherently," racial. Are we to suppose that something in white and Negro pupils unequalizes them? If so, what? If not, how can separation affect their equality—how can it *inherently* unequalize them?

Or is it the Court's meaning that the inherency, the necessity, resides not in race difference but in the imposed conditions of segregation: that the moment segregation occurs, inequality occurs; that there is a law or form of necessity at work in nature such that if there is segregation, inevitably there is inequality. But now, however wise the Court may be, it has no authority to tell us this. It is not science or philosophy speaking. In science and philosophy there are powerful reasons against the supposition of any necessity in nature. There is necessity in logic, and derivatively in mathematics, but only when certain logical tenets have been assumed (some logicians reject them). In nature, including racial nature, necessity is only a loose ascription, not needed and nowadays not much found in the advanced stages of scientific study.

So it is groundless to assume that segregation inherently means—necessitates—inequality.

Still, the alleged inherency might be there by virtue of other, inexplicit, considerations. Anything inherent is such by (a) nature, or (b) reason or by (c) prescriptive definition. Thus, size is inherent in a body, the conclusion of a valid piece of reasoning is inherent in the premises, and "native-born or naturalized" is inherent in the definition of "American citizen." Now inherent inequality in racial separation in sense (a) is not apparent in any indisputable showings of fact before the Court or the learned world. Nor does sheer reason, sense (b), know of such inequality — it is not an axiom or postulate of reasoning, hence not inherent in reasoning. So it seems to be something laid down theoretically or arbitrarily, something prescribed by definition, sense (c). But in what definition or prescription of "separation" are we to find inequality inherent? Not, I dare say, in any that are met in science, reason, or practical affairs. And the Court favors us with none. We are accordingly justified in concluding that there is none in evidence.

This must mean that the Court has not *found* inequality inherent in separation, but has only uttered a dictum declaring it so: a dictum without clear, positive warrant. The allegation in the South of dictatorial pretensions on the part of the Court is not, therefore, groundless.

Certainly there is some *difference* between separated things—difference of time or place, for instance—though not necessarily the difference signified by "unequal." Mere separation, as of a piece of chalk into two pieces, may do no more than destroy an identity. Things separated are of course not identical. Separate educational facilities are inherently unidentical.

Does the Court mean *inherently unidentical* in its dictum, rather than *inherently unequal?* If so, then no one can disagree. But such a finding would be pointless inasmuch as the Constitution does not guarantee identical protection, but only equal protection. The Federal Government and likewise the states are powerless to guarantee identical protection of law, since their instrumentalities and operations have to be diverse, separated, not just one.

Still, "equal" does mean identical, in some generic, overriding sense, just as "similar" does. Pennies, for example, are identical in monetary value. Similarly, "equal protection of the laws" may be presumed to mean identical protection, in some sense. In what sense? The Court does not say (though reason would say identical in quantity or character of provision or action). Instead, it tacitly abandons equality and demands out and out identity. It does so even when it has just declared, "the opportunity of an education . . . where the State has undertaken to provide it, is a right which must be made available to all on equal terms."[2] On equal terms—here the Court seems inexplicit or confused, saying "equal" when what it now must mean is "identical."

Since identity of schools is impossible, the Court puts all of them in violation of the law, or at any rate all those in each jurisdiction that have the same grades. Had it stood on *equality*, this unbelievable consequence would not have followed. But in that event it almost certainly would have been obliged to specify or to indicate the need of specified means for securing equality. This might have elucidated "equal protection," a term designating something to which the Court saw no bar, on previous occasions, in segregated schools. To justify its dictum that separation means inequality, the Court did not hesitate to repudiate previous findings, going so far as to say, "Any language in *Plessy* v. *Ferguson* contrary to this finding is rejected."[3] (In *Plessy* v. *Ferguson*, decided in 1896, the Court had held that segregation did not signify inequality and was a legitimate exercise of the police power.[4])

(2) *Separate facilities are invariably unequal?* If it cannot be maintained *a priori* that inequality is inherent in separation, what can be said for the alternative possibility, that separate educational facilities are in fact invariably unequal? At any rate this can be said: that the evidence must be exhaustive, a complete enumeration of cases and none of them unfavorable to the proposition. But of course we have nothing of the kind, and no prospect of having it. To be sure, there is much evidence to support the proposition that separation according to race heretofore carried a probability, perhaps very high, of inequality. But there is evidence the other way, too. The Court acknowledges this, remarking, "there are findings below that the Negro and white schools involved have been equalized, or are being equalized, with respect to buildings, curricula, qualifications and salaries of teachers, and other 'tangible' factors."[5] (This, so far, is contradictory to the proposition that separate facilities are inherently unequal.) Then the Court says, "Our decision, therefore, cannot turn on merely a comparison of these tangible factors in the Negro and white schools involved in each of these cases." It is as if the Court had reached its decision extraneously and were now looking about for presentable "grounds." Where shall it turn? What reasons will suffice it? The Court's answer is this: "We must look instead to the effect of segregation itself on public education."[6]

Now in the determination of cause and effect, in a matter so complex as this, the bench has no special competence. It can only look to those who do have such competence, and even they, as persons possessing a little philosophy know well, may misconceive cause and effect. The Court shows no compunction, however, against venturing into the matter. When it has finished, what we have is, chiefly, the aforesaid dictum, that inequality is inherent in separation.

The effect of segregation, whatever it is, has been accumulating for a century or more. Anyone who looks to it must expect to be occupied at great length, and perhaps in some dismay, if the purpose is to comprehend it well. The Court, however, seems to have been quickly satisfied, though it announced that it "must consider public education in the light of its full development and its present place in American life throughout the Nation."[7] It is content to refer to an opinion of the Supreme Court of Kansas and to certain psychological and sociological studies which, it says, give ample support to that opinion. The Kansas court's opinion states:

"The policy of segregating the races is usually interpreted as denoting the inferiority of the Negro group. A sense of inferiority affects the motivation of a child to learn. Segregation with the sanction of law, therefore, has a tendency to retard the educational and mental development of Negro children and to deprive them of some of the benefits they would receive in a racially integrated school system."[8]

Segregation "is usually interpreted as denoting the inferiority of the Negro group"—of what legal significance is this? Obviously it is dressed-up hearsay, like saying that being criminally accused is usually interpreted as being guilty. Who are the interpreters and when did they supplant the judicial process in determining questions of law? And what if segregation is usually interpreted as denoting Negro inferiority (a highly questionable supposition)—of what significance is that to the constitutional right of equal protection of the laws? It is only a hearsay ascription, of no probative force. Moreover, not all unequals are cases of unequal protection of the laws. Privates are unequal to generals and probably they are keenly aware of it, but that is no proof of unequal protection of the laws; and by staying to themselves privates have less cause for repining over the difference than they might have otherwise.

Yet from the mere anonymous ascription of inferiority the Kansas court, now seconded by the Supreme Court, goes on to infer that segregated Negro pupils do in fact have "a sense of inferiority." On such grounds, with such a precedent, one could prove one's neighbor a traitor and oneself a hero by starting the right kind of hearsay.

Conceivably, Negro children in communities where they are very numerous and have their own traditions and ways, are without the sense of inferiority contemplated by the judges. Conceivably, too, the sense of inferiority would be engendered or intensified if they were put in school with the whites. If one is going to look to the facts—"look to the effect of segregation itself on public education"—one will need to go carefully into such possibilities. In any event, if the facts are to govern, the Court must submit to them itself; which is to say that if anywhere the facts show equality in all respects, then the requirement of equal protection of the laws must be found satisfied. In such cases there will be, under the Court's chosen criterion of effects, no justification for ordering desegregation. Now it may be that such equality is to be found nowhere. But the Court cannot rule out the possibility, under the criterion it has adopted; it can only wait and see, meanwhile ordering, as far as its jurisdiction allows, the appropriate relief for those duly found to have been denied equality.

If the Court is indeed submitted to the facts, how can it rest on the Kansas opinion? The proposition in that opinion that segregation is usually interpreted as denoting Negro inferiority is contrary to the earlier finding in *Plessy* v. *Ferguson*. It misses altogether the reason that commonly underlies segregation, namely, physical, anthropological difference—difference extending down to protopathic levels and having nothing to do with inferiority, equality, or superiority, in any respect.[9] Not to perceive or respect this is surely not to follow a policy of finding out and submitting to the facts.

At best the Kansas court's proposition about racial inferiority— that being thought inferior by others, Negro pupils therefore feel inferior—is only a hypothesis,[10] of a kind which courts have no status to prove or disprove. So far, therefore, as the Supreme Court decision rests on that, it is not factually determined. No court can determine a question of fact which is to any degree esoteric and which the savants find as yet indeterminate (it would be ludicrous for a court to "find" the tenets of Freud or Einstein either true or false, for example, and it is no less ludicrous for it to "find" one way or the other on questions concerning race). To perform the judicial office of determining legal rights, as in the school segregation cases, does not require judges to take the part of impostors in spheres beyond them.

If the inequality the Court speaks of is indeed inherent in separation, then there was no point, other than illustration, in looking to the concrete facts; and if those facts were to govern, then the alleged inherency of inequality was immaterial. Just where then are we, or rather the judges? On the one hand, a hypothesis, indemonstrable at law; on the other a promised showing—a sweeping national survey— which the Court, however, omits to give; the little that it does give is indirect, vague, undiscriminating, and partly hearsay. Little wonder that the decision goes against decisions of the same Court in the past.

The proposition that separate facilities are inherently unequal is bound up with a further illogicality in the Court's exegesis. The Court says: "In *Sweatt* v. *Painter* in finding that a segregated law school for Negroes could not provide them equal educational opportunities, this Court relied in large part on 'those qualities which are incapable of objective measurement but which make for greatness in a law school.'" Then it says, without any showing of supporting evidence, that like considerations "apply with added force to children in grade and high schools."[11] No matter, then, how far equal the measurable qualities and opportunities are, here the unmeasurable ones make a decisive difference. (The Court's term, "objective measurement," is a bit specious; for measurement is *per se* objective.) In any event, if the qualities in question are incapable of measurement, as the Court says, how can they come under the equal-protection guarantee? For what is not measurable is incapable of being found either equal or unequal.

Since the decisive difference between schools is found in qualities which are unmeasurable but which "make for greatness," possibly we should try to discover in this greatness the comparison needed to settle questions about equality. But if there are no measures for the qualities that constitute greatness (itself a quality), where are we to find measures of greatness? The Court gives no hint, and we possess no barometer ourselves, apart from what the Court has ruled out when it rules out all measurables. All else that can be cited by way of telling whether a school has greatness, is, or is tinged with, partisan sentiment pro and con—proud loyalty to one's own school, supercilious diffidence or disdain towards others. Greatness being left indeterminate, we have in it no gauge of differences between schools and hence no test of whether any two schools are equal. Again the Court's decision proves to be speciously grounded.

If two schools have equal resources and standards (these are measurable), wherein are the pupils denied equal opportunity? It must be observed that opportunity is original and prospective, and that what is made of it is another matter altogether, a matter of results. Lincoln's opportunity, for example, is hardly to be judged by his accomplishment; for other men of no such accomplishment had like opportunity. What is done with a public property in a given locality—a park or hall or schoolhouse, for example—in contrast to a duplicate of it in another locality within the same jurisdiction, is no measure of their comparative value originally. It seems wholly unreasonable to say that, given equal provisions and standards, opportunity is not equal.

If the results are unequal, clearly that is evidence of different use of opportunity; and if the difference is highly correlated racially, that is evidence of racial difference of some kind, not necessarily of unequal opportunity.

The Court virtually says: Abandon equality, require identity. But the Constitution does not require identity, only equality. Then let identity—identical schools for white and Negro—be prerequisite to equality. Hence: "Separate educational facilities are inherently unequal."

Let identity be prerequisite to equality? Such (if it is indeed back of the Court's reasoning)[12] is an injunction which no court is competent to issue. Courts cannot prescribe to the mind. They have no jurisdiction over human reason. The Supreme Court has no more authority to make the concept, identity, prerequisite to the concept equality, as here, than the Legislature of Indiana had to ordain that the circumference of a circle is exactly 3.2 times the diameter (once the lower house of the Legislature voted to do that, to the amusement of the enlightened world).[13]

If it is not by the identity presumption that the Court would justify its doctrine, what plausible way is left? It will not consider facts which are measurable, or "tangible," but only facts of a different order; such, it says, as "make for greatness" in a law school, and in a grade school or high school all the more, namely, "reputation of the faculty, experience of the Administration," and so on. But these are just as compatible with educational equality in separate schools as they are with inequality. The Court, however, finds them greater in white schools. So that makes an inequality.

Looking for something inherent in the white schools to account for this inequality, what do we find? Under the circumstances only this, that they are white. Then does the Court mean that white schools are superior just by virtue of white characteristics? Is the inherency it asserts in its dictum simply racial? What else could it be, since the Court admits there is equality "with respect to buildings, curricula, qualifications and salaries of teachers, and other 'tangible' factors"? If, then, the inherency is simply racial, the Court's dictum, made explicit, is this: Separate white and Negro educational facilities are inherently unequal because of inherent white superiority.

It is difficult to believe that the Supreme Court would stand on such a ground. But when it admits equality in all tangible respects—in all respects that education itself takes into account in making school appraisals—what alternative is left? One might retort, "But the white schools have had great advantages in those respects, and their superiority is really due to nothing but that." Possibly that is the case. But if so, it only goes to show that all that was needed was to insure as good for Negroes; that is, insure equal provisions. On that premise, the Court could hardly have reached the decision it did reach. It would have had no reason for going beyond the separate-but-equal standard of *Plessy* v. *Ferguson*. Since it repudiated that standard altogether, the conclusion seems to be that the Court founds its troublesome inherency doctrine in white superiority.

This, if true, is astonishing for a further reason. It puts the Court in the position of abolishing racial distinction at law by paradoxically recognizing such distinction and making it the ground of the abolition. It is as if to say, Let there be a law against law. After this transmutation of reason the Court's repudiation of its rule in *Plessy* v. *Ferguson* is less puzzling. The first Justice Harlan, dissenting from the majority in the decision in that case, said, "There is no caste here. Our Constitution is color-blind . . ."[14] That, to be sure, was hardly a point then, since the Ninth and Tenth Amendments reserve to the people and states all their powers that have not been relinquished in the Constitution, and among these was the power, recognized by the Court then as coming under the police power, of racial segregation. Nevertheless, the present Court, if its *inherency* premise is what it appears here to be, puts itself in the odd position of rejecting the idea that the Constitution recognizes no color. Thus the Court seems to make racial superiority, and therefore color, a strong reason for its decision.

One might argue that this is not the true foundation of the decision; that the true foundation is the effects of segregation, namely, arisal of a sense of inferiority in Negro children, loss of motivation, and finally retardation in school work. But white pupils were segregated, just as Negro pupils were; hence they must have got the inferiority sense too, none, of course, being immune to what inheres in the condition of all. There is, however, no evidence that the white pupils had such a sense.

If it is thought that the intent of the Court was not that segregation *per se* but segregation of the racial minority with sanction of law is what engenders the alleged inferiority feeling, then consider the following: There are places in the South, entire counties in Mississippi and Alabama, for example, where the white population is decidedly the minority. In these the white children must have evolved a sense of inferiority, on the supposition here. But there is no evidence, and no hint in the Court's opinion, of that.

The example of segregation in other spheres is instructive. Jews and Orientals are isolated, practically segregated minorities, in some places. Are they therefore characterized by feelings of inferiority? Hardly. Conquered peoples, too, are often segregated, or ostracized, as were those of the South after the Civil War, the Germans after the first World War, the French during the last war, and many others down the course of history. But it will hardly be thought that these were commonly afflicted with the sense of inferiority. So it is by no means the case that the sense of inferiority is inherent even in oppressed minorities.

One further ground that might be advanced in support of the Court's decision—one intimated by the Court—is that even if there were equality of the intangibles as well as the tangibles, there would still be inequality in this: opportunity for exchanges between the pupils, for the manifold forms of learning from one another, which are a notable aid to instruction.[15] This would be as much as to say that unless Negro pupils can associate with white pupils in school, they are deprived of equal opportunity and hence of equal protection of the laws. But pupils, their thoughts and personality, are not exigible *opportunities,* not facilities—white pupils are not facilities for Negroes. Then to say, as the Court seems to say, that without these the Negroes are denied equal protection is to say that without sharing white characteristics, white life, they are denied equal protection. This, *prima facie,* is nonsense.[16] The Constitution does not guarantee Negroes white qualities, white companions. It guarantees nobody any companions, it leaves all to find their own.

But, it may be said, there is a distinction: white pupils, white characteristics, on the one hand; public facilities on the other—and public facilities cannot, under sanction of law, be set apart exclusively for whites without discrimination and hence denial of equal protection. Certainly there is such a distinction. But that implies nothing concerning which of the facilities are to be used by which pupils. The school authorities have to determine that. Equal protection is no more cognizant of white and colored than it is of fat and thin—it does not measure color and is not measured by color. The trouble is that the Court has confused the pupils and the facilities. It is treating the white pupils as somehow a facility to be shared, utilized, to an extent even sacrificed. Perhaps it did not mean that; perhaps its opinion is too loosely expressed to convey its meaning accurately. Regardless of that, the source and identity of what it finds to be "inherently unequal educational facilities" is just the distinctively white characteristics and achievements. In other words, the difference between equal and unequal facilities is white pupils; which means that white pupils are now to be *facilities (sic)* for the education of the Negroes. As such, in the eyes of the Supreme Court, they are subject to assignment like other facilities.

It comes once more, to this: The Court is using racial inequality to try to outlaw racial inequality; compelling white persons to accord to Negroes, by personal association, the benefits of tacitly acknowledged white superiority. In the deepest sense of the word a person's mind, spirit, character are properties. The autonomy, the inalienability of such properties is nearly synonymous with liberty. The dragooning of them by law into the service of other persons, even so in childhood, is a palpable and to a heedful mind odious violation of personal integrity and independence; a violation and deprivation of liberty and property and of the Fifth Amendment guarantee of them.

The part of the Constitution that was at issue is Section 1 of the Fourteenth Amendment:

"All persons born or naturalized in the United States, and subject to the jurisdiction thereof, are citizens of the United States and of the State wherein they reside. No State shall make or enforce any law which shall abridge the privileges or immunities of citizens of the United States; nor shall any State deprive any person of life, liberty, or property, without due process of law; nor deny to any person within its jurisdiction the equal protection of the laws."

A citizen who has not been deprived of any privilege or immunity by due process of law has every privilege and immunity that any other citizen has: what everyone is entitled to, anyone is entitled to. This, it seems, is undeniably implied in the second sentence of the Amendment; and it is a proposition which cannot be denied without self-contradiction. Similarly, with respect to persons, whether they are citizens or not, whatever protection everyone is entitled to, anyone is entitled to. Applied to the segregation issue, this makes impossible, logically, the denial to a Negro pupil of what is allowed a white one of like educational status.

But there are conditions. Everybody is privileged to walk in the street or sit in the park or have his house saved from burning down, but not everybody at once. Local regulations are required. All the children are entitled, if not compelled, to attend school, but not the same school since it may not for numerous reasons accommodate all. Local authority has therefore to provide other schools. It also has to ordain suitable measures for their operation. Suppose now that the authorities in some localities are satisfied on probable grounds and in good faith that putting the races together will produce strife, debase the educational work, and so impair the general welfare. What are they to do?

The Supreme Court has inclined in recent years, I believe, to uphold state laws imposing restraints on labor unions when not in conflict with acts of Congress, thus deferring to state legislative judgment concerning general welfare.[17] I doubt that any such law in a segregation state expresses a general-welfare judgment half as much as do the segregation laws, which were not in conflict with, but indeed were paralleled by acts of Congress on the subject. We might suppose that if state judgment concerning general welfare is controlling in such a matter as the security of labor in making a living, which is the main import of unionism just here, it would also control in maintaining peace and good order; for without that, not much of a living can be made or lived. Ironically, nearly everything that makes for segregation comes under the head of peace and good order.

The Court's written opinion in this case is an exceedingly loose thing. It promises to make an elaborate review, forgets that, jumps about, turns back on itself, takes liberties with fact, reason, and law, and comes to rest in the dogmatic edict about "inherent" inequality. It is a hurried confabulation, flung at history, fact, and the Constitution. The comparison between it and the opinion in *Plessy* v. *Ferguson,* which it renounces, is the comparison between a hodgepodge and a polished, finely reasoned essay.

Had the Court strictly applied the equal-protection requirement of the Constitution, in 1954, we might by now have had standard tests and procedures for seeing that colored children did receive equal advantages, and the race barriers or the edge of the Negroes' grievances would in all likelihood have been lessened. Had the Court taken notice that the Constitution makes no guarantee of identical public facilities for all, but only of equal facilities, it might have gone on to make a strict application of the equality requirement. The Court's unanimous logical blunder of supposing that equality is "inherently" the same as identity, precluded all of that.

A logical blunder is not just a blunder; not just an error of judgment or piece of imprudence, not something that can be overlooked or condoned in good spirit.   It is something intolerable. The intolerability may not appear immediately, but it is there, like an unpaid debt. If for a time we seem to have gained some good regardless, that is at the cost of sacrificing some other good. In the present case what is immediately sacrificed is (1) the axiom that equals are or may be discrete; (2) the idea that educational objects are measurable far enough for educators to be able to pronounce them equal or unequal; (3) the Tenth Amendment.

Over (1) no earthly court has any jurisdiction. To give it up would be all but unthinkable. A great part of knowledge and practice of all sorts, and doubtless much that goes on in the Supreme Court itself, would be at an end. To give up (2) would make present educational machinery unworkable. And (3) to abandon the Tenth Amendment would be to abandon statehood in all but name. (Of course, if reason governs, any judicial decision entailing the undoing of any part of the Constitution undoes itself.) Yet a further loss, as these come home to us, will doubtless be the loss of confidence—in the Court, the Constitution, and the law.

1 *Loc. cit.,* p. 495. 2*Ibid.,* p. 493. 3 *Ibid.,* p. 494.

4 The Court there said: "Laws permitting, and even requiring, their separation in places where they are liable to be brought into contact do not necessarily imply the inferiority of either race to the other, and have been generally, if not universally, recognized as within the competency of the State legislatures in the exercise of their police power. The most common instance of this is connected with the establishment of separate schools for white and colored children, which have been held to be a valid exercise of the legislative power even by courts of States where the political rights of the colored race have been longest and most earnestly enforced." 163 U. S. 537, 544.

5 *Loc. cit.,* p. 492. 6 *Ibid.* 7 *Ibid.* 8 *Ibid.,* p. 494. 9 *Cf.* ch. 8.

10 Indeed, "hypothesis" is much too fair a term to designate the mixture of presumption, surmise, and fallacy so conspicuous in the Kansas court's utterance. Something is "usually interpreted as denoting the inferiority of the Negro group" —by whom is it thus usually interpreted, and what is the source of the court's information that it is? Surely it is not so interpreted by all Negroes, or even whites. A very nebulous statement, obviously unworthy to ground a judicial decision. From it the court leaps to the inference (as if it followed implicitly) that separated Negro children *have* the sense of inferiority. And from that it infers with like positiveness that segregation "has a tendency to retard the mental development of Negro children." There is, however, not the slightest connection between this last statement and the one just before, nor any connection between that one and the previous. The whole is a piece of reasoning in which something "usually interpreted" a certain way—hearsay, merely—is assumed to involve inevitably what the alleged interpretation asserts, which in turn is taken to necessitate a precise, factual result. What have we in this but obvious, transparent fiction?

11 *Loc. cit.,* p. 493.

12 Possibly the Supreme Court did not assert "Separate educational facilities are inherently unequal" arbitrarily, but drew it somehow from the reasoning implicit in the Kansas court's opinion (*ibid.,* p. 494). That reasoning, exhibited in logical form, goes as follows:

Most segregation is interpreted as denoting inferiority of the Negro.

Wherever there is a feeling of inferiority in school pupils their motivation to learn is affected.

Therefore segregation under law has a tendency to retard the educational and mental development of Negro pupils.

Wherever there is such a tendency the Negro pupils are deprived of some benefits they would receive in an integrated school.

[Therefore they are denied equal protection of the laws.]

Of course the first conclusion does not follow—its terms are not contained in the premises, and so it is no more deducible from them than would be some such proposition as "Segregation may be a stimulus to excel." Supposing, however, that the conclusion were true on other grounds, then it and the last premise still would not yield the further conclusion (which would be the Supreme Court's) that segregated Negro pupils are denied equal protection; for that conclusion, which is about an actuality (alleged) goes beyond the last premise, which is about a mere tendency or possibility. To obtain that conclusion a premise such as "Whatever under law retards mental and educational development is a denial of equal protection of the laws," would be needed. But then we might with equal validity conclude that poverty is a denial of equal protection, and similarly that luxury, ennui, unhappiness, bad health, bad luck, all of which exist under law, are one and all a denial of equal protection. Then the question might fittingly be asked, Why not drop the subject or, alas, consider suicide?

From all of which it must be clear that "Separate educational facilities are inherently unequal" cannot seriously be regarded as a proposition logically deduced from the presumptions in the Kansas court's version of segregation.

[13] An account of this is given in *Indiana Academy of Science Proceedings,* vol. 45, pp. 205-210.

[14] 163 U. S. 537, 559.

[15] In *Sweatt* v. *Painter,* to which the Court refers, it was said: "Few students and no one who has practiced law would choose to study in an academic vacuum, removed from the interplay of ideas and the exchange of views with which the law is concerned." 339 U. S. 629, 634.

[16] In *Plessy* v. *Ferguson* the Court said, of a Negro required to occupy a segregated railway car, "he has been deprived of no property, since he is not lawfully entitled to the reputation of being a white man." *Loc. cit.,* p. 549.

[17] Cf. Charles L. Black, Jr., *The People and the Court,* New York, Macmillan Company, 1960, p. 152: ". . . much latitude is given [by the Supreme Court in recent years] to the judgment of state authorities. For example, even the so-called 'right-to-work' statutes . . . were sustained against federal constitutional objection." Citations: *American Federation of Labor* v. *American Sash and Door Company,* 335 U. S. 538 (1949); *Lincoln Federal Labor Union* v. *North-western Iron and Metal Company,* 335 U. S. 525 (1949). See also an article by Fred Ellis on "The Edge of No-Man's Land," 18 *Louisiana Law Review* 149-161.

CHAPTER 3

BROWN v. BOARD OF EDUCATION (II)

To say, as the Supreme Court said in *Brown* v. *Board of Education*, that separate educational facilities are inherently unequal, is just a way of saying that only with integration is there equality of facilities. It is to say that equality means integration.

If we demand justification for that statement, it will have to come, as remarked in Chapter 2, from pure reason or from exhaustive showings of fact or else from prescriptive definition, since these are all the demonstrative possibilities. The first two of these alternatives have to be rejected for reasons we have seen. If the remaining one is to stand, serious questions arise.

Suppose, to take an illustrative parallel, that we are told, "Only the unselfish are free." How is that known or proved? It is neither. It is only taken for granted. The person who takes it for granted is only putting forth a belief or assumed definition. He is prescribing the definition: " 'Free' shall mean unselfish."

He is of course at liberty to do that. But his prescription, or belief, may not be accepted by others. They may prefer to adopt their own, differing from his and perhaps also from one another. When, however, it becomes necessary for them to agree upon a definition or rule for all, it is no longer a matter of everyone to his taste. The long and difficult task of enacting a law or amending a constitution is strong reason to suppose that the terms finally adopted are not to be put aside lightly. Rather, they are to be scrupulously respected unless and until repealed or amended; for otherwise the whole business and function of lawmaking is defeated.

The proposition, "Equality means integration," states a definition which the Supreme Court has now prescribed to the country. This definition is not in the Constitution and is not clearly implied by anything the Court cites in the Constitution, nor does the Court intimate that it is. It is an altogether new meaning given by the Court to the equal-protection clause of the Fourteenth Amendment. It radically changes the meaning of that clause, when applied to public education, from what, legally, it had been ever since the adoption of the Amendment. How is this change justified?

The day after the Court's decisions were rendered, Senator Daniel of

Texas gave in the Senate a resumé of previous decisions on school seg-regation and some account of the history of the segregation question.[1] Senator Daniel was a member of the Senate Judiciary Committee and, before he became a Senator, was Attorney General of Texas. He had, he said, "lived with this problem for several years."

He pointed out that the separate-but-equal thesis had originated not, as some supposed, with the *Plessy* v. *Ferguson* decision in 1896, but long before in a Massachusetts law, which was sustained by the Supreme Judicial Court of that state in 1849[2] (this is noticed in the *Brown* v. *Board of Education* opinion). He remarked that many other Northern states had followed suit and had been sustained in the courts, among them New York, New Jersey, Connecticut, Ohio, Indiana, Illinois, Michigan, and that even now there were only sixteen states which prohibited segregation. Then he gave digests of five previous cases in which, he said, the Supreme Court had upheld the separate-but-equal policy,[3] thirteen cases in which other Federal courts had done so, and fifty-nine such cases in state courts.

The Court's break with the past in its decisions of 1954 was not just a break with *Plessy* v. *Ferguson* and the line of decisions uphold-ing segregation from the time of the Fourteenth Amendment's adop-tion. There is reason to say that it was a break with the intention of the Amendment itself. The Court said: "In approaching this problem (of the effect of segregation on public education), we cannot turn back the clock to 1868 when the Amendment was adopted . . ."[4] The part of the Amendment at issue is the equal-protection provision, in Section 1: "No State shall . . . deny to any person within its jurisdic-tion the equal protection of the laws." The Court's pronouncement might mean (1) that it could not go back to the meaning of "equal protection" in 1868, that is, the intent of those who adopted the Amendment; or it might mean (2) that it could not go back to con-ditions of that time, such as educational conditions. The Court expresses itself on both the intent and the conditions.

Concerning (1) the intent, it says that although the legislative history of the Amendment was covered exhaustively in the arguments before the Court, and although the Court has made its own investiga-tions of the subject, the results are "not enough to resolve the problem with which we are faced."[5] Then it says that although the intent of the most avid proponents at the time the Amendment was adopted is clear, as well as that of the most avid opponents, what others in Con-gress and the ratifying legislatures had in mind cannot be determined with any degree of certainty.

Here an ambiguity is apparent, between ascertaining the intent of the Amendment with regard to education, and resolving the problem before the Court. If the two are one and the same, how can the Court resolve the problem without determining the intent? If they are not the same, does the Court mean to disregard or go beyond the intent? And if the intent, the meaning, is indeed beyond determination, does that not make the equal-protection clause practically void as far as education is concerned? For to be beyond determination is to be not this, not that, not the other—nothing identifiable; which is to say, a practical nullity.

Suppose the alternative (2), that the meaning of not turning back the clock to 1868 is not something having to do directly with intent but rather with conditions at that time. Here again we run into trouble. How will the educational conditions of that time assure us of the meaning of "equal protection"? The Court itself says that they are "an additional reason for the inconclusive nature of the Amendment's history" (sic).[6] They varied widely and were much different from today, which moves the Court to add, "As a consequence it is not surprising that there should be so little in the history of the Fourteenth Amendment relating to its intended effect on public education."[7]

With that the Court concludes the matter of intent. Its entire treatment of the subject is confusing. We do not know why there is any reference to educational conditions in 1868 by way of ascertaining the intent, when the Court has already pronounced the intent unascertainable. One might ask, Should we look to conditions in commerce, for example, then or now, in order to fix the meaning of "equal protection" in that sphere? Or to health or crime or political conditions in order to fix the meaning concerning them? Is "equal" to be determined by what it applies to, not by the definition it bears? If so, we cannot say that 1 will equal 1 unless we are told 1 what, and what the conditions are; which is but to say that "equal" may mean unequal and hence that equal protection of the laws is a dream. If on the other hand "equal" is not to vary so, what is the point of dwelling on the conditions of 1868 (apart from deference to the appellants, who dwell long on it in their brief, to no clear result)? Might this be the explanation: that the Court is laying the ground for what is to come —that it is preparing to substitute effects, or conditions today, in place of intent?

Agreements, contracts, laws all have intent, since they are by nature prospective and instrumental. Ascertaining their intent and applying them in its light is a large part of the judicial function. Is it indeed the case that the intent or meaning of the equal-protection clause is indeterminate? If so, then it must be a dead letter. The Court gives no citation of authorities to support its conclusion of indeterminate intent, or meaning.

Inasmuch as the Court in the past has often had to construe and apply the Fourteenth Amendment, and therefore has had to determine its meaning, it seems an aspersion on the competence and integrity of judges in the past to say now that the intent, or meaning, is indeterminate. In 1899, for example, Justice Harlan, delivering the opinion of the Court in *Cumming* v. *Richmond County Board of Education*, a Georgia case alleging denial to Negro school children of rights guaranteed by the Fourteenth Amendment, had no hesitancy in declaring: "Under the circumstances disclosed, we cannot say that this action of the state court (temporary suspension of a Negro high school) was, within the meaning of the Fourteenth Amendment, a denial by the State to the plaintiffs and to those associated with them of the equal protection of the laws or of any privileges belonging to them as citizens of the United States."[8] The Court was not then perplexed over the meaning of the Amendment. It gave no sign of encountering in it anything indeterminate.

In 1879 in *Strauder* v. *West Virginia*, the first case, I believe, in which the Court had to test a state law concerning race or color by applying to it the Fourteenth Amendment, it held that the Amendment "was designed to assure to the colored race the enjoyment of all the civil rights that under the law are enjoyed by white persons, and to give to that race the protection of the general government, in that enjoyment, whenever it should be denied by the States."[9] It said in *Virgina* v. *Rives*, "the plain object of . . . the Constitution . . . was to place the colored race, in respect of civil rights, upon a level with whites."[10] It said in *Takahashi* v. *Fish and Game Commission*, "The Fourteenth Amendment and the laws adopted under its authority . . . embody a general policy that all persons lawfully in this country shall abide 'in any state' on an equality of legal privileges with all citizens under non-discriminatory laws."[11] In *South Carolina* v. *United States*, it also said: "The Constitution is a written instrument. As such its meaning does not alter. That which it meant when adopted, it means now . . . and as long as it continues to exist in its present form, it speaks not only in the same words, but with the same meaning and intent with which it spoke when it came from the hands of the framers, and was voted on and adopted by the people of the United States. Any other rule of construction would abrogate the judicial character of this court, and make it the mere reflex of the popular opinion or passion of the day."[12]

The Fourteenth Amendment grew out of a civil rights bill which was introduced in the House of Representatives by James F. Wilson of Iowa, chairman of the House Judiciary Committee, who expressed himself on the intent, touching schools, as follows:

"Do they (the provisions of the bill) mean that in all things civil, social, political, all citizens, without distinction of race or color shall be equal? By no means . . . nor do they mean that . . . their children shall attend the same schools. These are not civil rights or immunities."[13]

In *Plessy* v. *Ferguson* the Supreme Court held that the Fourteenth Amendment "could not have been intended to abolish distinctions based upon color, or to enforce social, as distinguished from political equality, or a commingling of the two races upon terms unsatisfactory to either."[14]

Senator Daniel, in his address after the decisions of 1954, stated: "Simply to keep the record straight, I wish to call to the attention of the Senate that at no place can there by found an interpretation of the 14th amendment, the equal protection clause, or any other clause, which indicates that it was intended to do away with the separate but equal schools established for the white and colored students in almost all of the States that voted upon the amendment before it became effective in 1868. Practically all of the States had separate schools at that time . . .

". . . Nor can there be found any indication on the part of those who wrote the 14th amendment and the States which subsequently ratified it, that there was an intention to prohibit a separate school system, if that system provided equal advantages for both races. On the other hand we do find considerable evidence of the fact that those who proposed the amendment and passed upon it did not think it would prohibit separate schools."[15]

Senator Daniel pointed out further, giving numerous citations, that Congress had never enacted a law requiring the mingling of white and colored pupils in public schools or colleges, but had defeated many proposals of the sort; that schools administered by the Federal Government for the emancipated slaves, after the Civil War, were separate Negro schools; that the Civil Rights Act of 1875 eliminated proposals for mixed schools; that the public schools of the District of Columbia, which are conducted under laws enacted by Congress, were always segregated both before and after the Fourteenth Amendment.

On the evidence of history it would be only willfulness to maintain that the Amendment was intended, in the sense of having behind it the majority resolve, to prohibit segregation; and willfulness to deny that it was effectively understood, with the support of judicial decisions again and again, to allow segregation. Yet the Court now says that it is out of the question to tell the intent of the Amendment, and gives as its reason this: that we cannot tell what was in the minds of those in Congress and in the ratifying legislatures who were neither avid proponents nor avid opponents of it.

This, certainly, is a most strange standard. In order to ascertain the meaning of a law we must find out what was in the minds of those voting on it who did not speak out avidly for it or against it? By, such a test it would be impossible to tell the meaning of anything whatever in the Constitution down to the Eighteenth or Nineteenth Amendment, since we should have to probe the minds of the silent in Congress and the legislatures, the vast majority of whom are now dead. Mind-reading is not, of course, a method of construing law.

A commonplace of construction is that the usual definitions of terms under question be assumed; and the term "equal," in "equal protection of the laws," which is the focus of the entire segregation issue, was not usually defined, either in 1868 or since, I believe, as *identical*. Usage, therefore, does not support the Court's restriction of the meaning of "equal." As we have seen in Chapter 2, it would be out of the question to treat "equal protection" as "identical protection" uniformly. [16] A further means of establishing intent is to study the contemporaneous action of the lawmaking bodies in relation to the matter at issue; and since Congress defeated mixed-school proposals[17] and allowed segregation in the District of Columbia schools from the first, and many states allowed or required it, one cannot reasonably say that segregation was contrary to the intent of the Amendment. It must therefore be concluded that the Court was not speaking with reasonableness when it pronounced the intent of the equal-protection clause to be beyond retrospective determination.

When all is said, is the phrase "equal protection of the laws" vague, ambiguous, indeterminate, unintelligible? Not in the least. Nevertheless, the Court thought fit to invite the parties to argue its meaning, with respect to public education at the time of adoption of the Fourteenth Amendment. It was not much thanks to them when the Court pronounced the result indeterminate. This, to borrow a figure from a famous philosopher,[18] is as if you raised a dust and then complained that you could not see. The appellants' counsel even produced an example of a Mississippi Senator[19] supporting Sumner's force bill, not mentioning, however, that the Senator was lately a Union army officer, from Connecticut, and was elected by Negroes at a time (Reconstruction) when most of the white citizens of Mississippi were disfranchised.[20] A good deal of dust is raised by such as this; and so the Court could say that new light, new directions were needed before it could tell the meaning of "equal protection." Thus it could seem to justify its shift from its office of applying the law, the clear, incorrigibly clear, mandate, "equal protection of the laws," to the novel business of appraising psychological data.

The concluding section, No. 5, of the Fourteenth Amendment reads: "The Congress shall have power to enforce, by appropriate legislation, the provisions of this article." Such power was indeed in Congress from the first, under Article I, Section 8 (18) of the Constitution: "The Congress shall have power . . . To make all laws which shall be necessary and proper for carrying into execution the foregoing powers, and all other powers vested by this Constitution in the government of the United States, or in any department or officer thereof." The express reiteration of this congressional enforcement power in the Fourteenth Amendment may therefore be taken to be especially significant. The Thirteenth Amendment, adopted shortly before (1865), contains a like reiteration.

There is in law a maxim for construing legal instruments, including laws themselves: *Expressio unius est exclusio alterius*[21]—the assertion of one alternative is the exclusion of another; that is, to adopt one alone of a number of courses is to reject the others. Under this it would seem that Congress, having alone been vested with power to enforce the Fourteenth Amendment, is the sole agency of the Federal Government to ordain measures for securing the rights set forth in it, including the right of equal protection of the laws. Undoubtedly the nullification of the law, in this case the nullification of the whole jural reality of a century or more respecting segregation, and the substitution of its very opposite, is legislation. The Supreme Court, having done that, is therefore chargeable with usurpation of the power of Congress. The usurpation goes farther still. Since it transformed a provision of the Constitution, it was usurpation of the power of the states also, they, not the Court, having jurisdiction, with Congress, over constitutional changes. The Court, though subject to the Constitution, overruled and reversed the Constitution. This would sound like dictatorship if we heard of it occurring in other countries. Of course it is not, with us, due process.

One might say that Congress had failed to act; that the guarantee of equal protection was not fulfilled; that the Supreme Court, as the guardian of constitutional rights, had the duty of securing them to those who were denied them.

But Congress had acted.[22] It enacted measures[23] for the direction of public education in the District of Columbia, measures allowing segregation, and these were locally duplicated over much of the country, as far as segregation was concerned. Having originated and submitted to the states the provisions of the Fourteenth Amendment, having applied them in education (as, it must be presumed, it intended them), and having seen its idea of equal protection upheld repeatedly in the courts, including the Supreme Court, what was there for it to do but maintain the status quo? Until the Court's reversal of itself in 1954, anything else would in all likelihood have got for Congress a reversal before that tribunal, in view of the fate of previous attempts to prohibit school segregation. Certainly Congress might have gone farther than it did along the path it had made; it might, conceivably, have ventured to establish criteria of equal protection in education and provided means of assistance for satisfying them without infringing states' rights. That, however, was discretionary entirely, and the policy uniformly followed by Congress, allowing and even providing for school segregation, can only be taken as expressing the congressional will, not congressional indifference or neglect.

Since there cannot be superiors or inferiors among equals, and since all are equal before the law, the law cannot assume any pupils in any one category to be unequal. Respects in which they may in fact be unequal are not, therefore, material to their status before the law. In slightly different terms, there are two realities: (1) the law, (2) those subject to it. Equality is in (1); it is not, strictly, equality of men but of law. It is the law's uniform incidence, real or potential, upon them; it is their right to equal public benefits and immunity to discriminatory burdens or penalties. To say that all are equal before the law is just a way of saying that a law is uniform and applies uniformly to every one to whom it applies at all.[24] The law is blind to individual distinctions within a class (save, rarely, in enactments for the relief or reward of individuals under peculiar circumstances). It is itself equal protection, unless not duly enforced. To it as to the census-taker, inferiority and superiority, like handsome and ugly, tall and short, do not exist.

A law cannot, therefore, presume to rectify alleged inequality among persons as such, and *a fortiori* cannot make forced use of superiors to elevate inferiors. Superiors and inferiors, to repeat, do not exist to it. When inferiority, or the feeling of inferiority, is alleged in behalf of the Negro pupils it is the same as to admit, so far, no case and hence no cause, as yet, for relief.

The Supreme Court gets around this by a stratagem. Into equal protection it writes equal opportunity, and into that, integration. Before, the white pupils were to be facilities to the Negroes; now, opportunities. Can the law use them so? Does not the privileges-and-immunities guarantee, given in the same sentence of the Fourteenth Amendment as the equal-protection guarantee, bar that? Does not the Court in singling out the white children discriminate against them on account of race as much as the segregation of colored children discriminates against the colored? Segregation forces the colored children out, the Supreme Court forces the white ones in. If one forcing is discriminatory and wrong, in a society of legal equals, how can the other be right?

It is of course true that the presence of anybody is to anybody else an opportunity of some kind, and that the presence of white pupils may be a favorable opportunity for colored pupils, though it may be in some schools an adverse opportunity, one for friction and disturbance not previously known to them. But such opportunities are in no sense the kind the law provides. They are only incidental. The presence of people on the street corner is an opportunity but not an opportunity the city provides in providing the street. It is only incidental to the provided opportunity, and so are the contacts and exchanges among pupils. To confuse such things is to confuse the incidental, the adventitious, accidental, and casual, with the essential.

Further, for "protection" the Court now substitutes "effects of protection." Since "equal protection of the laws" is far different from "equal effects of protection of the laws," it is little wonder the Court "cannot turn back the clock to 1868" (at that time such license in the Court probably would have evoked impeachment demands). Now "equal protection" is even turned into a self-contradictory conception, for in order to bring equal results the protection will have to go much farther for many pupils than others, even so far in some cases as to look like an attempt to make silk purses out of sows' ears; and this of course will be unequal protection. Thus "equal" is dissimulated into "unequal" in the name of equal protection of the laws.

The very assumption of results as a standard here is illicit. Results of the law's protection, being beyond the terms of the law, are not the protection; hence they are not what the Constitution guarantees. Accordingly they cannot determine either equal or unequal protection. All manner of results of the protection are possible, especially in education. The test of equal protection is not in them but in the administration of the law or, possibly, in whether the law itself discriminates and so implicitly ordains inequality, such as unequal provisions for people of the same legal standing. The determination of this will have to be made according to some objective standard or measure, showing a less-than, greater-than, in the very terms of the law's provisions or enforcement; nothing else can prove *equal* or *unequal*.

Nothing of the kind is found in *Brown;* only the dictum that separate educational facilities are inherently unequal. This dictum no more establishes unequal protection than it does equal protection. It is no more pertinent to the question of equal protection than its like would be to the determination of the majority ownership of shares of a corporation or the outcome of a horse race. It is no more an application of the equal-protection standard than it is of the *habeas corpus* right or the prohibition against *ex post facto* laws.

It might be thought that the measurement test is inappropriate. But if things are not in some way measurable, and measured, they cannot be pronounced either equal or unequal, inherently or otherwise. To say that they are unequal (or equal) is then patently a misrepresentation. It is saying that a test has been made when it has not. It is patent falsity.

That the Kansas law *per se* projected a less-than, greater-than, was not shown or even alleged. It looked on white and black alike, as so many *x's*. Inherent inequality, unequal protection, was therefore foreign to it.

On a line between white and black where does one find or look for or even think of equality or inequality? Inherently, in itself, the line is of course not unequal; and drawn between colors or between colored objects, it neither equalizes nor unequalizes. In recognizing racial lines the law is therefore doing nothing pertinent to equality or inequality; hence it is doing nothing pertinent to the guarantee of equal protection. Only what it does on the two sides of the line is then pertinent.

To say that it cannot reach out equally to those on both sides of the line is palpably untrue. It can dispense its benefits and bestow its care as well to both sides of the street as it can to one side. This, if it were a question at all, would be a question not of law but of something too elementary to occupy serious thought—such as whether right and left, east and west, may balance. And if it were questionable whether the state could reach out equally in this case, how much more questionable would it not be that it could do so in the case of male and female, native and naturalized, for example?

First the state must determine what protection, what laws, there shall be, and enact them. It may, without infringement of the equal-protection right, enact any law that does not project or impose a less-than, greater-than, on any person of the same legal status as another. In determining legal status it must often differentiate on natural lines both persons and provisions for them; otherwise infants and lunatics would have the same standing as the most gifted and accomplished, if any there were. The consequences of that for the state and civilization are not hard to imagine. Though the determination of status goes on perpetually, it can never be challenged on the ground of unequal protection when that ground itself is amenable to no measure of equality or inequality. School segregation is, or need be, only an administrative expedient: only the law recognizing and following lines which nature has sharply drawn. This is not discrimination. Equal and unequal do not pertain to it. Hence unequal protection is not involved in it. In order to find that it was involved, a showing beyond reasonable doubt would be necessary, since nothing less could establish either *equal* or *unequal;* and, absent both, no such showing is possible. The Supreme Court has said: "It is but a decent respect for the wisdom, integrity, and patriotism of the legislative body, by which a law is passed, to presume in favor of its validity, until its violation of the Constitution is proved beyond a reasonable doubt."[25] "Even if the wisdom of the policy [of a state] be regarded as debatable and its effects uncertain, still the legislature is entitled to its judgment."[26]

Federal power cannot, without forcible, lawless aggression, prescribe to a state what laws it shall enact, hence what protection it shall give; it cannot therefore prescribe, without such aggression and in violation of the Tenth Amendment, either integration or segregation.[27] Equal protection applies *to* these, *it* cannot decree either. Being but a measure, equal protection must await the appearance of something to measure. The gist of what the Supreme Court has done in the entire segregation controversy is to confound the measure and the measurable, through the dissimulation now apparent. Such is the way of judocracy.

Under the Court's inherency concept anyone could be summarily convicted or acquitted of anything. For, as in *Brown,* no showing or hint of what alone could prove the inherency need be given. A bare edict suffices. This is indistinguishable from judicial despotism.

It leads on to the naive assumption by some, including the present administration in Washington, that not to integrate is inherently wrong, wicked, perverse. Respect for fact, which indeed very soon comes round to respect for other people, declines everywhere and by some is fatuously abandoned. They surmise that race and its consequences are nothing. Their doctrinaire term "racism" is made current, signifying that it is all a vicious mistake to think that Africans but a few generations removed from cannibalism are any different from other people.

Who would not wish to see his fellow men, just as men, free of all stigma? In their capacity of men simply, all are equals by definition; not by definition of law but of pure reason, being each simply one of the species. It seems therefore contrary to nature and to the foundations of law to mark any of them as if they were miscreations.

Moreover, the Constitution, in the parts that concern civil rights, is a reflection of this natural state of equals. The public schools, like other public instruments, are further reflections or extensions of it. So the schools must be open to all alike, taking no cognizance of accidents of color. In providing the street it is true that the city did not provide the crowd on it and the consequent opportunity this might afford for those who care for crowds. But it provided something else not noticed, which made that opportunity, namely, that any and all might pass there. The street has no color bar and knows no stigma in the passersby. The state knows none, so far as this natural condition of equals is always reflected in its acts. Accordingly, the schools, unless through misfeasance, know none.

So it would seem. But the state, the law, is not everything. Like the equality of men, it does not go very far. It is little more than a minimum base of operations. A man who pays the taxes it exacts, keeps his agreements, and keeps out of mischief, only slightly notices it and is as little noticed by it. What makes inequalities is above this base, in the free interaction of the distinctive powers of individuals.

But soon these powers generate tension and disturbance and the state is entreated to control them. The concern of the state for sobriety, health, and public welfare expands; measures for securing these are constantly required. Differences between men become more conspicuous. Stratifications occur. Presently the respect in which all men are equal passes from notice and soon it is only nominal.

All this comes about through the exercise of constitutional rights and privileges, and especially, with us, the property right, secured in the Fourteenth Amendment along with equal protection of the laws. An agent of this process, created by it and reciprocally creating it, is public education. Suppose now that in a miscellaneous population ethnic differences are sharp and remain unextinguished for generation after generation; that they are reflected in the public school; and that one expression of them is segregation. We are brought to the antithesis of that formal, primal state of equality at which color, race, ethnology does not count at all.

This evolution, from equality to inequality and aversion, is not the product of prejudice. It was not planned. It is only the state of nature at an advanced stage. Men are still equal as before—equal as members of their species, as featherless bipeds, as ones. But they are extremely different also, and nothing in the nature of things prohibits the impression of their differences on their institutions. Nothing in our Constitution prohibits this. Nothing in it prohibits segregation *per se*, for example.

Nor, too, does anything either in the Constitution or in the nature of things inhibit aspiration of the underdog or sympathy with him. Such aspiration and sympathy give a new direction to socio-political evolution. A contest between the new and old takes rise. The present juncture is a high point in this contest.

When the Supreme Court resorts to Negro psychological considerations, saying that segregation engenders inferiority feeling and retards educational motivation, it is only recognizing one side of the contest. That may be the side the world sympathizes with, so adding momentum to the evolutionary process; yet there is a white side also—white abhorrence, or, psychologically, withdrawing reaction, and its derivative dispositions ("fixations," "complexes," "mechanisms") are not nothing. As long as the Court was making a psychological case of it, it would seem only fair to have heard and considered that side. Possibly it has an impressive psychology too. Possibly the Court has one of its own.

What, though, has this to do with the legal question, the only question before the Court? If the Constitution is silent on segregation, as it is, and if it allows very broadly for socio-political evolution, as it does, what is there to require either segregation or non-segregation? The answer is in history. The states, under their constitutionally reserved powers, had the option themselves, exclusively, between these alternatives, and some of them, in their constitutions, made segregation mandatory, some made it permissive, and the rest prohibited it. There was no Federal requirement.

To surmount this, the Court had to go beyond the Constitution or else to stretch some part of it to fit the purpose. In the Brown case it did the latter, making "equal protection" reach from the bare x-status of equals before the law all the way up to the coverage of one party's psychology, though not the other's, psychological justice not being, presumably, the even-handed genius that presided heretofore at the bar. In the Bolling case, with which the next chapter deals, it did both: stretched the Constitution as before and ventured out beyond it.

If the aspiration of the appellants and their sympathizers was for something more than the relief to which they might have been entitled according to previous rulings, then they were bountifully rewarded, the Court having put aside some eighty-six years of the Constitution in the act of gratifying them.

Further concerning effects as a constitutional test. Since equal protection of the laws presupposes the laws, it follows them and applies only where they apply. If no law touching some matter, then no equal protection at law concerning that. Equal protection no more guarantees any *thing* than the equal right of all to the pursuit of happiness guarantees any happiness. In particular, it no more guarantees equal effects of the protection than the right of all to pursue happiness guarantees equal happiness to all.

If effects were indeed a judicial test, nobody would know how to take a law—how either to obey it or enforce it—since nobody would know in advance what the effects would be (certainly not psychological effects). So this is an impossible standard. It is a flouting of the law by the bench.

A law is strictly normative, a certain punctuality for the government of all. It is a command of the state, let the effects be what they may. The state through its legislative organ, will judge of the effects of a law and determine whether to retain it, amend it, or repeal it. If a judge presumes to "invalidate" a law merely because of its effects, he is usurping legislative authority.

To see directly how untenable the Supreme Court's position here is, consider this: I go to court suing for equal effects of the tax law or public health law, for example. Under what law am I suing? What law guarantees me equal effects? I demand equal feelings, or deliverance from inferiority feelings, in consequence of my obedience to the law. Equal to whose? By what test of equality? What lawyer of any standing will take my case? I must be in dreamland, lured by the example of the Supreme Court.

How far amiss it is to take effects as a judicial test of law may be instructively shown in a parallel case outside of law. Here is a provision found in a labor contract, pertaining to the authority of arbitrators (arbitrators adjudicate questions arising between the parties to such contracts):

"The arbitrator shall have the authority to interpret the contract to make conclusions of fact based upon the evidence submitted at the arbitration proceeding and to apply the contractual provisions to said facts. He shall have no authority to add to, detract from, alter, modify

or amend any of the provisions of this agreement . . . His decision shall
not be based upon consideration of factors such as the effect upon
productivity of a particular result, its consequences to the morale of
the shop or his judgment as to whether tensions would be heightened
or diminished."[28]

Whereas the Supreme Court takes it to be axiomatic that a law
may be judicially tested by its effects, or, say, by the Court's approval or disapproval of them, here in the world of work and affairs
any such standard is roundly repudiated. Perhaps the parties to the
contract had had the experience of seeing their agreements riddled
by arbitrators who presumed to impose extraneous, impertinent
standards, and had firmly resolved to have no more of that. They
had committed themselves to a contract, one not for securing any
precise effects but, quite the contrary, for maintaining certain relations between themselves.

Effects are not a standard, but an admission of the lack of a
standard, since they will be indeterminate because the law applies
to indeterminates—individuals, x's. What will be the legitimate
effects, what the illegitimate ones? The law must have said before
the judges can say, otherwise it is not law that the judges are administering. If the law has not said—as of course it has not—yet the
judges presume effects as a standard, then the judges are guilty of
usurping legislative power and the rights of the electorate represented
by legislative power.

A man of no principle, who does not scruple to break a commitment if he sees a gain in doing so, is a perfect parallel of the *effects*
policy. With him the end, any effect agreeable to him, justifies the
means. When the Supreme Court looks to effects rather than to the
law, it is not far from emulating such a character. Its disposition
that way did not originate with *Brown*. Twenty-odd years before
Brown it said, "the statute must be tested by its operation and
effect."[29] Well before that it sensed the impropriety: "The argument, we admit, is not always the most conclusive which is drawn
from the consequences urged against the adoption of a particular
construction of an instrument."[30] But today effects are a flying
standard of the Court. Thus:

"The essential and inevitable effect of this redefinition of Tuskegee's
boundaries is to remove from the city all save only four or five of its
400 Negro voters while not removing a single white voter or resident.
The result of the Act is to deprive the Negro petitioners discriminatori-
ly of the benefits of residence in Tuskegee, including, *inter alia*, the
right to vote in municipal elections."[31]

This was a gerrymandering case from Alabama. Had it not concerned the Negro, who is now so prominently a concern of the Supreme Court, it might have been expected to go the way of previous gerrymandering cases before that Court. As recently as 1946, in *Colegrove* v. *Green,* the Court had said that electoral district lines are "of a peculiarly political nature and therefore not meet for judicial determination,"[32] and further: "Of course no court can affirmatively re-map the [Illinois] districts so as to bring them more in conformity with the standards of fairness for a representative system. . . . It is hostile to a democratic system to involve the judiciary in the politics of the people."[33] That the Court today is peculiarly adept at overcoming such "hostility" and at involving itself "in the politics of the people" will be a natural inference after its exploits that way in the recent Tennessee reapportionment case.[34]

Ironically, the opinion in *Colegrove* v. *Green* and that in the Tuskegee case were by the same judge, Mr. Frankfurter. He strives to distinguish them, saying that *Colegrove* was a matter of "a dilution of the strength" of the votes of some, whereas in Tuskegee "a readily isolated segment of a racial minority" had been singled out "for special discriminatory treatment,"[35] against the Fifteenth Amendment. Indeed, nothing of the kind. The white people, not the Negroes, were the minority in Tuskegee—1,310 white, 5,397 Negro, according to the last census before the change in the town's boundaries. (The Court, as we have seen, is not too particular about facts when integration is at issue.) Only if the state had denied or abridged the voting rights of Tuskegee residents on account of race, color, or previous condition of servitude would this be a violation of the Fifteenth Amendment; and of course the right to vote is not denied or abridged by a mere boundary line between voting districts. The Fifteenth Amendment carries no guarantee of where a Negro or anyone else shall vote. As long as he can vote when others in his district can, the guarantee is unabridged. If a state could not draw district lines, a voter could vote wherever he pleased and the whole political fabric which the Court was so anxious to protect in *Colegrove* would be destroyed. If a state is not free to delineate its subdivisions according to its sovereign judgment, is it free to determine the location of a road, a schoolhouse, hall, or park, or free to mark out zones of any kind or to allot police or fire protection—is it free to act at all: is it a state?

Justice Frankfurter took note of the shape of the remapped Tuskegee, an irregular figure of twenty-eight sides, which to him was a picture of racial discrimination. In *Colegrove* v. *Green* there were comparable maps of voting districts, one each in Alabama, California,

Illinois, and Pennsylvania, the map for Alabama showing the congressional district that contains Tuskegee and having, like one or two of the others, fifty or more sides.[36] Probably these boundaries separated white, Negro, Japanese, Indian, Poles, Republicans, Democrats, and so on, just as Tuskegee separated white and Negro. And that was all right, in Justice Frankfurter's eyes, in *Colegrove*. How odd the difference a concentration of Negro blood can make in judicature!

Soon after the Tuskegee aberration Mr. Frankfurter was again declaring it the sovereign right of states to mark out the voting districts as they saw fit. Dissenting in the Tennessee reapportionment case, he cited this passage in a recent (1950) Supreme Court decision upholding the Georgia county-unit system, an extreme example of electoral inequity: "Federal courts consistently refuse to exercise their equity powers in cases posing political issues arising from a state's geographical distribution of electoral strength among its political subdivisions."[37] He said also concerning the Tennessee decision: "The Court today reverses a uniform course of decisions established by a dozen cases, including one by which the very claim now sustained was unanimously rejected only five years ago."[38]

Here was a very versatile judge, one who might be likened to a pendulum, though in his swinging back and forth on the Constitution he was not very different from his colleagues. Swinging back and forth is a familiar exercise of the Court today; only, the swinging of some of the judges sometimes crosses the lines swung by the others, as in this instance. Imagine the *Constitution* a pendulum, swinging with the judges, meaning now this, now the opposite! Imagine Madison, Hamilton, and the other originators, and the ratifying states, dedicating themselves to such a plaything! What government, what law, could rest on that?

What is contemplated in the *effects* standard of *Gomillion, (Tuskegee)* and *Brown?* In *Brown* it is equality of feelings—absence of any feeling of inferiority. In *Gomillion* it would be difficult to say, the Court being concerned only to determine whether the Alabama Legislature intended to separate white and Negro elements. But what effect could that have, of any consequence to the Fifteenth Amendment? Nothing in that Amendment forbids such separation; nothing in it prescribes where a person shall vote. And a court cannot try intentions.[39] If effects were indeed the test, the law would have to prescribe them and the means of ascertaining and measuring them. Of course neither the Fourteenth Amendment, the Fifteenth Amendment, nor Congress has done that. So the Court is overreaching them all and decreeing its will.

When it is supposed that the Constitution, in particular the Fourteenth Amendment, precludes any law on racial lines, the mistake is made of assuming that a legal recognition of such lines implies inferiority on one side. It no more does that than tax schedules do. Equal protection in any feasible, efficacious form can hardly be given without differentiations and classifications. Without these, a new-born babe would have to receive the same benefits as a nonogenarian or a heavy-weight champion. All lines would vanish. But if there are classifications at all, it will be arbitrary to say there cannot be classifications according to whatever criteria the state finds meet, not excluding race. For the state is sovereign and has all the options or powers of sovereignty not surrendered to the Federal Government in the Constitution; and nothing in the Constitution precludes the option of making race a criterion.

Attributes of the individual or type of individual are not comprehended by the plain terms of the equal-protection guarantee and so cannot be reckoned by the state as a condition of its protection. But as a condition of the kind and, other things being equal, the extent of the protection to be given, many attributes may be reckoned; otherwise the pauper, the plutocrat, the juvenile, the insane, the criminal, the average man must all receive exactly the same. Other things being equal, so long as all receive equal shares it cannot reasonably be denied that the guarantee is fulfilled. The "other things being equal" proviso is, however, critically significant. It means differentiations, classifications, among the recipients. Equal protection is relative to these. If for some reason the state chooses to classify persons according to size, color, language, attainments—according to special attributes but without disparagement of the guarantee to *persons*—nothing in the terms of the guarantee stands in the way. Or if this is denied, then the state's protection cannot vary at all: it must be identical for everyone, and all laws pertaining exclusively to children, women, the aged, depraved, rich, poor, and so on are void. Race no more qualifies or detracts from *person*, to which alone the guarantee pertains, than does age, sex, health, or occupation.

Unless the state can distinguish between people (still according them equal protection, *ceteris paribus*), all that it can do is such as bears equally on every one of them. What will that be? Not taxation as we know it, obviously. Nor education, or none beyond a primary grade, since grades would mean inequality. Probably the only thing left for the state to do would be to patrol the roads, put out fires, bury the dead (in a potter's field). If it arrested a juvenile, he (or she) would have to be put with felons, on the same terms; only, there could be no felons, or juveniles either, since that would mean classifications transcending the mere *person*. It is doubtful that criminal acts could be even recognized, let alone punished, being not of the mere *person* but only of persons having certain attributes.

Failure to acknowledge the differences here between the mere person and individual attributes, is probably not unintentional. By not acknowledging it, partisans may hope to cancel racial distinctions and make believe that only the person, the common denominator of all, matters. But then the Negro would gain nothing. What is common to all, he has already. What he wants is something that is not common: white status or the extinction of Negro status. He wants the recognition of natural attributes to be prohibited; or he wants to be classed as having attributes he does not have. He would use what is only common as if it included what is distinctive: he demands a box seat on a general-admission ticket, on the naive supposition that the lowest-class ticket must be good anywhere.

Lest the fallaciousness of this be apparent, and with it the factitiousness of the Supreme Court's school decision resting on it, integrationists have another appeal. They cry Injustice. "Both the Negro and white communities of Birmingham know that very real and deep injustices have been inflicted on Negro citizens of that city for a long period of time."—Attorney General Kennedy.[40] If this means that white people violated law in dealing with Birmingham Negroes, of course that was injustice. But it calls for citations at least, of which the Attorney General gave none. Perhaps he meant only that segregation *per se* was unjust in Birmingham.

The tag "unjust," if applied without a full and impartial trial, is by any forthright standard unjust itself. It gives only one side, like a picket's sign, "Unfair to Union." Consider:

"Birmingham went to war. Thousands of enraged Negroes surged through the streets, flinging bricks, brandishing knives, pummeling policemen. A white cab driver was knifed, his taxi overturned and burned. A policeman was stabbed in the back and a white youngster's arm was slashed from shoulder to elbow. Negroes put a torch to a white man's delicatessen, fought off firemen as they arrived to put out the blaze. Two Negro homes nearby went up in flames, then three more white men's buildings. The rioters, bathed in the flickering orange light of the flames, looted a liquor store and screamed into the night: 'White man, we'll kill you!' "[41]

All of this followed bombings of Negro houses, which followed a month of organized violation of law by Negroes, in the form of marching in the streets in defiance of a city ordinance and a court injunction. "The Negroes of Birmingham are some of the toughest in the United States," remarked Roy Wilkins, one of the heads of the National Association for the Advancement of Colored People.[42]

Where are justice and injustice in this? One might say the injustice is behind it, in segregation. But then justice might be said to be behind that, in the open recognition of profound natural differences which if not kept at bay will engender conflict on slight provocation. Part of the integrationist strategy is to deny racial differences, a strategy which is clouded with injustice itself if you conceive of justice as excluding misrepresentation. Evidently the Attorney General presumed that there are no very significant racial differences or that the equal-protection clause extinguishes any there are. In either case he was profoundly mistaken. Some of the evidence will be given in subsequent chapters.

It is quite illegitimate, hence unjust, at law, to condemn for what the law does not condemn, and doubly so to do it in the name of justice. It overlooks all the questions of justice and forgets that one's own idea or sentiment of justice is only one's own. Others have theirs. Lest the consequences be a war of all against all, we have a system of government for fixing the definitions or standards and deciding issues under them. The fact that others do have a voice proves that justice is not the behest or utopian vision of one man. Just as *person*, the lowest common denominator, enshrined in the equal-protection clause, is presumed by integrationists to endow any one of us with status equal to that of anyone else, not just before a law court but in the natural distinctions of man, so here the bare private, unexamined idea or word "justice," of a single individual, is fancifully presumed to carry authority over all other individuals.

The law duly applied is the only justice at law. Beyond that, justice is a private ideal, of only such pertinence anywhere as philosophical demonstration may establish for it. If an Attorney General or President can prescribe justice, he can as well prescribe guilt, liability, rights, property, and so on without limit. An autocrat, like a judocrat, mistakes himself for law.

Further concerning differentiation by race (or by sex, age, occupation). What more is that than recognition of the obvious? How does recognition of an individual for what he obviously is deprive him

of any right? Of what right would it deprive him? Of the right, it is
said, of equal protection: "In the reflected light of the implementation decree, the full meaning of the decision of May 17, 1954 [*Brown*],
clearly emerges: laws based upon racial classifications are necessarily
discriminatory and discriminatory legislation is unconstitutional *per
se*."[43] But equal protection is a right only of the person, implying
nothing, precluding nothing, with regard to his race. The person protected by the Fourteenth Amendment is indifferently white, red,
yellow, brown, black. So it is wholly impertinent to say that racial
separation deprives the *person* of his constitutional right. It no more
does that than it eliminates him from the census (will integrationists
now say that racial classifications used in the census are unconstitutional?). Accidents, inessentials, are no test here. The only test
is the reach and application of the law: Does it reach out equally
to all those, respectively, to whom it pertains?

But it is on the accidents, and them alone, that the Brown decision
bears: the whereabouts, the associates, the attitudes, the mere in-
cidentals of the person. Now the person, the legal entity entitled to
equal protection, is none of these. The person is only an instance of
homo sapiens, in some category marked out by the law. The category may ignore ethnic lines, as in taxation, public alms, criminal
sanctions, for example; or it may be confined to them, as in provisions
for Indians; or while ignoring the lines in its provisions it may adhere to them in administration of the provisions, as in school segregation. Were no such categories admitted, there would be no correlative legal provisions, and whatever the state did provide would
have to be laid out indiscriminately before rich and poor, sick and
well, young and old, male and female. One trial would be the end
of that. Darwinian natural selection would quickly eliminate all but
the powerful, avaricious, and unscrupulous.

Of course it may be that race—not the mere formality of differentiation according to race, but the racial facts themselves—does
mean discrimination at the hands of people at large. But that is immaterial; it is not discrimination at the hands of the state. Nevertheless, now that inferiority feeling is unconstitutional (!) states must
take care not to allow it to be induced by anything they do. Accordingly, to insure the validity of their acts, the states, we may assume,
must now implement each act with a procrustean isopathic device
guaranteed to equalize people's feelings.[44] Looking afar, one may
envision SCUR, a desolate new world, that of the Supreme Court's
Universal Robots. In SCUR no one will dare to raise a feeling, let alone
a head.

A cloud of unthinking, darkened by partisan dispositions, covers the whole segregation-integration question. It arose in the Supreme Court when segregation was pronounced inherently unequalizing—as well might it have been called mystically unequalizing, the term "inherently" being hardly more intelligible in the Court's use of it than "mystically." As the consequences of that proposition have unfolded, the cloud has spread and darkened, reaching a high pitch when in the name of "justice" the President and Attorney General condoned lawbreaking.[45] Minds not blinded by this cloud, and seeing that the "inherently unequal" doctrine derives from demonstrable falsity, must be disturbed indeed about the administration of justice today. If the highest court for any reason cannot respect the plain terms of the equal-protection clause or is blind to patent fact and reason, and if the highest officers of the executive branch are so carried away by the Court's aberration that they mistake autocracy for justice, where are we?

But, it may be said, the right of assembly and expression is inalienable and is an overriding constitutional right. This will not withstand even casual examination. If not regulated, the right of assembly and expression could supersede and mortify all other rights. Exercised in the form of massive demonstrations, it could paralyze a community and generate chaos—counter demonstrations, having back of them the same constitutional right as well as the often-cited Section 242 of Title 18 of the United States Code prohibiting deprivation of any constitutional rights, would suffice for that. Soon would follow military rule and the eclipse of the rights of all.[46]

There is no implicit contradiction in saying that the right of assembly and expression involves none of this. The right is satisfied as long as realized *somewhere,* as in Union Square in New York or in a park in Birmingham. To say that it must be realized *anywhere* is to deny the right of others to pursue their lawful ways. The others, or the community as a whole acting through the authorities, can decide whether they shall have to witness a demonstration just anywhere or not; otherwise their rights are denied. Here is the whole trouble: one element, spurred on by Washington, claims exaggerated rights for itself at the expense of the rights of others. A month or more of that produced the strife at Birmingham. A very little thought and respect for the rights of all, on the part of Washington authorities, must have moved them to anticipate what happened there. To the contrary, they gave the violators encouragement and behaved throughout as if aiming for such an outcome: it would excite the country and make way for new legislation for "rights"—save the mark!

Racial dispositions can hardly be condemned as mere partisanship; for what are they but nature asserting itself? Segregation kept them at bay. Now they are to clash without restraint, except by riot troops. The only civil remedy envisioned by integrationist Washington is legalized make-believe: make-believe that there are no significant differences between white and black, that racial spirit and incipient racial conflict are only fictitious. Good fiction is worth something, but bad fiction is worth nothing. Without reason and in defiance of palpable realities this *naïveté* presumes that racial extremes amount to nothing or can be written off at the will of a few men in Washington: that the most heterogeneous population in the world is one great family without differences. Self-deception, resolute unwillingness to see, ever ready to abuse the other side with the epithets "unjust," "irresponsible," "bigoted," "indecent"—such is the policy.

Suppose it became the Washington policy to regard the great recent increase in crime as only make-believe. Suppose unemployment, crop surpluses, and the soaring national debt were resolutely dismissed as all a state of mind. And suppose that people who took these hard realities seriously, who lived under them and suffered by them, were continually criticized for narrowness, bigotry, obstinacy, injustice, defiance, by persons at a distance who hardly even thought of going to the scene and facing the facts before passing judgment. It is unthinkable? But let race and politics and judocracy go to work; the like of all this becomes a fixed policy in Washington and in the editorial North, with respect to realities behind segregation in the South (or in South Africa or wherever black and white are massively juxtaposed). A government which closes its eyes to the realities and feigns constructions of the Constitution making them impossible, even though they existed under it from the first and with continual acknowledgment by Congress, the Executive, and the courts, is either dreaming or naively, if not willfully, defaulting in the performance of government's most fundamental function.

When the sufferers are at length aroused far enough to initiate a plan of self-defense, in the form of state-originated amendments to the Constitution to shield themselves against the aggrandizement at Washington, especially that of the Supreme Court, what is the Washington reaction? This, for instance: "President Kennedy spoke critically of the proposed amendments at his news conference. He said he believed that the efforts to pass them would 'come to nothing, and I will be glad when they do'."[47]

Could President Kennedy have been thinking of the portentous remark of the late Justice Jackson: "There is no doubt that if there were a super-Supreme Court [just that is what is intended in the proposed Court of the Union amendment], a substantial portion of our reversals of state courts would also be reversed"?[48] Whatever the President might have been thinking, what he said fitted nicely with the Washington outlook on the states today, the outlook of imperial authority peering down on its subjects.[49]

Ten years after *Brown* this should be no surprise. *Brown* dethroned fact and reason. If the Constitution, which was a monument of fact and reason, can be thus undercut by nine willful men, does it really stand today? It is only by fact or reason that anything stands.

---

[1]*Congressional Record,* 83d Congress, 2d sess., vol. 100, pt. 5, pp. 6742 ff.

[2]*Sara C. Roberts* v. *City of Boston,* 59 Mass. 198, 206.

[3]*Hall* v. *DeCuir,* 95 U.S. 485; *Plessy* v. *Ferguson, loc. cit.; Cumming* v. *Board of Education,* 175 U.S. 528; *Berea College* v. *Kentucky,* 211 U.S. 45; *Gong Lum* v. *Rice, loc. cit.*

[4]*Loc. cit.,* p. 492. Compare this admonition from the Court on a previous occasion: "It is never to be forgotten that, in the construction of the language of the Constitution . . . we are to place ourselves as nearly as possible in the condition of the men who framed that instrument." *Ex parte Bain,* 121 U.S. 1, 12 (1887).

We are, we are not; we can, we cannot; the law is, it is not: this from the highest court! Why *not* recur to 1868 to find the meaning of the Amendment? If the meaning was not fixed then, in the utterances and acts of the authors, when could it have been fixed? For the Amendment has not been amended. To refuse now to recognize and uphold what was enacted then is to repudiate the constitutional reality established then. Such refusal is a betrayal of the oath of judges to uphold the Constitution.

[5] *Loc. cit.,* p. 489. [6]*Ibid.* [7]*Ibid.* [8] *Loc. cit.,* p. 545.

[9]100 U. S. 303, 306. [10]100 U. S. 313, 318.

[11]334 U. S. 410, 420. [12]199 U. S. 437, 448.

[13] *Congressional Globe,* 39th Congress, 1st sess., p. 1117.

[14] *Loc. cit.,* p. 544. [15] *Loc. cit.,* p. 6746.

[16] In *Hall* v. *DeCuir, loc. cit.,* p. 503, outlawing a Louisiana Reconstruction statute which prohibited segregation in common carriers, one of the justices (Clifford), concurring, said ". . . equality does not mean identity . . . equality of rights does not involve the necessity of educating white and colored persons in the same school any more than it does that of educating children of both sexes in the same school . . . any classification which preserves substantially equal school advantages is not prohibited by either the State or Federal Constitution, nor would it contravene the provisions of either."

[17]It twice defeated proposals by Senator Sumner of Massachusetts for mixed schools, in 1872 and 1874.

[18]Berkeley, *Principles of Human Knowledge,* London, Thomas Nelson & Sons, 1945, Introduction, 3.

[19]Henry R. Pease, *Congressional Record*, 43d Congress, 1st sess., vol. 2, pt. 5, pp. 4153-4154. See also: James W. Garner, *Reconstruction in Mississippi*, New York, Macmillan Company, 1911, p. 243; Dunbar Rowland, *History of Mississippi*, 2 vols., Chicago, S. J. Clarke Publishing Co., 1925, vol. 1, pp 139 ff.

[20]In this regard the following commentary, found in the 1954 *Report* of the Georgia Commission on Education, p. 48n, is noteworthy:

"As a matter of historical accuracy, it should be remembered that the Fourteenth Amendment was never legally adopted. Eleven States were excluded from representation in the Congress which submitted it. All the Southern States except Tennessee rejected it, and their subsequent ratification was compelled by military force. In order to ratify in Tennessee it was necessary to arrest two members of the Legislature. New Jersey, Oregon and Ohio withdrew their ratification. The Union was then composed of 36 States, and 27 were necessary for ratification. The concurrent resolution of Congress dated July 21, 1868, declaring the amendment ratified, stated that 25 named States had ratified, and included in this list were New Jersey, Oregon, and Ohio. Other States subsequently ratified to bring the total to 32, as stated in the note to this Amendment in the United States Code, but included in this total were the Southern States which ratified at bayonet point, and New Jersey, Oregon and Ohio, which withdrew ratification. No effort was ever made to cause the Amendment to be submitted by a Congress composed of representatives from all 36 States."

For a comprehensive account of the Fourteenth Amendment ratification proceedings see Walter J. Suthon, Jr., "The Dubious Origin of the Fourteenth Amendment," 28 *Tulane Law Review*, 22-44. See also the address in the House of Representatives, July 12, 1909 by Congressman, afterwards Secretary of State, Cordell Hull, *Congressional Record*, 61st Congress, 1st sess., vol. 44, pt. 4, p. 4404.

[21]Although this principle is known by this name, I believe, only in law, it is by no means an exclusively legal principle, but rather a corollary of a principle of metaphysics that every determinate thing is exclusive of everything else. If, conceivably, this did not hold, then no distinctions at all could be made in anything, and all that is before the mind would be a cloud of indefiniteness, indistinguishable from nothingness. This is behind John Marshall's proposition, "Affirmative words are often, in their operation, negative of other objects than those affirmed . . ." *Marbury* v. *Madison*, 1 Cranch 137, 174. Professor Charles L. Black, Jr. comments: ". . . Marshall reasoned that the constitutional inclusion of some items in the original jurisdiction [of the Supreme Court] implied an exclusion of all others—a highly doubtful argument from implication." *Op. cit.*, p. 200. But it is not an argument. It is an expression of one of the *grounds* of all logical argument: that a thing, A, is not not-A, that a true proposition is not a false one. Without this ground, argument could not begin—there would be nothing to argue about. Further, all logical argument is "from implication" and if no logical error is made there is no such thing as a "doubtful argument from implication." Although the inclusion of some things in a given class leaves indeterminate the question whether other things are included, that is so only formally, and subsequent showings of fact may remove the indeterminacy. The sovereign, "We the people," in establishing the Federal Government delegated certain powers to it, including certain jurisdictions to the Supreme Court. Does the fact that it delegated these jurisdictions imply that it delegated others? No. If it did, that would imply that whenever *some* is determined, *all* is determined,

since *some* would always imply *more* and so ultimately *all*. This is of course contrary to both reason and fact and wholly foreign to the conception and content of the Constitution.

The Supreme Court itself can be seen to stand on the *expressio unius . . .* principle when it refuses to render advisory opinions. For it deals with "cases and controversies," and advisory opinions would fall outside these. The Constitution says in Article III that the Court's jurisdiction shall extend to cases and controversies, but does not say *only* to them. Obviously, in refusing to go beyond these the Court is restrained by the principle that what lies beyond is excluded from its jurisdiction.

Amendment IX states, "The enumeration in the Constitution, of certain rights, shall not be construed to deny or disparage others retained by the people." Why this? For the good reason, doubtless, that without it such rights, not being enumerated among those protected, might be ruled out on the *expressio unius* principle. So this is a further recognition of that principle in the Constitution itself.

Again, the first article of the Constitution vests Congress with power, among others, to tax, to borrow money, maintain an army and navy, and make war . . . and to all these it superadds the power to make laws for carrying them into execution. It does not say that *only* Congress shall have this latter power, but of course it means that. Similarly the Fourteenth Amendment gives Congress power to enforce its provisions but does not say that *only* Congress shall have that power. If now the Federal courts can set themselves to enforce the Fourteenth Amendment, why may they not tax, make war, etc.? It is not long since the Supreme Court was pointedly reiterating, "It is not said that the judicial power of the general government shall extend to enforcing the prohibitions and to protecting the rights and immunities guaranteed in the Fourteenth Amendment." *Fay* v. *The People,* 332 U. S. 261, 283. So the Court itself, when it pleases, acknowledges its limitation. "It is curious," remarked Judge Learned Hand, that in the school-segregation cases "no mention was made of section three [*five?* of the Fourteenth Amendment], which offered an escape from intervening, for it empowers Congress to 'enforce' all the preceding sections by 'appropriate legislation'." *Bill of Rights,* Cambridge, Mass., Harvard University Press, 1958, p. 55.

In one of the school cases the Court says "the Fourteenth Amendment applies only to the States." *Bolling* v. *Sharpe, loc. cit.,* p. 498. Why *only?* For the Amendment does not say *only.* Of course the reason is *expressio unius est exclusio alterius.*

One further instance. The Supreme Court has taken occasion to curb the President on this same ground. It said in *Youngstown Sheet and Tube Co.* v. *Sawyer:* "In the framework of our Constitution the President's power to see that the laws are faithfully executed refutes the idea that he is to be a lawmaker. The Constitution limits his functions in the lawmaking process to the recommending of laws he thinks wise and the vetoing of laws he thinks bad." 343 U. S. 579, 587. Now the Constitution, enumerating the powers of the President (Article II), does not say that they are *only* those enumerated. But here is the Supreme Court saying as much, and this in 1952, the year it heard the school cases. And in saying that the President's specified power refutes the idea that he has other powers, the Court is as much as saying that the Fourteenth Amendment in specifying that Congress shall have power to enforce it, refutes the idea that the Supreme Court has such power. *Et tu, Brute!*

22 In fact Congress had acted long since, rather broadly, and had been counter-

acted, vetoed, by the Supreme Court. "The Civil Rights Act of 1875, the principal sections of which were declared unconstitutional by the Supreme Court some years later [*Civil Rights Cases,* 109 U. S. 3 (1883)] marks the culmination of the efforts of Congress to enact laws for the enforcement of the Fourteenth Amendment. The Republicans had been overwhelmingly defeated at the election in the fall of 1874 when the proposed Civil Rights Bill had been one of the main issues, and when that party again had the majority in all branches of the Government. . . ." Horace E. Flack, *Adoption of the Fourteenth Amendment,* Baltimore, Johns Hopkins Press, 1908, p. 277.

23 14 Stat. 216 (1866); 14 Stat. 342 (1866).

24 How, then, can there be graduated tax rates, as on incomes? Obviously they discriminate, and hence abrogate the equal-protection principle. It is immaterial that the rich are able to pay; for before the law, where all are equal, rich and poor do not exist. We cannot have it both ways; either the principle of equal protection of the laws is unreal, and that much of the Fourteenth Amendment is a deceit, or else the tax law cannot bear unequally on us. Alternatively, if the graduated income tax scale is somehow reconciled with equal protection— how, will ever remain a mystery—then we are not equals before the law. The worst pessimists speak of two classes of citizens, first and second. The true number now will have to be at least as many as the number of levels in the income tax scale.

Further, it will not do to say that not the person but the property is what is taxed; for then there could not be differential income tax rates. An income of a million dollars would yield the same tax, no matter how many or how few persons shared it. The inequality of income tax rates is a precise and telling measure of inequality of the protection of persons.

25 *Ogden* v. *Saunders,* 12 Wheaton 213, 270.

26 *West Coast Hotel Company* v. *Parrish, loc. cit.,* p. 399.

27 Cp.: "The Fourteenth Amendment does not profess to secure to all persons in the United States the benefit of the same laws and the same remedies. Great diversities in these respects may exist in two States separated only by an imaginary line." *Missouri* v. *Lewis,* 101 U. S. 22, 31.

28 Agreement between Continental Oil Company and Refinery Employees' Union of the Lake Charles area, Lake Charles, Louisiana, April 23, 1962, p. 36.

29 *Near* v. *Minnesota,* 283 U. S. 697, 708.

30 *Slaughterhouse Cases,* 16 Wallace 36, 78.

31 *Gomillion* v. *Lightfoot,* 364 U. S. 339, 341.

32 328 U. S. 549, 552.   33 *Ibid.,* p. 553.   34 *Baker* v. *Carr,* 369 U. S. 186.

35 *Gomillion* v. *Lightfoot, loc. cit.,* p. 346.

36 Geometry is a singular criterion for judging a political subdivision. Would a square or circle be the ideal and any irregular polygon illicit? Why? The city of Pittsburgh, for example, resembling the figure of a barking terrier more or less, or Cincinnati, comparable to the outline of a five or six-way wreck, might expect to rue the day they should happen to be called to answer in the Supreme Court.

37 *Loc. cit.,* p. 279. 38 *Ibid.,* p. 266.

39 The Supreme Court has said: "This court could not, even if it would, weigh different motives." *Bailey* v. *Drexel Furniture Company,* 259 U. S. 20, 27. In words of John Marshall, it "may well be doubted how far the validity of a law depends upon the motives of its framers." *Fletcher* v. *Peck,* 6 Cranch 87, 130.

Though motive and intent are distinguishable, motive without intent is blind, and intent without motive is void. Effective intent is inseparable from motive.

[40] Associated Press, May 4, 1963.

[41] *Time,* May 17, 1963, p. 25.   [42] Associated Press, May 19, 1963.

[43] Albert P. Blaustein and Clarence C. Ferguson, Jr., *op. cit.,* p. 153.

[44] How would judges or others measure feelings, in particular Negro pupils' feelings, to determine whether they were inferior? Was there in possession of the Kansas court or the witnesses it credited a suitable passionometer? If so, what was its description? (All apparatus used in scientific investigations must be carefully identified in creditable reports of the investigations.) What was its register in this instance? Why was it not used on the white pupils? Since it was not, how could judges or others determine that the Negro register was inferior?

The silence on these questions in both the Kansas court and the Supreme Court opinions is eloquent testimony itself that here was no real showing of fact, that the inferiority feeling was only ascribed, not proved. And even if the idea of determining the alleged inferiority by scientific measurement is dismissed, the case is not saved; for then all is a matter of guesswork or of clashing polemical opinion, proving nothing.

[45] "Crime," observed Justice Brandeis, "is contagious. If the government becomes a law-breaker, it breeds contempt for law; it invites every man to become a law unto himself; it invites anarchy." *Olmstead* v. *United States,* 277 U. S. 438, 485.

One of the reasons given by President Kennedy for urging integration legislation was that "new Negro demonstrations could erupt into a race riot." Associated Press, June 5, 1963. But when violence against school integration was threatened in Little Rock the Supreme Court said "law and order are not here to be preserved" if it meant blocking integration! *Cooper* v. *Aaron, loc. cit.,* p. 16. Violence, one might infer, is now a legitimate resort for Negroes, but not for whites. This should not surprise if we remember that from falsity, such as we have seen at the foundation of *Brown,* anything may arise.

Three days after President Kennedy's appeal the National Council of Churches of Christ "called for mass demonstrations" and for members of the Council's governing board "to personally involve themselves in demonstration." Associated Press, June 8, 1963. In Gadsden, Alabama, where daily parading by Negro demonstrators had gone on without police interference, one of the leaders gave word that a court injunction duplicating one in Mississippi which had been sustained by the United States Supreme Court would not deter the demonstrators—on the contrary, "we will become more radical and there will be no more truce periods." Birmingham *News,* June 18, 1963. The supposition frequently voiced by clerics that a person cannot reject integration and still be religious (or Christian) betrays an odd parochialism, if not a denial of religious freedom. Religious spirit manifests itself in many modes and circumstances, including the communion of homogeneous and subtly segregated Christian congregations.

[46] The Supreme Court hitherto said: "But neither the [Fourteenth] amendment—broad and comprehensive as it is—nor any other amendment, was designed to interfere with the power of the State, sometimes termed its police power, to prescribe regulations to promote the health, peace, morals, education,

and good order of the people." *Barbier* v. *Connolly,* 113 U. S. 27, 31 (1884). Cf. *Cox* v. *New Hampshire,* 312 U. S. 569 (1941).

[47] New York *Times,* May 19, 1963.   [48] *Brown* v. *Allen,* 344 U. S. 443, 540.

[49] The latest Washington move is a concentration on the interstate commerce clause of the Constitution to see whether it can be extenuated into a prohibition of segregation in places where goods from outside the state are sold. The power of Congress "to regulate commerce with foreign nations, and among the several states" is presumed to imply power in Congress to compel a restaurateur, for example, to serve Negroes.

Of course lawful *commerce* between a merchant and a supplier beyond the state terminates, in a given instance, upon consummation of the transaction. Thereafter there is no commerce in that case for Congress to regulate. The goods are the purchaser's quite as certainly as if they had originated on his premises; hence if Congress can deny him the right to hold them, that is, not to sell them to anyone he does not choose to sell to, so can it deny him, by reason of its *interstate* commerce jurisdiction, the right to hold the product of those premises, or even the right to hold the premises themselves rather than sell to a Negro (or to anyone else whom Congress might choose to patronize). Or, to change the case slightly, if an oil company wants to cross your land with a pipe line, or a gunpowder or fertilizer manufacturer wants to put up a factory on it, you cannot stop them, Congress willing. Thus ownership, one of the most elementary rights, totters with the Constitution.

It is also argued that if you don't serve Negroes, you place a burden on interstate commerce. A crude dissimulation—what does not exist cannot be a burden. Magic carpets do not exist, but that is not a burden on travel. Not everyone can stay at the Waldorf, but there are other places to stay. Moreover, *bona fide* commerce makes its way by finding or creating the channels suited to it. And is commerce everything? Do the constitutional guarantees of liberty and property fade before it? Even the equal-protection right will be sacrificed if anyone is compelled to sell his property or skill to a private party against his will; for the terms cannot be equal where the law compels one party to accede to the other's bidding. That, further, is involuntary servitude, which is prohibited by the Thirteenth Amendment.

Two sentences beyond the interstate commerce clause the Constitution confers on Congress the power "to coin money and regulate the value thereof." Will Washington presently be moved by this to regulate one's spending, perhaps going so far as to say you cannot refuse to buy from a Negro, just as it would now say you cannot refuse to sell to him?

Caveat emptor (let the buyer beware) still holds, though perhaps uncertainly, and is significant here. It signifies that the terms of sale and hence the decision whether to sell and hence to whom, are with the vendor. The transaction is, however, a bargain, a deal. Unless the right to deal, to buy or not to buy, to sell or not to sell, is no more, government cannot coerce either party and hence cannot require merchants to serve anyone against their will. Or if the merchant can be so compelled, cannot the clerk, the cook, the waiter, barber, doctor? Else discrimination, unequal protection. What if the services of these are grudging, long delayed, unsatisfactory, and priced sky high? Will Washington create an army of inspectors to go with Negro travelers and test, appraise, and fix the price of all services, even standing over diagnosticians and surgeons with threats of injunctions?

Further, is it true that just because licensed and subject to state regulations, a private business is a public service as said by Justice Douglas in *Lombard* v. *Louisiana,* 10 L ed 2d 338, 347? Surely nothing but a public utility is a public service legally. If being subject to state surveillance is being a public service, then everybody and nearly everything is a public service. There seems to be an equivocation here. The proposition is that a store, for example, renders a service which has become a public interest. Is everything with a public interest subject to Federal control? There is a public interest in churches, morals, play, the arts, intelligence, and life *per se.* Are these, therefore, subject to Washington? Of course the public interest in them and in private business is different from the public interest in a bus line or electric service, for instance. Only in a region such as the foglands of SCUR would confusion of such interests occur.

Confusion is not all. Some uncertainty having arisen about staking everything on the interstate commerce clause, proponents of the 1964 Civil Rights Act turned directly to the equal-protection clause of the Fourteenth Amendment for support. What might have been thought a mortifying if not fatal obstacle met them there, in the fact that the Supreme Court, in the famous *Civil Rights Cases, loc. cit.,* had voided the Civil Rights Act of 1875, which was founded on that clause and contained all the public-accommodation features of the 1964 law. But if there was any mortification or any misgiving about flouting the Court's decision, rendered in 1883, it hardly came into public notice. Rather, the sentiment seemed to be that the Court today, "in the light of [its] recent record of reversing old civil rights rulings" (*Time,* July 12, 1963, p. 20), would oblige with a timely reversal here too. The jest about the Court now belonging to the Negro and why don't the white folks get them one too, connects rather piquantly with this.

CHAPTER 4

BOLLING v. SHARPE

In *Bolling* v. *Sharpe* the Court held that segregation violates the due process clause of the Fifth Amendment. The clause states that no person shall "be deprived of life, liberty, or property without due process of law."

In support of its decision the Court stated the following grounds:

(1) That although the equal-protection clause of the Fourteenth Amendment does not apply in the District of Columbia (since the Amendment applies only to states), "the concepts of equal protection and due process . . . are not mutually exclusive." (This and the following quoted passages are found at 347 U. S. 497, 499, 500.)

(2) That discrimination "may be so unjustifiable as to be violative of due process."

(3) That classifications "based solely upon race . . . are contrary to our traditions and hence constitutionally suspect."

(4) That "liberty under law extends to the full range of conduct which the individual is free to pursue, and it cannot be restricted except for a proper governmental objective."

(5) That segregation "is not reasonably related to any proper governmental objective."

(6) That segregation "thus . . . imposes on the Negro children of the District of Columbia a burden that constitutes an arbitrary deprivation of their liberty in violation of the Due Process Clause."

(7) That segregation having been found unconstitutional in the states, in the Brown decision, "it would be unthinkable" that it should be upheld in the Federal jurisdiction.

Let us consider these grounds.

Now it is not logical to say, as seems to be said in (1), that just because two concepts are not mutually exclusive, the one can substitute for the other. More than non-exclusiveness is needed for that. The concept of integrity and that of wealth, for example, are not mutually exclusive, but that does not make one of them a substitute for the other.

The Court does say this: "The 'equal protection of the laws' is a more explicit safeguard of prohibited unfairness [*sic*] than 'due process of law', and, therefore, we do not imply that the two are always interchangeable phrases." (We might wish there were no safeguards of unfairness at all, prohibited or other; but this is the language, and thought, of our highest court!) In different language the meaning appears to be: Equal protection is in one sense more than due process, hence the two are not always interchangeable.

Does this justify interchanging them in the present case? Not at all. It does not preclude it, true; but neither does it entail it. It simply leaves it undetermined so far—which is as far as the Court goes.

It is not in fact interchangeability the Court needs here. Less will do. All that is needed is to bring due process under equal protection, so as to apply to the present case the decision in the Brown case. Yet that, if it were done, would be a gross anomaly. Due process applies expressly to all persons to whom the Constitution applies; equal protection expressly applies only to persons under the jurisdiction of states. Accordingly, to bring due process as such within the scope of equal protection as such, would be to include the greater within the smaller, an impossibility. And in fact, equal protection may exist without due process; as when, through either lax or harsh enforcement, different persons receive the same protection but not due process. So it is out of the question to justify due process by translation into equal protection.

This may be shown another way. Due process, it might seem, surely involves equal protection; for in any one type of case due process is one self-same thing, and all who receive it must thereby receive equal treatment, equal protection. This implies that if any are denied equal protection, thereby they are denied due process. Since by the Brown decision segregation is denial of equal protection, it seems to follow that the plaintiffs in the Bolling case were denied due process.

Ostensibly, such reasoning is irrefutable. But there is more to be said. Two juries, given the same evidence in accordance with all applicable rules of procedure, may return opposite verdicts. Judges on the same bench may reach different decisions and courts may reverse other courts or themselves on the same issue, as the Supreme Court has ofter done. The incidence of the law upon the parties concerned is then antithetical: the law's protection in like cases is unlike, unequal. Yet the parties were accorded due process.

It is thus evident that due process does not mean or require equal protection. Neither of them is a guarantee of the other. In trying to derive one from the other or to justify one by the other, the Court was therefore making an attempt against reason.

A further point, on which all the foregoing depends, may be noted. The Court is relying not on law or fact, so far as (1) is concerned, but simply on reasoning. It is assuming that, *logically*, things which are not exclusive of each other are in some cases interchangeable. That depends on what things they are—the bare form or logic does not guarantee it. The Court needed to specify; needed to state what there is of due process that is interchangeable with equal protection. By so doing it might have increased our understanding of the Constitution. By not so doing it left itself open to accusations of illogicality or arbitrariness. If a sophomore in a logic course reasoned similarly, concluding, for example, that because justice and mercy are not mutually exclusive, they can be taken to be interchangeable and hence that he could legitimately expect mercy in place of justice and so pass his course despite his F's, I am afraid he would find otherwise.

Our (2), or second ground of the Court's decision, attaches in the Court's published opinion to the ground formulated above as (1), thus: "But, as this Court has recognized, discrimination may be so unjustifiable as to be violative of due process." There is, however, no apparent connection between this and the question of (1), which is the question of how due process is related to equal protection. If something is violative of due process, of course it is unconstitutional, regardless of how or whether it is related to equal protection, since due process is an independent provision of the Constitution. If then the Court means there is a connection, why is it not shown? And if it does not mean that, what is the point of introducing, adversatively, this observation about due process?

Though due process is a somewhat complex and elusive idea, one does not have to be a jurist to see that discrimination—denial of legal rights, imposition of illegal sanctions, favoritism—might go so far as to make a travesty of law, and *a fortiori* of due process. Was that done in the District of Columbia schools? Just where is the line between discrimination of the type "so unjustifiable as to be violative of due process" and (what is evidently contemplated by the Court at this point) discrimination that is not so unjustifiable?

Here the Court gives three citations. The first, *Detroit Bank* v. *United States*, tells us only this, bearing on discrimination: "Unlike the Fourteenth Amendment, the Fifth contains no equal protection clause and it provides no guaranty against discriminatory legislation by Congress. Even if discriminatory legislation may be so arbitrary and injurious in character as to violate the due process clause of the Fifth Amendment . . . no such case is presented here."[1] The next citation (*Currin* v. *Wallace*) says: ". . . that Amendment [the Fifth], unlike the Fourteenth, has no equal protection clause . . . If it be assumed that there might be discrimination of such an injurious character as to bring into operation the due process clause of the Fifth Amendment, that is a different matter . . ."[2] The last of the citations (*Steward Machine Company* v. *Davis*) is this: "[The Social Security Act is valid] though we assume that discrimination, if gross enough, is equivalent to confiscation and subject under the Fifth Amendment to challenge and annulment."[3]

The essence of the first passage is that the Fifth Amendment does not guarantee equal protection, but that *if* discrimination may be so extreme "as to violate . . . due process . . ." The second is less positive: "if it be assumed that there might be discrimination of such an injurious character . . ." The last *assumes* that discrimination amounting to confiscation would violate due process. There is no finding here, no assertion that discrimination *is* or even that it may be an abrogation of due process. All that is set forth is a condition, a hypothesis without a thesis or consequent: if discrimination may go so far—. It is like saying, "If communism should spread over the earth—." (Perhaps the Court had in mind a subsequent citation more to the point, *Hirabayashi* v. *United States*, 320 U. S. 81, 100, but for some reason omitted it here.)

This is a long way from what the Court now calls a recognition, in the cited passages, that discrimination "may be so unjustifiable as to be violative of due process." The word, "if," likewise the equivalent, "assume," is a small word, but it cannot be stricken out at will. If it could, then I could say, "If I am king," thereupon strike the "if," and, behold, I am king!

Passing to (3), have we here a legal ground? The proposition is that classifications according to race are "contrary to our traditions and hence constitutionally suspect."

Our traditions are not the law; and being "constitutionally suspect" is not necessarily being unconstitutional. Federal financing of education, for example, is contrary to our traditions but is not, one may presume, unconstitutional. At any rate there are continual efforts in Congress and the executive department to bring it about. Some of the "social" legislation of the last generation was so far contrary to our traditions as to be unthinkable—literally beyond comprehension— to many persons at the time of enactment. The Supreme Court itself has had some ups and downs in this regard, now finding a law incompatible with our way, again finding it compatible. It is sometimes said that the republican form of government is not found among us (hence is not traditional), and yet not only is it not unconstitutional, it is even guaranteed to every state by the Constitution (Article IV, Section 4).

The statement that classifications based solely upon race are contrary to our traditions is disputable. Indians are for some purposes treated as a race, and the Constitution singles out the untaxed ones in its very first article and again in the Fourteenth Amendment, for the purpose of excluding them from congressional representation. But the fact that the great majority of Negroes in the United States had always been segregated, including those in the District of Columbia under the Supreme Court's eyes, refutes the statement that race classifications are contrary to our traditions. Such classifications come much nearer to being part of our traditions than contrary to them. That may be unjust and deplorable, but it is a fact. Were it not a fact, probably there would have been no segregation cases before the Court.

It is worth a moment to notice the citations on the point of constitutional suspiciousness. There are two, both of them concerning California Japanese in cases before the Supreme Court. In *Korematzu v. United States* the Court said: "... all legal restrictions which curtail the civil rights of a single racial group are immediately suspect. That is not to say that all such restrictions are unconstitutional. It is to say that courts must subject them to the most rigid scrutiny. Pressing public necessity may sometimes justify the existence of such restrictions; racial antagonism never can."[4] In the other citation it is said: "The Fifth Amendment contains no equal protection clause and it restrains only such discriminatory legislation as amounts to a denial of due process . . . legislative classification or discrimination based on race alone has often been held to be a denial of equal protection."[5]

To acknowledge that conditions may exist under which racial restrictions may lawfully be imposed, except that racial antagonism is not one of them, is as much as to concede a hypothetical justification for segregation.[6] Is school segregation a matter of racial antagonism? Of course it may be, but again it may not. Racial difference is not the same thing as racial antagonism. Tradition, custom, even aversion, is not necessarily antagonism; and a strong showing of friendliness of white people towards Negroes is found in many Southern communities. When it is acknowledged that "pressing public necessity may sometimes justify" racial restrictions, the way is opened for school segregation, and not on grounds of "race alone" but of the public interest, in such respects as peace, good order, educational welfare. Consequently, when that avenue is closed entirely, as in the school cases, the possibilities judicially recognized in these citations are summarily denied.

So the Court opens itself to the charge of arbitrariness. And arbitrariness is not just an epithet. It means or is the substitution of willfulness for reasonableness, of a man's fiat in place of proof. No one, including a law court, can say that racial restrictions may in some circumstances be legitimate and then issue an order unconditionally prohibiting them. That is patent contradiction. The effects come home in such form as confusion, insecurity, distrust, disorder.

The next one of the Court's grounds, (4), is little short of baffling. Is it a play on words? Or an entanglement in words? If my liberty "extends to the full range of conduct" that I am "free to pursue," what does that mean? I presume it means that I am at liberty to do what I am free to do. But since "liberty" is only a synonym for "freedom," derived from a Latin word meaning freedom, all that this tells me is that I am free to do what I am free to do. Well! And what is that? Am I free to enroll at any school I wish? Am I not subject to enrollment regulations? Not even if, as in the District of Columbia, they are sanctioned by Congress?

But the enrollment regulations and the law behind them may have exceeded constitutional bounds, and that is just what this case alleges. In particular, it alleges that they abrogated the due-process guarantee. In what way?

The Court, in finding that they did so, gives this answer: Segregation imposes on the Negro pupils "a burden that constitutes an arbitrary deprivation of their liberty in violation of the Due Process Clause."

If segregation is arbitrary, if it deprives of one's liberty, who but the tyrannical would uphold it? But it had been upheld from the first, in a long, unbroken line of decisions by state and Federal courts, including the Supreme Court. In all these cases therefore, according to the Supreme Court now, the judiciary must have been arbitrary and must have deprived people of their liberties, in violation of the Constitution and, we may add, of the judges' oath to uphold the Constitution.

This is a disturbing implication of the Bolling decision. The Supreme Court, by its own words, on its own grounds, is pronouncing its predecessors, Brandeis, Holmes, Stone among them, to have flouted or forgotten an ever applicable provision of the Constitution and to have assumed arbitrary power in doing so. Is this reasonable? Here again the Court lays itself open to accusations of arbitrariness.

What is the purpose of its citation of a passage from the 1896 case *Gibson* v. *Mississippi*, saying that the Constitution forbids discrimination at the hands of government, in the sphere of civil rights? If the Constitution does that, if it unconditionally forbids such discrimination, as the Court's language may suggest, why is the instant case,

Bolling, not settled forthwith? For if there must be no such discrimination, and if segregation is an instance of it, there is no more to be said. But not so. There is indeed more to be said.

In the place cited the Court declared: "In the administration of justice no rule can be applied to one class which is not applicable to all other classes." This is expressive of the equal-protection requirement (the question at issue in *Gibson* v. *Mississippi* was equal protection, not due process). It is also a recognition of classes (racially distinguished classes, it so happened). And the same Court, one month afterwards, in *Plessy* v. *Ferguson,* held that racially separate schools are no violation of equal protection. There was no intimation that separation of classes, in itself, meant unequal protection.

So the cited evidence of *Gibson* v. *Mississippi* is no support for the proposition that racial separation is unequal protection. On the contrary, it acknowledges the compatibility of racial separation and equal protection. If then separation is not unequal protection, and if you are bent on proving denial of due process of law by way of unequal protection, as the Court is here, this is wholly barren ground. The trap that was to destroy the enemy isn't there.

The remaining citation here, *Steele* v. *Louisville and Nashville Railroad Company,* decided in 1944, is of a ruling that a railroad employees' union could not discriminate against any of its members on account of race, under the Railway Labor Act. Presumably the bearing of this is not that what holds under the Railway Labor Act holds also in education, but rather that racial segregation is in itself discrimination. But this would only clash with the citation just before, where segregation is admitted to be compatible with equal protection and hence is not discrimination. The comparison here is still quite far-fetched: railway employment rights, or provisions, on the one hand, educational rights, or provisions, on the other. In the first there was found inequality of a kind. In the second there was not—the educational rights, or provisions, in the white and Negro schools in the Brown case were found to be equal. So again the Court went hunting and bagged no game.

Passing to the next one of the Court's grounds, (5), we find a singular judicial presumption: that of a "proper governmental objective." With what warrant does the Court venture to pronounce to the United States a proper (or an improper) governmental objective?[7] It is itself a creature of governmental objectives, not their author or judge. We alone, who are sovereign, are the author and judge. The phrase, "appropriate legislation," in the Fourteenth Amendment and other parts of the Constitution explicitly giving enforcement powers to Congress, might be thought to involve "proper objectives" and so to justify judicial review of the propriety of the District of Columbia's segregation objectives. But we have here two very different things; an objective and the means to it. Although the Court might judge the means (laws, regulations), under the "appropriateness" clause, to the extent of saying whether they were manifestly irrelevant or absurd, with what authority shall it judge the objective so long as it is not *prima facie* unconstitutional? And of course nothing that has been judicially sustained again and again without fail, and often by the Supreme Court, can be that.

In fact it rules out the objective, whatever it was; for to say that segregation is not reasonably related to any proper governmental objective is tantamount to doing that. How can the Court go so far without pretensions to omniscience? Does it know in advance all governmental objectives, including the many particulars of peace, health, good order, and know that segregation might be reasonably related to none of them? That would be *ultra vires*. Here the Court's silence—it says not a word to justify its pronouncement—invites a very different explanation, the one we have seen before: arbitrariness. For whoever judges without grounds, or with such only as he dares not to disclose, judges arbitrarily (if he can be said to judge at all and not just to make edicts).

Only by resorting to an *ad hoc* conception outside the law—"Separate educational facilities are inherently unequal," a proposition we have seen to be a presumption against fact and reason—did the Court seem to warrant its decision in the Brown case; and the Bolling decision rests heavily on that one. The Court has not demonstrated, has not shown by clear derivations from the Constitution, that segregation is *per se* unconstitutional. In the absence of such showing, it cannot justly chastise the District of Columbia with imputations of improper, unconstitutional objectives.

Having nevertheless done that, the Court goes on in (6) to declare segregation in the District of Columbia an arbitrary deprivation of liberty and hence a violation of due process. It arrives at this by inference from the presumption of an improper objective. But unless that presumption is justified, of course it cannot stand as a premise; and the Court has ventured to give no justification for it (the bare dictum, patently untenable, that separate facilities are inherently unequal, is not a *justification*). That (6) is untenable is accordingly inescapable. In short, lacking a ground, a conclusion cannot be drawn; from nothing comes nothing.

The last ground, (7), concerns, in the Court's words, the unthinkable:

that something unconstitutional in the states, as segregation is according to the Brown decision, should yet be constitutional in the District of Columbia is unthinkable. But it is not unthinkable that something applicable exclusively to the states should be inapplicable elsewhere; and the equal-protection clause of the Fourteenth Amendment, on which the Brown decision rests, is applicable exclusively to the states.[8] On the contrary, that the equal-protection clause be constitutionally applicable elsewhere when expressly limited to the states by the Constitution, is unthinkable—at least logically, consistently, unthinkable.[9]

The Court cites the case of *Hurd* v. *Hodge,* a Washington, D.C. case concerning enforcement of private covenants against sale of real estate to Negroes. There, after citing Section 1978 of the Revised Statutes, which reads "All citizens of the United States shall have the same right, in every State and Territory, as is enjoyed by white citizens thereof to inherit, purchase, lease, sell, hold, and convey real and personal property," the Court said: "We have no doubt that, for the purposes of this section, the District of Columbia is included within the phrase 'every State and Territory'."[10] The purposes of the section, however, are confined to real and personal property. There is a reference to *Talbott* v. *Silver Bow County,* where opinions of Marshall and others are cited in which it was held that the District of Columbia is in some sense a state. But it is also noted that Marshall held that a territory "is not a distinct sovereignty. It has no independent powers. It is a political community organized by Congress, all whose powers are created by Congress, and all whose acts are subject to Congressional supervision."[11] Since this fits the District of Columbia exactly, the sense in which the District is a state must be admitted to be peculiar, to say the least, and clearly not the sense in which the fifty members of the Union are states.[12]

Now, in the instant case, the Court says it is unthinkable that "the same Constitution would impose a lesser duty on the Federal Government [than on the states]." Just wherein is that unthinkable? Presumably in this: it would contradict some other constitutional provision. What one? The Court gives us no hint. But by logical construction it is easily seen that the provision would have to be one guaranteeing to persons residing in territories the same rights as those guaranteed to residents of states. There is of course no such provision.

If the Constitution imposes the same duty on the Federal Government as on the states, how is it that the Federal Government made the inhabitants of the District of Columbia voteless in national elections, while the citizens of the states voted in such elections under ample provisions of the Constitution? Why hasn't the District of Columbia two Senators and at least one Representative, as guaranteed to the states by the first article of the Constitution? These are matters which the residents of Washington have by no means found unthinkable— they have thought long, hard, and sometimes sourly about them; and Congress, which ordained the restrictions and also established and perpetuated school segregation there, must be presumed to have found them not unthinkable.

Even if the District of Columbia is "included in the phrase 'every State and Territory'," that is not enough to ground the Bolling decision. Nothing in that phrase or in the cited provisions of the Revised Statutes pertains to school segregation. Citizens white or black can enjoy all the rights there stated with or without school segregation. They did so before the Bolling decision.

The differences between the District of Columbia and the states at the time of the Bolling decision are seen in the following:

"The District of Columbia has no representation in Congress and no voice in the selection of the President, not by reason of any constitutional provision relating particularly to the District, but because such rights are conferred only on the people of the states . . .

"Full voting representation in the Senate and House and a share in the election of the President can be provided only through a constitutional amendment."[13]

Since the Brown decision invalidated segregation by application of the equal-protection clause, which constitutionally applies only to the states and not to the District of Columbia, application of the clause to the latter must require supplementary constitutional warrant; which would mean a constitutional amendment. So the Court has virtually amended the Constitution or else founded the Bolling decision on nothing. If the first, it was done without due process and by usurping the amending power from the states; if the second, the decision is but an *ipse dixit*.

Ironically, the Court finds that segregation in this case involves violation of due process. Indeed it does, on the Court's own showing; but violation on the part of the Court itself. For only by extending the Constitution beyond its expressly limited coverage does the Court give the appearance of a ground for its decision. Now such an extension may lawfully come about only as the Constitution prescribes, namely, by amendment through action of the states. That is the due, prescribed process. The Court's arrogation of authority to amend is then a patent violation of due process. In such an instance it is no reply to say that a judicial construction is not an amendment. Extending the coverage of a constitutional provision beyond the states when the Constitution expressly directs it to the states only, is not a matter of construing a document. It is a matter of adding to the document.

The plaintiffs' reliance on the due-process clause was sophistical in the first place, inasmuch as due process is not a form for stretching the Constitution (so as to make the equal protection clause, for instance, extend beyond its terms); rather, due process is a safeguard against such a thing, and well it is, for if you can stretch the Constitution here you can stretch it elsewhere and presently deprive of any right, including due process. And the Court's reliance on "unthinkability" is no less, in fact even more, sophistical. For what it calls unthinkable is only what the limitations of the Constitution implicitly allow and what Congress, surely not without thinking, had ordained.[14] "Unthinkable" is a rhetorical, not a constitutional criterion.[15] Judges who find the distinctions established in the Constitution unthinkable are admitting a singular limitation of mind, one that literally unfits them for their office.

Perhaps they meant only to throw up their hands, like frightened women. In that case they needed to recuse themselves *en masse,* and step down. Is it wrong that the District of Columbia is under special civil disability? Perhaps the states would gladly accord the lush capital equal rights; but they have not done so, and even though it were a desideratum, that would be no ground, no law, on which to rest a judicial decision. Desires, including the Supreme Court's, are not laws and it is not the function of the Court, but of Congress and the states, to translate them into laws, if they please to do so.

Concluding its rebuke of President Truman in *Youngstown Sheet and Tube Company* v. *Sawyer* the Court thundered: "In the framework of our Constitution the President's power to see that the laws are faithfully executed refutes the idea that he is to be a lawmaker . . . The Founders of this Nation entrusted the lawmaking power to the Congress alone in both good times and bad times."[16] This was in 1952. Two years afterwards the Court, by the sophistical means we have seen in both the Brown and the Bolling case, was making law itself, even making a virtual amendment to the Constitution.

Peculiarly sensitive about the equal-protection guarantee, a midcentury Supreme Court judge comes to think with it, see with it, commune with it, and so to give rise to anticipations that equal-protection sentinels may presently stalk the states in practically all that they do. Not stalk them with the intention of seeing whether they perform acceptably in every single category, but only in such categories as may possibly show a trace of color or race. No sentinels that we know of are to watch for inequalities where, for instance, the aged, the juvenile, rich, poor, sick, lunatic, jobless, destitute are concerned. Only the Negro is to have this extraordinary solicitude; the equal-protection watchdogs will growl only if they sense some denial or some slight to him.

Why this favored status for the Negro, since under the equal-protection clause no one is preferred? Some will suspect one reason, some another, a few openly alleging politics. Still darker possibilities may be intimated.[17] A certain progression is discernible: "Negro" becomes practically synonymous with *de facto* "inferiority status;" but what is inferior is not equal; hence the conclusion, now near unto sanctification: racial classifications under the eye of the law are in violation of the Fourteenth Amendment. Notice that the inferiority is not inferiority before the law, but before the white population. So there is a premise at work making equalization of the protected the meaning of equal protection of the laws.

That the Court should be bewitched by race when the Amendment concerns race no more than anything else; that the equal-protection right should be so far to the fore and all the number of rights reserved to the states by the Tenth Amendment left out of sight; that a court should discriminate among the laws, so generating unequal protection, unequal justice, by them—all of this, to give back to the Supreme Court what it flung out on the country, is "contrary to our traditions and hence constitutionally suspect."

---

[1] 317 U. S. 329, 337. [2] 306 U. S. 1, 14. [3] 301 U. S. 548, 585. [4] 323 U. S. 214, 216. [5] 320 U. S. 81, 100.

[6] Justice Stanley Reed, now retired, who participated in the decision of the Brown and Bolling cases, said in an address to the California bar, October 3, 1957: "The law is geared to human needs. Rights even of the First Amendment are subject to the elemental need for order without which the guarantee of civil rights would be a mockery." — Privately printed text, p. 20. It is noteworthy in this regard that the preservation of order was the officially stated purpose of the governor of Arkansas in using the state militia to forestall integration at a high school in Little Rock in September, 1957, and that the officially stated purpose of President Eisenhower, in sending in the Army, was to uphold a district court decision calling for integration. There were many criticisms of the governor, but what Justice Reed says here hardly a month afterwards seems a vindication of him. Cp. below, p. 106.

[7] No doubt the objective of school segregation in the District of Columbia was more or less complex, but a fair presumption would be that in addition to education, it included health and morals—the general welfare (which is an express objective of the Constitution). That these declined under integration,

after the Bolling decision, is evident in the disclosures made in a congressional investigation, which concluded with numerous reform recommendations made by the investigating subcommittee. A majority of the subcommittee recommended a return to segregation. *Report of the Subcommittee to Investigate Public School Standards and Conditions, and Juvenile Delinquency in the District of Columbia,* pp. 46-47. Some details of the findings in this investigation are given here, in ch. 14.

Even judging the means to an objective is, on the part of a court, almost certainly an impertinence and usurpation. The legislature, not the court, is the author of the means. Shall the court presume to tell the legislature that it does not know its business? Perhaps it doesn't and perhaps the court does, but that is immaterial since the judges have no authority to substitute their legislative ideas for those of the legislators. "Congress is of necessity the exclusive judge of what is needful and proper, when the means chosen conduce to the end and are not forbidden." Thomas M. Cooley, *General Principles of Constitutional Law in the United States of America,* 3d ed., Boston, Little, Brown & Co., 1898, p. 107.

In a government of separate, coordinate powers, such as ours, it is only when the legislative branch unquestionably oversteps its bounds that the judiciary may warrantably impose a check; and so long as a legislative act is reasonably related to a constitutional purpose, which in view of the wide discretionary powers of legislators can only mean not patently, not unquestionably contrary to such purpose, it cannot be disturbed by the judiciary without usurpation of legislative power and therefore, with us, subversion of the Constitution. School segregation, again and again approved by Congress and many states and consistently sustained by the Supreme Court from the first, was not without a purpose. For example, under the heading "The Public Health and Welfare" the National School Lunch Act was legislated by Congress in 1946, with provision for segregation. It is officially described as "a measure of national security, to safeguard the health and well-being of the Nation's children" (U.S. Code, 1952 ed., Title 42, secs. 1751, 1760). Until 1954, school segregation had not been denied to be a legitimate exercise of the police powers of the states; powers which are instrumental to the purposes: peace, health, good order, and morals, which in turn are subalternates of the general-welfare purpose of the Constitution. See further *Buchanan* v. *Warley,* 245 U. S. 60, 65, with citations.

8 Justice Frankfurter, though joining the other justices here in bringing the District of Columbia into the state category for purposes of the Bolling decision, had said a few years before: "Marshall . . . rejected summarily the notion that Citizens of the District [of Columbia] are included among Citizens of 'States'. It is suggested that other provisions of the Constitution relating to 'States' apply to the District. If the mere repetition of an inaccuracy begets truth, then that statement is true, not otherwise." *National Insurance Company* v. *Tidewater Company,* 337 U. S. 582, 653, 654. His clerk, Alexander Bickel, writes: "That word ['State'], he stated, cannot be broadened to include the District of Columbia." 69 *Harvard Law Review* 4n.

9 It is noteworthy that the Court's language here is conditional: "unthinkable that the same Constitution would impose a lesser duty on the Federal Government"—*would* impose, not *does* impose. Would, under what condition? Presumably under the condition that the controverted part of the Constitution, the equal-protection clause, applied beyond the states. Since it does not apply

beyond the states (unless we are to disregard the express terms addressing it to the states and not beyond), the condition contemplated is contrary to fact. The Court's whole contention at this point, if the language can be taken straightforwardly, is founded on such an idea as this: "If the Constitution extended farther than it does extend"—an idea which is of course wholly impertinent. And if this reading is disputed, what sense does the Court's utterance make?

10 334 U. S. 24, 31.   11 139 U. S. 438, 445, 446.

12 A few years afterwards the Court held that the territorial rights of some of the states bordering the Gulf of Mexico extended three times as far out to sea (10.3 miles) as those of the others. *United States* v. *Florida,* 363 U. S. 121. The flexibility of the Court's powers of thought must have increased in the interim; for whereas in 1954 the supposition that a resident of a state might have rights under the due-process clause which a resident of a territory did not have was "unthinkable," now (1960) it was thinkable even that a state should have rights which other states, including contiguous ones, did not have.

13 Laurence F. Schmeckebier, *The District of Columbia, Its Government and Administration,* Baltimore, Johns Hopkins Press, 1928, pp. 854-855.

14 Senator William E. Borah, of Idaho, whose prestige in the cause of liberalism was unsurpassed in his day, evidently found the traditional race distinctions not unthinkable. See his remarks on the subject quoted below, pp. 302f.

15 David Hume, a very eminent thinker, observed that "the contrary of every matter of fact is still possible [thinkable]; because it can never imply a contradiction, and is conceived by the mind with the same facility and distinctness, as if ever so conformable to reality." *Enquiry Concerning Human Understanding,* Oxford, Clarendon Press, 1902, sec. iv, pt. i, §21.

16 *Loc. cit.,* p. 587.

17 As when an interested agency sets out "to gather material which would be relevant to a court decision" which "has not yet been rendered by the Supreme Court." See below, pp. 121, 124.

CHAPTER 5

THE DECREES

It was one thing to declare separate schools inherently unequal and quite another to make them equal (*inherently* equal?). Congress alone has express power to enforce the provisions of the Fourteenth Amendment, one of which, the equal-protection provision, was the ground of the school decision. But Congress knew nothing of "inherently unequal" protection under school segregation, and did nothing about it. Taking matters in its own hands, the Supreme Court ventured to institute changes, not uniformly but variably, according to circumstances. A year after the decision, it remanded the cases to the courts of their origin,[1] charging them with the responsibility of issuing appropriate decrees. It said, in a unanimous opinion:

"These cases were decided on May 17, 1954. The opinions of that date, declaring the fundamental principle that racial discrimination in public education is unconstitutional, are incorporated herein by reference. All provisions of federal, state, or local law requiring or permitting such discrimination must yield to this principle. There remains for consideration the manner in which relief is to be accorded.

"Because these cases arose under different local conditions and their disposition will involve a variety of local problems, we requested further argument on the question of relief . . .

"Full implementation of these constitutional principles may require solution of varied local school problems. School authorities have the primary responsibility for elucidating, assessing, and solving these problems; courts will have to consider whether the action of school authorities constitutes good faith implementation of the governing constitutional principles. Because of their proximity to local conditions and the possible need for further hearings, the courts which originally heard these cases can best perform this judicial appraisal. Accordingly, we believe it appropriate to remand the cases to those courts.

"In fashioning and effectuating the decrees the courts will be guided by equitable principles. Traditionally, equity has been characterized by a practical flexibility in shaping its remedies and by a facility for adjusting and reconciling public and private needs. These cases call for the exercise of these traditional attributes of equity power. At stake is the personal interest of the plaintiffs in admission to public schools as soon as practicable on a nondiscriminatory basis. To effectuate this interest may call for elimination of a variety of obstacles in making the transition to school systems operated in accordance with the constitutional principles set forth in our May 17, 1954, decision. Courts of equity may properly take into account the public interest in the elimination of such obstacles in a systematic and effective manner. But it should go without saying that the vitality of these constitutional principles cannot be allowed to yield simply because of disagreement with them.

"While giving weight to these public and private considerations, the courts will require that the defendants make a prompt and reasonable start toward full compliance with our May 17, 1954, ruling. Once such a start has been made, the courts may find that additional time is necessary to carry out the ruling in an effective manner. The burden rests upon the defendants to establish that such time is necessary in the public interest and is consistent with good faith compliance at the earliest practicable date. To that end, the courts may consider problems related to administration, arising from the physical condition of the school plant, the school transportation system, personnel, revision of school districts and attendance areas into compact units to achieve a system of determining admission to the public schools on a nonracial basis, and revision of local laws and regulations which may be necessary in solving the foregoing problems. They will also consider the adequacy of any plans the defendants may propose to meet these problems and to effectuate a transition to a racially nondiscriminatory school system."[2]

Here the language and the sense are at least clear, which is a marked advance over some parts of the Court's original deliverances in the cases. Again, however, there are questionable presumptions and inferences.

It is taken for granted that separation means discrimination when, in the first paragraph, the Court speaks of "racial discrimination." As we have seen, separation does not necessarily imply discrimination. It is not necessarily for that purpose, nor need it have that effect. This, however, is a matter of only nominal significance now. The trouble begins when the Court commands that all laws "requiring or permitting such discrimination must yield . . . "

With what warrant is it held that racially separate public schools may not even be permitted? Suppose that in some districts separation is the will and preference of both Negro and white. By what authority does the Court forbid it? We know the Court's answer, though now we know also that it is arbitrary and specious: "Separate educational facilities are inherently unequal." Even if we were to concede, *arguendo*, that this is true doctrine, wherein would the mere existence of separate schools be a violation of it—wherein would they violate the equal-protection guarantee?

That guarantee is only against *denial*, by a *state*, of equal protection. Who is denied by the state if white families choose white schools and Negro families Negro schools? Nobody, of course; for people who have their preference are not denied. To be denied, would be not to have their preference. The Supreme Court, in prohibiting the possibility of their having that preference, is denying them the right of choosing their associates. This it does in the name of the equal-protection clause.

That is to say, from "no state shall deny to any person within its jurisdiction the equal protection of the laws" the Court is presuming to deduce the proposition that no state shall make provisions permitting citizens a free choice, racially, of schools. To put it another way, the Court is saying that because (1) the state cannot deny equality, therefore (2) it cannot permit citizens to reject equality (integration, that is). This is the inference. Is it valid?

To be valid, the inference must fulfill this requirement of logic: that (1) be incompatible with the denial of (2). For that to be, there must never exist a case in which these concur.

But there are countless cases in which they concur. In New York, let us suppose, there is at times no denial of equal protection; in particular, no denial of school integration. Yet thousands of the inhabitants freely reject integration. This, being a case of (1) with denial of (2), must accordingly be unlawful, by the Court's reasoning. New York, like perhaps all other large cities of the country, must therefore cease and desist from permitting it. Not only must New York insure that no one is denied integration, it must insure that no one is allowed segregation. Individual choice is therefore to be prohibited.

A parallel to this is instructive. No state may lawfully deny a qualified voter the right to vote. Does this imply, hence permit us to deduce, that no state shall permit a qualified voter not to vote? No state shall deny the right to own property; then none shall permit persons within their jurisdiction not to own property? Surely the Supreme Court will now have to ordain ways of redistributing the country's wealth, and of seeing that all qualified voters vote.

Since the Court's prohibition upon the mere permission of segregation is founded solely on reasoning (if it is not a purely arbitrary dictate), let us look a little more closely at the reasoning before proceeding. The reasoning is this: Given that a state is powerless to deny integration, it follows that it is powerless to permit segregation. Here "permit" is the negative, or more accurately an instance of the negative, of "deny," and "segregation" is an instance of the negative of "integration;" and we have: Since the state power to deny is something incompatible with integration, then the state power to permit is something incompatible with segregation. Formally it goes: Given that x excludes y, it follows that the negative of x excludes the negative of y.

But, as anyone with a little training in logic knows, the conclusion does not follow. In material affairs the negative of x coincides somewhere with the negative of y, and so refutes the conclusion that they are mutually exclusive.

Since the Court's prohibition upon even the permission of segregation is founded on this fallacious reasoning, that prohibition is untenable. If the Court persists in maintaining it, it will thereby defy reason in a fashion worthy of comparison with defying the multiplication table and the uses of mathematics generally.

The prohibition on racial liberty was soon in effect. In Nashville, the School Board, complying with a United States district court order to submit an integration plan, submitted one calling for three kinds of school, all-white, all-Negro, and mixed, leaving the choice to the pupil's parents in every case. The court rejected the plan and called for another, allowing only mixed schools.[3]

What, though, one may ask, if Negro pupils in Nashville should have had no effective choice—no integrated school to choose? It is a pointless question now; but all they would have had to do was to call upon the School Board to make good its offer to provide optional integration. Not satisfied with that, the district court, dutifully following the Supreme Court, called for more: for coercive educational amalgamation of the races, with its corollary denial of freedom of association.

The Court is making a fetish of race. Not only does it subordinate parts of the Bill of Rights to the Fourteenth Amendment;[4] it uses the Amendment as if to accomplish psycho-racial fusion. Consistently carried out, the decree against even voluntary segregation would require the methods of despotism, and the farcical gestures of New York City in trying to shuttle pupils back and forth to one another's schools so as to mix white and black, would be nothing by comparison.

It taxes reason to see how the executive branch of the Government, unless it has sunk to a position of incomprehension or of servility

before the Supreme Court, can turn its hand to enforce a dictate
denying people freedom to associate with those of their race under
protection of the law. That means denying elemental constitutional
right. It means a failure in our separate-powers system of government, a system which does not require or contemplate the submission
of one branch to aberration or aggression in another branch, but, on
the contrary, contemplates defense by each one against such misfeasance. To let the Court have its way when it patently errs, as
here, is to let the Constitution, which the President is sworn to preserve, be nullified.

What can the President legitimately do? It is apparent that he
can do either of two things. He can go to work as Lincoln did after
the Dred Scott decision, to show the abuse and error the Court has
committed and to bring about, if not a recall of the whole decision,
then a recall of as much of it as denies elemental liberties. Or he
can simply point out the error and refuse, as Congress long did, to
force it on the country. The worst this might do would be to restore,
officially at least, the pre-1954 state of affairs, a state of peace, morals,
and welfare assuredly not below that of the present. Now that lawlessness and violence are virtually a standard method for advancing
integration, not without Washington's indulgence, the consequences
of this change would not be difficult to foresee. And yet a President
who had the probity and firmness to perform the duty of preserving
the Constitution against judicial subversion would hardly lack the
capacity for dealing with organized lawlessness. It is a fair surmise
that judocracy would then voluntarily capitulate. The return to sanity
and integrity would open a new era in which a clear, forthright definition of where we stand on racial questions could be reached and
could be incorporated in the Constitution if it were a stand different
from that already written in the Constitution and declared again
and again in judicial decisions before 1954.

It is not consonant with the authority and responsibility of the
President to hold that he must enforce the decisions of the Court
regardless of what he may think of them. Though the Constitution
requires that he "take care that the laws be faithfully executed," it
also requires that he "preserve, protect, and defend" the Constitution itself, to the best of his ability. If he bows to the Court in everything, or in one disputable instance, he abdicates the office of preserver, protector, and defender. He thereby destroys the balance of
powers on which our system is founded. On May 16, 1954 school
segregation was lawful in many states and the District of Columbia,
under the Constitution judicially construed. Next day it was unlaw-

ful, though the Constitution had not been changed. As preserver, protector, and defender of the Constitution, could the President now turn upon it and stand ready to use force for carrying into execution this reversal—nullification—of it? If so, what are we to think of "the best of his ability"? He is in no way subservient to the Court here. Rather, he is, as the preserver, protector, and defender, subservient to no one. He is judge of both Court and Constitution.

If it is supposed that a President cannot directly check what he sees to be a nullification ("reversal") of the Constitution by the Court, but that he is limited to indirect checking, such as waiting for a vacancy on the Court and nominating for it someone he trusts (what an idea of *checking*!), then how can it be maintained that the Court can directly check him as it did President Truman in the steel crisis in 1952 or can directly check Congress as it does in pronouncing a congressional act unconstitutional? There is no more warrant in the Constitution for direct checking by the Court than by the other branches. Then only on a showing that our governmental system of co-ordinate powers, each a check and balance to the others, cannot hold up without the preponderance the Supreme Court has arrogated to itself, could it be maintained that the Court properly has this preponderance, this jurisdiction, over the other branches. Of course there is no such showing. If there were, it would be a showing that our system is not one of checks and balances but rather a nonarchy, an oligarchy of nine, unelected, out of the reach of all, ruling over Congress, the President, and the country. Of the many repugnant, intolerable consequences of such a doctrine, one especially is noteworthy here. The oath of the President to preserve, protect, and defend the Constitution would be desecrated, since he would be reduced to the role of rubber-stamping the nonocrats' decrees: he would be reduced, his high oath notwithstanding, to affirming, officially, solemnly, that the Constitution is not the Constitution; for that is what the Court does when, as in *Brown* and as we shall see more fully, it "reverses" itself.

In the first paragraph of the decrees we read of "the fundamental principle that racial discrimination in public education is unconstitutional" and in the third paragraph we are referred to "these constitutional principles" and "full implementation" of them. *What* "constitutional principles"? Only the one has been cited; hence this is a misleading reference, and the Court is lapsing into carelessness as before. Then it recognizes that "varied local school problems"

may arise under "these constitutional principles," and lays upon
school authorities the responsibility not only for solving them but
also for "elucidating" and "assessing" them, all to the satisfaction
of the trial courts. Why those courts and not the Supreme Court?
Because of "their proximity to local conditions and the possible need
for further hearings." What have proximity to local conditions and
possible need for further hearings to do with the authority of the
law of the land? Is not the Court's concession here a virtual admission of error and of encroachment on territory beyond the judicial
province? If the Fourteenth Amendment must hew to local conditions, is it not the province of Congress, through its enforcement
power, to say how? If the constitutional right of equal protection
of the laws is violated, what pertinency have "local conditions" and
corresponding equity considerations to the case? Constitutional rights
are indefeasibly above, not subject to, these varying conditions. It
is a tacit admission by the Court of something illicit—Usurpation?
Subversion?—when its decisions involve the compromise and degradation of a constitutional right (or what it erroneously takes to be
a constitutional right). Whatever can be thus compromised is not an
unconditional provision, like the equal-protection provision, of the
Constitution. In decreeing such compromise the Court was insensibly
decreeing the illicitness of its decision.

How could the trial courts know what to do? Ironically, the Supreme Court directed them to be guided by good-faith considerations
—by whether local authorities' action "constitutes good faith implementation of the governing constitutional principles." This after the
Court's own obliquities in the school cases! And the Court was to
demur, some years afterwards, to good faith as a standard, on the
ground that disproof of it is too difficult to establish![5] "Good faith"
is a rather vague standard in any circumstances, but especially here.
To any two men it may mean two different things. Before one of
them can pronounce the other guilty of bad faith, except in overt,
wanton misfeasance, he must see into the other's conscience and know
that he sees infallibly. He must not substitute his conscience for the
other's. Thus limited, it is not often that anyone can impugn the
good faith of another. But thus it is that the law of the land was
now to be administered.

Assuming their constitutional rights violated, why should the appellants have to abide this long, unpredictable process in order to
come into their own? Is the Constitution so loose and ineffectual?
Doubtless its authors would be surprised to learn that it is; and
assuming it not, we can only conclude that a miscarriage had oc-

curred, that the Court's decision did not stem from genuine constitutional grounds.

Still, having decreed a radical change in law and in the lives of thirty or forty million people, what could the Court do but allow a reasonable time for adjustments? Some would have allowed no time. Had the Court heeded them, disruption and chaos would almost certainly have occurred in many schools. The sudden nullification of laws and regulations, and lack of time and preparation for enacting new ones; the disturbance to financial commitments and projects; the probable revulsion in many communities, would have meant breakdown and closing of the schools.

So now local authorities had the task of "elucidating, assessing, and solving" the problems. Many men, many minds, many solutions. Is that equal protection? In the Brown decision the Supreme Court limited equal protection to identical protection, whereas here it laid down a condition which was practically certain to mean variations. This is repugnant to the equal-protection guarantee. In Nashville there must be no unintegrated school, but in North Carolina cities, I believe, the law was satisfied if one or two Negro pupils were in just one white school. Of course equal protection of the laws is not a patchery, one thing here, something else there, according to local temper and circumstance. It is no more dependent on pragmatic equity considerations than truth is dependent on convenience.

Having no constitutional power to prescribe directly to states how they shall conduct their schools, the Federal courts were now to prescribe indirectly (how often must they have admonished parties before them that one cannot do indirectly what one is forbidden to do directly!). Now they were to wait on the local school authorities to produce, at the courts' command, a schedule of integration measures: not, observe, to obey duly legislated measures on pain of sanctions duly legislated, but to produce the measures themselves to the satisfaction of the courts' inexplicit, esoteric will. It was as if the judge were to humiliate the condemned man before him by ordering him to come forth with his own execution program, though without calling it by that name.

Presently these authorities, after study and deliberation, and acting in good conscience, might come in with proposals such as: deferring integration, in any degree, until such time as community feeling was agreeable to it, say five, ten years hence; integration little by little, not all at once; integration only of pupils of approximately equal age and ability; caution against precipitate action, lest morale suffer and education with it. This would conform with the Supreme Court demand for local elucidation, assessment, and solution of the problem and also with the demand for "deliberate speed." To the calm onlooker it would only show that integration in some districts was little more than a dream. And all in full keeping with the Supreme Court's dictate.

When the Court ordered Negro pupils to be admitted to schools "as soon as practicable on a nondiscriminatory basis," it applied a criterion which was capable of fostering no end of confusion and delay. When would it be practicable, except when in harmony with the peace, good order, health, and morals of the community? And when was that to be, once the feelings associated with race, by nature and history, had been violently disturbed and were likely to continue so? Local authorities, acting in "good faith" as enjoined, could not deny or disguise the facts. Neither could the Federal courts if they, too, were to act in good faith. Ten, twenty years, or longer might be needed.

In the Court's phraseology the term "nondiscriminatory" is rather prominent. The Court assumes, as though it were beyond doubt, that segregation is discrimination. This is wholly arbitrary and unjustified if by "discrimination" is meant something unreasonable, unwarranted. Primordial racial dispositions being the probable source, segregation is no matter of discrimination in that sense, nor one of bias or prejudice—profound natural differences are not bias or prejudice, nor are they touched, let alone erased, by allegations of bias or prejudice. The Court, like integrationists generally, uses the term "discrimination" in a systematically misleading way, always giving it the sense of inequity, unfairness, hostility. Abundant evidence shows that the primary reason for segregation is nothing of that kind, though a spirit of that kind may in time arise under either segregation or integration. Everyone discriminates, in the sense of distinguishing or differentiating. To choose your own friends, live in your own house, eat, drink, and wear what you prefer is discrimination, but certainly it is not unfairness or hostility to anybody. Withdrawing, keeping your distance, is not discrimination, in the sense of unfairness or hostility. In not taking account of this distinction and in assuming that the color line is due to unfairness and hostility, the Court lays itself open, ironically, to suspicion of unfairness.[6]

There was to be required "a prompt and reasonable start" towards integration. Here again it is apparent that the Court was deferring to local conditions, as of course it now had to do since it, the Court, could not conduct schools, and the only alternative was to hazard breaking them up. The fiasco at Little Rock is illuminating now.

Having made a prompt beginning, the school authorities there decided that it was premature and petitioned for more time, proposing
to return to segregation for a period of two and one-half years.
Granted the petition in the Federal district court, they lost on appeal
to the circuit court, on the ground that popular resistance to integration was not a proper justification for delay; to which the Supreme
Court unanimously agreed.[7] And yet it was in part the recognition
of popular resistance in one form or another, and the need for time
to abate it, that led the Supreme Court to allow variable periods for
the transition to integration in its 1955 decree. Further, the Supreme
Court then deferred to the district courts on the question of how
soon integration must take place. Its Little Rock decision, if not an
outright contradiction of that concession, is at least very hard to
reconcile with it—you cannot consistently allow time needed for
adaptation and then, before adaptation has occurred, flatly refuse
to allow the time; you cannot leave to the district court the determination of the time needed and then, without a showing of grave
error on its part, annul the determination it makes. True, the law
cannot yield to violence as such, which occurred at Little Rock; but
the school board and the Federal judge were not doing that; they only
acknowledged the existence of conditions such as the Supreme Court
had foreseen and allowed for in its decree.

Complications could only be expected elsewhere. School boards
which might have initiated integration would be reluctant now to
act, lest the action be premature and irremediable. And since it was
a reasonable, not an unconditional, promptness that was required by
the Court's decree, there was no telling when, if ever, the beginning
might be made in some communities. Reasonableness does not respect
lawlessness, but on the other hand it does not disregard nature and
history.

Where a beginning had been made, the possibility was admitted
that the courts might "find that additional time is necessary to carry
out the ruling in an effective manner." Looking ahead, one could
see that integration in critical instances, whether begun early or late,
might not progress beyond the token stage for years; nor has it, in
many localities, ten years afterwards. The net gain for the Negro
after many more years may easily be nothing more flattering than
was the gain from his court-won right to serve on juries. Sometimes
there were hints in the press that token compliance was all that was
expected; and the Supreme Court's attitude encouraged the suspicion
that the judges themselves were not very sure beyond that. This is
rather like token segregation in dining cars years ago. The latter

was a bare recognition of the color bar; token integration begins to look like a bare recognition of the Court bar. Form has its place.

One remaining dictate of the Court pertains to school districts. The lower courts "may consider problems related to . . . revision of school districts and attendance areas into compact units to achieve a system of determining admission to the public schools on a non-racial basis . . . " Was this a hint to the lower courts to enjoin communities to make such revisions? A compact unit in Harlem would insure admission of Negro pupils only, while one in, say, the Garden District of New Orleans would mean the admission of white pupils only. Both, while meeting the compactness standard, would be in violation of the Court's "principle" that non-integrated schools are inherently unequal. To meet the integration standard, if such it might be called, white and Negro pupils might have to be shuttled back and forth, with all sorts of disconcerting consequences, as the experiment in New York has shown. Or does the Court intimate the advisability of gerrymandering, so as to reach from Negro sections into white sections and vice versa? If not that, what is the Court's point, or how is its integration ideal to be realized? Whatever the method, is not the Court presuming to draw or to require the lower courts to draw demographic or collectivistic lines through communities? Yet the Court had recently said in a related opinion, concerning voting rights, that no court could remap districts so as to bring them into conformity with "the standard of fairness for a representative system."[8]

Equal protection is an immediate, constant, unexceptionable right. It cannot wait or be deferred—that is nullification of it. If now integration is a requirement of equal protection, how could the Supreme Court, bound to uphold equal protection in its oath to uphold the Constitution, allow and contrive waiting? So far as it did that, it actually suspended the Constitution. The charge that it usurped the power of Congress and that it amended the Constitution in the school decisions, is hardly more serious than this.

Nearly ninety years after the Fourteenth Amendment was adopted we were yet, in some seventeen segregation states, to "make a start" towards compliance with it and were to have all sorts of lets and conditions on account of the likelihood that complying would not soon be "practicable"! Doubtless this would be incomprehensible to those who drafted and ratified the Amendment. It is incomprehensible *prima facie* when we recall that, according to the Court, segregation in the schools is "inherently" wrong. If that is so, segregation was a violation of the equal-protection guarantee from the first, since otherwise the wrongness could not have been *inherent*. Congress, the courts, and the President, all sworn to uphold the Constitution, must therefore have violated their oath and nullified the Constitution. This, surely, is too absurd. Congress expressly rejected compulsory school integration in the 1875 Civil Rights Act and again in the so-named act of 1957, three years after *Brown*. Eminent judges, such as sat on the Supreme Court when it unanimously upheld segregation in *Gong Lum* in 1927, can hardly be supposed to have lacked the acumen to discover the inherent wrongness, or to have lacked the probity to declare it, if it was there. To the contrary, we have seen that the inherency doctrine carries implications contrary to the most elementary reasoning, such as to make ordinary discourse and calculation impossible. It is no wonder the previous judges admitted no such "principle."

It is no point to say that we had to wait till 1954 to find out this wrong, by way not of law but of psychology. Empirical science, and particularly an unfledged science such as psychology, knows nothing of "inherent" wrong. It deals only with phenomena, events, states of affairs, which perpetually fluctuate, and its results today or this year may differ from those of last year (*Psychologies of 1925, Psychologies of 1930*, for example, are well known and indicative book titles).

Yet another anomaly in the Court's dispatch of segregation is to be seen in its order to the lower courts to require integration, in the instant cases, "with all deliberate speed." To deliberate and decide when and how a law shall take effect, as local authorities must now do—is that not a legislative prerogative? If it is, the Court again infringes the legislative province in presuming to dictate terms which only the legislative authority can legitimately ordain; while if it is not that, what is it? In other words, if the Fourteenth Amendment is not fully in effect and is now to be put in effect, at different times and by degrees, is it not the business of the amending authority (the states) or of the Amendment's specific enforcing authority (Congress) to fix the times and degrees?

So much inconsistency, paradox, anomaly, let alone suspension and compromise of the Constitution, is not to be seriously regarded as the consequence of anything contained in the Constitution. If the equal-protection clause entailed all of this, or any of it, how could the clause have endured for nearly a century? To speak summarily:

If equal protection means integration, then no forestalling of integration and no temporizing at the expense of integration, is constitutionally tolerable. But the Supreme Court decree expressly forestalls and temporizes with it. Hence equal protection does not mean integration.

If integration is not feasible at once, as the Court admits, and may never be realized fully under the terms the Court has laid down, that shows that it is extraneous to the Constitution and that in invoking and imposing it the Court is virtually amending the Constitution, in violation of the provision vesting the amending power in the states.

If integration is to be made a constitutional requirement, a lawful constitutional amendment securing it is necessary.

That an unqualified constitutional guarantee of rights—equal protection—should be rendered conditional, partial, impractical, and uncertain, by being made subject to conditions antithetical to it, is a plain contradiction in terms. That this should be done in the name of equity, under the Supreme Court's equity power, is an affront to equity, as if equity were a force for compromising the Constitution. Equity cannot modify the equal-protection guarantee; it cannot amend the Constitution. Is not the Court abusing the equity power for the sake of enforcing its doctrine that separate educational facilities are inherently unequal? Since that doctrine is inherently illogical, and incapable of factual vindication, there is no allying it to equity, without debasing equity.

Moreover, if equal protection resolves into a matter of equity, forthwith segregation is justified in a multitude of cases. For will it be equitable—reasonable, prudent, a fair give and take—to force children into contacts shocking to their nature and upbringing, with every prospect of friction, tension, and distraction? Is it equitable, or we might say educational, since here the two terms are practically synonymous, to impose conditions which are certain to cause uneasiness in pupils, their teachers, parents, and community, and hence likely to disrupt education? It might be *politic* to do this, if tyranny ruled and was bent on socializing or communizing everything. But it could not be *equitable,* since equity respects individuals and classes, while tyranny does not. The Court, as we have seen, overrode fact and reason to give us its doctrine, "Separate educational facilities are inherently unequal." Now, acting in the name of equity, it will have to override equity in order to enforce that doctrine.

Since race as such has nothing to do, constitutionally, with equal protection (the equal-protection guarantee is silent about it), the question of whether racial distinctions are to be made at law is a question left to the option of Congress and the states. Not to have made such distinctions within jurisdictions where race itself had already engraved them, jurisdictions where the Negro ratio was high, would probably have meant anarchy in the past. Now the Supreme Court holds that the mere mention of race is suspicious, as if equal protection precluded the thought of it. Yet the Fourteenth Amendment expressly distinguishes Indians, who in some classifications are counted a race. And the Court itself has ruled that a state "may classify persons and objects for the purpose of legislation;"[9] which of course a state must do, since otherwise the sick, the criminal, the rich, the poor would all be one, as would the farm, factory, yacht, cart—and government would be little more than a fiction.

If "race" is a suspicious term to the Court, the reason is hardly to be sought in the facts of life, where there are no secrets about it, but must be presumed to lodge in some peculiarity of the Court's mind. We might suppose, incidentally, that if the intent of the Fourteenth Amendment was to single out race for special safeguard under the equal-protection clause, the Amendment would so indicate, just as does the Fifteenth Amendment where "race, color, or previous condition of servitude" are specifically prohibited as bars against the right to vote.

Equal protection is not *equal* if it is more concerned about Negroes than about others. Its concern is just as great between white people as between Negro and white. The Court's sensitivity about the Negro is therefore in need of explanation. Until it is plausibly explained there is no gainsaying anyone who thinks he sees a connection between it and the Court's doctrine that separate schools for Negroes and whites are inherently unequal. If anyone chooses to believe that the doctrine came about of a purpose to degrade the equal-protection guarantee into an artifice for accomplishing integration, despite the cost to reason, constitutional law, and judicial probity, it is hard to see grounds for denying him.

Standing on that doctrine, the Court has seemed immune to question—at all events no question has been publicly raised, I believe, about the doctrine. And yet the doctrine cannot bear even casual examination. Evidence, educational facts and figures, could not show *inherent* inequality, since they concern matters of concrete fact, and "inherency" is not of that description. Rather, inherency is something *a priori*, or pre-determined, such that if you deny it, you contradict yourself; which in turn is because you yourself have laid down terms or definitions involving that. Thus you might say, for example, that perfection is something unattainable, "inherently unattainable," and when called to justify your statement proceed to exclude from the perfection category every attainable thing that might be cited to you, since if you conceded even one, it would refute you.

What would be your ground? A ready, forthright way of putting it would be this: "I will admit nothing to be capable of perfection." But this is mere obstinacy, arbitrary or capricious. Another person, perhaps arbitrary or capricious, perhaps wholly reasonable, might define perfection in a fashion the opposite of yours.

Similarly of "equal." If you exclude tangibles and measurables, as the Supreme Court does here, this term cannot be brought within ponderable, decidable bounds. Then anyone can define it as he pleases. Thus the Court can say simply, categorically, "Separate educational facilities are inherently unequal," which we can see to mean: "We will admit no separate educational facilities to be equal." Humpty Dumpty, in the fable, defined terms that way. But he realized what he was doing and was candid about it, condescending to say that it was not a matter of who was right but of who was boss. The Supreme Court is boss, true; but it is not above the law, but subject to it.

If the term "equal" can be subverted to such a purpose as racial homogenization, what might the judges not do with such a term as "freedom"? Its sense being far less precise than that of "equal," it is a ready vehicle capable of carrying even more dangerous freight than that one. Freedom of speech, freedom of press and assembly can be "interpreted" away more easily than racial black and white, as can the whole Bill of Rights. And if, by transmutation of "equal," the Court can successfully turn the constitutional prohibition upon state *denial* of equal protection into a prohibition upon state *permission* of voluntary segregation, which is only a variety of optional, free association, what can it not do in the way of transforming the whole Constitution? Either the Court is free to make any change in the Constitution or else it is not free to make this one, since this one has back of it no special judicial power. Persons under oath to support the Constitution are therefore caught in this dilemma: Uphold the Court's assumption of authority to make any change in the Constitution or else oppose its assumption of authority to make this one. If they choose the first of these alternatives, they will deny the constitutional provision by which the states reserve to themselves the power to alter the Constitution (Article V) and so will perjure their oath. To escape the consequences of that, they can only choose the other alternative. Thus a person of probity is bound to oppose what the Court has done.

Is there no protecting the Constitution against this corruption? There is indeed a protection, in clear, strong terms of the Constitution, applicable uniquely to the President. At inauguration the Presi-

dent takes the oath: "I do solemnly swear (or affirm) that I will
faithfully execute the office of President of the United States, and
will to the best of my ability, preserve, protect and defend the Constitution of the United States." This is an awful responsibility, or
else words mean nothing. Whereas judges are sworn merely to support the Constitution, like the lowliest constable or army private,
the President is sworn to do far more. Can he preserve the Constitution by mere lip service? Can he protect it by deferring to abusers
and destroyers of it? What does he mean when he swears to *defend*
it to the best of his ability? Andrew Jackson, for example, meant
much more than a formality of words and had no hesitancy about
resisting pretensions of the Court. Likewise Jefferson and Lincoln.[10]
President Eisenhower, from the playground at Newport, could only
say at the time of the disturbance in Little Rock that the Supreme
Court had spoken and that was final, no matter what he might think
of what the Court had said. Could he then have been aware of what
had befallen the Constitution he had sworn to preserve, protect, and
defend?

[1] Except the Delaware case, which was remanded to the Delaware Supreme
Court.

[2] 349 U. S. 294, 298-301.

[3] 159 F. Supp. 272. In Dallas, on the other hand, the Federal district court
made integration optional, and in only three schools, and not to start until 1961.
184 F. Supp. 402. In Houston the court rejected such a plan and ordered general integration, one grade a year, beginning with the first grade in 1960 (this
was within about one month of the Dallas decision). 312 F. 2d 191.

[4] Cp. the comment of Judge Learned Hand: "There is indeed nothing in
the discussion that positively forbids the conclusion that the Court meant that
racial equality was a value that must prevail against any conflicting interest,
but it was not necessary to go to such an extreme. *Plessy* v. *Ferguson* was not
overruled in form anyway; it was distinguished because of the increased importance of education in the fifty-six years that had elapsed since it was decided. I do not see how this distinction can be reconciled with the notion that
racial equality is a paramount value that state legislatures are not to appraise
and whose invasion is fatal to the validity of any statute." *The Bill of Rights*,
Cambridge, Mass., Harvard University Press, 1958, p. 54.

[5] *National Labor Relations Board* v. *Insurance Agents' International Union*,
361 U. S. 477, 490-494.

[6] In the past the Court recognized the distinction. It said in 1950 in *Henderson*
v. *United States:* "The right to be free from unreasonable discrimination
belongs . . . to each person . . . We need not multiply instances in which these
rules [for segregating Negroes in railway dining cars] sanction unreasonable
discrimination." 339 U. S. 816, 824f. This prohibits only "unreasonable" discrimination, not all discrimination—to prohibit all would be impossible since

that would mean obliterating all recognition whatever of differences, in defiance of life and the world. Discrimination is further considered below, pp. 187f.

7 *Cooper* v. *Aaron, loc. cit.,* p. 16.

8 *Colegrove* v. *Green, loc. cit.,* p. 553.

9 *St. John* v. *New York,* 201 U. S. 633, 636.

10 In vetoing the National Bank Act, President Jackson said: "The Congress, the Executive, and the [Supreme] Court must each for itself be guided by its own opinion of the Constitution. Each public officer who takes an oath to support the Constitution swears that he will support it as he understands it, and not as it is understood by others. It is as much the duty of the House of Representatives, of the Senate, and of the President to decide upon the constitutionality of any bill or resolution which may be presented to them for passage or approval as it is of the supreme judges when it may be brought before them for judicial decision. The opinion of the judges has no more authority over Congress than the opinion of Congress has over the judges, and on that point the President is independent of both. The authority of the Supreme Court must not, therefore, be permitted to control the Congress or the Executive when acting in their legislative capacities, but to have only such influence as the force of their reasoning may deserve." James D. Richardson, *Messages and Papers of the Presidents,* 1789-1902, n.p., Bureau of National Literature and Art, 1903, vol. 3, p. 1145.

Thomas Jefferson, some years after his Presidency, wrote: "[It is very dangerous doctrine] to consider the judges as the ultimate arbiters of all constitutional questions [and] one which would place us under the despotism of an oligarchy . . . The Constitution has erected no such single tribunal, knowing that to whatever hands confided, with the corruptions of time and party, its members would become despots. It has more wisely made all the departments coequal and cosovereign within themselves . . . *Works of Thomas Jefferson,* edited by Paul Leicester Ford, 12 vols., New York, G. P. Putnam's Sons, 1904-1905, vol. 12, p. 162.

"There are two measures which if not taken, we are undone. First, to check these unconstitutional invasions of State rights by the Federal judiciary . . . by a strong protestation of both houses of Congress that such and such doctrines, advanced by the Supreme Court, are contrary to the Constitution: and if afterwards they relapse into the same heresies, impeach and set the whole adrift. For what was the government divided into three branches, but that each should watch over the others and oppose their usurpations? . . . " *Ibid.,* p. 207.

" . . . The Judiciary branch is the instrument which, working like gravity, without intermission, is to press us at last into one consolidated mass . . . If Congress fails to shield the States from dangers so palpable and so imminent, the States must shield themselves, and meet the invader foot to foot." *Ibid.,* p. 196.

Lincoln refused to concede supreme authority to the Court. In his debates with Stephen A. Douglas he strongly opposed the Court's Dred Scott decision upholding slavery. He said: " . . . we think the Dred Scott decision is erroneous. We know the court that made it has often overruled its own decisions, and we shall do what we can to have it to overrule this. We offer no resistance to it." *Collected Works of Abraham Lincoln,* edited by Roy P. Basler, 15 vols., New Brunswick, Rutgers University Press, 1953-1955, vol. 2, p. 401. " . . . all that I am doing is refusing to obey it as a political rule." *Ibid.,* p. 495 . . . "Will you not graciously allow us to do with the Dred Scott decision precisely as you did with the Bank [National Bank] decision? You succeeded in breaking down the moral effect of that decision; did you find it necessary to amend the Constitution? or to set up a court of Negroes in order to do it?" *Ibid.*, p. **519**.

George Washington said in his *Farewell Address:* "The necessity of reciprocal checks in the exercise of political power, by dividing and distributing it into different depositories, and constituting each the Guardian of the Public Weal against invasions by the others, has been evinced by experiments ancient and modern; some of them in our country and under our own eyes. To preserve them must be as necessary as to institute them. If, in the opinion of the people, the distribution or modification of the constitutional powers be in any particular wrong, let it be corrected by an amendment in the way, which the state designates. But let there be no change by usurpation; for, though this, in one instance, may be the instrument of good, it is the customary weapon by which free governments are destroyed." *Writings,* Selected and Published by Jared Sparks, 12 vols., Boston, F. Andrews, and Charleston, A. Mygart, 1837-1839, vol. 12, p. **226**.

CHAPTER 6

THE COURT'S OWN EVIDENCE

It is the Supreme Court's finding—or premise, or doctrine—that compulsory segregation is detrimental on account of engendering a sense of inferiority, hence repressing the motivation to learn, hence tending to retard educational development, and so depriving Negro pupils of "the benefits they would receive in a racially integrated school."[1] This, the Court holds, means denial of equal opportunity and therefore denial of the constitutional guarantee of equal protection of the laws.

There is a seeming plausibility in the proposition that integration would be beneficial to Negro pupils; for it suggests a new and fairer order, with emancipation for all, promotion of racial understanding, attainment of more democratic and more humane relationships, and so on. There is, however, some reason the other way. Barriers so strong and so enduring as those between white and Negro may not be found to yield freely. There may be benefits to Negro pupils under integration, as the Court says, but again there may be detriments. To white pupils there may also be detriments.

Although no formula for educational or pedagogical equality has been established, the following is well recognized and even a commonplace: Where the range between capacities or aptitudes of pupils in the same class is wide, the superior pupils are held back by the inferior or else the inferior are soon frustrated. Equality or homogeneity of abilities seems to be the ideal; and when classes are sectioned pedagogically, ability is usually the criterion. If pedagogical equality with white children is what is needed to give Negro children the equal protection required by law, then it is by no means apparent that integration is the answer. Only a pedagogical answer would be proper, and it is hardly the province of a law court to give that kind of answer.

Government can in many circumstances command physical action, but it cannot command mental—cannot, for example, make a white child smile upon, befriend, or impart the fruits of its genius to colored children, or vice versa. Attributes of mind are subjective; the Supreme Court, the Federal Government have no authority in the subjective domain.

It follows that equal opportunity, equal protection of the laws, cannot be located in that domain. Equal opportunity and equal protection and indeed law itself are objective, not subjective. Were that not so, everyone might be a law unto himself, with chaos the consequence. The Court's appeal to "intangibles" is only a vague way of invading this domain. The "intangibles," the "benefits" are just the subjective qualities of white pupils, over which the Supreme Court has no more jurisdiction than the Kremlin.

There is an infallible way of testing the constitutional soundness of a judicial opinion. It is to find out whether contradicting the opinion involves contradicting some constitutional provision. If it does, the opinion stands, for if you cannot deny the opinion without denying the constitution, of course you cannot deny the opinion. But if denying the opinion does not involve denying some constitutional provision, then the opinion is shown to be constitutionally groundless.

What, then, is contradicted in our Constitution if we deny the proposition that the benefits of associating with white pupils—benefits deriving from the intelligence, accomplishments, and personality of the white pupils—are a right of Negro pupils? The equal-protection clause? The due-process clause? So the Court says. But wherein do these clauses provide or imply that the virtues of persons of one race shall be at the service of persons of another race?[2] Where does the Constitution give the Federal Government jurisdiction over anyone's personal traits? Where indeed? To justify such incursion the Constitution would have to provide substantially as follows: *In public establishments of education the acumen of the pupils shall be as common property, equally accessible to all without regard to race or color.* It would not suffice to provide just that the schools be open to all, regardless of race or color. That would be no guarantee of what the Court holds necessary for equal protection of Negro pupils, namely, benefits accruing to them from white pupils. To the contrary, the consequences to them, as remarked before, might be detriments, not benefits: friction, frustration, hostility. The Court does not rest with mere contact among the pupils. It requires the fruits—benefits, it believes—of contact. Nothing short of a constitutional provision such as the foregoing, fabulous though it is, would suffice for that.

What would the authors of the Constitution have said to such an article? What would people today who dread the omens of communism have to say if they were to consider what the Court has done and saw the personal communization it involves? What did the Great Emancipator, Lincoln, think of such a possibility? He expressed himself as follows:

"What next?—Free them [slaves], and make them politically and socially, our equals? My own feelings will not admit of this; and if mine would, we well know that those of the great mass of white people will not . . . We can not, then, make them equals.

"I have no purpose to introduce political and social equality between the white and black races. There is a physical difference between the two, which, in my judgment, will probably forever forbid their living together upon the footing of perfect equality; and inasmuch as it becomes a necessity that there must be a difference I . . . am in favor of the race to which I belong having the superior position.

"There is a natural disgust in the minds of nearly all white people, to the idea of an indiscriminate amalgamation of the white and black races . . . "[3]

Is the Supreme Court correct and Lincoln incorrect? That is, does mixing mean benefits, as the Court says, and never the opposite? Does the Court in thinking of benefits on one side forget the possibility of tension, discord, and disruption in the whole? The Court gives no intimation concerning that. It founds its decision upon the presumption that segregation deprives or has a tendency to deprive Negro pupils of benefits and hence deprives them of equal opportunity. That integration would secure them the benefits is, the Court says, a proposition "amply supported by modern [psychological] authority." What is the evidence for this statement?

The litigants supplied the Court a great abundance of evidence pro and con. The Court, however, takes judicial notice of scarcely any of it. Perhaps it found appellants and appellees at a standoff in this regard, as it did in regard to their contentions about the intent of the Fourteenth Amendment. Whatever the reason, the Court cited a few documents of its own choice to justify its aforesaid statement. Let us consider these documents, in the order of their citation by the Court.

Kenneth B. Clark, *Effect of Prejudice and Discrimination on Personality Development*. Midcentury White House Conference on Children and Youth, 1950. Mimeographed.

Presumably this is the Supreme Court's chief or favorite reliance among the works of "modern authority," inasmuch as it stands first on the list (unalphabetized). The title-page, however, bears this notice: "This document has not yet been revised to take account of suggestions and criticisms of the Technical Committee on Fact Finding or the Fact Finding Staff" (of the White House Conference). The author is a psychologist, of the College of the City of New York.

The document runs to 203 pages, and we may suppose that the whole of it received the Court's attention since no part is singled out for citation, by contrast with some other works cited. It is mainly a miscellany of excerpts from recently published writings on race and prejudice, but with extensive comment and criticism of them by the author.

Numerous passages indicate that race prejudice arises very early in children's minds. (The term "prejudice" seems questionable here, but it is used without questioning, throughout the document.) It seems established, we read, that: "Children are aware of racial differences as early as the age of three. This seems unquestionably true for Negro children of all skin colors both in the north and in the south."[4]

One of the studies quoted says that although individual children tend to grow tolerant as they grow older, this does not mean tolerant of Negroes. On the contrary, they are said to become less tolerant in that regard. Dr. Clark observes: " . . . the prevailing racial and religious attitudes [of society] exist in childhood at the pre-school ages . . . they develop with increasing clarity with age and . . . by the 6th grade they are relatively set in that they are practically indistinguishable from the attitudes of high school students."[5] Not only white children, Northern as well as Southern, but also Negro children are said to have "negative attitudes" towards the Negro. Studies by a half dozen or more psychologists show this to the satisfaction of Dr. Clark (who has carried out tests of his own in this field, using dolls of various degrees of darkness to elicit the children's preference and hence, he believes, their racial attitudes). From one of many such studies he quotes the statement: "Negro children reveal most vividly and often the feelings of insecurity resulting from anticipated rejection or insult from white children."[6] From another study, of Northern children: "Negro subjects, when required to make racial identifications, generally reacted with behavior indicative of uneasiness, tension or evasion, while there was no similar tendency among the whites."[7] He adds that Negro children in the North, on racial identification tests, show much more evidence of emotional conflict and personality disturbance than those in the South.[8]

What is the explanation, if that is not too much to ask, of such pronounced attitudes in young children? Dr. Clark, himself a Negro, is objective and cautious in what he says about that. He thinks there is too little information to justify a decisive answer; neither family, peers, neighbors, school, church, nor social or economic status, separately or in any combination, "exerts a significant restraining force on the development of negative racial attitudes in children and adolescents of America."[9] One study he cites concludes that "whether a child increased or decreased in prejudice apparently had no relation to how well adjusted he appeared to others."[10] Dr. Clark frankly concludes: "The problem of causality in the complex area of relationship between total personality and prejudices remains essentially unanswered."[11] "There appears to be some complex relationship between total personality structure of an individual and the amount and quality of his intergroup prejudices. This relationship is not capable of being stated at present in simple causal or specific terms."[12]

Prejudice towards the Negro, as Dr. Clark terms it, is found in an extreme degree among Indians—at least among the Croatans of North Carolina. He quotes from a study by Guy B. Johnson:

"The [Croatan] Indian, then, is forever on the defensive. His wish to escape the stigma of Negro kinship, and thus to be identified with the white man is uppermost in his mind . . . The child learns that the ultimate insult that anyone can give an Indian is to intimate that he has Negro blood. He stands ready to defend his personal honor and the honor of his whole group from such intimations from any one source. So intense is the feeling on this subject that one can only conclude that there is present in many persons a 'sense of guilt' which arises from the observed reality (Negroid physical traits) and which calls for constant denial of the reality."[13]

The Croatan "pattern," says Dr. Clark, appears similar to that of Mexicans in the Southwest. He suggests a similarity to that of "the Portuguese" in New England also. The white man is not alone in shunning the Negro.

Religion does not soften the "prejudice," according to Dr. Clark. He sees in a declaration of the Federal Council of Churches of Christ in America, entitled "The Church and Race Relations" (March, 1946), "an eloquent evidence that the pattern of segregation which characterizes interracial relations in the American culture permeates the church . . . this would seem to be as true for the Catholic church as it is for Protestant denominations."[14] Further, in dealing with "the problem of changing the attitudes of the prejudiced individuals" one "cannot be sure that the racial and religious attitudes of a substantial number of the available personnel are such that they would accept the premise that prejudice is undesirable and that a goal of therapy should be an elimination of these hostile attitudes."[15]

Paradoxically, Dr. Clark regards prejudice as a requisite to well-being. He states that "for children, adolescents and many adults the existence of someone to look down upon is a necessary factor in the development of their self-esteem and aids in their struggle for ego-security. This certainly is in itself not detrimental to the personality of these individuals. Prejudice cannot be objected to with any degree of validity on these grounds."[16]

According to another finding, "one cannot base his objections to racial and religious prejudices on the grounds of any demonstrated detrimental effects of these prejudices upon the personality structure of prejudiced individuals."[17] From Arnold M. Rose's *Studies in Reduction of Prejudice*, Dr. Clark quotes this sober judgment: "Race attitudes are known to be so deep and tenacious, that any careful study which has given us evidence that a change of attitudes has effected is a distinct contribution to knowledge."[18]

Dr. Clark draws on the annals of psychiatry and psychoanalysis, as well as those of psychology. For example: In a study of Negroes in a mental hospital "delusional material involving denial of color and ancestry was not an uncommon finding." The investigators "assert that their case material illustrates 'the striving of the Negro toward identification with white society' and that 'the color conflict takes many forms ranging from conscious "passing" to frankly illusional material'."[19]

From a psychoanalytic source, which he quotes at some length on the subject of race riots, we read that "psychologically, Negro race riots are violent outbreaks of infantile father hatred," that the Detroit riots of 1943 were a "continued manifestation of the infantile sibling rivalry reaction patterns," and that such things are: "the reaction to the arrival of a newcomer into the family, an infant brother or sister. This reaction is associated with a desire to prevent the younger sibling from growing up and competing." Moreover, here, in repressed herd aggression, with its concomitant sense of guilt "lies the very secret of the constancy, tenacity, and the intensity of social, racial and religious prejudices . . . "[20]

One psychoanalyst, G. B. Bovell, cited by Dr. Clark, finds the root of race prejudice in a more familiar department. Quoting him, Dr. Clark says:

"In discussing racial prejudice and sexual virility, Bovell states that there is a complex of inherent inadequacy which motivates the white race against their darker fellows.

" 'It is the revelation of an inherent constitutional or somatic weakness. The erotic consciousness of this somatic inadequacy is degrading and therefore objectionable to the striving for virility and racial esteem; it is a foe to the ego-ideal of the white . . .' "[21]

Dr. Clark himself says: "The presence of a rejected minority offers a socially approved object for the expression of ego-needs, ego-protective phantasies, vanity, pretensions, patronizing and condescending attitudes and other behavior which seem so essential to the average, matter-of-fact human being and for which the society does not offer him any outlet with the same impunity in any other area."[22]

This idea Dr. Clark carries further in the proposition that the Negro is denied "equality, status and security" in America because of the white man's "desire for status and an enhancement of his subjective feelings of having obtained a superior status." He remarks that in other nations "with similar motivations" (South Africa and Australia) "the pattern of racial prejudice and persecution is even more severe."[23] Again quoting Mr. Bovell, he adds: " 'This continuous drive toward the ego-ideal results in certain stereotyped attitudes toward the darker races, attitudes which are peculiar to the whole white family'."[24]

Nevertheless, Dr. Clark is ambitious for changes. He speaks of "the problem of changing the attitudes of the prejudiced individuals," and farther on he says: "If we are going to combat prejudice we are required to take our stand on the moral and *realistic* grounds that (1) these prejudices inhibit social progress, defined in humanistic terms; (2) they are manifestations of man's more primitive propensities to debase and harm his fellow human being; (3) they seem in a complex way to be related to the maintenance of destructive social tensions and conflicts and drain energy away from the task of constructive solutions to many and vast social problems; and (4) they distort, constrict, humiliate and in extreme cases destroy the personalities of the victims."[25]

It is noteworthy that the remedies envisioned in this have no relation to legislation or to litigation. There is no complaint that the law is the source of any of the troubles, or that the law has in any way fallen short, although it is complained that family, neighbors, the church, and society are all ineffective. The condition complained of is never taken to be other than a positive, natural one—one even said to be a requisite to the well-being of "children, adolescents and many adults"—and the remedies contemplated are not juridical but "moral and realistic."

If it is the case, as Dr. Clark believes, that too little information has been obtained for anyone to give a reliable explanation of the racial attitudes of children, then it is hard to see how the Supreme

Court can draw on this work for an explanation, let alone a decision. And if, as Dr. Clark holds, it is not now possible to fix the cause of such attitudes, or prejudices, as he calls them, even more dubious is the reliance the Court places here; dubious, however, not because of Dr. Clark's data but because of the Court's use of them. The Court, as far as it rests here, is virtually saying that these data prove that segregation causes inferiority feeling. Dr. Clark, on the contrary, finds the whole question unanswerable as yet.

His evidence concerning racial attitudes is in substance as follows:

That what is termed racial prejudice is present very early—by or before the age of three;

That even Negro children have it—have a prejudice against the dark-skinned;

That it is found north and south (the tenor of Dr. Clark's citations might be taken to be that it is the same north and south);

That Northern Negro children show much more emotional and personal disturbance than Southern Negro children;

That the prejudice is independent of social adjustment;

That social, including institutional, influences on it are unknown;

That Negro children in contact with white suffer mental disturbance more than the white;

That Negroes in mental hospitals betray attitudes of race renunciation.

On such evidence it would not be unreasonable to suppose that this defeated state of mind attributed to the Negro arises naturally from racial differences. In strict science that almost certainly would be the initial supposition. Dr. Clark, however, surmises that it is a social product, socially perpetuated. This is hard to reconcile with the finding that it is unaffected by social adjustment. Even if it were a social product, that would not keep it from being a racial or biological one also, and more fundamentally so, inasmuch as race might be the remote cause even though social force were the proximate cause. Furthermore, what social force produces it? Dr. Clark is not sure, nor can he well be, having found the available data unindicative. That itself, along with the finding that Negroes in contact with white people show mental disturbance, strongly suggests a racial cause, whether in the white or the Negro.

But it is a tenet of some writers today, among them, I gather, Dr. Clark, that race is more or less fictitious. Yet he says, "a knowledge of 'racial differences' exists as a part of the pattern of ideas of Negro children from the age of three."[26] How could there be knowledge of racial differences, and so early, if they were unreal? Presumably, the idea is that they do appear but are illusory. In that case the idea of such differences might be expected to be eradicated with some ease. Instead, the evidence brought out is that it hardens and even stands as a characteristic of the white man the world over. That is not the way of anything merely illusory.

Regardless of the nature of the differences, they were found, and were likable or unlikable to the children (chiefly unlikable). Since it can hardly be assumed that so elemental a thing as a child's likes and dislikes, north and south, segregated and unsegregated, is unnatural, and since, with regard to the Negro, these persist, become fixed, and characterize a large portion of mankind, it would be unreasonable to assume that they are about nothing. What they are about is what is ordinarily called race, and in particular the Negro race. If there is no such race, then the child, the youth, and the adult are deceived. This is too improbable. Dr. Clark's evidence goes to prove, if anything, the opposite of the doctrine that race is a myth only.

To admit that racial or color preference is a natural thing, regardless of whether it is in the blood or arises only from heteroracial contact, is to admit half the segregationist's case. The other half the segregationist and conceivably also the strictly scientific social writer may derive from that. He may cite evidence such as this item with which Dr. Clark opens his monograph:

"Between sobs Mary sputtered to her mother, 'Johnny called me a nigger. He said that I stink . . . He can't play with me any more . . . because his mother said he is not supposed to play with niggers . . .' 'We wanted [said the mother] to save our children from that. That's why we moved from the South. We wanted our children to be born in the North and not know what it means to be hurt because they are colored. But there is no escape.'"

Now it may be imagined that one reason why the white boy's mother is so adamant is that she perceives the same thing the boy has perceived. Further, in a mature white person, by contrast with a child, there may be numerous other perceptions of Negroes which are unfavorable; such as sloth, crudity, laxity. It does not matter very much that in some Negroes none of these are found, since in a great many they are found (see, for example, Professor Norman A. Brittin's article in the *Antioch Review*).[27] Yet the exceptional Negro, one may say, ought not to be segregated or stigmatized, even though others are. I take this to mean that his accomplishment, intelligence, or personal respectability ought to exempt him. Regardless of the merit of that view, which to many minds is very high, there remains, to others, an insuperable barrier: color, with all its connotations. So, on the one hand, the idea or dictate of conscience that there ought not to be a color bar; on the other, the primordial fact that there is such a bar. With segregation, reproach of conscience to one party; without it, revulsion of sensibility to the other. To indifferent or unperceiving persons neither horn of this dilemma means anything, perhaps; while to some others they both are intolerable. This is not necessarily a result of prejudice or malice. It may be due to elemental facts, just as the susceptibility of some Orientals to fainting in the presence of Caucasians is not traceable to prejudice or to any idea, but to revulsion of sensibility.

It is somewhat puzzling that anything so pronounced, persistent, and widely met as this fundamental, protopathic disposition should be overlooked or disregarded in a study concerned to discover not only effects but also causes and remedies. To look for a social explanation of something so personal, primordial, and persistent amidst whatever social variations, is like searching in the clouds for something on the ground. In fact the evidence here seems to declare emphatically the explanation: primitive, pathic revulsion. Nevertheless, Dr. Clark shows no bias in giving the evidence, and he often criticizes Negrophile views. He is, however, strongly preoccupied with social, or socio-logical, viewpoints and usages. In such preoccupation there may be obstacles, even antipathy, to strict objectivity and hence to scientific work, as may be judged from this example quoted from a certain Cantril: "There can be no such thing as 'impartiality' for any social scientist who is in the stream of things ... any pretense of impartiality is more than likely to lead only to social irresponsibility."[28] This, it can be confidently said, is thoroughly unscientific. If it were even a little characteristic of science, then science would be compromised, would lose its authority and autonomy, and would be liable to domina-tion by doctrinaires, all at the great cost of knowledge and human welfare. It is possible that, although quite objective with his data, Dr. Clark in his determination to allow only a sociological explana-tion of them is closing his eyes to the real explanation.

Heedless of that, the Supreme Court offers this document as evidence that school segregation induces inferiority feeling in Negro pupils. I find nothing in it giving the slightest support to that supposition; and the Court points to nothing of the kind. This is certain: What is in a child's mind at the age of three was not originated in it at a segregated school at or after the age of six. Possibly segregated schooling makes it stronger, but possibly it does not—there is nothing here to show.

Not only does the monograph fail to supply the Court's alleged support; it contains next to nothing on inferiority feeling in Negro pupils. Rather, its concern is racial "prejudice." And the cause of this "prejudice" is found to be just about everything and nothing. To which is added the finding of Dr. Clark that in the present state of knowledge in this field, causal judgment is out of the question.

Since the evidence here is confounding and is of doubtful relevance to the Court's thesis about inferiority feeling, we may wonder whether the Court gave it serious consideraton. If it did, how could it judge that such evidence supported its decision? If it did not, what was the purpose of citing it as support of the decision? Regardless of what may be thought about the right or wrong of segregation, this is apparent: the hand of justice is exceedingly hard to find in the Court's utilization of this document.

Helen Leland Witmer and Ruth Kotinsky, editors, *Personality in the Making, the Fact-Finding Report of the Midcentury White House Conference on Children and Youth.* Chapter VI, "The Effects of Prejudice and Discrimination." New York, Harper and Brothers, 1952.

At the outset the authors point out, as many others do, that not much is known concerning this subject because "there is little in the scientific literature on the precise effects of prejudice and discrimination on health of personality."[29] They admit that, "Unfortunately for scientific accuracy and adequacy, thoroughly satisfactory methods of determining the effect . . . have not yet been devised, nor has a sufficient number of studies dealing with the various minority groups been made."[30] In support of this they quote from Otto Klineberg's *Characteristics of the American Negro:* "Completely satisfactory research in this field will have to wait until psychologists have devised more adequate measures for the study of personality."[31]

This marked sense of limitation is by no means confined to the authors of chapter VI. The book is a digest of contributions by more than a hundred participants in the Midcentury White House Conference, and contains a preface in which we read: "In reviewing the materials assembled for the Conference, the Technical Committee on Fact Finding shared a widespread feeling that there is great need for tested knowledge in the social and psychological sciences . . . All agree as to the importance of proving or disproving what dynamic psychology holds to be true, for example, concerning personality development during the early years of life, and its implications for the subsequent years. All who work in the fields pertaining to child life and child development are acutely aware of great chasms of ignorance."[32]

It is then no surprise that much of what is said here is conditional or tentative, in terms such as "may be," "is likely," "seems," "appears." A careful reader will discount the whole accordingly. Nevertheless, the Supreme Court offers it as authoritative evidence for its proposition that segregated schools are detrimental to Negro pupils. Let us see what the chapter tells us in that regard.

The authors draw from various studies such findings or indications as the following:

That Italian children in New York, rejected or prejudicially treated by others, showed signs of inferiority feeling, maladjustments, introversion, emotional instability;

That the behavior of Negro children indicates rejection of their own race: it reflects "forces toward increasing rejection of the Negro, which are in line with the mores of the dominant culture; forces which arise out of a need for self-acceptance; and forces toward aggressive retaliation against whites;"[33]

That Northern Negro children two to four years old showed feelings of uneasiness and evasiveness when required to identify themselves racially, perhaps reflecting "the psychological insecurity and the uncertainty concerning status which characterize most adult Negroes;"[34]

That "even very young Negro children are likely to manifest emotional conflict in regard to their racial identity. They are ambivalent in their feelings about themselves and the group to which they belong, on the one hand accepting derogatory stereotypes of the Negro and, on the other, feeling inferior and resentful about being so classified;"[35]

That with consciousness of race comes "awareness and acceptance of the existing cultural attitudes and values attached to race"[36] and that this is perpetuated in older Negro children and college youth;

That "the stereotype of the typical Negro" in the minds of Negroes "is not indicative of a high degree of intra-group morale;"[37]

That in the United States at large, Negro children show "a pattern of personality disabilities which seems to be associated with the inferior and rejected minority status of the Negro," a pattern which "includes not only subjective feelings of inferiority, low self-esteem, ambivalent attitudes toward [their] own group, but also either overt or indirect hostility against both whites and Negroes;[38]

That "all whose economic status is very low are likely to be regarded as socially inferior and to be discriminated against."[39]

Considerable is said also about prejudiced and discriminatory types of character. For example:

That some social scientists find prejudice and discrimination "even more detrimental to the emotional well-being of the prejudiced person" than to the victims, though the authors judge the attitudes of such persons to be "only on exaggerated reflection of the attitudes that are prevalent in the society;"[40]

That extreme prejudice may reflect many types of motive: it "may be an expression of unresolved guilt, anxiety, and emotional conflicts" or it "may spring from basic, universal needs" such as "status needs, hostility needs—and the need for a socially approved hostility object," and group affinity and conformity needs;[41]

That to combat prejudice "we must take our stand on moral and realistic grounds;"[42]

That as we noticed in the Clark study, "race attitudes are known to be so deep and tenacious that any careful study which has given us evidence that a change of attitudes has been effected is a distinct contribution to knowledge;"[43]

That "ethnic hostility and prejudices have anxiety and insecurity as their roots" and can only be curbed "individually and socially;"[44]

That the problem of prejudice is complex and is usually regarded in too simple terms by reformers.

It is hard to see why this miscellany was cited by the Supreme Court as scientific authority for the proposition that school segregation causes inferiority feeling and educational detriment in Negro children. The essence of it is that although a good deal is indicated or believed which is more or less relevant to that proposition, nothing decisive has been established. It is a serious if not fatal admission for the authors to point out that satisfactory and sufficient research has not yet been carried out and that thorough procedures for determining causes and effects in this sphere do not exist.

This casts doubt on many statements by authors cited in the chapter, and signifies contradiction and confusion foreign to the nature of science. It discredits the Court's finding; for it is the Court's own witness and it does not bear out but is nearer to controverting that finding. If it shows anything, it shows that Negro children are conscious of race status, a status of inferiority, well before school age, in unsegregated kindergartens and in contacts with white children, regionally and nationally.

So the Court misses the mark when it uses this evidence to outlaw school segregation. If removal of inequality through dispelling inferiority feeling was the aim, the Court should have outlawed social status altogether; which is to say it should have outlawed American life; for in American life, as in the life of other nations and in nature at large, status is as common as large and small, superior and inferior, approval and disapproval. In Chapter 5 of the Witmer and Kotinsky volume we read:

"Studies carried on by one school of anthropologists over the last twenty years have shown that American society is considerably stratified, and that each of the social status levels (identified as upper, middle, and lower) has a way of life that differs somewhat from the others.[45]

"In the work of the anthropologists . . . there is much evidence that low income and low social status go together and that children from the lowest level of American society are looked down upon and discriminated against. To be shamed and made to feel unworthy, to be told by word or deed that one is inferior and of little account interferes seriously with the healthy development of personality, it has been made clear."[46]

The evidence here and in the Court-cited chapter, since it points beyond the school and locates the source of inferiority feeling not in the school but in the system of American life, would, ironically, have been better support for a decision favorable to segregation than for the decision the Court rendered. What, then, are we to think of the Court's use of this evidence? That the Court did not seriously examine it? That the Court's mind was so firmly made up already that not even the doubts and reservations of the authors moved it to look more closely and critically? That the citation of this work was more a formality, a respectful gesture, than really a corroborative reference?

Max Deutscher and Isidor Chein, "The Psychological Effects of Enforced Segregation: A Survey of Social Science Opinion." *Journal of Psychology*, Vol. 26, Second Half (1948), pp. 259-287.

This is a digest of opinions solicited by the Commission on Community Interrelations of the American Jewish Congress, from 849 social scientists (anthropologists, psychologists, sociologists), of whom 819 were in the United States. The purpose was "to gather material which would be relevant to a court decision" on "the legality of enforced segregation, regardless of equal facilities," a decision which "has not yet (this was in 1948) been rendered by the Supreme Court."[47] A questionnaire was sent out with a letter which stated the purpose to be that of "providing legislative bodies, courts and the general public with a consensus of responsible scientific opinion." The letter also said, "Each reply is important because it is essential to assure a truly representative opinion of competent social scientists."[48] Some 406 of the questionnaires were sent to persons in nine Northeastern states, 71 to thirteen Southern states, and 342 to the remaining states and the District of Columbia. The total number of replies, domestic and foreign, was 517.

The questionnaire included the following statements of belief, with a request that the recipient signify one:

"I believe that enforced segregation has detrimental psychological effects on members of racial and religious groups which are segregated, even if equal facilities are provided.

"I believe that enforced segregation does not have detrimental psychological effects on members of racial and religious groups which are segregated, if equal facilities are provided.

"I have not as yet formed an opinion on this issue."[49]

A large majority of the replies (90.4 per cent) were in the affirmative; only 2.3 per cent were in the negative.

Space for comments was provided in the questionnaire, and it appears that a good many who answered did comment.

Concerning school facilities the compilers give this summary of opinions: "Even where they reject the actuality or possibility of 'equal facilities,' the gist of these comments is the emphasis upon the essential irrelevance of the physical facilities with reference to the psychological effects under consideration."[50]

Some of the comments against segregation were:

"The result of this denial is personality distortion, disillusionment, cynicism, and other overt behavior which is definitely anti-social itself. I do not see how an intelligent and self-respecting individual can escape the blighting effects of segregation if he is a member of a group toward which a policy of segregation is directed."

"The facts of psychological detriment to those being segregated and the possible detrimental effects of a feeling of guilt among the segregators seem so obvious that it seems hardly worth investigating."

"The effect is primarily to cause insecurity and inferiority with compensatory defense mechanisms, withdrawals, aggression, etc."

"In the present racial and religious struggle which is bound to become more serious, the most severe 'psychological' damage is being done the segregated groups through the development of a martyr-point-of-view."

"Segregation, even with equal facilities, seems to cause those in the minority group to regard themselves as different, as being discriminated against, and sometimes as being persecuted."[51]

" . . . the ambiguity of status created by a society which insists on the fact that all men are born free and equal, and then turns about and acts as if they were not is even worse [than other effects of segregation] . . . Human beings simply cannot function efficiently in such situations if they have strong feelings and are strongly motivated— as many, if not most or all, members of discriminated against minority groups are—with regard to these situations."[52]

The compilers mention that a small number opposing segregation "indicate their belief that some individuals gain psychologically from being members of segregated groups while others are harmed thereby."[53] They also give examples of comment favorable to segregation, some of which are:

"While the bad psychological results of enforced segregation on both parties are unquestionable, it may be the only way to prevent much more serious trouble based on incompatibility of the cultures of the groups involved, long established hostile attitudes, etc."

"However, I should not like to make the statement that the elimination of segregation if unwisely carried out would have no detrimental effect. Even worse prejudice and conflict than exist now might result from such measures."

"Colored children on an average are 1½-2 years younger mentally than whites at various grade levels. Where the colored make up a relatively large proportion of school community, nonsegregation would mean combining older colored with younger whites."

"However, the matter is simplified in these questions; segregation is in part a function of ethnic and racial cohesion, which in turn is a *naturalistic* phenomenon."

"Natural segregation occurs everywhere in nature, in business (all auto agencies in same neighborhood) . . . The matter of segregation, legal or by social pressure, is a vastly complex matter, affecting the institution of private property, security, attitudes, and a score of other aspects."[54]

The questionnaire asked for the grounds of the beliefs expressed, and brought out these: the respondent's own research—29.2 per cent of the answers gave this; others' research—61.1 per cent; one's own professional experience—66.5 per cent; others' professional experience—47.6 per cent; personal opinion, value judgment, ethics or moral belief—3.1 per cent. There were 6.8 per cent of the replies which gave no grounds.

The investigators recognized the need of taking precaution against bias in their questionnaire, but they say: "There is no feasible way of controlling the possibility of introducing a bias through the mere statement of the reason for the study and thereby focusing the attention of the respondents on the consequences of their answers."[55]

In itself, the suspicion of bias, as well as the assumption that the answers might be influenced by the end in view, is disturbing to one's confidence in the results of this investigation. There comes to mind, since the end in view is the law court, a query of this kind: "Do you solemnly swear that the testimony you are about to give is the truth, the whole truth, and nothing but the truth, so help you God?" The reasons for Messrs. Deutscher and Chein's misgivings are perhaps not much different from those behind the oath requirement at the bar.

Whether the anticipation of a Supreme Court decision was biasing or not, the following remark on the survey, made by the authors in introducing the results, must have struck readers as a singular disclosure:

"It was oriented toward determining whether prevailing social science opinion is that enforced segregation does or does not have *detrimental* effects, since the court decision will be based on whether enforced segregation is considered to be a violation of the rights of citizens."[56]

How could Messrs. Deutscher and Chein know, years in advance, what the decision was to be based on? One might suppose they were *amici curiae* or even confidants of the Court.

Scientifically, opinion is of little or no moment. Fact and reason are all that court. Of course fact and reason are often imbued with opinion, but this has to be excluded in order for science to take rise and do its work. Of an opinion, only the ground, provided it is factual or logical, is scientifically significant (a ground often turns out to be only some further opinion or piece of hearsay, fallacy, biased or inadequate information, and consequently without scientific significance).

Somewhat fewer than a third of the persons answering the questionnaire gave, as their ground, research they themselves had carried out. What that research was, its extent, scientific status, and relevance, is not intimated in the findings of Messrs. Deutscher and Chein. Nearly two-thirds of the answers gave others' research as their ground. Of what character that research was, by whom, and of what significance to segregation, we are again not informed.

The high percentage, 66.5, of respondents resting on their own professional experience gives more positiveness to the results. Scientifically, however, and also legally, it is needful to know what that experience was, of what bearing on segregation, how extensive, whether scientifically organized and interpreted, and so on. The published results leave all this in question.

The category, "others' professional experience," is puzzling. If it means others' scientific research, it is only a duplication; if it does not mean that, which seems more likely, then it may, since it is second or third hand, turn out to be only impression, hearsay, or distortion. One cannot testify very competently of another's toothache, heartache, or experience of any kind. It was for that reason that behaviorism took rise in psychology.

The 6.8 per cent who gave no grounds are a further puzzle. Were they only prejudiced, one way or the other? The questionnaire called for responsible opinion; was theirs not responsible? Or were they only more candid than the majority?

Since the center of segregation is in the South, we should expect a poll to be concentrated there in order to be fairly representative. Not so in this case— quite the opposite. Only 6.2 per cent of the answers were from Southern states, whereas 72.9 per cent were from Northern states. Suppose the 72.9 per cent were from persons having little or no first-hand acquaintance with segregation in localities where the Negro ratio was as high as it is in the South; would it be reasonable to give them the same individual weight as the answers from the South? No; statistically, scientifically, it would not. Nothing is said about this, however; and yet the poll is probably regarded without questioning, by the Supreme Court as well as others.

Where all that counts is opinion, the majority opinion rules—at least it rules the majority. But in science it is evidence, reason, demonstration that rules, not opinion, unless where science is as yet only pioneering or for some reason has not succeeded in its task; and even then opinion is always subject to negation and discredit by a minority, even a minority of one. A lone opinion, as of a Galileo or Pasteur, may overthrow all the others, not because of being an opinion or of being theirs but because of the scientific warrant they are able to produce for it.

If in spite of this we presume that the majority opinion of a selected number of scientists establishes a scientific truth, as the Supreme Court evidently presumes, what must be our ground? Something, assuredly, going beyond science; some presumption of knowledge or authority overreaching science. What is such knowledge or authority? The Court does not tell us. It gives no hint. It seems unaware of any presumption. In such circumstances an authoritative pronouncement is commonly called, in law, arbitrary or capricious. Observe that what is before us here is not a body of expert testimony taken in court under the wise safeguards of the rules of procedure, including cross-examination. Nor of course is it common knowledge. Its capacity to adjudicate between the contentions of the parties is therefore nil. Moreover, the cautions we have met in the two previous studies, that fiindings in this sphere are not to be taken conclusively and that reliable standards for conducting investigations have not been established, discredit everything here so far as it is positively, unconditionally, asserted. Suspended judgment is all that can justifiably result under these circumstances.

It was therefore improper in the extreme for the Supreme Court to treat this miscellany of half-knowledge as support for any decision, let alone a decision nullifying and reversing the law of the land. But judges who have compromised fact and reason are only acting in character when they presume to compromise science also. The judges who sat in the Virginia and South Carolina school segregation cases, before whom appeared many expert witnesses pro and con, found the showings inconclusive just as some of the contributors to the writings cited by the Supreme Court do. A close, impartial, scientifically enlightened consideration of the Deutscher and Chein poll itself, independently of the grounds for the opinions it elicited, would almost certainly result likewise; for the poll is by no means unanimous in the outcome, and, we repeat, the minority judgment in inconclusive scientific work may turn out, with the progress of science, to be the correct one. Such a consideration is especially pertinent here in view of the fact that the poll was so one-sided—for one person polled in the region where segregation was concentrated, fifteen were polled elsewhere. It would be pointless to say that science is not a matter of region, or that so many more psychologists and sociologists are in the North and West than in the South; for the problem, the phenomenon, was chiefly in the South, and to be comprehended it had to be studied on the scene. The work of a single individual at close range, such as that of Professor Norman A. Brittin, represented in a subsequent chapter here, may be more instructive than the polled opinions of any number far away, of whom very many may be no better qualified to give judgment than Americans are qualified to judge the policy of the British Government in Africa, for example.

Isidor Chein: "What Are the Psychological Effects of Segregation under Conditions of Equal Facilities?" *International Journal of Opinion and Attitude Research*, Vol. 3 (1949), pp. **229-234.**

In this paper Mr. Chein summarizes and interprets the poll conducted by him and Max Deutscher, which we have just considered. His principal observations with respect to the poll's bearing on segregation appear to be the following:

"On the face of it, since equal facilities are in fact not provided, the proposition that enforced segregation does have detrimental psychological effects, even under conditions of equal facilities, seems impossible to prove. Yet, its correctness seemed quite evident to us as psychologists . . .

" . . . I have myself had occasion to argue . . . that facts are not established scientifically by holding a poll among scientists concerning their preferences . . . I believe . . . that if there turns out to be a clear consensus on a given issue . . . this consensus should be given due weight as representing the soundest conclusion which can be reached on the basis of the available evidence and pending further evidence.

" . . . one may ask how, if the provision of equal facilities is indeed largely a fiction, it is possible for so large a group of scientists to arrive at such agreement with regard to propositions which specify equal facilities as a condition."[57]

Mr. Chein undertakes to answer the foregoing question on four grounds.

"1. There are some instances in which approximately equal facilities are actually provided.

"2. It is possible to study children developmentally. There is evidence to indicate that Negro children, for instance, become aware of status differences associated with segregation long before they become aware of, or appreciate the significance of, the difference in physical facilities. In general, however, judging from the comments this area of research has received relatively little attention.

"3. . . . there is relatively little difficulty in finding otherwise comparable groups of unsegregated individuals which differ in the quality of the facilities available to them; and similarly in the case of different segregated groups. In other words it is possible to eliminate segregation as a variable and to assess the effects of the differential facilities . . . Again, judging from the comments, this is an area of research which has not been sufficiently exploited.

"4. It is often possible, especially in clinical studies, to identify the factors which are associated with specific psychological effects. Insofar as the factors thus identified are unrelated to the available facilities, one may reasonably infer that those same correlates will be found under otherwise similar conditions of segregation even if equal facilities are provided.

" . . . there is virtually nothing in the published literature which is explicitly devoted to this problem . . . The discrepancy between the negligible amount of published research . . . and the widespread agreement that enforced segregation is harmful, even when equal facilities are provided, is striking."[58]

In scientific work the idea that a proposition which "seems impossible to prove" may nevertheless seem quite evidently correct, is too paradoxical or too superficial to receive much credit. It is axiomatic that any scientific proposition, short of the principles of science, is capable of proof or disproof (otherwise it will have no cognitive meaning and so will fall outside the purview of science). There are indeed many instances in the history of science—a history which could be fairly well depicted by such—in which propositions as yet unproved nonetheless "seemed quite evident." But they didn't seem "impossible" to prove. The possibility, rather, of proving them, and the patient devotion of scientists to the task of proving them—of Copernicans to proving the heliocentric hypothesis, and Darwinians to proving the evolutionary hypothesis, for example— was what kept the propositions before the scientific world. If a proposition *is* an impossible one, then it does not seem, to a logical mind, a true or correct one; its impossibility excludes that, *a priori*. Psychologists who are convinced of the truth of a proposition and at the same time of the impossibility of proving it, are not acting the part of scientists. They are closer to dogmatism than to science.

No one of judgment would question the truism, "a clear consensus on a given issue should be given due weight." But what is the due weight? Not, surely, as Mr. Chein himself admits, a concession that something is scientifically established just by a poll. All that the poll establishes is the sense—sentiment, attitude, impression—of those polled. Fifty million Frenchmen can be wrong, as the world saw in 1940.

When Mr. Chein states that "there is virtually nothing in the published literature which is explicitly devoted to this problem" (enforced segregation with equal facilities), he is virtually saying that there is little or nothing with which to prove the hypothesis that segregation has detrimental psychological effects. If his purpose had been to discredit the opinions polled, little that he might have said would have accomplished it better.

His suggested investigations to confirm the hypothesis may appear promising, since they would supply evidence in place of mere opinion. It may be remarked, however, that, under number 2 of these, additional evidence that Negro children are very early conscious of status might go as far towards disproving the hypothesis as it would towards proving it; for if the sense of status arises very early it is probably due to preschool awarenesses—racial, social, economic, for example—rather than to school segregation.

His proposals 3 and 4 involve certain procedural tenets which, because of easily overlooked shortcomings in them, call for some attention. Under 3 we would choose (a) "comparable" groups of pupils from a number of unsegregated schools where the facilities were unequal, and (b) such groups from a number of segregated schools where also the facilities were unequal. Mr. Chein presumes that in (b), effects of, say, different curricula, school equipment, and teachers' qualifications could be determined independently of segregation, and similarly, in (a), independently of non-segregation. What would that prove concerning segregation? Nothing, so far. More studies would be needed, of segregated and non-segregated schools having comparable facilities as well as comparable pupils. (Incidentally, a kindred study has been made, of unsegregated pupils from comparable socio-economic environments, with results unfavorable to integrationist contentions. See pp. 332f.)

In all of this it is a matter not so much of facts and figures as of methods; meaning not the research steps taken but the rationale behind them. Certain methods defined and expounded by John Stuart Mill in his *System of Logic* and commonly used, exemplify this. The requirements of these methods are exceedingly difficult to satisfy, because of indefiniteness in experimental data and also because of underlying assumptions of exhaustiveness and exclusiveness in the data. And for further reasons beyond the concern of this book, there is grave doubt whether the methods establish causal connection at all.

Mr. Chein's proposal number 4 is subject to these limitations plus another. He assumes that, given some clinical symptom, let us say stuttering, and given that it is not correlated with school facilities but with something else, then it remains correlated with that, even if different facilities are provided. Suppose the stuttering is correlated with a repression of some kind, and the repression continues. The idea, by virtue of the assumed correlation, is that the stuttering will continue. Suppose that segregation is substituted in place of repression, and the feeling of inferiority in place of stuttering; then, as Mr. Chein would say, the feeling of inferiority is correlated with segregation. In general he means that by this kind of procedure it may be shown that segregation has such and such correlates wherever it occurs, regardless of whether school facilities are equal or not. This, it will be seen, would accord with a decision even that equal facilities do not insure psychological equality (of course nothing insures that).

Since he speaks of "specific psychological effects," Mr. Chein must mean not simply correlates back of them, but causes—effects imply causes. Or if he does not mean that segregation causes such and such psychological effects but only that it is correlated more or less with them, then the Supreme Court has no ground here for its proposition that segregation causes inferiority feeling. Correlations are limited to cases in hand. If correlations found in an integrated Chicago school, for example, apply to schools in Clarendon County, South Carolina, there must be a connecting link, such as causation. Anything less would leave open the possibility of exceptions. Because of concentrations of Negroes in South Carolina, and other circumstances, it might turn out that the exception was in fact the rule, and so not to be judged by results elsewhere. It is an absolute requirement of scientific method that in order for results obtained in one situation or context to hold of another, the other must be strictly similar. In the Chein study and project we have not the slightest evidence that that is the case.

If causation is assumed, worse trouble arises. To suppose that complex psychological data are so finely differentiated and so rigidly connected as to permit the application to them of ironclad causal connection, is to go far beyond the data themselves. It presupposes that what is true in a sample of cases in this field is true in all such cases whatever. This is a leap in the dark. It is of course not in the data, but wholly additional to them. So far as the data go or may ever go—they are extremely diverse—it might as well be false as true. But without this leap, Mr. Chein's proposal number 4 cannot be maintained.

In view of these limitations it must now be said that the last three of his four grounds carry little promise of proving one thing or another; of proving it, that is, in the sense of putting it beyond scientific doubt. (A clue, a rough indication, a conditional possibility is not a proof, and constitutional law can hardly rest on anything so dubitable.) Separately and together these grounds fall far short of resolving what Mr. Chein hoped they would, namely, the anomaly of a poll which by a heavy majority tells us that segregation is bad even where facilities are equal, though facilities never are equal!

The remaining one of the four suggested grounds, number 1, only makes things worse. It says that there are cases in which "approximately equal facilities are actually provided," whereas the first quotation from Mr. Chein says "equal facilities are in fact not provided." His remark that between the poll's result and the slender body of research back of it there is a "striking" discrepancy, will hardly be denied. No less striking is the anomaly of a poll in which we find that something which is said never to have been known to exist is yet asserted, as if on the authority of science, to have such and such specific effects.

There is a further anomaly. Mr. Chein, having conducted his poll, sees inconsistencies and now ponders measures for finding out whether the result is really true. Not so the Supreme Court. Why? Because it has not thoroughly considered these writings and realized their uncertainty? Because it is not in fact relying much on them? Because, venturing into fields removed from the judicial office, it has erred and strayed? Then, since the purpose of the poll was to inform the Court, and the Court has accepted the information at face value, Mr. Chein and others "similarly situated" are now spared the labor of justifying the poll's results by scientific investigation.

The Court must have esteemed the poll highly, since two of the rather few citations it gives pertain to it. Presumably the Court takes the poll as science or a substitute for science. If the first, the Court must have peculiar ideas of science and how it is achieved. If the other, the Court's requirements must be very easily satisfied. In either case judicial proof is something very much less than the lay world has believed. And in either case justice and the law are also less.

Theodore Brameld: "Educational Costs," in Robert M. MacIver, ed., *Discrimination and National Welfare,* New York, Harper & Brothers, 1949, pp. 44-48.

In the five pages of the Court's citation here the principal items seem to be:

That costs of discrimination include "social losses" which are "difficult to measure numerically but which follow from an inadequately educated population," such as "the cost in unhappy, inefficient, poorly trained workers which results from denial to the Jew or Negro of his right to the kind of education he desires and deserves;" "the loss in sheer ignorance which in turn causes people to behave unintelligently as consumers, voters, parents;" "the cost in delinquency, crime, poor relief."[59]

That "social scientists are almost unanimously agreed that the white people and the Christian people of the United States suffer more from the effects of discrimination than do the minority groups themselves."[60]

That a Philadelphia study "apparently shows that even very little school children develop prejudice as they soak up the beliefs and habits of discrimination maintained at home or in their neighborhoods."[61]

That persons of "different races, religions, nationalities fail to enrich one another and cultural learning is narrowed and distorted."[62]

That one of the most important effects of segregation shown in a poll of social scientists (this is readily seen to be the Deutscher and Chein poll) is "the tremendous cultural loss that results simply from the isolation of groups from one another."[63]

That "another detrimental effect of tremendous importance may be epitomized by the term 'social neurosis,' as in the frustration and aggression of white children, and their parents, in Gary, Indiana, when Negroes were admitted to white schools, followed by counter frustration-aggression among many Negroes;" and in clannishness and clustering, as in Jewish and Negro fraternities.[64]

That such forces "cause boys and girls to develop prejudice, distrust, guilt feelings" and "to substitute over-simplified, stereotyped thinking for honest, particularized thinking about their fellow human beings."[65]

Mr. Brameld mentions still further costs, as in "confusion of values;" "domination of reason by passion;" "sacrifice of integrity (witness the distortions by officials of universities and colleges regarding the [Jewish] quota system—certain college authorities have actually admitted that they would not admit Jewish students in any considerable numbers, even though they had to close their doors);" "denial of truth or value seeking through free consensus attained by participation of all groups."[66]

Several remedial steps are proposed by Mr. Brameld: (1) support of the President's Committee on Civil Rights (this was in 1949) and of fair employment practice legislation, "which should of course include all educational workers;" (2) tests of the "constitutionality of segregated schools and quota systems right up to the Supreme Court;" (3) support for the minority's struggle" for "equal salaries and equal tenure" and for the efforts of teachers to organize strongly, autonomously, in the same way that other workers, intellectual and manual, organize;" (4) institution of tests for prospective teachers, to determine "the amounts and kinds of prejudice" they have—he intimates that it is questionable to certify teachers without such tests, lest they "help perpetuate in the classroom the very prejudices already incipient in their own students;" (5) "intercultural education for children in the schools;" (6) "perhaps most imperative" of all, upholding "an audacious conception of education which glows with the magnetic vision of an order in which all people are at last equal and free, not merely in theory, but in every aspect of day by day practice."[67]

It must be very difficult to demonstrate that the "social losses" cited here are due to discrimination. For just what is a social loss, and how are we to judge that discrimination was its cause? Anything called a social loss, even such a one, presumably, as depletion of population, will presuppose a standard of gain and loss, and this standard will almost certainly be only putative if it is not implicit in or at least consistent with public policy; and if it is so related to public policy, then redress of it is possible at law.

Social science cannot prescribe the standard, it can only propose it. For its own purposes it can of course invent and abstractly apply standards at will. But it has no jurisdiction, it is not representative, and what it takes for a standard is strictly presumptive unless it is the policy of or prevalent in society. Absent the standard, then absent the loss. If there is such a thing as social science (which is sometimes questioned), then it can ascertain a society's standards by abstraction from its ways of life, and can compare them with the laws and with other societies' standards, offering proposals of its own. But it can hardly do more.

According to what standard is it said by Mr. Brameld that we are suffering social losses in such forms as inefficiency and unhappiness of workers? Or in behaving "unintelligently as consumers, voters, parents"? To every Republican, I suppose, a Democratic vote is unintelligent. But then, so is a Republican vote to a Democrat. Neither Democrats nor Republicans, nor the supporters of this cause or that, regardless of party, concede that their vote is properly subject to critical appraisal by sociologists. They consider the secret ballot of higher value than any opinion of sociologists on its exercise. And there the matter ends.

It ends there because of what, with us in this country, is a superior standard: freedom. Self-government, we hold, is better than good government by others. It is pointless to tell us about "social losses" when avoidance of such "losses" would mean compromise of freedom.

To show that these supposed losses arise from discrimination would be exceedingly difficult. May they not arise from all sorts of circumstances? If social science goes far, probably it will find that what the integrationist calls discrimination or prejudice is far less a thing of that kind than it is an expression of natural disparities and contrasts between people.

Is it certain that different peoples *fail* to enrich one another, as Mr. Brameld thinks, by holding apart? Is it so simple as that? Much evidence goes to show that when some come together what they chiefly enrich is battlefields. Mr. Brameld's Gary instance is a miniature of this. And is isolation *per se* bad? To the Greeks of antiquity—a great example of culture—other peoples were barbarians. It can hardly be assumed that the cultivated life is assured by, or depends on, the indiscriminate mingling of peoples.

Can "confusion of values"—who does not experience this at times? —and "domination of reason by passion" be summarily charged up to discrimination and prejudice? Psychiatry, I dare say, will not give much support to this allegation. It knows too many other causes.

But administrators of the Jewish quota system in colleges (under which the number of Jewish students admitted may be limited to a certain percentage) are certainly fair game for Mr. Brameld if, unlike the painfully explicit one he quotes, they have to resort to hypocrisy. Is it really hypocrisy, however, or, as he puts it, "sacrifice of integrity"? Is it never merely reserve, for reasons of delicacy?

Is truth and value-seeking a matter requiring "free consensus attained by participation of all groups"? What if some groups do not wish to participate, or prefer other ways?

Among Mr. Brameld's proposals for social reform is one which appeals to many high-minded persons: fair-employment-practices legislation. Although this has now been enacted by Congress, in the 1964 Civil Rights Act, great opposition to it exists. Because of discrimination? Not because of incompatibility with things in the American system which are held dearer?

The proposal of "equal salaries and equal tenure" wholly disregards merit. It is naive communism.

The proposed test for teachers, to find out and exclude the prejudiced, might disqualify many of the best, for it is well known that zeal for unpopular causes, which is easily mistaken for prejudice, is a frequent concomitant of superior pedagogical ability.

The last of the proposals illuminates all the others and all their author's objections and criticisms before. The aim of making all people "equal and free, not merely in theory, but in every aspect of day by day practice" is not just communistic, it is wholly utopian. Little wonder that, with it as a standard, discrimination and prejudice should seem rife among us. It is not the American standard and is not compatible with it, nor, probably, with itself.

Free enterprise means free undertaking and says nothing about the proceeds. But, with us, it contemplates and in fact involves the right of the enterprising to possess the proceeds. Its principle is that of earning. If all earn the same, they receive the same, provided the principle is respected, and if they should by chance save the same they would have the same and so, presumably, exemplify the Brameld ideal of equality of all. But if, as with us, they earn unequally or husband their earnings unequally, results are unequal: advantages, disadvantages, inequalities. So his ideal is not compatible with the American system.

Further, free enterprise is not economic enterprise only, but what we may call talent and effort enterprise. The fruits of this are of all kinds, not just of the economic kind. Different, unequal talents or endeavor—different, unequal results. To these results Mr. Brameld would have to apply, continuously, a leveling, redistributing, robotizing operation, since otherwise he could not be assured that all would be equal "in every aspect of day by day practice."

But he also proposes that in every aspect of day by day practice all are to be free. Presumably this means unrestricted or, if restricted, then equally restricted. Suppose that, being free, one infringes another's enterprise or outrivals him so far that his endeavor sinks low. Restraints will have to be applied, for otherwise only the stronger will now be free. But if restraints are applied, then freedom of the strong is denied. We then have the dilemma: With restraints the strong are not free; without them the weak are not free. Hence the internal inconsistency of Mr. Brameld's ideal.

Why is such an ideal put before us by the Supreme Court? It means asking us to turn from the system prevailing in the United States since the adoption of the Constitution to a system very nearly the opposite, one of pure communism, adumbrated for us in SCUR (above, p. 66). Why does the Supreme Court appeal to this and other such "modern authority" for support of its decision?

There is one clue. As we have seen, the Court takes effects, results, as its standard in judging whether segregated schools are unequal, saying that segregation causes inferiority feelings even if there are equal school provisions. So the Court must be thinking of equal protection of the laws in about the same way Mr. Brameld thinks of equality in "every aspect of day by day practice." There is, however, this difference: Mr. Brameld candidly and zealously admits that his is an "audacious conception," while the Court makes believe that its is a deduction from the United States Constitution! And Mr. Brameld applies his to "every aspect" of daily affairs, while the Court confines its to racial affairs, for the present at least.

To countless persons whose lot is inferior, who doubtless are oppressed by feelings of inferiority in consequence, this must seem like discrimination in favor of the Negro. Let them take heart. The same "modern authority" that here inspires the Court's racial integration, envisions integration in "every aspect of day by day practice". And the same sentence of the Fourteenth Amendment under which the Court assumes authority to integrate the races, must allow it to assume authority to integrate life, liberty, and property as well. Now anything goes. But the Constitution goes farthest—into eclipse.

E. Franklin Frazier: *The Negro in the United States*, New York, Macmillan Company, 1949, pp. 674-681.

The eight pages of this citation contain very little concerning education. In substance it is: Segregation has always meant inferior schools and inferior teachers; inferior schools "have caused a high rate of illiteracy to continue among Negroes since Emancipation;" "the resulting mental isolation of Negroes continued a half century" and was only partially overcome by migration from the South to the North during the first World War and subsequently; Negro incentive has been restrained by discrimination both in employment and in opportunities for training in the higher lines.[68]

The statement that segregation has always meant inferior schools and teachers is contradicted by findings in the cases before the Supreme Court, though it is possible that the difference between the date of the statement (the book was published in 1949) and the date of the cases (1952) will favor the statement somewhat. In the Brown case there was a finding of "substantial equality as to all factors."[69]

The statement that inferior schools "have caused a high rate of illiteracy" is strictly contrary to fact. Illiteracy is not caused by schools (though under today's pedagogy one may be tempted to say that it is perpetuated by some of them, without regard to race). A nonentity (such is illiteracy) is not *caused*.

To say that mental isolation of Negroes has resulted from inferior schools by way of illiteracy presumes that a clear causal connection between such isolation and the schools is established. No evidence of this is given here, and though such a connection may be surmised, that is a very different thing from showing that it exists. The possibility that indolence, inferior capacity, heritage, and kindred attributes are causes of such isolation is disregarded. Further, "mental isolation" is a figurative term. Active minds are not isolated from knowledge or the world.

But it can be presumed, in agreement with the author, that restriction of opportunities for employment in the better lines has hurt incentive. Even this, however, may require qualification. It might hold of only a small element. Instead of repressed incentive, some cases may disclose only shiftlessness. Compare the Japanese in California, and the Jews the world over; if anything, restriction of opportunity has been a spur to incentive in them.

The easiness and presumptiveness with which causal connections are asserted in this book, as in much other writing on its subject, must arouse apprehension in the thoughtful reader. This is a field where, instead of the clear and distinct showings needed for the assertion of such connections, we have a complex of uncertain forces which may be very difficult to distinguish and exactly connect. Of these, do we really know that discrimination is the cause of so much? If so, how? Unless thorough and comprehensive investigation has been made, under criteria well known to be reliable and applicable (these, we have seen, are acknowledged to be lacking in this field), the assertion of causal connection is premature and may be deceptive.

A term much used in such writings, and now strained into a cliché, is "stereotype." The author of the book here says that white people in the South don't know Negroes as human beings, but know only "the stereotype" Negro, and that rarely does the Negro know the white except by stereotype. This can be no more than a surmise— to set such limits to so many people's acquaintance is a very odd pretension. But it leads to the question, whether a great deal now current in writings about the Negro is not stereotype too. For instance, the idea, always recurring and hardly ever questioned, that the Negro's lot is all due to white discrimination. There are many Negroes in Southern communities who by ability and industry have attained good positions, including public office. If, having blamed discrimination for so much, writers would consider why it exists, and if the victims would try the experiment of seeing themselves as others see them, the results would doubtless be illuminating. To do such a thing the writers would require a reorientation, from that of the impressionist and the promoter to that of the scientist. Supreme Court citations from their writings, if the Court, after its misadventure this time, should try again, might be more dependable then.

Gunnar Myrdal, *An American Dilemma: The Negro Problem and Modern Democracy.* New York, Harper & Brothers, 1944.

This the last of the Court's citations in the category of what it calls modern psychological authority is by far the most considerable of them all. But it is not a work in psychology, except to a minor degree. Rather, it is primarily sociological. As the Court gives no place

references, but only the indefinite "see generally," we are left to find
in it what we can. That is very much indeed. Yet since the Court's
concern here is only to justify its tenet that segregation causes inferiority feeling in Negro pupils, we can confine our notice to what
seems to bear on that and to the general tenor of the book.

It is a massive two-volume work, running to 1538 pages. It was
inspired and commissioned by the Carnegie Corporation of New York,
with the purpose of providing "a comprehensive study of the Negro
in America." In order to insure freedom from bias, sectional, national,
or racial, the Corporation looked abroad for a man to supervise the
project. Professor Myrdal, whom it chose, is a Swedish economist,
of the University of Stockholm, and a former member of the Swedish
Senate. He brought with him to the United States another Swedish
scholar, Richard Sterner, as an assistant. He also had the assistance
of Arnold Rose, now of the University of Minnesota. In addition,
there were scores of collaborators in the United States who contributed researches to the project. For some reason, which perhaps will
be gathered as we proceed, there is prefixed to it a notice stating that
the Carnegie Corporation "is not to be understood as approving by
virtue of its grant any of the statements made or views expressed
therein." And Frederick P. Keppel, the president of the Corporation,
remarking in a foreword that "it is inevitable that many a reader
will find in these volumes statements and conclusions to which he
strongly objects, be he white or colored, Northerner or Southerner,"
appeals to them to "make every effort to react to these statements
intellectually and not emotionally." In reading it, one who has pon-
dered the Supreme Court's reasoning in the segregation cases may
wonder whether the Court heeded this appeal.

The appeal suggests another question: How did Professor Myrdal
react to the matters treated in his book? Of that, we have an indication in his concept of social science. This he regards not as science
in a rigorous sense but as a technique of reform, or "social engineer-
ing." Everything about it carries valuations, he holds, meaning by
"valuation" an "idea about how reality . . . ought to be or ought to
have been;" and so "a 'disinterested social science' is, from this view-
point, pure nonsense. It never existed, and it never will exist."[70]

There is, he says, a "rationalism and moralism which is the driving
force" behind social science, "whether we admit it or not."[71] He says,
"The scientific facts of race and racial characteristics of the Negro
people are only of secondary or indirect importance for the social
problem under study in this volume." It is "the popular beliefs, and
they only, which enter directly into the causal mechanism of inter-

racial relations."[72] And such beliefs, touching race problems, are "opportunistic and have the 'function' to defend interests."[73]

Just what is "America's Dilemma" about?

It is concerned with "the disparity between American ideals and behavior" with respect to the Negro.[74] The "dilemma" arises over what the author calls "The American Creed," which consists of "ideals of equality and liberty," made "the highest law of the land" through the Declaration of Independence, the Preamble to the Constitution, and the Bill of Rights.[75] The dilemma is stated as follows:

" . . . the ever-raging conflict between, on the one hand, the valuations preserved on the general plane which we shall call the 'American Creed,' where the American thinks, talks, and acts under the influence of high national and Christian precepts, and, on the other hand, the valuations on specific planes of individual and group living, where personal and local interests; economic, social, and sexual jealousies; considerations of community prestige and conformity; group prejudice against particular persons or types of people; and all sorts of miscellaneous wants, impulses, and habits dominate his outlook."[76]

A further version of the dilemma is this:

"There is plenty of discrimination in the North. But it is—or rather its rationalization is—kept hidden. We can, in the North, witness the legislators' obedience to the American Creed when they solemnly pass laws and regulations to condemn and punish such acts of discrimination which, as a matter of routine, are committed daily by the great majority of the white citizens and by the legislators themselves. In the North, as indeed often in the South, public speakers frequently pronounce principles of human and civic equality. We see here revealed in relief the Negro problem as an American Dilemma."[77]

Professor Myrdal and his associates were four years compiling the materials and writing the book. As the director of the project and principal contributor to it, Myrdal was given a free hand. The range of the book may be indicated as follows. There are forty-five chapters, treating such matters as: American political ideals; ramifications of the Negro problem; racial characteristics, ancestry, and beliefs; population and migration; economic status of the Negro from slave days onward; Negro occupations and income; the Negro in politics; the Negro and the law; social inequality; segregation, caste, and class; Negro attitudes and actions with regard to Negro status; the Negro church, school, and press; the Negro and the war.

It is a conspicuous theme of the author that race is a myth. He speaks of "the fateful word *race*" but takes satisfaction in this: "By inventing and applying ingenious specialized research methods, the popular race dogma is being victoriously pursued into every corner and effectively exposed as fallacious or at least unsubstantiated."[78]

If there is no race, of course there is no racial inequality. The supposition of such inequality he calls a dogma, like the supposition of race itself. If biological and psychological evidences have indicated such inequality, he assumes that they were biased or not scientific. If anthropological evidences indicated it, they were one-sidedly construed: a white man is really "much nearer" than a Negro to the apes; for his thin lips and straight hair signify closer kinship to them than do the Negro's thick lips and woolly hair.[79] If it is alleged that Negroes are personally objectionable on account of a peculiar odor, Professor Myrdal replies that he himself has not noticed any difference between white and Negro in this respect, adding, "Even if it were established that Negroes had a different odor, it would not explain why this odor is considered offensive. Likes and dislikes in smells of this sort are a matter of personal taste and cultural conditioning."[80] And, "Even if one felt that the Negro was repugnant in his physical appearance to some white men, scientific knowledge could reveal to him that antipathies of this sort could be removed, and new ones avoided."[81] He mentions a certain experiment in which there were taken samples of white and Negro perspiration in a gymnasium and olfactory tests were made, with results not complimentary to the whites.[82]

There attaches to the Negro "an historical memory of slavery and inferiority."[83] But although it is a widespread belief that Negroes are inferior to whites in intelligence, and although psychological tests show this to be so, the supposition that it is due to innate Negro deficiencies is mistaken, according to Professor Myrdal. Those who believe that the inferiority is innate have "not been able to discern the influence of gross environmental differences, much less the influence of more subtle life experiences" and, moreover, their observations have been "limited and biased."[84] White people hold "false beliefs" concerning Negro racial inferiority.[85] Yet "inferior the Negro really is; so he shows up even under scientific study. He is, on the average, poorer; his body is more often deformed; his health is more precarious and his mortality rate higher; his intelligence, performance, manners, and morals are lower."[86]

"On the inherited inferiority of the Negro people there exists among white Americans a whole folklore, which is remarkably similar throughout the country."[87] "Being a Negro involves—everywhere in

America, and independent of social class—having an inferior status."[88]
There is a rigid and intricate caste system for maintaining this status.

Nevertheless, Negro apologists uphold the doctrine that their race
is equal to the white in natural endowments. "If a Negro leader publicly even hinted at the possibility of inherent racial inferiority, he
would immediately lose his following. The entire Negro press watches
the Negro leaders on this point."[89] Booker T. Washington, though
he went far in making concessions to white opinion, "never dared
to allude to such a possibility" as innate Negro inferiority.[90] Robert
B. Moton wrote that the Negro " 'would never admit that his blood
carries any taint of physiological, mental, or spiritual inferiority.' "[91]
Moton was speaking of Negro-white amalgamation. This is a subject
which occupies Professor Myrdal at considerable length.

Like many other attitudes of white persons towards Negroes, the
opposition to intermarriage is, according to him, more or less a
"rationalization," or specious reason intended to conceal the real
reason. And the real reason, he holds, is fear of social equality.
That is to say, it is not revulsion towards amalgamation as such, but
fear lest the social barrier between white and Negro be broken down.
He says:

"The fixation on the purity of white womanhood, and also part of
the intensity of emotion surrounding the whole sphere of segregation
and discrimination, are to be understood as backwashes of the sore
conscience on the part of white men for their own or their compeers'
relations with, or desire for, Negro women [sic!] . . . Our practical
conclusion is that it would have cleansing effects on race relations
in America, and particularly in the South, to have an open and sober
discussion in rational terms of this ever present popular theory of
'intermarriage' and 'social equality,' giving matters their factual
ground, true proportions and logical relations."[92]

Myrdal seems surprised to find that even from a liberal-minded
Northerner:

"The response is likely to be anything but pleasant if one jest-
ingly argues that possibly a small fraction of Negro blood in the
American people, if it were blended well with all the other good stuff
brought over to the new continent, might create a race of unsurpassed
excellence: a people with just a little sunburn without extra trouble
and even through the winter; with some curl in the hair without the
cost of a permanent wave; with, perhaps, a little more emotional
warmth in their souls; and a little more religion, music, laughter,
and carefreeness in their lives."[93]

From Kelly Miller, the Negro author of *Out of the House of Bond-*

age and other works, Myrdal quotes the following: "It must be taken for granted in the final outcome of things that the color line will be wholly obliterated . . . A physical and spiritual identity of all peoples occupying common territory is a logical necessity of thought."[94]

From W. E. B. DuBois, another Negro author, Myrdal quotes this statement: " . . . a woman may say, I do not want to marry this black man, or this red man, or this white man . . . But the important and vicious demand that all colored folk shall write themselves down as brutes by a general assertion of their unfitness to marry other decent folk is a nightmare."[95]

Social inequality between white and Negro is found by Professor Myrdal to be contrary to the American Creed. The Creed, he says, precludes any resort to social sanctions, to say nothing of economic and legal ones, for securing such inequality.[96] White people, "whether they know it or not . . . are dwarfing their minds to a certain extent by avoiding contacts with colored people."[97] In employment there is in general, he thinks, no excuse for denying the Negro equal opportunity. He contemplates a "breakdown of discrimination" in the labor market and says: "By attacking the color bars everywhere, it is possible to minimize the change needed in any individual establishment if the Negro is to be completely integrated into the economic system."[98] And to break down prejudice and raise the Negro's status, he favors "everything which brings Negro and white workers to experience intimate cooperation and fellowship."[99]

Myrdal senses in the white American's concept of the Negro an "irrational element."

" . . . It is like the concept 'unclean' in primitive religion . . . The one who has got the smallest drop of 'Negro blood' is as one who is smitten by a hideous disease. It does not help if he is good and honest, educated and intelligent, a good worker, an excellent citizen and an agreeable fellow. Inside him are hidden some unknown and dangerous potentialities, something which will sooner or later crop up. This totally irrational, actually magical, belief is implied in the system of specific taboos . . .

"In this magical sphere of the white man's mind, the Negro is inferior, totally independent of rational proofs or disproofs. And he is inferior in a deep and mystical sence. *The 'reality' of his inferiority is the white man's own indubitable sensing of it, and that feeling applies to every single Negro.* This is a manifestation of the most primitive form of religion. There is fear of the unknown in this feeling, which is 'superstition' in the literal sense of this old word."[100]

The italicized sentence is meant as a value statement, or moral judgment of the author's, and, in conformity with a practice throughout the text, it is so printed in order to distinguish it from sentences meant as factually or logically warranted statements.

In spite of much that he says in praise of America, Professor Myrdal indicts us generally. He says that "the Negro problem in America represents a moral lag in the development of the nation . . . "[101] He says we entertain "whole systems of firmly entrenched popular beliefs concerning the Negro and his relations to the larger society, which are bluntly false . . ."[102] but he tells us that "the conquering of color caste in America is America's own innermost desire."[103] Throughout his pages the Negro appears as a blameless victim of our ways. "There is no single side of the Negro problem . . . which is not predominantly determined by its total American setting."[104]

The Supreme Court must have found little or no evidence in this book to support its proposition that school segregation induces inferiority feeling in colored children. Perhaps that explains the absence of page references in its citation of the book. At all events, the evidence in it of Negro inferiority is overwhelming and it is evidence of inferiority long existing and without regard to schooling. Different interpretations of the inferiority are given, but Professor Mrydal and others are firmly disposed to take the environmental one and maintain that innately, in the blood, there is no difference between Negro and white. Presumably the Supreme Court is not concerned to pass upon that. Its stated concern, its reason for turning to this and the other cited writings, is to prove its proposition that public school segregation induces feelings of inferiority in Negro pupils.

To my finding, the closest thing in the book to what the Court required is, ironically, the contrary observation that some Negroes, including the prominent apologist W. E. B. DuBois, who was also a teacher, "prefer the segregated school, even for the North, when the mixed school involves humiliation for the Negro students and discrimination against Negro teachers."[105] Humiliation being an acute sense of degradation or inferiority, it is apparent that this observation supports not what the Court presumes but the opposite: that to prevent inferiority feelings on the part of colored pupils, segregated schools are better than mixed schools. And humiliation for white pupils in mixed schools in more intimate respects than for the colored, is a common and direful expectation in communities with large Negro population ratios.

Professor Myrdal is admittedly an advocate. Though the Court's citations are given as scientific evidence, he is at times scornful of scientific standards, notably the standard of objectivity, or submission to facts. He belittles it in such eminent American sociologists as Sumner, Giddings, and Ogburn—defenders of "the old do-nothing (*laissez-faire*) bias of 'realistic' social science,"[106] he calls them; "do-nothing" because their aim was not the reformer's aim of redirecting the course of affairs [but the scientist's aim of thoroughly comprehending and explaining it, regardless of its direction].

He has taken a large, miscellaneous body of work by other hands and marshaled it around certain themes of his own, two of which are his so-called American Creed and American Dilemma. He says he came by the former in this way: "He was requested to see things as a stranger. Indeed, he was asked to be both the subject and the object of a cultural experiment in the field of social science . . . As he, in this problem — to which he had previously given hardly a thought — was nearly stripped of all the familiar and conventional moorings of viewpoints and valuations, he had to construct for himself a system of coordinates. He found this in the American ideals of equality and liberty."[107]

But is there an American Creed? Not just a sentiment or conviction of some of us but a nationally avowed and sustained doctrine? If so, just what is it and where may we find it? To speak again and again of *the* American Creed, as Myrdal does, is to take for granted that there is one and one only and that we adhere to it as a nation. And yet it is most unlikely that Americans, differing so much among themselves, agree on anything that can seriously be called a creed, unless we call the law of the land a creed (even it may leave doubts). The congressional un-American Activities Committee, were its tenets expressly set forth, would perhaps, by inverse implication, bring us as close as anything else to an official answer. But what that committee has defended as well as what it has opposed is anything but an American creed, pro or con, to judge by the voluble criticism that has dogged its career.

It is of course not impertinent for Mr. Myrdal to cite the Declaration of Independence, the Preamble to the Constitution, and the Bill of Rights, nor for him to abstract from them the idea of liberty as a cardinal tenet of Americanism. But what liberty? The liberty we possess is that specified in the law, as in the Bill of Rights, plus unspecified forms residual in us after the law has set its bounds. Our freedom of assembly, of expression, and of religion is independent of race or color: it exists equally with or without regard to them and neither gives nor takes away so far as they are concerned. Now Myrdal would draw from this a specific right of the Negro to mix with the white, and by implication a legal duty of the white to mix with the Negro; otherwise there is no point in his appeal to the Bill of Rights in the hope of striking down the color bar.

This is quite incredible. The Bill of Rights neither mixes nor un-mixes, but leaves that to us; and just in that—in the freedom of choice, the autonomy of the individual—is the glory of it.[108] The Swedish stranger misapprehends. He would read compulsion where our cherished right reads freedom. He must have overlooked Article X of the Constitution, which reserves to the states the determination of their policy concerning all matters not delegated by them to the Federal Government.

Equality undergoes an extension the same as liberty, at Myrdal's hands. From "All men are created equal" he would infer that all are entitled to equal opportunity, or perhaps it is from "ideals of equality and liberty," which he calls "the highest law of the land," that he would infer it. Now it is obvious that equality of opportunity, however much we cherish it, is not a corollary of our being created equal. Equality as members of our species, or before the law, or in the sight of God, is no guarantee of equality in one another's sight or under the terms and standards of one another's callings, affiliations, and so on. We do indeed have a certain equality of opportunity, in a formal sense, which is this: We are not denied it or disqualified for it by law. But this absence of legal disability is an empty form, by no means the same thing as possession of qualifications for any and all positions and pursuits. Those qualifications must be supplied by oneself and one's heritage. They are not a peculiar bestowal of the American Government. Nor is it Negroes alone who fall short in them; countless white people also fall short, and some Negroes qualify where whites do not.

We might ask, Equality of what opportunity? The opportunity for Negroes to mix everywhere and in everything with whites? Regardless of the whites' wishes? The whites claim no such opportunity either with respect to one another or to other races. It would be the end of individual liberty. But Myrdal would deduce it from "ideals of equality and liberty." It is evident that he gives these ideals a different sense from that of the Declaration of Independence, the Preamble to the Constitution, or the Bill of Rights.

"What," he asks, "do the millions of white people in the South and in the North actually think when, year after year, on the national holidays dedicated to the service of the democratic ideals, they read, recite, and listen to the Declaration of Independence and the Constitution? Do they or do they not include Negroes among 'all men'?"[109]

This is rhetoric about rhetoric. If Mr. Myrdal had been less a stranger, he would have known that Fourth of July oratory is not a good measure of American thought and jurisprudence. He would also have known that the proposition, "All men are created equal," is, to speak unreservedly, a stock enigma, rarely uttered except to be amended or disputed. Had he remained with us longer and read the debates in Congress on the proposed Fair Employment Practices Commission law, he could hardly have thought that equality of opportunity, in a concrete, universal sense such as he intends, is an article of faith here. Of course we say, formally, contemplatively, that there is always room at the top and the poorest boy can become President, but in saying it we do not mean to cancel the conditions, of which there are very many, all part of our system. The Swedish stranger overlooks these. He also overlooks the fact that a few years after the Declaration of Independence there was written into the Constitution a provision, in the first Article, reckoning a slave to be, or to count as, three-fifths of a man, and an untaxed Indian not to count at all. Much later, on the eve of the Civil War, the Supreme Court said:

" . . . In the opinion of the Court, the legislation and histories of the times, and the language used in the Declaration of Independence, show, that neither the class of persons who had been imported as slaves, nor their descendants, whether they had become free or not, were then acknowledged as part of the people, nor intended to be included in the general words used in that memorable instrument . . .

"They had for more than a century before been regarded as being of an inferior order, and altogether unfit to associate with the white race, either in social or political relations; and so far inferior, that they had no rights which the white man was bound to respect and that the Negro might justify and lawfully be reduced to slavery for his benefit . . . "[110]

The Thirteenth and Fourteenth Amendments, abolishing slavery and commanding equal protection of the laws, are silent about the past and its judgment of the Negro. Out of all this Mr. Myrdal might have constructed the answer to his question, whether "all men" in 1776 or subsequently included the Negro. To find the American creed, if there is one, he would have been well advised to study the facts more, even though, to his purpose, facts, admittedly, were only secondary.

America is in a dilemma? Over race questions? Many a Negro

citizen may be in a dilemma because of his lot, but the supposition that the country as a whole was so beset twenty years ago when this book was written does not ring true. We were not, as the dilemma metaphor presumes, impaled on the horn of adhering to a fancied creed at the expense of abandoning the color bar, and the horn of keeping the color bar and renouncing the creed. There was really no such creed. It is an abstraction and distortion: an abstraction by reason of being isolated from its conditions, and a distortion by reason of confusing the idea of equality before the law with equality, through cancellation of the conditions, of opportunity. And since there was not such a creed, there was not such a dilemma.

So Professor Myrdal is systematically misled throughout his book. This may not detract from the polemical value of the work, but polemical value is something different from pure factuality—and only the latter could have the probative force the Supreme Court required. It must also be said that at many points where he is recounting observations and episodes, and not carrying out his apologia, what he says is beyond criticism. Further, the book contains many inform- ative, instructive, and disturbing passages from distinguished works of others. Yet in the main it is vitiated by the author's renunciation and distrust of scientific objectivity. He is capable of such an utter- ance as this: "To the knowledge of the present writer, there is no piece of research on the Negro problem which does not contain valu- ations, explicit or implicit . . . The attempt to eradicate biases by trying to keep out the valuations themselves is a hopeless and mis- directed venture."[111]

Myrdal thinks all science is similarly biased. He says that "every choice involves valuations. One does not escape valuations by re- stricting his research to the discovery of 'facts'."[112] (The mockery of the term "facts" signifies a challenge of the idea that there are facts, and intimates that impression and attitude are everything— though elsewhere he laments having to "base our generalizations on impressionistic observations."[113]) On the contrary, choice in science is commonly made according to objective, neutral standards, such as logicality, probability, measurability, workability. It would be quibbling to say that these in turn have behind them a choice or preference, as of more knowledge rather than less, more power rather than less, and so on. Myrdal deprecates "research that is simply factual and without use for practical or political efforts."[114]

So we are to understand that the mountain of material he had available from his collaborators as well as other authors past and present, was biased throughout and that nothing better can be expected. Conceivably, t, 　　　　 T. 1any would deny it. But if it is correct, it 　　　　　　 M. e case. For since bias is given sway, the b t i, 　　 W. 　　 Eastland, for example, must be acknowledge, 　　　　 S. 1at of Professor Myrdal, with the consequenc, 　　　n he antithesis of Myrdal's, is as respectable a, 　　　　uld distinguish good bias from bad, and introduce criteria ... ging the good to the fore.

Now this is too naive. It puts him in a real dilemma. For either he will have to admit that the criteria are but further biases, and thereupon yield to the adverse party's right to counter with criteria of its own, or else he will have to admit that they are not biases, but objective standards, and so contradict his own supposition that science is not objective.

Though bias in some sense is a very common trait, there is no denying that some minds and disciplines rise above it. Generally, in the procedures of science, ways are established or continually sought for excluding it. Without that, we of course can trust neither findings nor interpretations of findings. In this author's work it is apparent that the inspirations called the American Creed and American Dilemma are so far biasing to him that they have kept him from seeing the Negro clearly or from seeing the facts of American life and history clearly or from giving an ingenuous accounting of them. It is one thing to sense injustice and say so; another to cast a shadow over just and unjust alike, out of biased vision.

In a writer admittedly biased, who assumes all others to be biased, it is not surprising to find incongruities and contradictions. He announces that his value premises, as he calls them, will be put in italics to distinguish them from the rest; yet among the rest are far more—premises, conclusions, dicta—that are doctrinal or optative and therefore valuational in his sense of the term. He relegates science to a secondary place, accuses it of bias, and presumes it to be socially determined, yet again and again appeals to it as an independent and conclusive authority. He treats morals relativistically, yet indicts America for "moral lag" (to be consistent, he must indict no one, since, relativistically, all are *ex hypothesi* equal in moral authority). He assumes that when people believe something to be real, it is real, yet also assumes it the business of social science to criticize and refute popular beliefs about the Negro "when they are wrong;"[115] likewise he admits an "indubitable sensing"[116] of Negro inferiority, yet denies it is real. He rejects the idea of a reality such as general welfare, yet invokes the Preamble of the United States Constitution, with its general-welfare clause, and assumes his American Creed and

American Dilemma to be realities. He is satisfied that if it came to pass overnight that all American Negroes were turned white and their past was obliterated from our minds, soon we would be aware of no difference between them and ordinary Americans.

There is a well known intelligence study of white and Negro school children by the psychologist George O. Ferguson, Jr.,[117] with results decidedly favorable to the white. He found that the darker the Negro skin, the lower the pupil's standing on the tests. Myrdal, without seeing his work and on the strength of a summary of it by another author, calls him a biased investigator.[118] He says, "He dismissed the possibility that social differences may have caused the differences in performance."[119] On the contrary, as Professor Myrdal would have seen if he had consulted the study, this is what Ferguson said:

"Of course it may be held that social conditions make it impossible for colored ability to assert itself. There may be potentially eminent men among the Negroes who are not able to attain their commensurate achievement on account of environmental conditions. On the other hand, it may be said that the best opinion, as that of Galton, holds that eminence is independent of circumstance; that innate power can be neither crushed nor created by adverse or favorable influences."[120]

Myrdal, however, will not be downed. "Subsequent studies," he contends, "have not been able to corroborate Ferguson's finding . . . "[121] And yet a more elaborate study some years later by the psychologist Joseph Peterson,[122] and other studies to which he refers, did give corroborative evidence. Myrdal, without considering Peterson's very careful and exacting work, now declares:

" . . . Even if a correlation were found, it would not prove that the high intelligence was caused by white ancestry, since socio-economic differences between mulattoes and full-blooded Negroes would first have to be held constant, and since it would first have to be proved that the inheritance of intelligence does not involve dominant or recessive genes and that the parent population were representative samples of the total Negro and white populations (which they were not) and that passing [of a Negro for a white, that is] and differential reproductivity did not bias the sample of mulattoes."[123]

This extreme requirement, a set of conditions practically unattainable, would make all experiment in this field out of the question. It is a reduction to absurdity. Still, Myrdal asserts the "right to feel confident in the results of the scientific trend, on the part of scientists (sic), toward finding no psychic difference between Negroes and whites."[124] And he thinks it credible that there are as many Negroes as whites in the highest ranges of intelligence.[125]

Well, the right to believe what you please comes in very conveniently. Science, however, is not so disposed. Instead, it bows to the facts and would be quick to disown any instance of bending the facts to anyone's creed or preference.

Philosophically, procedurally, in every way, it is faulty to advance as an explanation of a phenomenon something that cannot be brought to light, or to maintain the *argumentum ad ignorantiam* that because the adversary has not disproved your contention, it must stand. To assume that environment is the sole explanation of Negro-white differences in intelligence tests when you have so defined environment that it is beyond actualization, is little different from explaining heat by phlogiston or disease by divine wrath. Moreover, environment is only a stage, on which the scenes are continually changing under the agency of those having the genius for direction. It is no explanation of history to say that it would have been different if the forces that made it had not been what they were, or to call those forces a deprivation of lesser or non-existent ones. We do not explain what is by what is not.

But if you are determined to think the contrary, it will be no surprise if you run into paradox and confusion. Applying a phantom standard, you can accuse America of moral lag. You can call race a myth, see nothing amiss in amalgamation, and wonder why there is segregation. "One is amazed," says Professor Myrdal, "to see how often, even today, white people go out of their way to help individual Negroes . . ."[126] Amazed, however, only if one is too much a stranger to the facts or so biased as not to comprehend what one sees. Science is never amazed.

On the premise of inherent equality of Negro and white faculties it is easy to maintain that where investigation shows Negro inferiority it is ostensible only, and to blame the white man for it. Thus it will be held that the white man has imposed artificial but insuperable handicaps on the Negro and now misconceives the results as shortcomings of the Negro. Going on, you may say that even after centuries of this and the fixation of a system of beliefs to justify it, there is uneasiness, surrounded with self-deception, on the part of the white. You allege that he has invented no end of stereotype characters which he attributes to the Negro, and that in doing so he has practiced deception on himself. This last is called rationalization.

This term, in the sense it bears here, is a commonplace of psychology, where it means giving a specious, deceptive, *ad hoc* reason for an act or attitude. It means, more particularly, that one has been either disingenuous or naive about one's behavior. In other words, a knave or a fool.

According to Myrdal, it is a "rationalization" that explains, for instance, the South's abhorrence of intermarriage, the real reason being the desire to prevent social equality and so to perpetuate white supremacy. And, he says, it is nothing but a rationalization of the desire to prevent social mingling, or even mixed seating, when the white person makes Negro odor an excuse against these. The whole idea of racial barriers is taken to be a rationalization of the resolve to maintain segregation and discrimination in religion, education, law, politics, housing, breadwinning, and recreation.[127] Myrdal even speaks of "needs for rationalization" and says "the scientist becomes influenced" by such.[128]

But how does anyone know that another's explanations are rationalizations? Since A is not privy to B's mind, how can he, except conjecturally and quite presumptuously, pretend to belie B's reasons and to state the true ones? How are we to know that in accusing B, A is not guilty of rationalization himself? And even if the reasons people give for their opinions are unsubstantiated by other people, that may not be decisive. They may have further, unstated reasons known only to themselves which they do not care to, or know how to, articulate.

Putting aside the psychological findings, suppose it is true that there are no inherent differences of mentality between Negro and white, and that Negro apologists are therefore justified in denying Negro inferiority. Then it must be an unlikely hypothesis that mingling of white and Negro pupils is necessary for equal educational opportunity: things, talents, which are intrinsically equal do not require equalizing. So the weight of the Myrdal book will be against the Supreme Court's doctrine concerning inferiority. And if on the other hand it is the case, as the Court holds, that segregation engenders a sense of inferiority, that sense, in the face of the book's denial of natural inferiority, must be only superficial or illusory. Now it would be an exceptional Negro school or teacher who did not dispel such superficiality or illusion, especially with race consciousness what it is among Negroes today.

On the evidence of the book there is no reason to suppose that school segregation does engender a sense of inferiority, illusory or other. Why then does the Court cite it as support for that idea? Unless we presume that the Court gave it, an admittedly biased book, only superficial attention (a reluctant presumption, considering the gravity of the issue and the express purpose of the citation), we are left to our own surmise—for instance, the surmise that the endorsement expresses the endorser, and hence that the bias of the book reflects a like temper in the Court. And since the bias of the book includes the idea that race is a myth and race purity little more than a joke; that intermarriage is as nothing and amalgamation therefore not to be reprehended; that it is un-American for white people not to accord social equality to Negroes; that white people are dwarfing their minds in not carrying on social relations with them; that intimate fraternizing between white and Negro workers is desirable; that the line between white and Negro is hypocritically drawn and superstitiously maintained by the white people;—for such reasons it is easy to understand the suspicions and allegations of some persons that the Court has become partisan and even Communistic. Had the Court's critics examined this and some of the other cited writings on which the Court founded its reversal of previous segregation decisions, their indignation would probably have been greater than it was; for the facts here, in black and white, exceed the phantoms of suspicion and rancorous imputation that have come forth in Congress and elsewhere.

Because of the admitted bias of the book, to say nothing of unadmitted and therefore more insidious bias, the Court casts discredit on its own judgment in offering the book unreservedly as scientific justification for its decision. The Carnegie Corporation was more judicious. It divested itself of responsibility for everything in the book, as we noticed at the outset. And the Corporation president, foreseeing objections to it from all sides, thought fit to appeal to readers to look upon it with detachment. Had the Court looked upon it that way, or, what is the same thing, with judiciousness implied in classing it as scientific evidence, probably the book would not be found among the citations.

A sharp inconsistency throws all these writings into question. On the one hand we have, in the Witmer and Kotinsky compendium, the caution that too little is known or likely to be known by present means to justify scientific conclusions about the formation and development of mental disposition in children or its bearing on their future; on the other hand we have a large number of conclusions on the subject, vehemently maintained (as in the Deutscher and Chein poll) and presuming unquestionable justification. If it is the case that information is inadequate and proof is out of the question, these conclusions are all discredited, and sound judgments concerning effects of segregation on the minds of Negro children cannot now be made. And if the authors Witmer and Kotinsky and their numerous corroborators are wrong, then it must at any rate be shown or probably indicated wherein that is the case.

The Supreme Court intimates no doubts, no questions, no reservations. Evidently it was aware of no serious inconsistency. Did the Court not read closely enough to see inconsistencies? It appealed to science and offered these writings as science, but from them we learn that science is not established in this territory. So it cannot be maintained that science is the foundation of the Court's momentous decision unless the Witmer and Kotinsky evidence, to say the least, is ruled out. On the Court's own showing, therefore, the supporting ground alleged for its decision is lacking.

Not only is the scientific ground lacking. There is a shortcoming in the whole body of citations, of such obviousness and significance to a person moderately acquainted with such matters that it discredits the conclusions almost as much as the inconsistencies discredit them. It is this: In none of the citations is there a recognition of fundamental differences between white and Negro such as to create a barrier between them. One or two writers touch upon the possibility, but reject it summarily. Evidences of it, however, lie before us in many a page of their writings. Strictly scientific interest would be alert to such a thing, and scientific investigation would not dismiss it but pursue it with the same zeal that motivates any bona fide scientific undertaking.

Further, it must be cause for doubt, in a critical reader (and in a law court too, if the court is going to venture to make critical determinations in non-legal affairs), that all these writers should have no positive explanation of so powerful a thing as racial attitude. So far as they show us, racial attitude is unaccountable or is too superficial to be recognized as a fundamental reality. They incline to think that race is fictitious and hence that race differences are only specious. Of course, on such premises, intense, persistent racial attitudes will be unaccountable—will have to be assumed to come from nothing or to be only adventitious. Prejudice, it is true, is almost uniformly asserted by these writers to lie back of white people's rejection of the Negro. But this is only taken for granted, not positively shown. If prejudice is so common, why so? I suppose it is not something simple or self-caused. To impute it to other people without plausible show-

ings is presumptuous and question-begging and contrary to science
and justice.

What is established? Or if we cannot say established, what is most
consistently affirmed or denied concerning effects of school segregation, in these evidences?

The answer is that nothing is established concerning effects of school
segregation; for that is a subject which (we learn) has not been
investigated.

What is contended or conceded or more or less evidenced, of bearing on the school-segregation question, is mainly the following:

1. Too little is known of race matters in the lives of young children
to justify causal assertions about them.

2. Negro children show race consciousness by the age of two or
three years, and with it some antipathy towards their own race.

3. Inferiority sentiment in Negro children seems to be associated
with the status, one of inferiority and rejection, of the Negro people.

4. There is a sense of uneasiness among Negro children, and more
so in the North, where white contacts are freer, than in the South.

5. The best hope for improving the Negro's status lies in moral
awakenings.

When the Supreme Court declares that school segregation causes
inferiority feeling in Negro pupils, and when it decrees integration as
a corrective, it practically reverses the findings of its authorities. Then
it offers these findings as justification of its decision. In other spheres
the like of this would prompt demands for a sanity investigation.

---

[1] *Loc. cit.*, p. 494.

[2] Not this, not to acquire something from the white, but only to throw off
the stigma he has imposed; no longer to be set apart and excluded, but to be
let alone, racially, like others; to be unhandicapped and free;—such, it might
be sympathetically urged, is the aim of integration.

But the Supreme Court assumes in *Brown* v. *Board of Education* that the
Negro pupil does acquire something from the white pupil, namely, benefits
(above, p. 108). It says that if not allowed the opportunity to acquire these
benefits the Negro pupil is not on a footing of equality with the white and so
is denied equal protection. The first point in the sympathetic defense, that
the Negro is asking for nothing from the white, is therefore beside the mark.
Probably there are many Negroes who are not asking for such benefits; but
that is immaterial, since the Brown decision is founded on a premise of such
benefits.

The next point, throwing off the stigma the white man has imposed—has this a factual backing? Did the white man impose a stigma? Go back to the beginnings: men in a state of savagery, resembling the white man in hardly anything except being of the genus *homo,* captured and carried off into slavery. Where is the stigma? That is surely a misnomer as yet. The great differences between them and their masters are deeply imprinted on the white man's mind and remain so. When, generations afterwards, under a system of equal rights, these differences are still reflected in the white man's disposition, that is not an imposition of a stigma on the Negro. Interracial reaction is no more a stigmatizing than international or interorganic reaction. The integrationist, if he seriously considers the facts, must see that a political formula, such as equality before the law, has no anthropological force. It can no more extinguish race than it can bleach skin or straighten hair. It is formal only, taking people at their lowest common denominator, as units, 1's, x's, all alike, as in the census, their manifold differences, including primordial affinities and aversions, remaining untouched. Beyond the legal formality, people are not equal, but unequal, in countless respects. The biblical text "The last shall be first and the first last," realistically regarded, acutely rebuts the supposition that all are equal before God.

The Negro ought not to be set apart, since he is equal to every other before the law?—An erroneous inference. Being equal before the law does not imply being equal before other men. It is not an *entrée* to their society.

Finally, the desire to be unhandicapped and free is not peculiar to the black man but is a universal aspiration, of a kind. It is one, however, which is likely to lose itself in the clouds of make-believe. Where, in a world of countless human differences, of claims, counter-claims, fixations, and aggressions, is this eldorado to be found? Where are natural differences and their cumulative fruits canceled by a mere edict, judicial or other?

What is gained by enlisting sympathy for the segregated, white or non-white, on grounds which disregard racial realities? Sympathy is a human offering, to palliate the misfortunes or deficiencies of a fellow creature. But, like equality before the law, it has no capacity to unmake natural differences among us. Where it goes so far as to disguise or deny such differences, what is it but a deception? Sympathy is not the law. The best it can achieve is response in kind, a reciprocity of sympathy. That cannot be coerced, but only won or found. So it was, in the South, before the integration militance.

Throughout the integrationist contention there runs a systematic deception. It would replace palpable, elemental facts with their opposites, and tries to veil these with abstractions: equality before the law, for example, a cover for forcing repugnancies on white people. Over these repugnancies it maintains another cover, of silence, a shield against having to acknowledge them, or a tacit, unventured denial that they are repugnancies. Or it tries to divert attention from them by intimating that we ought not to consider them.

Equality before the law does not involve rights beyond the law, such as rights of Negroes to personal status with white people. A man is rarely before the law, rarely reduced to an equal, a mere x or 1; but he is almost all the time before other men, where he is a person, a unique individuality not reducible. The theory of integration is that reducibility in the first respect involves it in the other respect. But this theory is never openly stated, whether because integrationists are too astute to expose it or too far in the clouds to see it. Of the patent subversion of law, fact, and reason in *Brown* it merely says that the decision is law and so must be obeyed. In place of openness, respect for facts, submission to reason, it maneuvers to circumvent or vacate all of them. Its course resembles that of a traveler with a forged passport.

[3] Roy P. Basler, *Abraham Lincoln: His Speeches and Writings,* Cleveland, World Publishing Co., 1946, pp. 292, 359, 445.

[4] P. 29.   [5] P. 44.   [6] P. 64.   [7] P. 65.   [8] Pp. 68 ff.   [9] P. 59.

[10] P. 60.   [11] P. 121.   [12] P. 151.   [13] P. 75.   [14] Pp.194-195.   [15] P. 125.

[16] P. 154   [17] P. 153.   [18] P. 165.   [19] P. 81.   [20] Pp. 146, 148.   [21] P. 149.

[22] P. 131.   [23] P. 13.   [24] P. 149.   [25] Pp. 125, 154.   [26] P. 28.

[27] Quoted below, pp. 325 ff.   [28] P. 18a.   [29] P. 136.   [30] P. 139.   [31] P. 140.

[32] Pp. ix-x.   [33] P.141.   [34] *Ibid.*   [35] P. 142.   [36] *Ibid.*   [37] P. 143.

[38] P. 145.   [39] P. 135.   [40] Pp. 147, 153.   [41] P. 152.   [42] P. 153.   [43] P. 155.

[44] P. 156.   [45] P.117.   [46] P. 119.   [47] P. 259.   [48] P. 286.   [49] P.261.

[50] P. 280.   [51] Pp. 273-274.   [52] P. 276   [53] *Ibid.*   [54] Pp. 281-283.   [55] P. 261n.

[56] P. 260.   [57] Pp. 230, 232.   [58] Pp. 232, 233, 234.   [59] P. 44.   [60] *Ibid.*   [61] *Ibid.*

[62] P. 45.   [63] *Ibid.*   [64] Pp. 45-46.   [65] P. 46.   [66] Pp. 44, 47.   [67] Pp. 47, 48.

[68] Pp. 674-675.   [69] *Loc. cit.,* p. 492.   [70] Pp. 1027, 1064.   [71] P. 1024.   [72] P. 110.

[73] P. 111.

[74] P. liv.   [75] Pp. xix, 4.   [76] P. xliii.   [77] P. 67.   [78] P. 92.   [79] P. 116.

[80] P. 1213.   [81] P. 585n.   [82] P. 1213.   [83] P. 54.   [84] P. 148.   [85] P. 76.

[86] P. 97.   [87] P. 54.   [88] P. 640.   [89] Pp. 62-63.   [90] P. 63.   [91] P. 62.

[92] P. 591.   [93] P. 57n.   [94] P. 64.   [95] *Ibid.*   [96] P. 573.   [97] P. 644.

[98] P. 385.   [99] P. 654.   [100] P. 100.   [101] P. xix.   [102] P. xlv.   [103] P. 1021.

[104] P. xlix.   [105] P. 901.   [106] P. 1052.   [107] Pp. xviii-xix.

[108] Autonomy of the individual in his exclusively individual capacity, that is; it holds of or within that individual, not necessarily between him and others. Bills of rights, though they may throw safeguards around the individual, shielding what really is individual, such as the person, his private action, and expressions of his thought and conscience, draw their power from beyond the individual, in our case the concert of individuals, "we the people." Though the personal freedom of an individual includes association, it does not necessarily include, say, miscegenation, since that is more than association, namely, the prospect of progagation, hence of genetic effect on the population, the people. Since the people are sovereign, they, not the individual, have the last word on miscegenation, permitting it in some states and prohibiting it in others.

[109] Pp. 88-89.

[110] *Scott* v. *Sandford,* 19 Howard 393 (1857). This is the renowned Dred Scott case.

[111] *Op. cit.,* p. 1043.   [112] *Ibid.,* p. 1058.   [113] P. 1061.   [114] P. 1058.

[115] Pp. xlv, 110.   [116] P. 100.   [117] See pp. 157 f.   [118] *Op. cit.,* p. 1217.   [119] P. 145.

[120] *Archives of Psychology,* No. 36 p. 128.   [121] *Op. cit.,* p. 1217.

[122] See p. 159.

[123] *Op. cit.,* p. 1217.   [124] P. 146.   [125] P. 147.

[126] P. 592.   [127] Pp. 58, 59.   [128] Pp. 106, 1035.

CHAPTER 7

OTHER EVIDENCE

After what we have seen of the grounds invoked by the Court in support of its tenet that school segregation induces inferiority feelings, it will be useful to turn to evidence of another kind. Although the Court refers to "modern authority" in psychology, it does not venture to specify any finding of scientific psychology as a support for its stand. Its reliance on Gunnar Myrdal's book suggests that it credits the thesis of that book that the innate mental abilities of white and Negro are equal. But between that thesis and the proposition that segregation induces inferiority feelings, there is a difficulty.

If two peoples are equal in endowments, especially endowments of mind, is it plausible to suppose that separation will make one of them feel inferior? It may do so, yes; likewise it may not—there is no logical necessity that it should, and the factual evidence of history hardly supports the supposition, as we have observed before. If inferiority feeling does arise, it strongly suggests implicit inferiority, either in endowments or in antecedent status.

If it is inferiority in endowments, then Myrdal's thesis is discredited; if it is not that but inferiority in pre-school status, the Court's tenet is discredited, since the feeling will not have originated at school but in conditions prior to school. So there is an incompatibility between the Court and its witness. This does not mean that if the Court is wrong, then Myrdal is right; both of them may be wrong—in fact Myrdal admits there is no way of conclusively proving his thesis,[1] and the evidence of another of the Court's witnesses, Dr. Kenneth B. Clark, weighs heavily against the Court's doctrine, as we have seen.

The question of how the abilities of white and Negro pupils compare has engaged many psychological investigators. Forty years ago numerous attempts to find the answer had already been carried out. In 1916 the late Professor R. S. Woodworth, one of the most prominent American psychologists, published in the *Psychological Bulletin* a digest of the results. Since then other studies of the question have been made. It was in that year that the work of George O. Ferguson, Jr., which Myrdal criticizes, was published (see above, p. 149).

Ferguson gave four standard intelligence tests to grammar school and high school pupils, 486 white, 421 Negro, of three cities in Virginia

—Fredericksburg, Newport News, and Richmond. Using the results of two of the tests (the other two "did not show any considerable differences in the general inter-racial comparison"), he found among the Negro pupils a decided correspondence between color and score. Those with the highest degree of white blood (three-fourths) averaged approximately 94 per cent of the white pupils' score on one test while those with no white blood averaged only 66.7 per cent and those of intermediate color had intermediate scores. In general, he thought "it is probably correct to say that pure negroes, negroes three-fourths pure, mulattoes and quadroons have, roughly, 60, 70, 80 and 90 per cent, respectively, of white intellectual efficiency."[2]

Summarizing his findings and those of other investigators before him, he stated:

" . . . the average performance of the colored population of this country in such intellectual work as that represented by the tests of higher capacity, appears to be only about three-fourths as efficient as the performance of whites of the same amount of training.

"The negro's intellectual deficiency is registered in the retardation percentages of the schools as well as in mental tests. And in view of all the evidence it does not seem possible to raise the scholastic attainment of the negro to an equality with that of the white."[3]

Three years after Ferguson's work a kindred study was made in Indiana by S. L. Pressey and G. F. Teter and published in the *Journal of Applied Psychology*, Vol. 3 (1919). Tests employing the Pressey Group Point Scale for Measuring General Intelligence were given to 187 pupils in Negro schools and 2,800 in white schools. (Professor Pressey's tests have been widely used and through them he has attained a prominent place in American psychology.)

Some of the findings were:

"Negro pupils averaged below white pupils of the same age on all the tests (there were ten tests, each comprising twenty items).

"Negro pupils making about the same average score as white pupils were two years older than the white pupils and one grade below them."[4]

Allowing that the results were influenced by the fact that the Negro pupils came from "a psychological environment which is subtly but powerfully different" from that of the whites, and also allowing for the fact that the tests were prepared for white pupils and given by white testers, the authors concluded that some of the differences were nevertheless too marked to be explained by these circumstances.

"A poor average ability," they said of the Negro pupils, "seems unmistakably indicated—a poor ability inadequately compensated for in the schools by a greater retardation, and so leading to lower grade standards as well . . . There is the definite suggestion here of a more elementary and less highly developed ability among colored children."[5]

One of the most comprehensive studies in this field is by Joseph Peterson, entitled "The Comparative Abilities of White and Negro Children," and published in *Comparative Psychology Monographs,* vol. 1 (1922-23). Dr. Peterson, of George Peabody College for Teachers, was assisted by a staff of a dozen psychologists and educators. Tests were administered to 1,726 white and 1,424 Negro school children in Arkansas, North Carolina, and Tennessee. They were standard tests, including the Haggerty, Myers, Otis, and Pressey tests, well known to students of psychology, as well as one of Dr. Peterson's own devising, intended to find out reasoning ability independently of environmental influences. Some of the findings were:

On the first four tests there was "an undeniable race difference in the mental abilities tested," expressible thus: On the average, 82 per cent of the white children exceeded the median (dividing line between the upper half and lower half of the scores) of the Negro children.[6]

The average I.Q. of the Negro pupils was found to be .68; of the white pupils, .88. The author observes: "There is little doubt that training factors are somewhat influential in these test scores; but the race difference persists, and even increases somewhat, where the schools for both races are best and most nearly equal."[7]

Of the remaining test, which was given to 299 white and 314 Negro pupils in Nashville, he says: "From every standpoint, then, so far as our criteria in this test are concerned, the white children are markedly superior to the Negro children, particularly in functions such as sustained attention to the essential elements of a complex situation . . . Indeed, taking all the criteria of the test together we find the 8-year-old white children to be considerably superior to the 10-year-old Negro children, even though, in these two groups, 60 per cent of the whites are from the poorest white schools tested—probably some of the poorest in the city—while 97 per cent of the 10-year-old Negroes are from the Negro school judged to have the best native ability of the colored schools . . . "[8]

Correlations between the scores and the degrees of color in the Negro pupils led to this conclusion: "Our results with young subjects [pupils], in agreement with those of investigators studying older subjects, both Negro and American Indian, indicate an increase of ability to achieve success in simple abstract learning with an increase in degree of white blood."[9]

It is well known that Army intelligence tests in the first World War showed, with minor exceptions, a pronounced difference between white and Negro, in favor of the white. There is a recent study of results of such tests (Army General Classification Test) given to ground crews of the Air Force Service Command during the second World War. This study is the work of Byron E. Fulk and Thomas W. Harrell, of the University of Illinois, and was published in the *Journal of Applied Psychology*, vol. 36 (1952). Messrs. Fulk and Harrell used the scores of 2,174 white and 2,010 Negro soldiers. In order to equalize the education factor, they grouped the scores according to years of schooling, which ranged from zero to thirteen or more.

At all levels the whites surpassed the Negroes. That is, whites with no schooling surpassed Negroes with none, those with one year surpassed Negroes with one year, and so on throughout the fourteen levels. The average for the whites was a score of 95.1; for the Negroes it was 68.5, or 28 per cent below the whites.[10]

There have been numerous studies of social relations among Negroes and between Negroes and whites, an example of which is a monograph entitled *Problems and Emotional Difficulties of Negro Children,* by Mary Regina Goff (Columbia University, Teachers College, 1949). This considers race cleavages in childhood in New York City and in St. Louis. The author found, among other things:

That the darker the Negro child's color, the more difficulties the child experienced in social contacts.[11]

That Negro children gave evidence of early awareness of race barriers, and learned to restrict accordingly their expectations in society at large.[12]

That from social contrasts they inclined to "develop enduring inferiority feelings which pervade all avenues of development, lowering aspiration levels and stifling individual abilities."[13]

That parental instruction was not usually an effective counterfoil to the attitudes thus engendered; and that it "appears improbable that, with the additional experiences which children will have in Negro-white relations, better ways of dealing with situations will follow."[14]

That in St. Louis 40 per cent of Negro parents interviewed accepted segregation on the ground that it "lessened chances of embarrassment in public places."[15]

Dr. Mary Ellen Goodman, a sociologist at Wellesley College, has made a very painstaking study of the genesis of racial attitudes in

unsegregated nursery school children in Massachusetts. Her findings
are set forth in her book, *Race Awareness in Young Children*, (Cambridge, Mass., Addison-Wesley Press, 1952). Among the findings are
the following: that racial awareness arises as early as awareness of
age or sex;[16] that a very common reaction of the white children to
the Negroes is to call them "dirty" (the Negroes themselves do this
at times);[17] that in this reaction "the unfavorable associations build-
ing around the attributes of Negroes are implicit;"[18] that "four-year-
olds, particularly white ones, show unmistakable signs of the onset
of racial bigotry;"[19] that the Negro children never (in this study
upon a group of 46 white and 57 Negro) assume superiority to the
white—"over half . . . convey a sense of inferiority to whites;"[20] that
the Negro child's "most central special problem is one of self-rejection, arising out of a learned set of values which make his person
and his kind unattractive to him;"[21] that white qualities, on the other
hand, fascinate the Negro child, as in this pathetic manifestation:
"Often they stroke, fondle, ruffle, or just lightly touch the hair of
white children. White children, significantly enough, very rarely
make the same gesture."[22]

The degree of Negro color is already significant, in the nursery
school, even though "racial identity is deliberately and consistently
ignored"[23] there. A Negro child's mother is "particularly likely to
dwell upon the topic" and the child can also hear it discussed "by
almost anyone else who knows, as all Negroes know, how important
are shades of color, kinky versus 'nice' or 'good' hair, 'fine' features
versus 'coarse' ones, etc."[24] (The author objects to "white," considering it "an unfortunate term . . . just as inaccurate as 'black',," and
would like to substitute "brown" or "browned" and "bleached"—
she does not admit that there are black people in the United States:
"What we actually have here is a brownness continuum which proceeds without a break from dark brown to the extreme bleach of the
extreme blond."[25])

She finds that the Negro children, four years old, "can sense that
they are marked, and grow uneasy." In some "the high degree of
race awareness . . . is startling."[26] Negroes who have migrated from
the South, "partly in search of an escape from the white-over-brown
formula . . . have not found it."[27]

Since these children were under no racial distinctions, we cannot
suppose that the poignant consciousness of such distinctions so soon
manifested by the Negro children came from discrimination or prejudice. Dr. Goodman's showings, especially of the spontaneous rejection of Negro children by the white and even by themselves, leave

hardly any room for doubt, and her remark that in this bare, un-
learned act there is implicit the system of racial lines later to appear
must be vexing to those who want to think that such lines are artificial and arise out of prejudice and meanness, not out of primordial
nature. She goes on to say, pitifully, that the Negro child in whom
self-rejection occurs "badly needs help."[28] Indeed. And what kind
of help is indicated? Etiologically, separation; the source of the trouble being contact with the white, elimination of that is plainly indicated as the remedy. If a child falls into bad company, with de-
moralizing consequences, no one doubts that what he needs is to be
removed from such company. If a man or a people cast their lot
with others so different that attrition occurs at once, and in time
becomes overwhelming, is there any question about the cause or the
cure? Do they need *help?* What help? It would be fatuous to say
that a Moslem needs to *help* a Frenchman fraternize with him or
vice versa, when one cannot endure the other. Hot does not need to
help cold. Whatever need there is, in such affairs, is the need of
seeing and respecting the facts and not mistaking oneself, or one's
idealizations and ambitions, for the facts.

Even more fatuous is it to say, like the Kansas court and the Supreme Court, that Negro children need integration lest they develop
inferiority feeling. In the nursery school it was integration that gave
them that feeling. It gave them the yet worse feeling, self-renuncia-
tion. Face to face with the white, without imposed barriers of any
kind, they soon discovered barriers not of anyone's making. To ignore these and to impose on the country a dictate presuming them
non-existent, which the courts did, is a betrayal of the children and
of the country. In one respect it is a greater betrayal than even that.
It either falsifies fact or sophistically conceals it or, blinded with
partisan purpose, sees it not: it flouts the truth. Done in the name
of the law of the land, this makes corruption the public policy. It
stands then as an encouragement to all kinds of misrepresentation,
misunderstanding, partisanship, malignment. Under its authority the
most fanciful conceptions are vindicated. Honesty becomes "prejudice." One need not go to the facts, as did Dr. Goodman. Instead,
this: "A white child in the South is not born with anti-Negro prejudice, but that child, from its earliest days, sees others who differ
from itself only in skin color discriminated against and segregated.
The child must come to the conclusion, from the observed fact of
segregation, that those against whom discrimination and segregation
are practiced constitute an inferior type of human being." In other
words, the child, say of age four, reasons it out and from the *idea* of

discrimination and segregation *infers* his way to prejudice. Nothing undergone, felt, suffered. Quite a feat for a child, one might say, and very odd that the Massachusetts children gave no sign of it, yet quickly showed what, according to this, we should have to term "prejudice."

Such a visionary account of elemental realities is found in a publication by the American Jewish Congress, reprinted in part in *Race Prejudice and Discrimination,* by the Negro sociologist Arnold Rose, p. 539. In another book by that author, *The Roots of Prejudice,* certain "theories" of the rise of racial "prejudice" are formulated, one of which he calls "the dislike of difference theory," by which he means the idea that prejudice "always arises instinctively against people who are different."[29] He says: "When some people are asked why they dislike Negroes, they will say it is because they are so black and dirty, or because Negroes are dangerous. Others will say ... you cannot treat a Negro as you can a white man, because a Negro is like a child or an animal and cannot act like a man." To this he replies: "All these statements are expressions of prejudice. They assume that there is something about the minority group which naturally causes the majority group to regard it as inferior."[30]

Another "theory of prejudice," he says, "is that people become prejudiced because of unpleasant experiences with members of minority groups. It is true that a bad experience with a person can make one dislike that person ever afterward. But why should the dislike be turned to all people with the same color of skin or the same accent? If a fat person does one some harm, one does not forever thereafter hate all fat people."[31]

Still another "theory" concerns "scapegoats." "Everyone," he says, "uses a scapegoat," meaning that everyone is more or less frustrated and tries to even matters by making believe that others, not he, should bear the blame. According to this, the Southern Negro is a scapegoat; "so much prejudice and violence against Negroes" is due to frustrations of Southern people.[32]

To science there is a repugnancy in summary pronouncements concerning matters of fact, unless they are conclusively supported with evidence. Unsupported, they are, literally, expressions of prejudice. Take the proposition that anyone who says he dislikes Negroes because they are "black and dirty" is only indulging in an "expression of prejudice." Who could know that? A single instance to the contrary overthrows it. The nursery-school children ("at least half, ... of both races") called the Negroes black and dirty in rejecting them, and Dr. Goodman, who can hardly be considered a segregationist, judges it to have been "the result of the child's own and independent observation." She adds: "No one need have taught him to describe a Negro as 'dirty', and he need have heard no one else do so."[33] Prejudice seems so remote from this that only prejudice itself, of another order, could offer it as an explanation. Abraham Lincoln will not be thought prejudiced against Negroes, yet he gave a reason for separating them from whites which scarcely differs from the one evinced in the nursery school—natural aversion of the white ("disgust" was his term for it).[34]

Take next the supposition that the alleged prejudice against Negroes is significantly connected with numerical differences—that it arises from offenses of individuals in the minority against those in the majority; and the inference that since a person does not reject all fat people merely because some of them have given offense, it is unreasonable to reject the Negro race on account of offensive qualities seen in individual Negroes. In localities where the Negro is in the majority, in the United States and Africa, rejection of him still occurs and is probably even more pronounced;[35] so numbers don't explain (talk about "minority groups" in this connection often seems to be just a veil to conceal the reality, namely, the peculiar aversion of white to Negro, something quite independent of numbers). And the idea of proving the white rejection of the Negro irrational, by analogy with the fat, is an idea in which a student of logic would see violations of all the rules of analogy. Reason is not the determiner of protopathic reactions. Pink and orange, for example, are not *reasoned* to be a disagreeable combination, and one does not *reason* away a bad taste or nausea.

The "scapegoat" simile is even more far-fetched. How, the facts being what they are, could anyone demonstrate that Southern "frustrations" cause "so much prejudice and violence against Negroes"? He would have to show, for one thing, that assault, murder, and rape have no part. It would be hardly more unreasonable to suppose that Northern "frustrations" cause Northern aggression against segregation in the South. Here is another instance of make-believe posing as science, or "social science." Still another: "If Negroes do not always behave like fully responsible people, that in itself is due to prejudice."[36] The ease with which this author (one of Gunnar Myrdal's collaborators in *An American Dilemma*) assigns causes might call, if what he says were taken seriously, for explanation; and doubtless one of the first explanations to suggest itself would be that he was not going to facts, or was not aware of what is necessary to establish causal connections between them, and was only indulging in prejudice himself.

Negro society itself has been studied in much detail, with findings which have some relevance to the Supreme Court doctrine that school segregation generates inferiority feeling in Negro pupils. Under auspices of the American Council on Education an inquiry into Negro life in Chicago, and especially the role played by color, was carried out some years ago by Walter A. Adams, Buford H. Junker, and W. Lloyd Warner. The findings were published in 1941 in a volume entitled *Color and Human Nature.*

Chicago Negro society was found to be, socially speaking, a close parallel of American society at large. But racial or at least physical traits were a powerful determiner of position, both social and occupational, within the Negro society as well as within the whole city; "such traits as skin color, hair texture, and Negroid features have an exaggerated importance in determining social and vocational success . . . and consequently are bound to have far-reaching consequences in the formation of personality." Since color was "in very large measure the basis of high or low position in the Negro social hierarchy" it was judged to be "the most important single element that determines for better or for worse the development of Negro character."[37]

Not only was color such a determiner; shade counted also: "shade of skin color is definitely associated with social or class position. Lightskin persons by and large are at the top of the scale, and darkskin individuals are at the bottom."[38] And the potency of color, socially, politically, nationally, came out in a manner "more acute and painful" as the individual Negro approximated "those behavior traits and general standards of the larger society for lack of which the race is usually reproached.

". . . It is as if American society wished not only to condemn Negroes as inferior beings with unacceptable, if picturesque, modes of living, but also to punish those who change their ways and most completely accept traditional American values. The more intelligent and sensitive, the more cultured and refined a Negro may be, and the more completely he assimilates and transmits the national ideals, the more seriously is he made to feel that his race, and race alone, bars him from enjoying the full rights of American citizenship."[39]

Here is an earthy example of the power of color in Negro Chicago:

"He [the speaker's father] just says he doesn't like dark women, and that's all there is to it. They just don't mean anybody any good. Why, one of my sisters is worse than my dad. We went to the same grammar school but she is so much lighter than I that she was hardly believed my sister. She has actually snubbed me right out in public."[40]

As with much other writing about race, it is easy to see that some of this is either fiction or else questionable interpretation of fact. For instance, the statement, "It is as if American society wished . . . to punish those who change their ways and most completely accept traditional American values." What reason have we to suppose so malicious a desire on the part of America? Is that the only explanatory conjecture the authors could manage? Much simpler would it be to assume that race *per se*, the color bar, is the power at work; an assumption clearly in accord with the authors' own findings concerning the color scale in the Chicago Negro world and likewise in accord with our stock of information concerning Negro-white barriers generally. In fact, is there not a degree of blindness where so patent an explanation is not recognized?

Nevertheless, such unalloyed facts as can be gathered from writings of this type speak with unanswerable force. If it is a true finding that status in the Negro city varies with color, of course there will be racial superiors and inferiors. This will mean that inborn inferiority is expressly acknowledged in the Negro community itself. The awakening to it may be assumed to occur before school age, in view of the evidence brought out in the Kenneth B. Clark study and the Goff and Goodman studies. Myrdal speaks of a shock experienced at this stage by the Negro child—"the shock of the Negro child when he first learns that he is a Negro and realizes the social import of this fact."[41]

After this experience is it plausible to assert that Negro children attending Negro schools are destined to *acquire* there, in the Supreme Court's words, "a feeling of inferiority as to their status in the community"? The evidence from the Court's own citations is that they have a settled realization of their status already and that it remains with them whether the schools are segregated or not.

Possibly a superadded sense of inferiority comes with segregated schooling. But possibly it does not—possibly the sense is even diminished in the close community of the Negro school and the zealous racial tutelage it affords. Possibly, too, the sense is intensified in the contrasts of the mixed school. Such evidence as the Court has vouchsafed to us points the latter way. And in the Goff study it is frankly stated that the prospect of better relations between white and Negro children through more extensive contacts is not favorable.

Not only does the evidence weigh against the Court's finding on the score of inferiority, it weighs against the decreed remedy as well, that is, against integration. The Court commands, Put white and Negro pupils together. The evidence points to distress for the Negroes if that is done. The Court virtually says, Integration will prevent or mitigate the inferiority feeling in Negro pupils. The evidence, concisely expressed, says that it will more likely induce and intensify it. This is clear: the Court's finding is not sustained by the evidence.

In another respect the decision is contrary to the evidence. It is known that Negro pupils are retarded, by comparison with white pupils—one of the social scientists quoted in the Court-cited Deutscher and Chein poll remarked that Negro pupils on the average are a year and a half to two years younger mentally than white pupils; and we saw that Messrs. Pressey and Teter found a retardation of two years. So the Court in requiring that they be placed beside the white pupils requires the schools either to hold back the white pupils or, where segregation has been the rule, to subject the colored ones to new humiliation. I have read somewhere that the judges declare emphatically they are not going to assume the role of school administrators. Surely, then, they must have thought too lightly of what they were doing. On the evidence of their own witness they have made that role such that in many localities (for in many the retardation will be much above the average) hardly anyone else can assume it without dismay.

It happens that there is a proviso in the Court's opinion which we have noticed before and which might be thought to save the case. "To separate them [Negro pupils] from others *of similar age and qualifications* solely because of their race," the Court says, "generates a feeling of inferiority as to their status in the community . . . " (The italics, not in the original, identify the proviso.) This is not an unqualified assertion that separation generates inferiority feeling. It is only an assertion that it does so in certain cases, namely, cases in which Negro pupils have qualifications equal to those of white pupils their age. Others, it might be supposed, are not involved. Consequently, one might expect the Court's decree to have been limited to cases in which Negroes have qualifications matching those of white pupils their age. That would have meant that in only a rather few segregated schools would desegregation have been required. In the greater part of the South probably no change at all would have been required.

Since, however, the Court's decision makes no exception but requires desegregation of the unequally qualified Negro pupils along with the rest, what are we to conclude? This, at least: that equality of qualifications was not in fact the controlling consideration, though in the Court's written opinion it clearly is. So now the inferiority doctrine is under another cloud; for the Court says that inferiority feeling is the result of segregating the equally qualified Negro pupil and says nothing of the unequally qualified, who, nevertheless, are to be mingled with their white superiors. So far as we are informed by the Court, there is no reason to suppose that the unequally qualified are subject to the inferiority sentiment, yet that sentiment is the Court's material ground for desegregation. Accordingly, they are to be put with their white superiors without reason and contrary to pedagogical principle.

So many inconsistencies, so much confusion, might seem to leave room for no more, short of chaos. But there is a variety we have left unnoticed. In the last chapter we saw there were serious questions about the methods and reliability of the psycho-social investigations on which the Court relied. There are questions, too, about the scientific status of this whole sphere of study. Since the Court has ventured to draw upon it for the decision of a momentous question of law, let us look briefly at the standing of this science, assuming it to be a science, for making decisive pronouncements on life and character.

When ninety-six Congressmen and Senators from the South published a declaration in criticism of the Court's decision (below, p. 254), a Princeton University law scholar, Professor Alpheus T. Mason, commending it, took occasion to say: "rather than rely on available judicial precedents, the Court invoked two of the flimsiest of all our disciplines—sociology and psychology—as the basis of its decision."[42] Without willful disparagement it can be said that this appraisal of the two disciplines is not limited to one man, but is rather common in university opinion.

Sociology, as a distinct department of knowledge, has only a petty place. Remove from it what it appropriates, sometimes with distortion, from other branches, such as psychology, history, and ethics, and there is little left to it: taking polls, breaking down the census, marking out and correlating groups, propagandizing. It has no very strict technical requirements: no mastery of logic, mathematics, philosophy, law, or of other scientific grounds, except, perhaps, elementary statistics. No doubt Myrdal's dictum that a wholly objective social science is impossible or futile reflects this propertyless, free-lance condition. A careful journalist could soon qualify as a sociologist, if he chose.

Not that sociological work is without respectability or usefulness. Quite the contrary. Neither does history, for example, stand out in rigorous technical or intellectual requirements, yet it is a cherished and ever rewarding subject; and sociology, we might say, is abstracted historical data, or history standing still. Only, it is not positively, indisputably science, and the Supreme Court employs it as if it were.

The supposition that psychology is a science with *prima facie* trustworthy findings and explanations is evident in the Court's uncritical appeal to it. If in the lavish bazaar of modern learning we were to look for something like a sideshow, this would be it. Fortune-tellers have only fortune-telling, aside from oriental blandishments, with which to catch the prey. Modern psychology has that and a great deal more. It tells your fortune by estimating your traits and matching them against the statistics from similar estimates of other people, to the firm persuasion of schools and colleges, which now maintain psychological annexes through which the pupils pass and which provide them a certificate of their character and destiny (not always to their own conviction). It offers proofs of occult, clairvoyant powers, called parapsychological, which are the occasion for violent disputing within the circle; proofs also about dreams, including a "law" to the effect that every dream is the fulfillment of a suppressed desire. It connects strategically with sex interests and has produced a whole mythology of sex and instituted a kind of sexual gospel. Transcending even this, it has adumbrated a mysterious power called "the subconscious" out of the lives of madmen, and persuaded a willing public that this shadowy thing dominates us all. Over the lives of a vast multitude psychology amounts to a thrall, which, in the more articulate, leads on towards that epitome of irrationality, existentialism. To many college students it is nothing less than an impediment to their intellectual progress.

Let it be said, however, that psychologists by no means agree on the reality of all that passes under the name of psychology. Nor do they agree that psychology is a science, or if it is, whether it has any proofs. In psychological writings, today as a generation ago, one may read laments about the state of the subject. Professor Kenneth W. Spence, of the State University of Iowa, for example, discussing a need of theoretic discipline, has this to say: "It is most imperative that psychologists attempt to formulate their theories in as precise and articulate a manner as possible, for it is only by means of such theorizing that psychology can hope, finally, to attain full fledged scientific statehood."[43]

It is the distinctive business of psychology, according to Professor E. C. Tolman, of the University of California, to ascertain the connections between a creature's physiological state, environment, heredity, training, and age, on the one hand, and its behavior on the other; connections, however, which turn out to be too loose to admit of a precise formulation. Professor Tolman introduced one of the chief concepts (or terms, for what it stands for is not new) of recent psychology, the "intervening variable." This denotes factors such as habits and drives, unknown to or uncontrolled by the psychologist in his experimental studies but assumed to intervene in the set of known conditions and with them to determine the creature's behavior.[44] Not only are there intervening variables, but variables both antecedent and consequent: antecedent—heredity, physiological condition, environmental stimuli; consequent—the behavior itself, or what the creature does in the circumstances. Variables from beginning to end, in short, so that what will happen in a given case (let us say in the behavior of a certain colored child in a certain school under certain conditions), is beyond determination.

We find many of the familiar terms of psychology brought into question in a recent book by Professor B. F. Skinner, of Harvard; such as "intelligence," "test," "individual difference," "trial and error learning," "phobia," "trait." Intelligence tests, he says, are arbitrary and not really quantitative (which means they are scientifically defective). Traits, which have been taken for granted, are far from certain. "Even when we define a trait as a group of responses, the unity or coherence of the group needs to be proved. Do all the responses which are taken to be evidences of aggressiveness, for example, vary together with a given condition of frustration? And are all conditions of frustration equally effective? In order to be sure of the unity of the trait, we have to show that each of the acts which 'expresses' it is controlled by each of the conditions specified as its cause—that each aggressive act, for example, is controlled to the same degree by every condition which can be described as frustrating."[45] Strictly, it would be out of the question to show all of that for it would require constant watching of the creature throughout its life, and infallible insight into its processes. Still, Professor Skinner says that it is the business of the kind of psychology he advocates to show it.

The late Clark L. Hull, of Yale, observed that "it can hardly be doubted that psychology in its basic principles is to a considerable degree in the thrall of the Middle Ages . . . "[46]

Mind, as a distinct reality, is likened to a ghost by Gilbert Ryle, the Oxford editor (ironically) of *Mind*, the most renowned philosophical periodical in English. He remarks that "the postulated interactions between the workings of the mind and the movements of the hand are acknowledged to be completely mysterious. Enjoying neither the supposed status of the mental, nor the supposed status of the physical, these interactions cannot be expected to obey either the known laws of physics, or the still to be discovered laws of psychology."[47] He goes on to argue that psychology is not a distinct study, let alone the master study of behavior; that it is "a partly fortuitous federation of inquiries and techniques" sharing the field with, among others, economics, politics, and the pursuits of teachers, examiners, detectives, biographers, historians, novelists, competitors, employers, and parents; that psychological measurements give little promise of leading to causal explanations of behavior; and that the idea of psychology as the science of mind, correlative to physics as the science of matter, needs to be abandoned.[48]

Uncertainty, it seems, is the rule: either the subject does not admit of exactness or correct methods have not been found or there is misconception all around. There is in Myrdal a mention of certain psychological tests in which a Negro psychologist and a white psychologist tested the same pupils, the Negro finding the average I.Q. of Negro pupils six points higher than the white psychologist found, and the white psychologist finding white pupils six points higher than the Negro found them.[49] After what we have now seen, perhaps this is not very surprising.

Law being normative, directive, the public policy, and not necessarily a scientific transcript of facts, it may or may not agree with the findings or ideals of psychologists and sociologists. Though it may be enlightened by such findings and ideals, yet it may not: it may itself be the wiser. In any event, psychologists and sociologists are not the lawmakers. Yet now the Supreme Court turns to them as if they were vicarious lawmakers, takes as a reality something not indeed found in them, and gives it legal status. This is one of two things: it is legislating by the Court and so usurping the authority of Congress, or it is virtually submitting the determination of a constitutional question to an extra-legal tribunal.

The Court's psycho-sociological citations demonstrate nothing about any effects of school segregation. In fact, they hardly touch that subject. What they seem most to show is race contrast and conflict which leaves its mark on colored children long before school age. And what must strongly impress a careful reader of them is the repeated caution that uncertainty pervades this whole region of study, and even that trustworthy methods are lacking. Did the Supreme Court not read with enough care to notice this caution, though it occurs repeatedly? If it did not, it can hardly escape the imputation of neglect or of incompetence to construe such materials. ("It is not within our competence to confirm or deny claims of social scientists as to the dependence of the individual on the position of his racial or religious group in the community."[50]) If on the other hand it did take notice of the cautions, can the inference of judicial bias be questioned?

So the Court cannot rest here. Its presumption that "modern authority" has established new grounds giving new meaning to equal protection of the laws proves illusory. The Court is therefore left where it was before, without grounds for a change, which means that it is left to precedent; which in turn means that it could only decide the 1954 cases in accordance with previous decisions, such as the decision in the Gong Lum case. The only alternative, if it can be regarded as an alternative open to a court of justice, was to render an arbitrary decision, one without grounds. In the name of an admittedly specious "science," and contradicting what it had said only two years before concerning its competence in such "science," that is what it did.[51]

[1] *Op. cit.*, pp. 147, 152.

[2] *Archives of Psychology*, no. 36, p. 125.

[3] *Ibid.* Cp: "An interesting comparison has been drawn between the various Central American republics where the population is of mixed Spanish and Indian origin, with a small percentage of Negro blood. 'It is a striking fact [says A. Grenfell Price, *White Settlers in the Tropics*, 1939, p. 122] that the progress, civilization and culture of the five Central American republics, Costa Rica, El Salvador, Guatemala, Honduras and Nicaragua, appear to vary in proportion to the percentage of white blood. Costa Rica and El Salvador possess the smallest areas and the poorest natural resources. Yet they contain the highest percentage of white population and they are far in advance of the three larger republics inhabited by a blend in which the Indian element predominates.' " Sir Alan Burns, *Colour Prejudice*, London, Allen and Unwin, 1948, p. 120.

[4] *Loc. cit.*, pp. 280, 282.   [5] *Ibid.*, p. 281.   [6] *Loc. cit.*, p. 91.   [7] *Ibid.*, p. 92.

[8] *Ibid.*, p. 118.   [9] *Ibid.*, p. 131.   [10] *Loc. cit.*, p. 34.   [11] *Op. cit.*, p. 53.

[12] *Ibid.*, pp. 83f.

[13] *Ibid.*, p. 84.   [14] *Ibid.*, p. 64.   [15] *Ibid.*, p. 73.

[16] *Op. cit.*, p. 217. Permission to reprint granted by the Anti-Defamation League of B'nai B'rith, holders of the copyright. The book is now published by Collier Books, New York.

[17] *Ibid.*, pp. 46, 47, 106, 107.   [18] *Ibid.*, p. 46.   [19] *Ibid.*, p. 218.

[20] *Ibid.*, p. 67. Comparing a Jewish and a Negro family, Dr. Goodman found that the Jewish one had "little sense of minority group status and no sense of inferiority." *Ibid.*, p. 76.

[21] *Ibid.*, p. 212.   [22] *Ibid.*, p. 137.   [23] *Ibid.*, p. 134.

[24] *Ibid.,* pp. 177, 178. This shows itself within a Negro family, when a ten or twelve-year-old girl who is darker than her sister "feels herself inferior, and suspects that when she is punished for some misdemeanor it is because she is colored . . ." p. 122.

[25] *Ibid.,* p. 197. To say there are no black people in the United States, one must not have looked far. In the Black Belt of the South I have seen spectacularly black ones—lamp black or bone black could hardly have been blacker. To say that the very blond are only bleached presumes that all were dark at some time (at descent from apes or the ape-like?). White *per se* is in no degree brown, either perceptually or physically.

[26] *Ibid.,* p. 217.   [27] *Ibid.,* p. 70.   [28] *Ibid.,* p. 212.   [29] *Op. cit.,* p. 28.

[30] *Ibid.*   [31] *Ibid.,* p. 29.   [32] *Ibid.,* p. 30.   [33] *Op. cit.,* p. 107.

[34] Above, p. 15. Cp: "There is no innate aversion of races to one another. The very fact that race mixture has taken place everywhere and at all times is the best possible indication that this is so." Otto Klineberg, *Race Differences,* New York, Harper & Brothers, 1935, p. 347. But racial aversion, to be real, need not be innate nor need it be inculcated. It may be born of contact. This is obvious in the nursery-school study. To establish the proposition that race mixture has taken place everywhere and always, a universal and perpetual record, something *ultra vires,* would be necessary. Probably a great deal of it is a result of sexual promiscuity, which doubtless may occur in spite of deep racial aversion. Cp. below, pp. 190, 209.

[35] The reaction of the white man in Kenya—either flight from the country, leaving his life's stake behind, or resolution to die in resistance, or moral resignation—as the day of the independence of that colony and of the ascendancy of the Negro drew near, is described by an English correspondent, Tom Stacey, in the New York *Times Magazine* of June 10, 1962.

[36] *Op. cit.,* p. 28.   [37] *Op. cit.,* p. 37.   [38] *Ibid.,* p. 293.

[39] *Ibid.,* p. 295.   [40] *Ibid.,* p. 135.   [41] *Op. cit.,* p. 151.

[42] New York *Times,* March 18, 1956.

[43] *Psychological Review,* vol. 55, p. 77.

[44] *Erkenntniss,* vol. 14, p. 389. See also *Psychological Review,* vol. 45, pp. 1-41.

[45] *Science and Human Behavior,* New York, Macmillan Company, 1953, p. 202.

[46] *Psychological Review,* vol. 44, p. 32.

[47] *Concept of Mind,* London, Hutchinson's University Library, 1949, p. 52.

[48] *Ibid.,* pp. 322ff.   [49] *Op. cit.,* p. 150.

[50] *Beauharnais* v. *Illinois, loc. cit.* p. 263. This was in 1952, the same year that the school cases came before the Court. Said the Court further: "Only those lacking responsible humility will have a confident solution for problems as intractable as the frictions attributable to differences of race, color or religion." *Ibid.,* p. 262. In the ensuing two years before the Brown decision, did the race frictions vanish or did the Court lose its "responsible humility"? Probably every integration decision it has made, beginning with *Brown* in 1954, is a patent contradiction of its 1952 declaration.

[51] There have been many studies of racial differences—so many that quite a number of studies of *them* are now to be found. See Audrey M. Shuey, *The Testing of Negro Intelligence,* Lynchburg, J. P. Bell Company, 1958, p. 3, for a list of the latter. The handful of instances noticed in this chapter is microscopic by comparison with the total, though it is perhaps sufficient to match the Supreme Court's handful. In any event if the requisites of scientific reliability

are lacking, if, as some investigators are frank to say, even proper methods are lacking, it matters little how numerous the studies are. Professor Klineberg, the author of one of the studies of the studies, says of studies of personality differences between white and Negro: "The problem [of racial differences in personality] is of especial importance, but there are in the meantime no satisfactory methods for its solution." *Op. cit.*, p. 207.

Yet the Supreme Court takes this massive uncertainty as "modern authority" and uses it to supplant the law of the land as hitherto determined by the Court itself.

Chapter 8

RACIAL REASONS

"And so, at the end of the last century, within the vast region enclosed by the coast of Africa, with its widely spaced forts, towns, and settlements of people from other countries, bounded on the north by the Nigerian Emirates, the Sahara, the Nile Sudd, and the Abyssinian massif, the West found itself in control of millions of people who had never invented or adopted an alphabet or even any form of hieroglyphic writing. They had no numerals, no almanac or calendar, no notation of time or measurements of length, capacity, or weight, no currency, no external trade except slaves and ivory (and on the west coast palm oil and mahogany, made accessible by the navigable rivers), no plough, no wheel, and no means of transportation except human head porterage on land and dugout canoes on rivers and lakes. These people had built nothing, nothing of any kind, in any material more durable than mud, poles, and thatch. The spade of the archaeologist might unearth the skeleton of primitive man a million years old, or stone implements alleged to date from 30,000 years back, but after that—nothing: nothing at all before the rubbish dumps of modern colonial towns. With a few notable exceptions, there were no units of government throughout the area larger than the tribe, and the tribe might amount only to a few thousand people and have half-a-dozen contending chiefs. Except in the west-coast region there were no towns, and even villages usually consisted of a very few families . . ."[1]

For this deathly specter of the heart of darkness we can thank Sir Philip Mitchell, a former Governor of the British colony of Kenya.

Between Africa and Europe, Africa and Asia, Africa and America, the difference is that between night and day. Between distinctive parts, such as Kenya and Germany, this difference is even intensified. Between a black man and a white man it is poignantly, protopathically, unspeakably manifest. Contacts between them bring results which mirror this natural difference.

Behavior, both human and animal, may be simply described as of a twofold character: reflex and, more or less, reasoned. There are psychological controversies over where the line is to be drawn between reflex and reason, or whether it is to be drawn at all, reason being sometimes regarded as nothing more than a compound of reflex, mechanical actions itself. By some, reflex action is thought to be the foundation of our dominant dispositions, including likes and dislikes. Explanations of conduct are considered incomplete or superficial if they do not come down to these psychophysical terms.

In all argument we rest on grounds, either directly or indirectly: axioms, postulates, fundamental presuppositions of some kind. These, not being inferences or deductions from others (since if they were, they would not be the grounds), are intuitive, direct, self-evident. I do not deduce that I have a toothache, I know it protopathically. That is, I feel it, suffer it, I do not infer it. I do not resort to reasoning to show myself that I like blue and dislike yellow, nor turn to someone else to tell me what I prefer, reject, or think.

> *I do not like you, Mr. Pell.*
> *The reason why, I cannot tell;*
> *But this I know, and know full well:*
> *I do not like you, Mr. Pell.*

When Professor Myrdal divined, as he terms it, "the white man's concept of the Negro 'race' " he pronounced it irrational and seemed surprised that it "cannot be grasped in terms of either biological or cultural differences."[2] Another might have observed that a toothache, too, is irrational, yet perfectly grasped, more is the pity, by persons to whom biological and cultural differences mean little or nothing. To be real, a thing need not be rational; that is, need not be logically warranted. It may be apprehended directly, intuitively.

Of course it is in a sense irrational in the three-year-old colored children to dislike dark skin, as Dr. Clark found that they did; likewise irrational in grown-up white persons to have the "natural disgust" remarked by Lincoln at the thought of amalgamation with Negroes. But dislike and disgust in matters so elemental can hardly be expected to carry logical certifications. Throughout experience some degree of attraction on the one hand and repulsion on the other occur to the attentive, sensitive mind. At the lowest range, on the plane of primordial, unpremeditated liking and disliking, all sorts stand equal. At higher levels liking and disliking are, or may be, more or less educated; as the liking of modern music or of fencing and the disliking of loose manners or of Longfellow. There is an immediate consequence: the formation of natural lines of separation. You may not like (or dislike) snow or football or dark skin or this or that people, but others do and that is the end of it. In Warren, Junker, and Adams' Chicago study we noticed this item of Negro testimony by one of the individuals questioned: "He (the individual's father) just says he doesn't like dark women, and that's all there is to it."[3]

A sentiment like this man's, intensified a hundredfold, may be recognized in an episode recounted by Paul Robeson, the Negro singer, from his youth. He said in an interview in the New York *Times*[4] some years ago:

". . . I was a freshman trying to make the football team. Rutgers had a great team that year, but the boys—well—they didn't want a Negro on their team, they just didn't want me on it.

"Later they became my friends, but every word of this is true, and though they are my friends I think they won't mind me telling it. On the first day of scrimmage they set about making sure that I wouldn't get on their team. One boy slugged me in the face and smashed my nose, just smashed it. That's been a trouble to me as a singer every day since. And then when I was down, flat on my back, another boy got me with his knee, just came over and fell on me. He managed to dislocate my right shoulder . . .

" . . . My brother came to see me, and he said, 'Kid, I know what it is, I went through it at Pennsylvania. If you want to quit school go ahead, but I wouldn't like to think, and our father wouldn't like to think, that our family had a quitter in it.'

"So I stayed. I had ten days in bed, a few days at the training table, and then out for another scrimmage. I made a tackle and was on the ground, my right hand palm down on the ground. A boy came over and stepped, hard, on my hand. He meant to break the bones. The bones held, but his cleats took every single one of the fingernails off my right hand. Every fingernail off my right hand! That's when I knew rage!"

Cruelty, brutality, stark inhumanity. But it would be illusory to suppose there is no assignable cause of them, or that the cause is nothing but sheer perversity. Capital punishment and war are cruel in the extreme, but not uncaused. Dispassionate regard may lead to the realization that the profound sentiment of white persons against Negro association, if crossed and provoked, may break out in riot and madness. To minds thus aroused, cruelty and savagery are not what they are to pure contemplation.

Nor is the white sentiment something evinced in maniacal outbreaks only. "In all walks of life the Negro is liable to meet some objection to his presence or some discourteous treatment." So remarks the eminent sociologist of a generation ago, W. I. Thomas, adding: "If he gain the affections of a white woman and marry her he may invariably expect that slurs will be thrown on her reputation and on his, and that both his race and her race will shun her company."[5]

One may reply that people ought not to shun their fellow men, it is not right. Does he mean there is a higher, moral law which supports his contention, and assume that he has an indisputable comprehension of it? Does he intimate that so many who evince the attitudes that Myrdal found are people less moral than he, or less comprehending? Modern analytical philosophy argues that when we say that such and such *ought* to be because of higher moral law, we are expressing recommendations, preferences, or visionary attitudes of our own, rather than giving evidence of a transcendental law.

Professor Myrdal was surprised to find that even in "a handful of rational intellectual liberals" in the United States who accepted amalgamation "in principle" there was an admission of "an irrational emotional inhibition against it" and that "even a liberal-minded Northerner of cosmopolitan culture and with a minimum of conventional blinds will, in nine cases out of ten, express a definite feeling against amalgamation."[6] Such surprise is indicative of a presumption that open-mindedness must subdue sentiment, a presumption which is not very conversant with facts.

To say, as Myrdal does, that scientific knowledge "could reveal" how antipathies towards the physical characteristics of Negroes "could be removed, and new ones avoided,"[7] is just short of make-believe. Scientific knowledge may show how all manner of things could be accomplished—if we were prepared to take the prescribed measures. There is the rub. It means, in this instance, the task of supplanting the likes of the nine-tenths of liberal-minded Americans Myrdal speaks of, and presumably all the illiberal-minded, with opposite likes such as those of Myrdal. His idea here is akin to his idea that those who speak of a peculiar Negro odor ought to "explain why this odor is considered offensive."[8] This is like calling on one to explain why pain is painful.

It is held by some that there is no such thing as racial repugnance. Myrdal, for example, intimating that barriers erected against intermarriage of white and black in the South are evidence that if there were no barriers there would be intermarriage, and that this is a disproof of repugnance, goes on to state: "Even the more general allegation that there is an inherent repulsion to personal intimacies and physical contact between the two groups is unfounded. The friendly behavior of Negro and white children untrained in prejudice and also the acceptability of physical contact with favorite servants are cases in point."[9]

The odd expression, "acceptability of physical contact," perhaps means tolerability of it under certain circumstances. Young children, to whom it probably refers, have only children's perceptions. As they mature, their powers are widened and sharpened—an elementary fact likely to be ignored by one who, like Myrdal, attributes everything to inculcated prejudice. They perceive what they did not perceive before, both directly and indirectly: physical differences, personal differences, social, racial, and historical differences. It is a careless presumption to say that this is due to indoctrination, for some are not indoctrinated and some do not respond to indoctrination received, yet they come to make many distinctions between white and colored. A young child may not perceive the difference between long and short, fact and fable, prudence and folly, white and Negro; but an adult does. Not to recognize this or allow for the possibility of it, discredits such an assertion as Myrdal's concerning physical contact.

His own evidence, like that of others cited in these pages, powerfully suggests the opposite of what he says; suggests, that is, a distinct awareness, a primary disposition of rejection, on the part of the white towards the Negro. It is immaterial that cases can be found to the contrary, for the like is true throughout the categories of nature. Even the lines between living and not-living, plant and animal, cannot be drawn with full assurance, but that does not cancel the distinctions between them. Between blue and green there are many shades, yet blue and green remain; so, too, of black and white. Nature differentiates and so segregates, though admitting some overlapping, and men impose lines of precision in many fields for the efficacy of their ordinances, such as the lines between up and down, today and tomorrow, adult and minor, oriental and occidental, white and Negro.[10]

Once the differentiation is established, classes form accordingly (natural segregation, this may be called) and are perpetuated by their own force. In Myrdal there are stories such as: Negroes and whites sitting around a stove at a country store in the South, the whites together on one side, the Negroes together on the other; Negro and white children playing together in Washington, yet racially divided, the whites talking only to one another, and the Negroes to one another; prisoners in what Myrdal calls "a progressive prison" in the North, playing ball in racial cliques "apparently always with minute observance of the color line."[11] To Myrdal the explanation is simple: discrimination against the Negro. He looks upon racial differences as if they were unreal or only superficial and would rub out with contact.

How can this view hold up against such a proposition as Myrdal's that in "the white man's concept . . . one who has got the smallest amount of 'Negro blood' is as one who is smitten by a hideous disease"?[12] Or against the Croatan's idea of "the stigma of Negro kinship," "the ultimate insult that anyone can give an Indian"?[13] Or against the conclusion by Arnold Rose that racial attitudes are known to be "so deep and tenacious" that the discovery of any effective change in them is something worthy to be regarded as "a distinct contribution to knowledge"?[14] Or against the conclusion that in South Africa and Australia "the pattern of racial prejudice and persecution is even more severe" than in America, and that over the world there exist "stereotyped attitudes toward the darker races, attitudes which are peculiar to the whole white family."[15] If Myrdal is correct in pronouncing racial differences only superficial, such findings as these are grossly erroneous, and a great deal of the work done by investigators in this field must be rejected. If he is incorrect, the greater part of the ground of his book is cut away.

There is a predisposition in social writers to subordinate the individual and to treat all matters socially, just as there is in the Negro press to treat everything racially, and in partisan pursuits generally to see and think from the standpoint of their own advantage. Is it not obvious, however, that a great part of life, including the social part, arises from and moves towards realities which are either not social at all or else only superficially social? But it would be a blow to the social doctrinaire's case to concede this. He could not then summarily dismiss the idea, for example, that race attitudes are expressions of primordial dispositions of individuals rather than results of social influences.

Some sociologists speak of consciousness of kind, the creature's immediate awareness of its fellow. The whites and Negroes around the stove, those on the playground, and those in the prison all illustrate that. In greater or less degree, so do Southerners, Englishmen, Jews, Republicans, actors, anglers, lovers, and so on throughout all well-defined categories of human and even animal life. Is this intuitive recognition something due just to social influence and in no way to original insight on the part of the indivual?

As there is consciousness of one's own kind, so there is of its opposite, perhaps to a higher degree. "All children," according to one psychologist, "develop negative reactions toward certain persons who come into the range of their experience. These may be based on physical appearance, gestures, voice, and general behavior."[16] A marked difference often amounts to opposition; not in the sense of hostility, but in that of utter rejection. Between a person of coarse qualities and one of refined qualities, between light and dark, white and albino, white and Negro, the feeling is unmistakable.[17] Though it may be repressed in some, in others it persists despite all endeavor. It is intuitive, palpable, protopathic. It is primordial nature expressing itself. The following account, distinguished by an objectivity hardly to be found in most of the writings cited by the Supreme Court, brings this out. It is by W. I. Thomas:

"In looking for an explanation of the antipathy which one race feels toward another, we may first of all inquire whether there are any conditions arising in the course of the biological development of a species which, aside from social activities, lead to a predilection for those of one's own kind and a prejudice against organically different groups. And we do, in fact, find such conditions. The earliest movements of animal life involve, in the rejection of stimulations vitally bad, an attitude which is the analogue of prejudice. On the principle of chemiotaxis, the microorganism will approach a particle of food placed in the water and shun a particle of poison; and its movements are similarly controlled by heat, light, electricity, and other tropic forces. The development of animal life from this point upward consists in the growth of structure and organs of sense adapted to discriminate between different stimulations, to choose between the beneficial and prejudicial, and to obtain in this way a more complete control of the environment. Passing over the lower forms of animal life, we find in the human type the power of attention, memory, and comparison highly developed, so that an estimate is put on stimulations and situations correspondent with the bearing of stimulations or situations of this type on welfare in the past. The choice and rejection involved in this process are accompanied by organic changes (felt as emotions) designed to assist in the action which follows a decision. Both the judgment and the emotions are thus involved on the presentation to the senses of a situation or object involving possible advantage or hurt, pleasure or pain. It consequently transpires that the feelings called out on the presentation of disagreeable objects and their contrary are very different, and there arise in this connection fixed mental attitudes corresponding with fixed or habitually recurrent external situations—hate and love, prejudice and predilection—answering to situations which revive feelings of pain on the one hand, and feelings of pleasure on the other. And such is the working of suggestion that not alone an object or situation may produce a given state of feeling, but a voice, an odor, a color, or any characteristic sign of an object may produce the same effect as the object itself . . .

"The examination of these external signs impresses us with the fact that race-prejudice is in one sense a superficial matter. It is called out primarily by the physical aspect of an unfamiliar people—their color, form and feature, and dress—and by their activities and habits in only a secondary way. The general organic attitude, growing out of experience (through reflex rather than deliberative experience), is that the outside world is antagonistic and subject to depredation, and this attitude seems to be localized in a prejudice felt for the characteristic appearance of others, this being most apprehensible by the senses. This prejudice is intense and immediate, sharing in this respect the character of the instinctive reactions in general. It cannot be reasoned with, because, like the other instincts, it originated before deliberative brain centers were developed, and is not to any great extent under their control . . .

"The Negro, for his part, not only loses race-prejudice in the presence of the white man, but repudiates black standards. In America the papers printed for black readers contain advertisments of pomades for making kinky hair straight and of washes to change the Ethiopian's skin; and the slaves returned to Sierra Leone in 1820 assumed the role of whites, even referred to themselves white, and called the natives 'bush niggers.'

"Race-prejudice is an instinct originating in the tribal stage of society, when solidarity in feeling and action were essential to the preservation of the group. It, or some analogue of it, will probably never disappear completely, since an identity of standards, traditions, and physical appearance in all geographical zones is neither possible nor aesthetically desirable. It is, too, an affair which can neither be reasoned with nor legislated about very effectively, because it is connected with the affective, rather than the cognitive, processes. But it tends to become more insignificant as increased communication brings interests and standards in common, and as similar systems of education and equal access to knowledge bring about a greater mental and social parity between groups, and remove the grounds for 'invidious distinction.' "[18]

Whoever recognizes primordial dispositions recognizes potential social, political, and moral types. Whoever denies such dispositions assumes us all to be alike originally, and to be molded entirely by social or other environmental forces. But where, on the latter view, will these forces in their great diversity and opposition have originated? That is, if men, like Robots, have no native inclinations or disinclinations, how will the social molders of men acquire them? An indoctrinator, whether individual or social, must be indoctrinated, or strongly inclined or disinclined, himself. How then does the first one in a given line of indoctrinators become indoctrinated?

If it is not by the arisal in him of attitudes to which he is predisposed by nature, which attitudes then motivate his actions, then it must be by reaction to his environment. Still, even in the latter case it is *his* reaction: but for *his* predispositions, it might have been an altogether different kind of reaction. So his predispositions are decisive, whether in his action or reaction. Similarly with types of men, such as Eskimo and African, white and Negro. Fundamental motives of inclination and disinclination, which is to say unalloyed nature itself, thus predetermine the dominant attitudes of white people towards Negroes.

It is true and not to be discounted that these predispositions may, in some, have been practically stamped in from outside; and those who teach the doctrine of social origin of our ways must presume such to be true of us all. But the stamp doesn't print uniformly, even when it does print. It prints only upon the receptive, those suitably predisposed. The first indoctrinator must therefore have transmitted his own dispositions, and those who took them up must have done so because of apposite dispositions in themselves. So the social-influence doctrine takes native dispositions for granted at some point. Among them it is reasonable, considering the evidence before us, to include dispositions towards personal qualities and types of person, conspicuously the Negro.

If these inherent dispositions are not admitted, the social-origin theory of attitudes towards the Negro encounters yet more difficulties. It may class the attitudes as chance arisals in the social flux, comparable to phobias, humors, ephemeral tendencies. That, however, will make them superficial and spotty, leaving their great tenacity and their extension over the world unexplained. And being, on this hypothesis, only chance, superficial things, coming from practically nothing, why are such attitudes not offset and eradicated by counter-prejudice or indoctrination? (Recall that one of the testimonials in K. B. Clark[19] is that it is a rare, signal event for that to happen. Phobias and fashions disappear, but race attitudes are admitted by social writers to persist without much change.) And why don't race affinities, instead of antipathies, arise from time to time, as we should expect if chance were the source?

Or the theory may presume race attitudes to be a matter of "training in prejudice," as it does with Myrdal, for instance. Why such training? What would motivate it? Without some deep-lying racial disposition, such as primordial inclinations, how account for anything of such magnitude and effect? Is the motive sheer malice? What is the evidence of that? If white simply doesn't like black, and takes lawful means to keep at a distance, is that *prima facie* malice? If so, then it will be malice to build a fence or to zone a city. Malice may sometimes be the motive, but to suppose that it generally is, would require showings far beyond any we possess.

Explanations like this, obviously putative, suggest in themselves the very thing they condemn in others, namely, prejudice. The admitted and avowed partiality of a Myrdal, with his profession that there can be no such thing as purely objective study of these matters —what is that but prejudice? And yet the materials before us abound in evidence favorable, on the surface at least, to Myrdal's contention. In the Clark study it is held that "someone to look down upon" is "a necessary factor" in our development;[20] and from the Witmer and Kotinsky study we learn of a "basic, universal need" of such a thing as a "hostility object"[21] (*sic*), which object, we are not surprised to read, may give rise to prejudice. Not only prejudice but also perversity, one might say. And perversity twice over, so far as Clark is concerned, for after declaring prejudice necessary he calls it "cancerous demoralization."[22] In writings on race the term "prejudice" is so freely used that we would not be far wrong in taking it to mean almost anything an author finds disagreeable in anyone else's views or showings.

Let us try to make the term "prejudice" clear. In unprejudiced usage, it refers to partiality in judgment or decision; that is, foreclosing or arbitrarily denying some relevant fact or consideration. It means unreasonableness, one-sidedness, unwillingness to face the facts. It denotes a mind not capable or willing, whether through native shortcoming, perversity, lack of education, lack of balance, or what not, to stand before the realities of the world and declare them unreservedly. It cheats by holding something back; or it smuggles in a private standard where we expect and are deceitfully given to believe that we have an open, public one. It is a miscarriage of judgment.

It would be prejudice to deny the best qualified man a job, an opportunity, or an honor—the best qualified according to the going standards. It would be prejudice not to consider all the qualifications or disqualifications, under the applicable standards, and prejudice to judge by unacknowledged, inapplicable standards. Disregard of anything relevant—relevant according to open, admitted standards—is prejudice.

On the other hand, prejudice does not qualify or attach to any bare fact. As law is distinct from facts to which it applies, so is prejudice. No sentiment or feeling, liking, disliking, or preference is prejudice. Consciousness of one's kind and affinity for it are not prejudices. Such things are personal data, and there is no jurisdiction over them except in the person who has them. The desire to avoid, the desire to come near, the desire to let alone are not prejudices, just as a toothache or laugh is not. Prejudice is a policy towards facts; a corrupt policy, yes, nevertheless a thing distinct from the facts.

Different peoples may of course have different regard for the same facts. A consensus is struck, becoming the law or prevailing standard, and differing more or less from one people to another. If one people passes judgment on another under its own and not the other's standards, that is prejudice; for it is a denial of the applicable, going standards and an arbitrary substitution of other standards. It is saying that our laws, the essence of our likes and usages, shall override yours. That is a pretension of tyranny. In a federation of states which have bound themselves as have the United States to give full faith and credit to one another's laws, it cannot lawfully occur.

One people's facts, whatever may be their laws and standards for dealing with them, cannot be truly denied by others, inasmuch as no fact can be truly denied. Perhaps others do not know these facts and never could know them, for they include the experiences, the ways, habits, dispositions, and history of that people. And to expect or demand that a people disregard such facts is quite arbitrary and of no more force than a reciprocal demand by them would be.

When, to take an example, Professor Myrdal belittles opposition to Negro-white amalgamation as if it were mere prejudice[23] he assumes that under some applicable standard, amalgamation is quite legitimate; or he assumes that there are no facts about it which are objectionable. Neither assumption holds, in many jurisdictions. He is therefore completely in error as far as those jurisdictions are concerned.

Prejudice is not predisposition simply. Kindness, hope, elevation are predispositions of many persons, but are not prejudices. To prove prejudice you must prove abrogation of a demonstrably relevant right or fact or standard. Where, for instance, there is no established but only an envisioned right, such as the vision of equality in everything, there can be no merit in the allegation of prejudice. To deny a Chinese admission to the United States or to deny a Negro a certain job or station, is not necessarily prejudice, for it may be that neither of them meets the applicable requirements. And to challenge the requirements is to set one's own vision above the law or standard, and at some point to set one's own disposition above that of others. This is what is done when the New York press, for example, ventures to prescribe to Southern states on the subject of segregated schools, segregated assemblies, and so on. We may, to be sure, contemplate and work for one standard for all, under which all are equal. But that is a different thing from imposing such a standard. Nothing less than a monarch of the world or a world soviet, willing to ignore the great differences among men, would suffice for that.

Morals, ethics, religion, singly and together, do not suffice to erase lines deeply engraved by nature. The disgust that Lincoln spoke of, the horror sensed by some, the profound inhibition Professor Myrdal discovered even in the most liberal white, are hardly resolvable into contemplative, ideal terms.[24] In New Orleans the Catholic archbishop condemned segregation, calling it morally wrong and sinful (though it had existed in the parochial schools for generations), and announced that it would be abolished. Directly there sprang up a league of Catholics opposed to abolition and it was not long until the church authorities suspended their plans.[25] Such was the resentment and defection in the congregation of a church in a nearby community when a Negro priest was assigned to it that the church had to be closed. In Baton Rouge a visiting Negro archbishop from Harlem, of the African Universal Church, upheld segregation and declared integration a sin, citing Scripture as his warrant.[26]

With fundamental likes and dislikes motivating so much of the white world's judgment upon race, what of Negro likes and dislikes? They are as real as any. When, however, they are set against those of white people it is just as with any other opposition: a question of which side has superior weight. Inevitably, in nature's balances some likes and dislikes of the inferior side are sacrificed (voted down, so to speak). That is the price of coexistence. The alternative to it is separation, or segregation.

Juxtaposed to white people, Negroes are constantly restrained by the color bar and can never be sure that it will not be pushed higher. Rejection and deprivation threaten them continually, no matter what the law says. In countless ways the white is able nearly everywhere to withhold advantage, opportunity, consideration, even hope.[27] Consequently there is little security for the Negro along the border between his people and the white except as the white, or the white and Negro together, voluntarily establish it. The border was not created by law but by nature. It is untouched by law.

The bar is implicit in the sentiment of revulsion or rejection. This is clear even in the evidence cited by the Supreme Court. Expressed, formalized, the sentiments are the bar; and the bar applied is segregation. To abolish segregation means and requires therefore extinction of those sentiments. Conceivably that may come to pass, but there is no reason to expect judicial decisions to accomplish it. The law is not a force itself but only an instrument of force. Let the white (or black) force be superior or maneuver itself into a position of advantage, and the law will be and do its will.[28]

In much writing on race the term "discrimination" is a companion to "prejudice," and is used presumptively, like that term. Thus it may be called discrimination not to play, work, associate with, or perhaps even marry the Negro.

Two senses of the term, which are universally recognized, are confused in such writing. In one sense it means favoritism, implying an abrogation of equal right; in the other sense it means a mental act, of discerning or distinguishing.

For discrimination to be attributable in the first sense, a premise of equality is requisite. For example, if we say it is discrimination when a white person refuses Negro association, we presuppose social equality between them, since without that as a standard nothing could be found contrary, and it would be pointless to cry discrimination. In particular, we would presuppose equality of esteem, of personal liking, and disliking, as between a white person's regard for the white and his regard for the Negro, if we were to say that the white's rejection of the Negro generally was discrimination.

That would be grossly erroneous. No such presupposition obtains. On the contrary, as the idea of social contact between white and black was revolting to Lincoln, so it is to untold numbers of white persons over the world today. The ground for the stereotyped accusation and lament, *Discrimination*, in cases of this kind therefore falls away.

In countless cases discrimination in the first sense of the term must be presumed to occur. But it takes the form of a demonstrable inequity. It occurs between whites themselves, between Negroes themselves, and perhaps between all sorts of men.

In the world at large, legal equality is the only equality we can take for granted, since only the law assumes all of us to be equal there. While this equality is invaluable as far as it goes, the fact is that it ordinarily touches so little of life that we are seldom conscious of it. What we are conscious of nearly everywhere is inequality. This is partly owing to discrimination in the second of the two senses we noticed.

In that sense we speak of a discriminating eye or ear, of discriminating taste, of discriminating a meaning, a value, and the like. Everybody can and more or less does discriminate thus, and the most acutely discriminative ore admired and envied. Discrimination in this purely perceptual, aesthetic sense, does not impose distinctions, but only discovers them. It does not distinguish between equals, nor find equality where equality does not exist. But the farther it extends, the finer the differentiation it makes, between men as well as things, and the more inequalities it finds. Likes and dislikes follow this progression, and actions follow likes and dislikes. One result is the development of customs and practices such as sociological writers impugn with their term, "discrimination."

That term, as they use it, is strictly inapplicable here. For in their use it is limited to the first meaning, namely, an inequity of some kind, a denial of equal right, whereas here it means something wholly different, namely, discernment, the perceptive grasp of what comes before the mind. It seems, too, that "discrimination," in those writers' use, carries over from the idea of equality before the law, whereas here it has no relation to the law. Here its field is the whole inner world of perception, a world which is beyond the authority of the law. We speak in the Bill of Rights of *the* freedom of expression; how much more certain is the freedom of perception!

Discrimination in this sense is naturally beyond criticism—who would criticize a fine sense of fact or a subtle insight into relations between facts? To act without discrimination is nearly the same as acting irresponsibly or promiscuously. The ants discriminate among ants, and birds discriminate and separate. In people, obtuseness or willfulness may see no distinction at many points, but fineness of perception, which does see distinctions, is hardly to be impugned on that account. A child or a dullard may not perceive avarice or liberality, cowardice or heroism, but a finer mind perceives them with the same immediacy as that of protopathic agreeableness and disagreeableness.

If an individual finds it intimately disagreeable to associate with another, that is final, he being the sole judge. If his kind finds it similarly disagreeable, that also is final. All else is a matter of toleration at a distance and of suitable measures to secure the integrity and welfare of each. The alternative would be some form of violation of their integrity, such as an attempt to force likes and dislikes. That would be an attempt against nature.

Nature, however, is not absolutely rigid, but to a degree fluid and evolutionary, and men's likes and dislikes may therefore change. One who hates bullfighting or jazz music or rude manners or unseemly presences may indeed come to tolerate them; but *he* will have to do it, he cannot be coerced in his sensibilities. Similarly a sect, party, or people: homogeneity or heterogeneity among persons and peoples are universal facts. Nevertheless, if like and dislike are left undisturbed they may form convenants under which their peculiarities are respected and secured and their potentialities allowed fulfillment. In political philosophy it is sometimes held that the institution of the state came about in this way, primitive men acceding to terms under which they relinquished their unlimited individual freedom in return for security against the ambitions of one another and the consequent war of all against all.

Where racial realities are not acknowledged, what prospect of racial accord can there be? And if it is supposed that there is no race, of course there is no race problem, unless it might be to convince ourselves that it is an illusion. The complete contradiction of this outcome, by palpable facts, must discredit the no-race theory and all that is founded on it.

Race is no mystery. Black and white, like and unlike, mine and thine are perfectly familiar. It may be regrettable and at times even tragic that the racial realities are what they are, but that does not cancel them or justify making believe that they are nothing. Finding some overlapping between abilities of white and Negro, social writers of the type the Court consulted presume there must be equality, and, like the Court, they seem to confuse equality with identity. Then they wonder why everything is not at one between the races and why barriers exist in all walks, and they answer: prejudice, discrimination. This has become almost an article of faith among them, which might be put: In the beginning was prejudice, and prejudice was with discrimination; and so forth. To admit that Creation was the source, however, would be fatal since it would intimate that nothing effective could be done against such attitudes, whereas the writers strongly urge positive measures. This in turn is as much as to admit that the attitudes are natural forces, having natural sources, and yet it is denied that there is anything in the Negro's nature to give rise to such attitudes. So we are left to think that they have come from nothing.

This is contrary to a principle, perhaps the most fundamental, of science: From nothing comes nothing; or, nature never produces something out of nothing. But for such a principle, science would be on a footing with superstition and would have to admit magic, mystery, and unintelligibility in everything. To maintain any scientific claim in support of their cause, racial apologists must accordingly admit the reality and weight of racial elements producing what they call prejudice and discrimination. These are in fact conspicuously shown in their own data, such as the racial antipathies of two or three-year-olds and the admission of universal rejection.

It is not prejudice or discrimination, in the pejorative sense of these terms, to shrink from what offends the sensibilities. Nor is it prejudice or discrimination to institute humane measures for minimizing such experiences. On the contrary it is by acknowledging and respecting personal differences that the amenities of life are secured and it is by securing these that polities are possible, and the different types of men able to live in civility and peace.

[1] Reprinted in *Africa Today*, ed. by C. Grove Haines, Baltimore, John Hopkins Press, 1955, p. 12. Cp.: "The Black races alone have not contributed positively to any civilization—as yet." Arnold J. Toynbee, *Study of History*, abridged by D. C. Somervell, 2 vols., New York and London, Oxford University Press, 1957, vol. 1, p. 54. This and the preceding observations might be crowned with an item from a missionary's report mentioned by William James: ". . . those black warriors who pursued Stanley's party on the Congo with their cannibal war-cry of 'Meat! Meat!' . . ." *Essays on Faith and Morals*, New York, Longmans, Green & Co., 1947, p. 328.

[2] *Op. cit.*, p. 100. [3] *Op. cit.*, p. 135.

[4] January 16, 1944, sec. 2, p. 1. Years afterwards, speaking in Australia, Mr. Robeson put the story in much less heroic terms. "When I was playing football if a fellow hurt me I wasn't bitter. I just waited my chance to knock him over and stomp right on his face." Quoted in George Sokolsky's syndicated newspaper column, December 8, 1960.

[5] Kimball Young, *Source Book for Social Psychology*, New York, Alfred A. Knopf, 1927, p. 500.

[6] *Op cit.*, p. 57. [7] *Ibid.*, p. 585n. [8] *Ibid.*, p. 1213.

[9] *Ibid.*, p. 590. Concerning "the friendly behavior of Negro and white children untrained in prejudice" compare the showings in Dr. Mary Ellen Goodman's study, above, pp. 160ff.

It may be noted that the "physical contact with favorite servants" is only casual, and quite a different thing from contact of white with white. The test would be whether white persons freely seek or welcome Negro contact rather than shun it; and the answer is almost universally No. Casual, accidental circumstances in which it occurs, likewise its occurrence in sexual promiscuity, count very little beside the known and powerful general disposition against contact. To say that it is only prejudice, legalized and institutionalized, that prevents contact, is no more than prejudice itself, in the absence of unmistakable evidence. In fact, a wall of prejudice of this kind, shutting out the spirit of open, impartial determination of questions, has been erected by integrationist propaganda, and the integrationist line, so to speak, now lays it down as a closed, settled matter that the explanation of racial rejection is only prejudice.

The term "prejudice" is even used by otherwise careful writers to denote not arbitrary, biased decision but mere natural disposition. For example: "The hard fact of the matter is that wherever two peoples distinguishable by real or imagined physical differences live contiguously, race prejudice exists." This is from a review of a Unesco book, *Race and Science*, in the *Saturday Review of Literature*, August 5, 1961, p. 19. To Unesco—and this seems to hold of the integrationist line generally—even the idea of race is a prejudice or mere doctrine: "Racial doctrine is the outcome of a fundamental anti-rational system of thought and is in glaring conflict with the whole humanist tradition of our civilization. It sets at nought everything that Unesco stands for." *Ibid.* The reviewer, John Greenway, who is an anthropologist at the University of Colorado, notes a "pervasive lack of objectivity" in the book and comments: "Considering the absolute universality of race prejudice (Cushing has even found it among birds), the real anomaly in this entire question is not why it persists but why the leveling philosophy that permeates this book arose to such importance in this generation. Unesco's predecessor, the League of Nations, rejected a resolution proclaiming the equality of all races. Not one of the authors considers the underlying cultural drift that is rapidly making nations into what Robert Frost called 'corn-meal mush' . . . "

The will to believe is rarely stayed by contrary evidence, and so Unesco could, in a previous volume, allow the inclusion of items such as the following, concerning Negro immigration to Great Britain: " . . . for some people it is as if the 'blackness' of the Negro diffuses itself over persons or objects around. Some of them speak of being 'contaminated' by his physical proximity and women, in particular, express special aversion to the idea of his hand coming into contact with their white skin." Kenneth Little, of the University of Edinburgh, in Unesco, *The Race Question in Modern Science*, New York, Whiteside, Inc. and William Morrow & Co., 1956, p. 203.

The United States Supreme Court has held that Americans are not free to restrict a neighborhood against the influx of Negro residents, 245 U.S. 60, 82. Compare the British: "There are instances of special clauses in the leases of houses and flats excluding a coloured person . . . Residents in the area are afraid that their peace will be disturbed and the neighbourhood acquire a bad name . . . Cardiff, Liverpool, and Manchester . . . all have specific localities known as 'the coloured quarter' . . . the white inhabitants of these British cities have much the same kind of feeling as the white inhabitants of American cities, of their own racial and social separateness from the coloured areas." Unesco, *Ibid.*, pp. 198, 199.

[10] What may fairly be called racial communists—those who would deny and nullify racial differences just by resolving that they do not exist—cling nevertheless to the term "Negro," indignantly insisting not only on the capital "N" (which the Supreme Court took up only fifteen years or so ago) but even on a certain prescriptive pronunciation, something between the Spanish original, approximately "naygraw," and "nigger." But just as the term "Negro" is used significantly, so is the term "race." Gradations of black towards white do not extinguish the Negro reality, just as gradations of spectral colors into each other do not extinguish pure colors. Justice Holmes remarked: "I am the last man in the world to quarrel with a distinction simply because it is one of degree. Most distinctions, in my opinion, are of that sort, and are none the worse for it." *Haddock* v. *Haddock*, 201 U. S. 562, 631.

[11] *Op. cit.*, p. 648.   [12] *Ibid.*, p. 100.

[13] Above, p. 112. Cp.: "The Haliwa Indians (North Carolina) absolutely balked at going to school with Negroes, and in order to maintain red supremacy they established a private school." C. Vann Woodward, in *Commentary*, November, 1958, p. 373. How would one know that the purpose was "to maintain red supremacy"? This assumes that maintaining supremacy is the only reason

for separation, a proposition which, though probably in agreement with the integrationist line, is sharply at variance with the evidence.

[14] Above, p. 113. [15] Above, p. 114.

[16] Kimball Young, *Social Psychology*, New York, F. S. Crofts and Company, 1930, p. 455.

[17] Repugnance of dark to light, not just of Negro to white, is often remarked in many lands and in remote times as well as today. It is noticeable even in Roman poetry: " . . . the coarse paws of some huge, raw-boned Moor, /whose hideous form the stoutest would affray,/if met, by moonlight, near the Latian way . . . " Juvenal, *Satires*, V, 53-55.

Two thousand years before this, in the time of the Pharaoh Sesostris III, the disposition of the Egyptians to the Negro was evidenced in the following royal notice posted at a boundary point on the Nile: "Southern boundary . . . ; in order to prevent that any Negro should cross it, by water or by land, with a ship, (or) any herds of the Negroes; except a Negro who shall come to do trading in Iken, or with a commission. Every good thing shall be done with them, but without allowing a ship of the Negroes to pass . . . going downstream, forever." James H. Breasted, *Ancient Records of Egypt*, 5 vols., Chicago, University of Chicago Press, 1906-07, vol. 1, pp. 293f.

"There does exist," says Sir Alan Burns, "for one cause or another, a real physical repulsion between individuals of different races." *Op. cit.*, p. 110. He mentions the case of a bishop who, "although he had striven and prayed all his life . . . had been unable to overcome his instinctive aversion from coloured people." *Ibid.*

[18] *American Journal of Sociology*, vol. 9, pp. 593-594, 607, 608, 610-611.

[19] Above, p. 000. [20] *Op. cit.*, p. 154. [21] *Op. cit.*, p. 152. [22] *Op. cit.*, p. 203.

[23] *Op. cit.*, p. 55.

[24] It is not confined to the white, who may even cause it himself. Cp. "There is no doubt that individuals differ in bodily odor; and it is certain that races do. Gilbert Murray tells of a Japanese waiting-maid who fainted at the smell of a number of Europeans and Americans sitting at dinner. Both Japanese and Chinese students have told the writer that they are quite aware of the distinctive bodily odor of the white race." Kimball Young, *Social Psychology*, p. 455. Professor Toynbee tells of remarks by a Japanese actress after a season in a London theater: " 'And the worst thing of all was the smell, the people in this country smell like lions and tigers.' The truth is that the Japanese, whose national odour is kept sweet and wholesome by a mainly vegetarian diet, are considerably distressed by the rank and foetid odour of the carnivorous peoples of the West . . . " *Study of History*, 12 vols., London, Oxford University Press, 1939-61, vol. 1, p. 231.

[25] Some years afterwards (1962), New Orleans public schools having been desegregated under orders from the Federal courts, the archbishop announced that the parochial schools also would be desegregated.

[26] Associated Press dispatches of February 20, 1956, and August 15 and 27, 1956.

[27] Berl I. Bernhard, the Staff Director of the Commission on Civil Rights, in an address at St. Louis, stated that "racial discrimination" reaches into "every region of the United States and into almost every area of life." Associated Press, August 8, 1961.

[28] Apologists for the Supreme Court today, if not the judges themselves, might

be said to presume that the law changes itself, without legislation. "Both decisions *(Plessy* v. *Ferguson,* 1896, and *Brown* v. *Board of Education,* 1954) were as much consequence as cause; both rested on the value systems of their times." J. W. Peltason, *Fifty-eight Lonely Men: Southern Federal Judges and School Desegregation,* New York, Harcourt Brace and World, 1961, p. 248. What does this mean but that Congress and the states can be ignored, the judges proceeding to read the law out of the times? But, without legislation, there is in fact no *law* in the times; there is only some set of dispositions and forces, which would first have to be made the law. The Supreme Court can no more make them law, without violating the first article of the Constitution, than any other nine men can.

There are judges possessed of such clarity of mind that they see through the sham, and of such probity of character that they will not "for their belly's sake / creep and intrude and climb into the fold;" they simply refuse a part in the whole subversive business. For example: Judge Ashton H. Williams, of Charleston. Inasmuch as he "thought the Supreme Court decision barring separate public facilities for whites and Negroes was based on unconstitutional grounds," this judge withdrew from a case, with these words: "Since as a Federal judge I have to follow that decision, I will disqualify myself because I have taken an oath to sustain the Constitution." United Press International, September 7, 1960. Supreme irony—a judge having to disqualify himself because of respecting his oath to uphold the Constitution!

Mr. Peltason has more to say on what the law is when it is made by judges, though with no suspicion of the ironies that play all about. "And as the general tides of public opinion have altered, judicial decrees have responded to these political developments"—today's judges, presumably, not even waiting for the "iliction returns." Without a hint of the comedy, of the farce upon *equal* protection, he remarks that in one jurisdiction in Kentucky total integration of the schools was required in one year, whereas in Georgia eight years was allowed for just a beginning and in Texas an indefinite time. *Ibid.,* pp. 115, 134.

Now *this* is law and the Constitution? Who seriously believes that? Not Congress, for instance—Congress, which alone has constitutional power to enforce the Fourteenth Amendment, sat for ten years without turning a hand to enforce the Supreme Court's decision in *Brown.*

CHAPTER 9

THE SUPREME COURT v. THE CONSTITUTION (I)

Not much attention to the bearings of *Brown* v. *Board of Education* is necessary to see that it makes a welter of constitutional rights. We have seen that the ground of the decision either justifies complete socialization by judicial decree, including the leveling of wealth, or else involves massive discrimination in favor of the Negro. The decision and the decrees applying it involve also the annulment of one of the most cherished constitutional guarantees.

The same sentence of the Fourteenth Amendment that guarantees equal protection of the laws, guarantees liberty: "No State shall . . . deprive any person of . . . liberty . . . without due process of law . . . " The state cannot, for example, arrest, imprison, or otherwise restrain anyone except for lawful reason. At liberty, each is his own master: his decisions and his courses of action are voluntary; he cannot be compelled to do what he does not will to do; he is a free agent.

Between free agents it is just as between sovereigns. Whether they associate is optional with each. Two conditions have therefore to be satisfied: willingly joining and willingly being joined. Compulsory segregation denies the first condition; compulsory integration denies the second. One is as much a deprivation of liberty as the other. Accordingly, if the state can deprive of liberty by way of the one, so it can by way of the other. It is admitted by the Supreme Court that the state can do this by way of integration, and is now even required that it do it. So, then, can it by way of segregation. To deny that it can by segregation is equally to deny that it can by integration. To deny either is to deny the state's sovereignty. Of course the Supreme Court cannot lawfully deny a state's sovereignty.

In its integration decrees the Court presumes to order the states to enact certain laws. On the very face of it such a presumption is ludicrous. That a court, itself a pendant of the law, should presume to dictate to a sovereign state what laws it shall have, is repugnant to intelligence. In this instance it is even more than repugnant—it verges on the contemptible—for the Court goes into the most gratuitous detail, as if presuming the states to be in tutelage to it.

But there is equal protection of the laws,[1] and one of the powers prohibited to the states by the Constitution is that of denying equal protection to any person under their jurisdiction; and the Court claims such denial as warrant for its school decision. Logically considered, equal protection has nothing to do with the content of any law, only with the law's uniform application. It does not *per se* "validate" or "invalidate" laws—that would make it a law above laws, and the Supreme Court a legislature above Congress and the states (this is boldly demonstrated in the Court's use of it to go down into the schools and presumptively outlaw certain psychological results—inferiority feelings—in the pupils, in *Brown* v. *Board of Education*). Equal protection is ancillary to the laws of the state, not constitutive of them. Without content itself, it is not a source of law and so cannot yield either an integration law or a segregation law; cannot secure even the enforcement of a law; can only require that if it is enforced, it is enforced uniformly on those it covers. It can only see that the law, of whatever description, *is* the law: general, universal in its sphere, unexceptionable. It is a legal afterthought, a standard perfectly realized, and hence not needed as a distinct entity, whenever the other provisions of the Constitution and laws applicable in a case are fulfilled.

Another constitutional ground which might be thought to justify integration is the right of assembly, secured in the First Amendment by a prohibition on legislation abridging "the right of the people peaceably to assemble . . . " Though it applies, in the Constitution, only to congressional action—Federal action—this prohibition has been so construed by the Supreme Court as to make it apply to state action also. Supposing it properly applicable to the states,[2] we meet the question, If the colored attendance is segregated by state action, is that not a restraint of assembly and hence a denial of constitutional right? Strictly, it is not that, although it is a restraint of social contact. As long as all who wish to assemble are within the assembly, it seems unreasonable to say that any are denied their right. Integration is not necessary to an assembly; not all elements have to be in immediate contact, and where natural and historical differences are so extreme that interracial contact is a threat to peace and good order, and hence to the right of assembly, it would be folly not to segregate.

In the Bill of Rights, in the words of the First Amendment, the assembly must be *peaceable;* hence if it is not that, it is not a constitutional right. Now a condition of peaceable assembly is mutual toleration. It would not be difficult to show that various other conditions, beyond outer civility, and tracing back to the springs of life, are in turn precedent to that, especially where racial differences are extreme and strongly color the history of the community. For example, a considerable degree of homogeneity, or at least the absence of conditions that generate clashes between radically different or irreconcilable elements, is requisite. If such conditions are present and persistent, then segregation lines naturally form and segregation suggests itself as the public policy. A policy of ignoring those lines and coercing all elements into unison is not really a policy, rather it is a defiance of nature and therefore a defiance of what could reasonably be called a policy. The extreme of putting free assemblies under military surveillance would be ludicrous, meaning the stifling of liberty in the name of liberty. Putting *peaceable* assemblies, the only kind safeguarded by the Constitution, under such surveillance would also be ludicrous, since it would mean that they were not peaceable. In fine, free assembly precludes forced, involuntary mixing, and peaceable assembly precludes unpeaceable mixing. "Legislation," said the Supreme Court in the past, "is powerless to eradicate racial instincts or to abolish distinctions based upon physical differences, and the attempt to do so can only result in accentuating the difficulties of the present situation."[3]

A mitigation of the integrationist's lot and no less of the segregationist's would be to provide mixed schools for those wishing them and segregated schools for others. By that standard, Northern states that do not thus provide segregated schools, which, I believe, is all of them, would incur the same kind of criticism they are accustomed to lavishing on the South, since both alike are denying the option between segregation and integration. Where the option is not desired, or is so little desired that satisfying it would be impracticable, argument and agitation over it become pointless. As we saw, this plan was offered in Nashville and was summarily rejected by the Federal district court,[4] in ostensible conformity with the Supreme Court's decrees in *Brown*. Simultaneously or subsequently Federal courts elsewhere in the South were countenancing both segregation and integration and the Supreme Court was countenancing them in it.

The ferment, strife, disorder, and disunion following the first attempts to compel integration, and persisting, even increasing, with the passage of the years, are a mirror reflecting the manifold obliquity of the Court's performance. There is much to be said of the antecedents of that performance, and particularly of the volutions of the Court in the feat of "absorbing" one part of the Constitution in another. By this, the Court would contrive to impose upon the states certain limitations which the states, as one condition of ratifying the Constitution, imposed on the Federal Government originally.

The First Amendment reads: "Congress shall make no law respecting an establishment of religion, or prohibiting the free exercise thereof; or abridging the freedom of speech, or of the press; or the right of the people peaceably to assemble, and to petition the government for a redress of grievances."

The Fourteenth Amendment reads in part: "No state shall make or enforce any law which shall abridge the privileges or immunities of citizens of the United States; nor shall any state deprive any person of life, liberty, or property without due process of law . . . "

Now the Court would read into the Fourteenth Amendment, under the word "liberty," the same prohibition contained in the First Amendment and so put the states under the same limitation as that Amendment puts upon Congress. The following extract from its opinion in *Palko* v. *Connecticut* in the year 1937 will attest:

" . . . In these [numerous issues heretofore decided by the Court, chiefly concerning freedom of speech, press, religion, and peaceable assembly] and other situations immunities that are valid as against the federal government by force of the specific pledges of particular amendments have been found to be implicit in the concept of ordered liberty, and thus, through the Fourteenth Amendment, become valid as against the states.

"The line of division may seem to be wavering and broken if there is a hasty catalogue of the cases on the one side and the other. Reflection and analysis will induce a different view. There emerges the perception of a rationalizing principle which gives to discrete instances a proper order and coherence . . .

"We reach a different plane of social and moral values when we pass to the privileges and immunities that have been taken over from the earlier articles of the federal Bill of Rights and brought within the Fourteenth Amendment by a process of absorption . . . So it has come about that the domain of liberty, withdrawn by the Fourteenth Amendment from encroachment by the states, has been enlarged by latter-day judgments to include liberty of the mind as well as liberty of action . . . "[5]

First, the Court brings immunities into the category of liberty. Obviously it was unnecessary to do that if the purpose was to secure for them the protection the Fourteenth Amendment gives to liberty, and in fact it was a derogation of immunities; for the Amendment unconditionally protects immunities, but not liberty. All it does for liberty is to protect it conditionally: protect it against deprivation by any state without due process of law. It gives no protection against deprivation of liberty *with* due process of law; and so the states are free to deprive of it, provided they adhere to due process.

Secondly, to make constitutional liberty amenable to this "absorption" operation, the Court indulges in a remarkable liberty itself. It presumes to put a limitation on what the Constitution leaves unlimited. It changes liberty to "ordered liberty." Then it asserts that that has been found to embrace the privileges and immunities that are constitutionally excluded from Federal limitation. Since the Fourteenth Amendment forbids the states to deprive of liberty (without due process of law), the Court can now say, speciously, that the states cannot deprive of the aforesaid privileges and immunities. And here it takes a further liberty, of omitting the qualifying condition, "without due process of law."

Thirdly, something called "the perception of a rationalizing principle which gives to discrete instances a proper order and coherence" is said to underlie this modification. What rationalizing principle? When much that issues from the Court is demonstrably at variance with elementary reason, it is reassuring to hear that the Court has found a rationalizing principle. It would be more reassuring if the Court would vouchsafe what that principle is; and still more reassuring if it did not keep secret what it means by "a proper order and coherence"—is it *constitutionally* proper? If it is, to show what it is, and whereabouts, in the purview of the Constitution, should be no difficulty. Or is it another limitation which the Court, in the face of its oath and obligation to support the Constitution, is presuming to impose on the Constitution?

Fourthly, a constitutional guarantee—liberty, "withdrawn by the Fourteenth Amendment from encroachment by the states"—is admitted to have been "enlarged by latter-day judgments." The rather odious term "judge-made law" is here frankly, naively, enlarged too, and may fairly be said now to include "judge-made constitution." To have this from the Court's own mouth must be cynically gratifying to the Court's critics, who have thought it for some time themselves. And yet the "enlargement" is really, demonstrably, nothing of the kind, though the Court's willingness to assume and declare it, is illuminating. Our "liberty of the mind as well as liberty of action" has not been constitutionally enlarged at all, though the Supreme Court's may have been (not constitutionally, but illicitly, by aggrandizement). Consider the Constitution's prohibition on *ex post facto* laws, whether Federal or state (Article I, Sections 9, 10). Implicit in it is a complete and conclusive answer to questions concerning the scope of constitutional liberty. It implies that liberty, with us, is a state of being without legal restraint: unless there is a law, one's acts cannot be restrained, constitutionally. Thus liberty, indirectly defined by the Constitution, is absence of legislated restraint. The Supreme Court can lawfully do nothing about that—neither enlarge nor diminish it. And only by diminishing the number or content of laws, only by superseding Congress and the state legislatures, could it presume to make such an enlargement; for Congress and the legislatures alone have legislative power. If then its decisions have enlarged liberty as it says, that is an open admission of usurpation. So the Court's critics need not have charged usurpation; all they needed to do was to follow closely, and presently they would have overheard the Court admitting it, as here.

In fine, these proceedings come to this: rights unconditionally guaranteed in the First Amendment are to be brought under the conditional guarantee of the Fourteenth Amendment; what Congress cannot touch according to the First Amendment, the states can take away according to the reservation in the Fourteenth. What then is the point?

The answer is plain. The Federal Government, in particular the Supreme Court, thus gains new power over the states. Whereas freedom of religious establishments, freedom of speech, of the press, and of peaceable assembly, are shielded *against* Federal power by the First Amendment, now they are to come *under* that power by the artifice of "absorbing" the substance of the First Amendment in the Fourteenth. The Constitution is turned inside out. The states are now like so many Frankensteins subject to being destroyed by the monster they have put in Washington.

The Court's "ordered" liberty is indeed ordered—ordered by the Court. "Ordered" liberty is a contradiction in terms. It is liberty under restraint, the liberty of a child in strings. It is also contradictory of the implicit definition of liberty in the *ex post facto* law prohibitions in the Constitution, a definition which leaves everyone a free agent except so far as the law, the will of the sovereign, forbids. Where the law forbids, it takes a toll of liberty, but that is by no means the same thing as imposing "order," or a strait jacket. Certainly public restraint is imperative, the only alternative to anarchy, nevertheless it is still optional. What it shall be, the state alone must decide. The state's decision, so long as it does not infringe other sovereignties, is no more subject, constitutionally, to Supreme Court confirmation than to Supreme Soviet confirmation.

Who originated the prohibition to which Congress is submitted in the First Amendment? Not the convention that wrote the Constitution, but the states—they would not ratify until thus guaranteed against congressional encroachment upon personal rights, including the right of peaceable assembly. Obviously, had it been conceivable to them that such encroachment might come from a court of justice; that the judicial mind might ever be so seduced or grow so perversely, so judocratically ambitious as to pretend to revise the Constitution, which is to say usurp the sovereign power of the states; in short, if they had feared that the Supreme Court might become a usurper as they feared that Congress might, then if they had not rejected the whole project of unification forthwith, surely they would have laid at least as strong a restraint on the Court as they laid on Congress. Who now encroaches on the right of association, or peaceable assembly? It is the Court. What the Constitution forbids Congress to do the Court now magisterially presumes to do. The sovereign states gave the law to Congress, now the Court turns upon them and gives the law to them. And yet the Court formerly acknowledged that "sovereignty itself is, of course, not subject to law."[6] Sovereignty has no legal superior.

We noticed just now that in adumbrating its "absorption" doctrine the Court said: "the domain of liberty [has been] withdrawn by the Fourteenth Amendment from encroachment by the states." In another case it said a few years afterwards: "while it is the Fourteenth Amendment which bears directly upon the state it is the more specific limiting principles of the First Amendment that finally govern this case" (the case concerned a state law which required school pupils to salute the flag, a requirement which the Court made out to be an abridgment of freedom of speech.)[7] Compare the Court's utterance on a previous occasion: "The first amendment . . . was not intended to limit the powers of the State governments in respect to their own citizens, but to operate upon the National government alone . . . The very highest duty of the States, when they entered into the Union under the Constitution, was to protect all persons within their boundaries in the enjoyment of these 'unalienable rights [life and personal liberty] with which they were endowed by their Creator.' Sovereignty for this purpose rests solely with the States."[8]

If now "the domain of liberty" has been withdrawn from "encroachment by the states," they cannot touch it. Any venture into it by them, any limitation they might impose, must then be an encroachment and therefore prohibited by the Fourteenth Amendment.—This novel pretension will not bear a moment's rational consideration. For if the states cannot encroach upon or circumscribe liberty, the consequence is anarchy: everybody is free to do as he pleases, no one is secure in anything, and the state is a mere fiction.

The language of the Fourteenth Amendment favors liberty not at all over life or poperty—and the state takes away these perennially.[9] Whatever power the state has over these two, it has over liberty also, by the parity of the terms of the Amendment. And there can be no reasonable doubt of the state's power; apart from such as it has relinquished or has submitted to, as in the United States Constitution, it is plenary, consummate power. The only restraint upon it is what the state itself may choose to undergo.

What the Court is about is clear enough, though its way of achieving it is protectively clouded. It would isolate liberty, putting it in a privileged place above both life and property. Now obviously this is in no sense warranted by the terms of the Fourteenth Amendment. But by the occult expedient of "transmitting" and "absorbing," the Court feigns to compass it just the same. These are its words: ". . . it is important to distinguish between the due process clause of the Fourteenth Amendment as an instrument for transmitting the principles of the First Amendment and those cases in which it is applied for its own sake."[10] Now the Court takes the "instrument" it has found in the Fourteenth Amendment and presumes to reach with it into the First Amendment, lift out the contents, and transfer them intact to a favored place in the Fourteenth. It presumes that they bring with them the impervious shield that keeps them beyond congressional reach in the First Amendment, magnified and adapted so as now to be equally effective against the states' reach.

Such a maneuver, once exposed, is repugnant to law and reason and, ironically, to due process of law, the "instrument" by which the Court professes to carry it out. It matches a type of high-level larceny in which the larcener contrives to induce the law to tie its own hands while he takes the goods. Another parallel to it is this: A group of men form a corporation, appoint managers, and draw up a set of regulations for their direction. The business prospers and the managers, like bureaucrats, begin to assert themselves. At length they are so consolidated and cocksure that, like the central government, they presume to lay down the law to the stockholders, who like states of the Union, presently find themselves stripped of their control and barely tolerated on the premises. The change has come about, you understand, by *absorption* of power *transmitted* (others would say illicitly appropriated) to the upstarts by the very *instrument* of rules regulating them. A note: It was not the managers alone who thus stood the owners on their heads. Outsiders had a part, in fact the greatest part, as members of a tribunal which the founders had established to uphold and apply the rules the owners had made; which tribunal, newly emboldened, now offers the rules themselves, particularly a certain artfully phrased one of them, call it due process of law, as bounden warrant for what they have done!

We might formulate the logic of the Court's stated position respecting Amendments I and XIV, to see how it supports what the Court is doing. Condensed, it seems to be as follows:

The federating states ordain in their Constitution that Congress shall not legislate concerning establishments of religion nor abridge the freedom of speech, press, or peaceable assembly (Amendment I). They ordain that they themselves shall not deprive anyone of life, liberty, or property without due process of law (Amendment XIV).

Therefore they ordain that they themselves shall not legislate concerning establishments of religion, nor abridge the freedom of speech, press, or peaceable assembly.

To any attentive reader it must be apparent that the conclusion does not follow from the premises. There is no logical connection between ordaining that Congress shall not do such and such at all and ordaining that the states shall not, except by due process of law, do the like. That the states, in the Constitution, prohibit certain congressional action and pledge themselves against similar action save in accordance with law—these are no more the same thing than orders to a deputy are the same thing as a resolution on the part of his chief. They are wholly independent.[11]

Perhaps it will be said that the case is not so simple as this; that something is overlooked, namely, due process of law; and that that is the main force impelling the Court to its decision. The fact that due process of law is avowedly taken as an "instrument" by means of which the Court accomplishes the "transmission" of the terms of Amendment I to Amendment XIV, which then "absorbs" them, goes to show that the Court itself relies on such a premise: the premise that due process of law is justification for extending to Amendment XIV the prohibitions contained in Amendment I. Let us consider that.

The Court has often had occasion to express itself concerning due process of law. In one of the cases here it said: "Much of the vagueness of the due process clause disappears when the specific provisions of the First [Amendment] become its standard."[12] Half a century ago the Court said: "Few phrases of the law are so elusive of exact apprehension as this . . . this court has always declined to give a comprehensive definition of it . . ." But then it adds: "The words due process of law were intended to secure the individual from the arbitrary exercise of the powers of government, unrestrained by the established principles of private rights and distributive justice."[13] Before this it held: ". . . 'due process of law' is equivalent to 'law of the land,' as found in the 29th chapter of Magna Charta . . ."[14] Recently (1952) it had this to say: "Due process of law is a summarized constitutional guarantee of respect for those personal immunities which, as Mr. Cardozo twice wrote for the Court, are 'so rooted in the traditions and conscience of our people as to be ranked as fundamental,' or are 'implicit in the concept of ordered liberty.' "[15] Lower courts have been equally inconsistent on the subject. "No definite definition—none but the most general—has been or can be given of 'due process of law.' The best the courts can do is to say, in each case as it arises, whether a given act or proceeding in the particular matter is due process of law."[16] And due process of law "means a general public law, binding upon all members of the community under all circumstances . . ."[17]

A cardinal formulation of law is thus now vague, now exact. Its meaning cannot be fixed, yet is firmly fixed. Too elusive for the Court to grasp, yet it is seized by the Court and given a panoply of attributes: tradition, conscience, "ordered" liberty. A magic wand held over the Constitution would scarcely do more than this.

But notice that due process of law is unconditionally held to be equivalent to the law of the land: law applicable to all alike. Where then is the vagueness? Where is the elusiveness? What is there about the law of the land to allow the slightest modification of it by a court? In particular, what is there to justify the Supreme Court in taking a provision of the Constitution as an "instrument" for it, the Court, to use for transforming state-imposed limitations upon the Federal power into limitations upon state power? The question answers itself. It would be absurd to suppose that the law of the land might be inverted or in any manner transformed by an agency charged, as is the Supreme Court, to do the opposite, namely, to support it, to maintain it as it is.[18] The law of the land is no instrument for its own destruction. It is no instrument at all, unless for effecting the will, or policy, of the sovereign, which is the states jointly, or the people. Moreover, the Court has long since rejected the crudely presumptuous idea that constitutional restraint upon the Federal Government extends to the state governments. It said:

". . . no limitation of the action of [the Federal] government on the people would apply to the state government, unless expressed in terms . . .

". . . Had the framers of these amendments [I-X] intended them to be limitations on the powers of the state governments, they would have imitated the framers of the original Constitution, and have expressed that intention.

". . . These amendments contain no expression indicating an intention to apply them to the state governments. This Court cannot so apply them."[19]

The Fourteenth Amendment came thirty-five years after this, but contains nothing making the First Amendment applicable to the states. That, however, is no check upon the Supreme Court of today and the recent past. A court that can "reverse" itself, making the law and the Constitution the opposite of what they were, while the sovereign sleeps or fiddles away, can do practically whatever it wishes. It can even toy with the covenant entrusted to it, abstract a part, transform it, and solemnly declare it a kind of catalyst capable of making another part absorb yet another. Or, in its own words, it can use one part, "due process of law," as an "instrument" for "transmitting" the content of the First Amendment to the Fourteenth, there to be "absorbed."[20] The Court seems totally oblivious of the plain, obtrusive fact that to do this requires alteration, is alteration, of the Constitution, something the states alone can lawfully do.[21] Even a passing regard for another part of the Constitution, Amendment X, which is just as real as any other and which commands the Court's fidelity just as much as any other, would check this rampant disposition of the judges to melt down the Constitution and recast it in their image.

Whatever is not law or process of law is *a fortiori* not due process of law. So the Supreme Court can never, lawfully, "use" due process of law to "make" or to conceal its "making" law. It is subject itself to due process of law—"the framers of the Constitution," said Marshall for the Court, "contemplated that instrument as a rule for the government of courts, as well as of the legislature."[22]

The Court is not sovereign, but the chamberlain of the sovereign. Judging cases under law is not exercising sovereignty but only applying the sovereign's previously declared will. Finding out and declaring minutiae of the law and applying them to cases is not lawmaking. The rather common supposition nowadays in writings on constitutional law that the judge, even in pronouncing and applying the law is shaping it, putting himself into it, is a piece of confusion. Though it is true that a judge sees with *his* eyes and decides according to *his* lights, that is trivial; what he sees must be there, made visible to all by his showing. Otherwise he fails. Other men make the laws, and made him only an intermediary between the laws and the facts of the cases coming before him, one who shall demonstratively determine the application of laws to cases; *demonstratively*—that is, objectively, logically, accurately, impartially ascertain the law and the facts and the bearing of the one on the other. It is a cardinal assumption of judgment, here as in the world at large, that the facts and the laws are apart from the judge or observer, who in his official capacity can only bow to them. In bowing he is not *making* or modifying what he bows to, though he is making it evident and articulate. If he is not content to do that but must seize the occasion to substitute his ego for either law or facts, let him cease his pretension to judgeship and offer himself as a messiah of some kind. A judge who has not the acumen to distinguish between law and himself, and the probity to respect the law of the land regardless of his own disposition towards it, is incapable of really taking the oath to support the Constitution, and of course utterly incapable of performing the office of a judge. Due process of law is not an "instrument" for betraying law or for aggrandizing the ministers of law.

"Due"—this term cannot, under a republican government, denote anything judocratic. Whatever might be said, sophistically, of taking other constitutional terms to mean now this, now that, at the will of the judges, "due" cannot fall into that category. If it did, it would mean not due process of *law* but due something—Pleasure?—of the judge; and since no one can prescribe to the judicial mind or to any mind, "due" would mean nothing. Due process, in its entirety, is the due of the law, not of the judge. The law does not know Judge A from Judge B. Yet we read, "In a word, what 'due process of law' today means in relation to state legislative power is the approval of the Supreme Court."[23]

So "due" may be such and such today and not tomorrow? But this cannot be, without disruptive consequences. "Due" is a fixity and cannot *per se* alter. To be due is to be certain, unambiguous, univocal. A due may be annulled by competent authority, or be superseded by a different due, but in the latter case it is univocal as before. If then due process of law is whatever the Supreme Court pleases to have it, it is abolished. The Court's presumption to change it destroys it, just as would a presumption to change a record or a promise. A thing cannot both be and not be at once. How could anyone, including the judge, know the law's due, or anyone's rights and obligations under it, if they were not already fixed and hence beyond judicial meddling?

Without law there is no due process of law. The process can occur only in applicaton, and only the law can be legally applied. So due process of law is not a determiner of law but is determined by law: it is but the law applied, fulfilled. It is to the law as a course is to action, in the phrase "course of action," or as conformity is to rules in "conformity with all the rules": not an entity, only a shadow (in which, however, the Supreme Court has been safe from peering eyes, if any happened to turn that way).

Since the law is precedent to due process, and the courts are not the law but organs of the law, such a thing as judicial prescription of the content of law, in the name of "substantive due process," is out of the question.[24] It makes no difference that a law, duly enacted, is tagged "unreasonable" or "arbitrary" (the tagger may be unreasonable or arbitrary himself). All that can reasonably, *logically*, be asked is whether it was enacted in accordance with the constitution and the procedures established in pursuance of the constitution. To demand more would be an infringement of prerogative. In a free people, under a republican government, such as the Constitution pledges to every state, there are no due laws. Where would they come from? There is no legal source above the state itself, or the people. It would presume a sovereign superior to the sovereign, and so be self-contradictory. If the Supreme Court ventures to lay down a law about what shall be a law, that is itself the supreme violation of due process. It is a nullification of republican government and a substitution of oligarchy.[25]

"It must be conceded," the Supreme Court has said, "that there are such rights [life, liberty, property] in every free government beyond the control of the State."[26] To reconcile this with the Fourteenth Amendment provision reserving to the states the right to deprive of life, liberty, or property by due process of law would require the delineation of a territory at once within and not within the world; one which was entirely out of reach of the state, yet which was partly, conditionally, within its reach: entirely out of the world according to the Supreme Court, yet within it according to the Constitution. This is impossible, a sheer contradiction in terms.[27] Judocracy, alert to opportunities for aggrandizing itself and not too particular about how it does it, affects to gloss over the contradiction by applying its wonder-working "instrument," due process of law. It seizes on the due-process proviso of the Amendment and transmutes it into a provenience under which the judges assume ulterior power. Due process of law must now satisfy *their* demand; through it *their* will is made the law. Since the maker is above his handiwork, the judges are now paramount to the law, including the Constitution, hence including the sovereign. Any doctrine of judge-made law, if not merely specious or meant to deceive, has to admit this; which is to admit judicial subversiveness and judicial despotism.

Still, in putting personal rights beyond the reach of authority, is not the Court defending all of us and fufilling the most cherished guarantee of the Constitution? Perhaps it will be thought that the Court is only recognizing inborn, natural rights of the individual. That is mistaken. The Court is not just pointing out the stars. It is, so to say, giving orders to the firmament.

Whatever may be thought of this pretension, the Court is fatally out of order in another point. It assumes that individual rights are superior to the state. Much in the utterances of the Court does not bear rational scrutiny, and here is a marked example. We have no rights at all except under the state. Beyond the pale, all that we have are primitive powers, which others, singly or in concert, may at will overpower. Our status is no better than savages', "solitary, poor, nasty, brutish, and short." To escape it we form a compact, or state, creating mutual security, and it is from this union that our rights take rise. Instead of having no authority over these, the state, their author and sustainer, has plenary authority over them; which is mutely recognized in the Fourteenth Amendment's reservation of power in the states to deprive of everything—life, liberty, property—by law. There are in us no personal rights *per se*, only natural attributes, as in any other natural beings.[28]

In this light, due process of law, an entity, the Court's fabulous "instrument," is nowhere visible. An afterthought, immaterial, in itself nothing, it registers zero. It was misrepresented. By conjuring with it the Court professes to work wonders: to turn a rule into the things ruled, form into content, mind into matter. The result is this stark nothingness, like the self-deception of the servile multitude in thinking the king was robed and crowned, when a simpleton could see that he was naked.

Even if certain of our endowments are held to be absolute rights,[29] it is obvious that they cannot be that now, after *Brown*, since that case allows one person, or many, as a right, to encroach on another, even to use him as a *facility*. And this is the extreme form of denial of personal right since it offends and to a degree sacrifices the very being of the individual, whereas restraint of speech, press, or religion, for example, is only a denial of expression, something secondary to his being, or person. To encroach on another individual cannot be a liberty, except in tyrants. It presumes one man or element to have special privilege over another, which of course would void equality and the guarantee of equal protection. Do the encroachers suppose that all are thus free, each to use the others as facilities? Then personal rights vanish and we are reduced to primitivism. *Brown*, therefore, did not vindicate personal rights. It extinguished them (or would if allowed to stand).

Sovereignty is the supreme liberty, the source of all civil liberty. So, substantially, the Supreme Court itself has said in other times: ". . . the greatest security [of liberty] resides in the right of the people to make their own laws and alter them at their pleasure."[30] Now that the Court, seventy-five years after, has possessed itself of its fabulous "instrument" for transforming the otherwise unaltered Constitution, this reads like something out of fiction.

To intrude on others, to violate the integrity of the person, is not only to sacrifice some part of his make and, under integration, to turn it into a public property, a *facility*, in the Court's language; it is also to forfeit one's own personal integrity by opening it to the like violation. Who, if he knew what he was doing or was not too low in the scale of being to care at all, could commit himself to that? Where a white person shrinks from thought of it—literally, he or she is appalled nowadays, especially in Northern cities, at the news that Negroes are moving into the neighborhood—the integrationist Negro seems to know no such compunction. Here, by comparison, his stature equals zero: to him intrusion on another, violation of personal integrity, is evidently nothing. He cannot understand that it is not nothing to the victim of his ambition. Thus he himself proves the reasonableness, the personal need, of segregation. In making his case he even more unmakes it.

We seem to be entering a new Reconstruction era, with the Negro holding sway somewhat as he did before. It might behoove him to take notice that the country at length tired of the farce the first time and put an end to it, leaving his ancestors in disillusion. Enthralled by the miracle at Washington, now as then, he is in no state to heed anything so sober as that. He is in a New Jerusalem where the first are become the last and the last first. "Equal protection," magically transformed, outtops all else, the most intimate rights and interests being dwarfed or extinguished before it.

Paradoxically, it is in the name of personal rights under the Constitution that the sacrifice of white to black has occurred. Ludicrously, we are in the position of upholding personal rights by grossly violating them, forcing one element upon another while it shrinks in revulsion, and then using it, the victim, chattel-like, as *facilities* to the other. We continually hear of the miserable lot of the individual in Russia; but compare: "Citizens of the USSR are guaranteed inviolability of the person." This is Article 127 of the Russian Constitution. I suppose some will say that it is only words, paper, a mask held up to the world. What then can they say of our example? That it, too, is now only words, changeable at the judges' will?

It begs the question to suppose that natural barriers between persons must be disregarded or rubbed out. Why must they? The Constitution, a shield to the individual amidst whatever barriers, is far more an acknowledgment of the barriers than a design for their obliteration. Shielding, you may say, can pass into excluding, and that is what integrationists oppose. But where personal rights are concerned it is indeed, naturally, a matter of excluding: they *are* exclusionary. Since integration aspires to end the exclusions, it means a corresponding extinction of personal rights.

Seeing that all racial barriers are to be leveled, might it not be an astute policy for facilitating action and for imbibing the full spirit of so revolutionary a change, to import Russian teams to guide and inspire us? On second thought it occurs that this, paradoxically, might not be the wisest choice. The Russians themselves, I believe, shun mixing with dark people.[31] Only the more abject Latin-American elements and some others of the South Seas, products themselves of mixing, could, of all the world's people, qualify racially. Whether they would have the wherewithal for the task is a different question. For the present, Washington is giving the lessons itself, in a more or less *sub-rosa* manner. We have had, for example, the anomaly of the Attorney General, an officer sworn to uphold the Thirteenth Amendment as much as anything else in the Constitution, attempting to cajole the proprietors of restaurants into surrendering their independence; not, observe, into providing equally for the Negroes without encroaching on white customers and risking the loss of their business and possibly the closing of the place, but simply to put the Negro with the white regardless of the white's inclination. What business has the Federal Government to resort to extra-legal acts, such as these, for attaining extra-legal ends, ends calling for the sacrifice of personal rights? The only difference between such arrogance and that of despots is the method.[32] As well might the Attorney General carry his aggression into adjoining fields and attempt to induce people not to speak or read or think.

Judges who are not without compunction for their oath must suffer torture when they subscribe to the desecrations of the Constitution that glitter through these wanton exhibits. Their commitment is as much against circumventing, breaking through, reversing the Constitution as it is for adhering to it—one is but the obverse of the other. They are sentinels charged to defend the constitutional position the same as a soldier is charged to defend a military position, with one difference: the treacherous soldier who opens the way for an invader or (a closer parallel) makes the invasion himself and delivers up the prize, will be put to death. The robed, exalted judge, transforming the trust reposed in him by the Constitution into license even to riddle the Constitution, rules in Olympian immunity and serenity.

[1] Equal protection involves the question, Equal to what? The answer is explicitly before us in the first section of the Fourteenth Amendment: Equal to the protection accorded to other *persons* (equal protection, in the Constitution, applies only to persons). The Federal (constitutional) requirement is therefore satisfied so long as the persons are equally covered. State requirements are another matter. In its discretion and under its powers acknowledged in Amendment X the state may differentiate and differently accommodate the persons subject to its jurisdiction without denying equality to any—difference is immaterial to equality: it neither makes nor unmakes equality. The only question will be whether a person has in fact received his share; and this can be answered only by objective determinations; otherwise, any decision can be legitimately disputed.

The equal protection clause of the Fourteenth Amendment regards racial differentiation no more than it does sexual, psychological, sociological, or pathological differentiation. If one of these is legitimate, so is another—else discrimination, and therefore unequal protection; and there is no question of the legitimacy, the legality, of differentiations according to sex or sanity, for example. Where nature differentiates so sharply that the result is a withdrawal, not to say flight, of one element from another, it is anarchic to say that the state cannot recognize the differences and adapt its provisions to them. That would mean that the state cannot act to prevent disorder, violence, lawlessness: that it cannot perform the first office of the state. What is the contrary, or Supreme Court conception? Evidently this: that nature must be over-ridden; the white person must not shrink or flee; there must be amalgamation (integration).

There *must*? Where in the Constitution is this laid down? Certainly nowhere. In *Brown* v. *Board of Education* equal protection is presumed to justify it. But the sole referent of equal protection is the person, the individual; all else is irrelevant. Whether he associates or falls in with this or that other person, is of no more bearing than whether he walks on this side of the street or that, or whether he follows the crowd or lives in seclusion. The imposition upon him of conditions for the enjoyment of an unconditional right, such as equal protection, is obviously incompatible with law.

[2] See above, pp. 197ff.

[3] *Plessy* v. *Ferguson, loc. cit.,* p. 551.

[4] *Kelley* v. *Board of Education,* 159 F. Supp. 272, 278. In New Orleans a Federal court itself drew up and decreed its own integration plan, such, I believe, as the school board of Nashville offered and the Federal court there rejected and forbid. The result all but emptied two schools, amidst scenes of violence. This occurred in 1961 and was sensationally publicized.

[5] 302 U. S. 319, 324-327.

6 *Yick Wo v. Hopkins,* 118 U. S. 356, 370. Cp.: ". . . the conduct of the [English] legislature . . . (*ex hypothesi*) cannot be governed by laws . . ." A. V. Dicey, *Introduction to the Study of the Law of the Constitution,* 1927, p. 426.

7 *West Virginia Board of Education v. Barnette,* 319 U. S. 624, 639.

8 *United States v. Cruikshank,* 92 U. S. 542, 552-553. See also *Slaughterhouse Cases, loc. cit.,* p. 75; *Maxwell v. Dow,* 176 U. S. 581, 604.

9 The Court itself hitherto said: "Both property and liberty are held on such reasonable conditions as may be imposed by the governing power of the state in the exercise of those powers [police powers, which "relate to the safety, health, morals, and general welfare of the public"], and with such conditions the Fourteenth Amendment was not designed to interfere." *Lochner v. New York,* 198 U. S. 45, 53 (1905).

10 *West Virginia Board of Education v. Barnette, loc. cit.,* p. 639. The Fourteenth Amendment repeats literally the due-process clause of the Fifth Amendment, with this effect: what the Federal Government is forbidden to do in the Fifth Amendment, namely, deprive any person of "life, liberty, or property, without due process of law," the states, too, are henceforth forbidden to do. This is no imaginary "transmission" or "absorption" but an original act imposing a limitation on state power. If there was any intention of lifting something from the First Amendment and "transmitting" it to the Fourteenth for "absorption," is it now to be supposed that the authors and ratifiers of the Fourteenth did not have the will to say so? They had every power; why should they dissemble or be secretive? It is an affront to their memory and to the intelligence of our time to confabulate this transmission and absorption make-believe and offer it in their name and in the name of law.

11 Cp.: "We have here two sovereignties [state and Federal], deriving power from different sources, capable of dealing with the same subject-matter within the same territory. Each may, without interference by the other, enact laws . . . Each government, in determining what shall be an offense against its peace and dignity is exercising its own sovereignty, not that of the other." *United States v. Lanza,* 260 U. S. 377, 382.

12 *West Virginia Board of Education v. Barnette, loc. cit.,* p. 639.

13 *Twining v. New Jersey,* 211 U. S. 78, 99, 100, 101.

14 *Hurtado v. California,* 110 U. S. 516, 521.

15 *Rochin v. California,* 342 U. S. 165, 169.

16 *State v. Sponaugle,* 32 S. E. 283, 284.

17 This was declared in *Charles J. Off & Co. v. Morehead,* 85 N. E. 264, 266. Cp. the following: "The larger and better definition of *due process of law* is that it means law in its regular course of administration through courts of justice." Thus the Court in a day past (1890), quoting Blackstone, 2 *Comm.* 13, 134 U. S. at 418. Cp.: ". . . law in its regular course of administration through courts of justice is due process, and when secured by the law of the State the constitutional requirement is satisfied; and . . . due process is so secured by laws operating on all alike, and not subjecting the individual to the arbitrary exercise of the powers of government unrestrained by the established principles of private right and distributive justice." *Leeper v. Texas,* 139 U. S. 462, 567.

Cp. also: "There are volumes of discussion of the meaning of the phrase 'due process of law.' There is also some loose and indefinite talk about life, liberty, and property. When, however, one seeks to ascertain the precise signification of 'due process of law,' he will not get a more definite idea from the decisions than from the concise, but necessarily rather vague, definition of Webster ['the general law, which proceeds upon inquiry and renders judgment only after trial'] . . ." Charles E. Shattuck in *Selected Essays on Constitutional Law,* compiled by a committee of the Association of American Law Schools, 4 vols., Chicago, Foundation Press, 1938, vol. 2, pp. 188, 200. Webster here is vague? Hardly. He is inclusive, but inclusiveness is not vagueness. Definition in one sense is nothing but a measure of inclusiveness, capable of being narrowed to where it covers only some one individual or expanded to cover everything. What is covered in Webster's definition here is as precise as the terms "proceed," "inquiry," "judgment," and "trial," all of which are fixed or capable of being fixed both analytically and practically.

When it is alleged that some clause or term of the Constitution is vague, it is a good chance that this is going to be used as ground for giving it a meaning after the liking of the alleger. Indeed, to a mind not thus motivated, there is probably nothing intrinsically vague—clouded, indeterminate—in the Constitution. Take "the general welfare," which to the vague-minded may seem an extremely vague term, in the preamble. To James Madison it was nothing of the kind, but rather a term which, considered in conjunction with the subjoined articles, bore a meaning "too obvious to be mistaken." Jonathan Elliot, *Debates in the Several State Conventions on the Adoption of the Federal Constitution,* 2d ed., 5 vols., Philadelphia, J. B. Lippincott Co., 1907, vol. 4, p. 552. The question is not whether a constitutional term is vague to someone today. It is, what did it mean as employed by the authors of the Constitution, not what it may happen to mean to the renovators who currently are striving to transform it *ad hoc.* And this is a question always admitting of impartial answer, according to the long-established canons of construction. Madison, in an exceedingly luminous passage concerning limitations of legal discourse, remarks that obscurity and ambiguity are more or less characteristic of the laws "until their meaning be liquidated and ascertained by a series of particular discussions and adjudications." *Federalist* 37. With him it is a matter of course, not something *ultra vires,* that the meaning be thus established.

Nevertheless, according to Justice Frankfurter, the words of the phrase "due process of law" are so "undefined, either by their intrinsic meaning, or by history, or by tradition that they leave the individual Justice free, if indeed they do not actually compel him, to fill in the vacuum with his own controlling notions of economic, social, and industrial facts with reference to which they are invoked." *Law and Politics,* New York, Harcourt, Brace & Co., 1939, p. 13. No; a judge cannot substitute his idea for a lawmaker's idea any more than a witness in court can substitute his version of an occurrence for another witness' version. If the vagueness is indeed incorrigible, then it leaves only indecisiveness and hence cannot ground a *decision.* Terms that do not yield their meaning to competent study are nothing more than abracadabra, hence are not laws, hence are not applicable. But it is hard to see how "due process of law" should be put in this category. In *Hurtado* the Court said, ". . . it is not to be supposed that . . . due process of law is too vague and indefinite to operate as a practical restraint." *Loc. cit.,* p. 536. Yet today we may read: "The modern interpretation of the 'due process' clause [is] an interpretation not dreamed of in 1787 . . . what it means [today] is, in effect, the approval of the Supreme Court." In these few words from Professor Corwin's *Court Over Constitution,* Princeton, Princeton University Press, 1938, pp. 38, 107, may be read the record of judocracy.

[18] It has always been doubtful that the Supreme Court has power, constitutionally, to nullify acts of Congress; supralegislative power, that is. The Court's reasoning in *Marbury* v. *Madison, loc. cit.,* pp. 177-179, where this power is thought to have been established, is seen in the following:

"It is emphatically the province and duty of the judicial department to say what the law is. Those who apply the rule to particular cases, must of necessity expound and interpret that rule. If two laws conflict with each other, the courts must decide on the operation of each.

"So if a law be in opposition to the Constitution; if both the law and the Constitution apply to a particular case, so that the Court must either decide that case conformably to the law, disregarding the Constitution, or conformably to the Constitution, disregarding the law, the court must determine which of these conflicting rules governs the case. This is of the very essence of judicial duty . . ."

In the Judiciary Act of 1789 Congress had conferred on the Court the power to issue writs of mandamus, such as the appellant Marbury was now asking (he had been appointed justice of the peace, but for political reasons his commission had been withheld). Denying Marbury's petition, the Court held that Congress though having express constitutional power to alter the Court's appellate jurisdiction, had no power to add anything to its original jurisdiction, and that the mandamus power was such an addition. This, it presumed, meant that the Court could nullify the addition—could nullify an act of Congress.

Though the Court may have to say that it cannot, faithfully to its oath to support the Constitution, apply a law which conflicts with the Constitution, that is not the same thing as nullifying the law. To nullify, it would have to assume power over Congress, power which is not to be found in the Constitution.

There was an alternative to nullifying the law. Without compromising the Constitution and without presuming any power over Congress, the Court could have rejected all claims under the law. It could have firmly minded its own business and let Congress alone. That would have been literally a checking and balancing of congressional power without encroaching on it, and quite in accord with the design of the Federal system. To be sure, it would have rendered the law inoperative, the same thing as nullifying it, virtually; but the law was self-nullifying, if logically incompatible with the Constitution, and the Court need only have pointed that out to give it the quietus. To point out a contradiction, and to refuse to countenance it is not to assume power of any kind, over Congress or anything else. It is only to fulfill a part of the business of a rational, responsible mind.

Marshall, the author of the Court's opinion in this celebrated case, went into transports of eloquence on the subject of the judges' oath to support the Constitution. Did he forget that Congress also takes an oath to support the Constitution? Did he suppose that the Supreme Court has a purer, fairer cognizance of supporting the Constitution than Congress has? We know now that it cannot be much if any purer or fairer, seeing that the Court so often repudiates its own "findings" of what the Constitution is or means (reverses itself again and again). It must be presumed that Congress is mindful of its oath, as judges are of theirs; and not forgotten that the President is under a higher oath than either, "to preserve, protect, and defend" the Constitution. Whenever the Court and Congress are at a stand, as they must be in any case in which the Court presumes to nullify a congressional act, the President must have power to resolve the conflict, by virtue of his superior obligation to the Constitution; or if not, then the power lies only with the sovereign, that is, the states or people, by means of constitutional amendment; certainly not with the Court, which is only coordinate with Congress.

The Court is to the law, and the sovereign back of it, as an auditor is to his client. It has no more power, constitutionally, to nullify a law on finding it contradictory than the auditor has to change a client's policy after a similar finding. Authority to expose and denounce error is not the same as authority to command correction of the error. Still less is it authority to strike down the maker of the error.

Nor has the Court, constitutionally, the power to review (nullify, reverse) its decisions of constitutional questions. These delineate the law in its application: the law of the land. Over that the Court has no power whatever, all such power lodging in the people and their agent, Congress. If it nevertheless assumes such power, it is virtually in insurrection. Its role admits of no turning back, no vacillation, since that would mean duplicity and discrimination in the law and hence unequal protection. Constitutionally, it can no more reverse a decision than a jury which has sent a man to his death can reassemble, reverse its verdict, and resurrect the man.

In our time the Court is presuming, deftly and obscurely but surely presuming, to "review" even the Constitution itself. When it ventures to employ a constitutional element (due process of law) as an "instrument" with which to bring about the "absorption" of one article by another, that is reviewing indeed—it is more: remaking. When it ventures to say that "neither liberty nor justice would exist" if "the privileges and immunities" of the Bill of Rights had not been "taken over" and "brought within the Fourteenth Amendment by a process of absorption" (*Palko* v. *Connecticut, loc. cit.,* p. 326) is it dreaming? Was there not liberty and justice in the country before 1868, when the Fourteenth Amendment was adopted? Or not until, long after, the Supreme Court began to "take over" such an such from one part of the Constitution and "absorb" it in another?

[19] *Barron* v. *Baltimore,* 7 Peters 243, 248, 249, (1833). Reiterating this ruling long afterwards, the Court said: "The first amendment . . . was not intended to limit the powers of the State governments in respect to their own citizens, but to operate upon the National government alone . . . [It and the nine other amendments adopted with it] left the authority of the States just where they found it, and added nothing to the already existing powers of the United States." *United States* v. *Cruikshank, loc. cit.,* p. 552 (1875).

[20] Before its "transmission" and "absorption" thaumaturgy, the Court went through a series of defections from its acknowledgment, at the time of Marshall, that the limitations imposed on the Federal Government by the first ten amendments, or Bill of Rights, had no application to the states. A sequence of cases in this category is cited by the Court itself in *Palko* v. *Connecticut, loc. cit.,* p. 324. In 1873, five years after the adoption of the Fourteenth Amendment, the Court said that the privileges and immunities of state citizenship "are left to the state governments for security and protection, and not placed under the special care of the federal government." *Slaughterhouse Cases, loc. cit.,* p. 78. In subsequent cases it repeatedly rejected the idea that the rights secured against congressional power were now secured against state power by the Fourteenth Amendment. *Maxwell* v. *Dow,* 1900; *Twining* v. *New Jersey,* 1908; *Prudential*

Insurance Company v. *Cheek,* 1922. In 1931 all this was changed. The Court that year struck down a state law against publicaton of any "malicious, scandalous and defamatory newspaper, magazine or other periodical" on the ground that such a law was "an infringment of the liberty of the press guaranteed by the Fourteenth Amendment." *Near* v. *Minnesota, loc. cit.,* pp. 706, 723. Since the Near decision it has been all but axiomatic with the Court that the rights protected by the First Amendment against congressional action are protected by the Fourteenth Amendment against state action. "The First Amendment, as made applicable to the states by the Fourteenth" is language indicative of that. *Everson* v. *Board of Education,* 330 U. S. 1, 8 (1947).

So now the Fourteenth Amendment means, according to the Court, what before, according to the Court, it did not mean. Where are we? In never-never land?

Where does the Fourteenth Amendment make the First Amendment applicable to the states? It does nothing of the kind in terms. Then it must do it by logical necessity if the later Court is to be vindicated—a logical necessity not comprehended by the earlier Court. But no such necessity is shown or even hinted. The logical test is whether the Fourteenth Amendment can stand independently of the First. To that the answer is plainly Yes: the Fourteenth would be fully intelligible and applicable, though the First had never been written, and vice versa. So they are logically independent of each other, and the Fourteenth no more entails the First than it does the Twenty-first (the one repealing the Eighteenth).

We find that liberty in one state is often quite different from what it is in another, just because the different states limit it—deprive of it—differently. How could this be if the Fourteenth Amendment, applying to all states alike, did not admit of it, and how can the Court single out any certain liberty for favor and say that due process of law precludes restriction of it? Due process puts no law or liberty above any other; it is not a law above law but only a mirror of the law.

Yet the Court speaks of "the preferred place given in our scheme to the great, the indispensable democratic freedoms secured by the First Amendment." *Thomas* v. *Collins,* 323 U. S. 516, 530 (1944). *Preferred* place—what, how, could that be? All laws duly enacted are equally laws, as all facts duly ascertained are equally facts. Preference, preferred place, can no more be an attribute of theirs than it can of, say, odd numbers over even numbers. So the judicial preference must be something wholly extrinsic, presumably something in the judges' minds, naively disclosed by their awkward phraseology. Elsewhere the Court has spoken of "equal laws," equal not in the sense that any law is as much a law as any other but in the sense, presumably, of similar laws, laws all alike here, there, everywhere (see p. 278). If this artless, empty conception meant anything, it would make nonsense of "preferred" laws. It would be pointless to say that some laws take precedence through being preferred laws. Of course some laws underlie others, as some beams of a house underlie others; but they are not *preferred* on that account. Calling them preferred gives the judges a little more latitude, whereby *their* preferences may gain a place and at length dominate (though a judge's preferences are no more the law than anyone else's). No part of the Constitution is constitutionally above or below any other. "We can hardly say that one [individual] right is more guaranteed than another," said the eminent English constitutionalist, A. V. Dicey. "To say that the 'constitution guaranteed' one class of rights more than the other would be to an English-man an unnatural or a senseless form of speech." *Op. cit.*, p. 196. The Supreme Court has said: "... as no constitutional guarantee enjoys preference, so none should suffer subordination or deletion." *Ullmann* v. *United States,* 350 U. S. 422, 428 (1955).

In any event it is no liberty of any person or element to encroach on another person, for that destroys the liberty of the other. The supposition that the state cannot act to prevent this, that it cannot secure liberty against violation by libel, for example, is itself inimical to liberty. Erected into a judicial tenet, it is a weapon for destroying statehood. " ... The preservation of the States and the maintenance of their governments," said the Court just after the adop-tion of the Fourteenth Amendment, "are as much within the design and care of the Constitution as the preservation of the Union and the maintenance of the National government. The Constitution, in all its provisions, looks to an indestructible Union composed of indestructible states." *Texas* v. *White,* 7 Wallace 700, 725 (1869). Integrationists, thinking only of one thing, forget this or care not about it. They see a great gain in liberty. Indeed: the liberty of violating the liberty of others. That is the self-destruction of liberty. The Supreme Court has now acclaimed it the law of the land, deriving, the Court supposes, from due process and equal protection; which is to say that due process and equal protection, veritable guarantees of the Constitution, are de-vices for destroying the Constitution. In the realm of reason what leads to absurdity is itself absurdity. Let the blood be on the judicial heads.

21 Cp.: "No honest student of the Constitution . . . be he judge, lawyer, or layman, will have the hardihood to assert that the Court was prompted by any compulsion of words to give the phrase 'due process of law' the sweep of scope, the vast vagueness, and the illimitable elasticity with which it was en-dowed when the Court, upon its own initiative transferred it from a proce-dural requirement of decency and fairness in matters of procedural law into a requirement that substantive laws dealing with matters of economic and social concern shall pass the scrutiny of the Court's censorship." Howard Lee McBain, in *Bacon Lectures on the Constitution of the United States,* 1928-1938, Boston, Boston University Press, n.d., p. 383.

22 *Marbury* v. *Madison, loc. cit.,* p. 179.

23 Edward S. Corwin, *Twilight of the Supreme Court,* New Haven, Yale Uni-versity Press, 1934, p. 89. The same author says further: "Today the clause [due process of law] is chiefly important as a restriction upon the substantive content of legislation and what it means is, in effect . . . [that] legislation must not be 'arbitrary' or 'unreasonable'; but what this means, inevitably, and all that it means, is that legislation must not be unreasonable to the Court's way of thinking." *Court Over Constitution,* pp. 107-108. But what is due under due process of law is to be read—seen, shown—in the terms of the law. What is due is predetermined by the law; hence the judge himself has really no voice in it—his only voice is the voice of the law. Only an *ad hoc* arbiter can make his own voice or "way of thinking" the determiner of a decision. Judges of constitutional questions are not *ad hoc* arbiters. Seventeen years before the foregoing passage in *Court Over Constitution* was written, the Supreme Court itself said of due process of law: "The due process clause requires that every man shall have the protection of his day in court and the benefits of the gen-eral law, a law which hears before it condemns, which proceeds not arbitrarily

or capriciously but upon inquiry, and renders judgment only after [the hearing] . . ." *Truax* v. *Corrigan*, 257 U. S. 312, 332 (1921).

[24] It is sometimes said that without certain content, such as guarantees of personal liberty, there can be no due process of law. *Twining* v. *New Jersey, loc. cit.,* pp. 99, 107; *Palko* v. *Connecticut, loc. cit.,* p. 325; *DeJonge* v. *Oregon,* 299 U. S. 353, 364. Obviously some authority must say *what* personal liberties, and that, obviously too, the sovereign, the state, alone can say. For judges to claim authority to say it, in any degree, is despotism to that degree; for it is lawmaking of the most fundamental kind; and the very first provision of the Constitution bars judges from any lawmaking.

Were personal liberty prerequisite to due process of law, there could be no due process in prisons, in the Army, in any rigid system. But, in fact, law still rules in all of these, and the most abandoned culprit in any of them has a due. Implicit in the law is the due process, and it is nowhere else; hence those who make the law also make due process of law. To suppose that in order to have due process of law you must have certain prescribed laws is like supposing that in order to think, you must have certain prescribed topics of thought. "Substantive" due process in that sense is an illusion arising out of juridical mist.

It is also a veil faintly concealing a face which would not dare to show itself. Not due *process* of law but due *content* of law is the real claim. Of course there is no such thing as due content of law. *Due* to what? Above the sovereign there is no other, hence no reference for "due." The sovereign —the people—under such restraints as it may have uniquely willed, alone ultimately determines the content of law. In slightly different words (words of the Supreme Court heretofore), this is but "the right of the people to make their own laws, and alter them at their pleasure." *Hurtado* v. *California, loc. cit.,* p. 535.

With us the sovereign is the people, and the Constitution is a tablet in which are mirrored the features of our literal constitution: our governmental dispositions, convictions, resolutions, and an outline of measures for effectuating these. To single out such features as the disposition towards religion or voluntary association or expression, and call them God-given rights is unrealistic. The disposition towards voluntary association (freedom of assembly), for example, is no more a right than a disposition towards rest when tired is a right. It is something anterior to rights.

The Supreme Court, in the "absorption" operation by which it presumed to incorporate in the due-process clause of the Fourteenth Amendment the freedom guaranteed in the First Amendment, said that "neither liberty nor justice would exist . . . [without] freedom of thought and speech." *Palko* v. *Connecticut, loc. cit.,* p. 326. The First Amendment unconditionally forbids the Federal Government to deprive of freedom of speech; hence, if that prohibition inheres in due process of law, as the Court says, then the states, too, must be unconditionally forbidden to deprive anyone of freedom of speech.

Consider the consequence. If speech were wholly unrestrained (unless among angels), then slander, libel, malicious falsity would ensue, civility would disappear, and violence and chaos would reign. Justice Black has said: "I have no doubt myself that the provision [of the Constitution against abridgment of speech or press by congressional act], as written and adopted, intended that there should be no libel or defamation law in the United States under the

United States Government, just absolutely none so far as I am concerned."
45 *New York University Law Review* 234, 567. Justice Black, being one of
those judges who by "transmission" and "absorption" have contrived to impose
on the states the prohibitions the states imposed on the Federal Government
in the First Amendment, must mean that the states, the people, are powerless
to protect the most virtuous character against the most vicious tongue or pen.
Which is to say that not the people but the vilest blackguard among them
is sovereign; which in turn is a fresh indication of the extreme dereliction of
the Supreme Court in presuming to legislate to the states, or else it is a tacit
acknowledgment that the "transmission" and "absorption" artifices are unreal
and that the prohibitions upon the Federal Government are not prohibitions
upon the states.   Consider: If a state can deny women the liberty of working beyond certain hours, as the Supreme Court has held that it can (*West
Coast Hotel Company* v. *Parrish, loc. cit.*), then of course the idea—the Court's
own idea—of inviolable personal rights, of which the right of contract, abrogated in that case, is among the chief, is an illusion. If physical well-being,
with its consequences for the public health and welfare, is, without more, justification for restricting women's hours of work, then *where* they work must be
immaterial, and so the state must have power to restrict their work in the home:
power to deprive them of ordinary liberty. The proverb, "A woman's work is
never done," is then tacitly reversed by the Supreme Court, and with it the
hallowed legend, "A man's house is his castle." There is another proverb, or
legend, which the Court cannot reverse: "Power always corrupts." But the
Court can illustrate that, and does.

The Court said that woman is "properly placed in a class by herself, and
legislation designed for her protection may be sustained even when like legislation is not necessary for men and could not be sustained." *Ibid.*, p. 395. Then
to deny that the state can classify according to race, for reasons which may
be equally compelling, is arbitrary, to say the least.

A yet more express vindication by the Court of the state's authority to deprive of liberty is seen in *Twining* v. *New Jersey, loc. cit.* There it was held
that the state can compel a defendant in a criminal proceeding to be a witness against himself. If the state can do this, what can it not do in the way
of abrogating liberty? And if the Supreme Court has transcendent power,
through "transmittings" and "absorbings," to turn constitutional limitations of
the Federal Government into limitations upon the state governments, it seems
hardly credible that the Fifth Amendment prohibition upon the Federal Government against requiring a defendant to be a witness against himself should
not be turned into a like prohibition upon state governments, with results
opposite to that in *Twining*.

25 Cp.: "Courts cannot nullify an act of the state legislature on the vague
ground that they think it opposed to a general latent spirit supposed to pervade or underlie the Constitution, where neither the terms nor the implications of the instrument disclose any such restriction. *Such a power is denied
to the courts, because to concede it would be to make the courts sovereign
over both the constitution and the people, and convert the government into a
judicial despotism.*" *Loan Association* v. *Topeka*, 20 Wallace 655, 669.

26 *Hurtado* v. *California, loc. cit.*, p. 537.

27 For an account of meanings—one might say of wars of the Court with
itself over the meaning—of the term "liberty" as judicially conceived, cf.

Charles Warren in the Association of American Law Schools' *Selected Essays on Constitutional Law*, vol 2., pp. 237-266.

[28] "A right," says Thomas M. Cooley, "in any valuable sense can only be that which the law secures to its possessor, by requiring others to respect it, and to abstain from its violation . . . Rights . . . are the offspring of law; they are born of legal restraints." *Op. cit.*, p. 247.

[29] Blackstone, for example, speaks of "the absolute rights of man," such as "the power of acting as one sees fit," "a right inherent in us by birth, and one of the gifts of God to man." 1 *Comm.* 125. Madison invokes "the rights of nature paramount to all Constitutions." *North American Review*, vol. 31, p. 544. The Supreme Court has declared "the rights of life and personal liberty" to be "natural rights of man." *U. S.* v. *Cruikshank, loc. cit.*, p. 553. Is this not a confusion between natural power and juridically established rights, or between natural, brute law and enacted, legislated law? In the state of nature a man no more has rights than a sparrow has them. Naturally, he has, *owns*, nothing. He merely *is*, of such and such characteristics and capacities. He may seize things around him, but equally may another seize them, and from him. Nothing above or apart, nothing but brute power, sustains either of the two against the other. Without a contract or code the word "rights" denotes nothing.

Natural powers are a condition and final sanction of rights. But they are not rights, any more than pleasure, pain, and death are rights (these are only states or events). On the other hand, even such a thing as a standard of living, highly particularized, can be made a right, through articles of agreement between competent powers; and has been so made by the United Nations ("Universal Declaration of Human Rights," 24ff.). But unless backed by adequate enforcement power such a right, or any right, is vacuous. A right is only a shadow of power delegated by the sovereign. Cf. Friedrich Paulsen, *System of Ethics*, Frank Thilly trans., New York, Charles Scribner's Sons, 1899, pp. 625 ff.

[30] *Hurtado* v. *California, loc, cit.*, p. 535.

[31] Cp. the following, by Robert F. Kennedy, the Attorney General, written after traveling in Russia (he was then counsel to the U. S. Senate Permanent Subcommittee on Investigations):

"In every city that we visited there were two different school systems. There was one set of schools for the local children—those of a different color and race [Mongolian?] from the European Russian children. State and collective farms were operated by one group or the other, rarely by a mixture of both.

"Although work is supposedly being done to minimize the differences, many of the cities we visited were still split into two sections, with the finer residential areas being reserved for the European Russians. European Russians coming into the area receive a 30 per cent wage preferential over local inhabitants doing the same jobs. The whole pattern of segregation and discrimination was as pronounced in this area as virtually anywhere else in the world." New York *Times Magazine*, April 8, 1960, p. 60.

An article in the *U. S. News and World Report*, August 1, 1960, tells of sharp discrimination against African students in the University of Moscow.

[32] All of this went on before the introduction in Congress of the 1963 civil rights bill. Cf. ch. 3, n. 49.

Chapter 10

THE SUPREME COURT v. THE CONSTITUTION (II)

The Supreme Court's adventure in *Brown* v. *Board of Education* has since inspired a lower court to lay down integration terms which allow us to see more distinctly and fully the meaning of that case. In a New York City suburb, New Rochelle, there ran a protracted controversy over whether to retain a public school in a certain Negro neighborhood. Negroes cried segregation; whites proudly denied it. A vote was taken and went against closing the school, which would have meant dispersing the pupils among other schools, mostly white. The integrationists then brought suit to force a change. They alleged that the school board had gerrymandered the district in order to insure segregation. They won the decision, in the Federal district court, a decision brought in on a stream of racial rhetoric flowing from *Brown*.

The court, Kaufman J., sharply criticized the board for not solving the "problem" of "racial imbalance" in the school (there were 454 Negro pupils and 29 white—figures which the court said "certainly [do] not afford the Negro children . . . the educational and social contacts and interaction envisioned by *Brown*").[1] Judge Kaufman spoke of "racists" (persons who, I believe, recognize that there are racial differences—something now not quite legal for one to do? Will it, I wonder, presently be wrong to recognize the fat, the insane, the evil, and will those who persist in recognizing them be stigmatized from the judge's bench as fattists, insanists, and evilists?). He questioned, not too obliquely, whether the school board were men of good will, and lectured them about "moral" obligation (integrationists do not hesitate to presume themselves moral exemplars, and show no compunction against damning their adversaries as immoral).

If some have doubted that *Brown* means racial amalgamation, this will perhaps bring them to see. Not just an education for the Negro but "social contacts and interaction" are, it says, the aim. Drawing further on *Brown*, Judge Kaufman declares "the necessity of giving these minority-group children the opportunity for extensive contact"[2] with the others; a strange thing, surely, for the New Rochelle school, where the whites were the minority and were not seeking the alleged "opportunity" but, it seems, were shrinking from it. No doubt the judge was looking beyond the school to the whole community and to what might be termed community miscegenation, in the name of education and of *Brown*. What else is meant by "the necessity of . . . extensive contact"—*social* contact—and "interaction"?

So we are to understand that the United States Constitution exacts of a white person a draft on his white nature, his presence, his person, for use as a *facility* for Negroes. A pound of white flesh, so to say, ordered to be served to the Negro; only, it is more than flesh and more than poundage. The first Justice Harlan is remembered for his maxim that the Constitution is color-blind.[3] Look now at the Supreme Court and at Kaufman. By their will the Constitution is made to see both black and white and to require that the white be served to the black. What if integration and the vision of miscegenation are so repugnant that some localities will give up public education? Since that is their right[4] it is idle to impugn them, or no more justified than it would be for them to impugn others for insensitivity to the noisomeness, to them, of Negro-white mixing.

Judges have no justicial options; none, that is, affecting law and reason. Beyond their distinctive business of seeing, showing, ratiocinating the law and the facts, they cannot go, without usurpation and the betrayal of the judicial office. If their decision is not implicit in the premises relevant—the law and the facts—it is not real, not the true decision of the case, any more than a doctored, falsified laboratory result is a true scientific analysis. "Interpretation" cannot yield it—what is not in the law as it comes to the judge cannot be put into it by him, since he has no legislative power and no business with such power. Without infidelity to his office and his trust he cannot yield to his own or others' sentiments, or "morals;"[5] these are not the law. What difference is there between yielding to that kind of temptation and yielding to other kinds, for example, favoritism, egoism, aggrandizement, so far as administering justice is concerned? How can a man who is qualified by character and enlightenment for the judicial office yield to any of them? But one may read:

" . . . the judicial solution of doubtful cases is not to be explained solely by reference to the juristic materials on which such solution purports to rest. These materials from the outset furnish *legally* adequate basis for a pro-plaintiff solution and similarly adequate materials for a pro-defendant solution. In this situation the court was not only presented with the opportunity, it was presented with the *necessity*, of making a choice between two bodies of juristic materials of approximately equal respectability and weight, and it did so, with the inevitable result of expressing a preference and of forwarding views as to which the law had hitherto preserved neutrality.

"In short, decision is choice; the very circumstance which produces doubtful cases guarantees the Court what Justice Holmes has termed 'the sovereign prerogative of choice' in deciding them . . . [6]

" . . . alternative principles of construction and alternative lines of precedent constantly vest the Court with a freedom virtually legislative in scope in choosing the values which it shall promote through its reading of the Constitution.[7]

". . . the Court is able today to approach the question of factual justification from either one of two opposed angles, according as it wishes to sustain a statute or to overturn it, and is able to cite an ample array of precedents in justification of either approach."[8]

The proposition that courts of law cannot decide "doubtful" cases without resorting to "preference"—this is too naive. On the bench a competent judge has no preference. He makes no choice, but makes the law and the facts so apparent, so clearly set out in the balances, that he need only read off the result.[9] If no preponderance, then the petitioner or appellant has not established his case and therefore is the loser. Were the judge to indulge his "preference," that would make him a partisan, either against one of the litigants or against the law itself. Subversion, betrayal, corruption all take rise here.

If we are so misled as to believe that a judge must be a lawgiver, we only inspire him to act the part. Protected if a Federal judge by his lifetime tenure, and flattered by the judolatrous complaisance of the bar, he does perhaps answer to Professor Corwin's image of him here. A consequence is that a man never knows today, in the United States, whether tomorrow he will be made a criminal or a fool, not by anything he may have done contrary to law but by what the Federal courts will do.

Look about and you may happen to meet such an exhibit as this: "The Court's occasional departures from its own precedents are themselves amply justified by precedent."[10] In other words, default is justified by default. On this principle, which we learn from a Yale law professor, aberration of every sort—deceit, treachery, murder, ruin—is justified, being amply precedented. Enlightened thus, we are prepared for a further lesson: "Americans used to speak of 'a government of laws and not of men'. This was, as we must now know, a naive formula. There is no law in the world without men, for men must always interpret and mold and apply the law."[11] But though lawmakers are men, the laws they ordain are not men, nor attributes of men; rather, they are bonds to which men have made themselves subject, not unlike the laws of nature to which they are subject.

From this author, Charles L. Black Jr., we have also the "insight" that judicial review exists for "imprinting government action with the stamp of legitimacy."[12] Now if such a conception had any plausibility it would cease with the first Supreme Court "reversal" of its own decision. Self-contradiction, which is what such a "reversal" is, is self-destruction.

Mr. Black means that the Supreme Court tells us what laws we shall have (if the Court can "legitimatize" laws as well as nullify them, and can curb the states, Congress, and the President by "interpreting" the Constitution as it wills,[13] obviously it is not just a court but an oligarchy with absolute, autocratic powers). Blackstone said, "to set the judicial power above that of the legislature . . . would be subversive of all government;"[14] but Blackstone, presumably, is in the discard now, along with Marshall, thanks to "insights" such as the Yale professor's. In fact our whole system is in the discard if, as this author's "insights" tell him, the will of the Supreme Court is now the alpha and omega of the law. How does this veritable revolution come about? Law, says Professor Black, "has to be expressed in words—or, more accurately, law *exists* as words. No word can be warranted to have a unique correct meaning, without ambiguity or penumbra, and, if such perfectly clear words do exist, it is all too obvious that a great many words used in law are not of their kind . . . The term 'common carrier' [for example] is not a term of entirely fixed meaning; its meaning can be divined only from its usage, and its usage has been vague and shifting."[15]

It is utterly mistaken to suppose that law exists as words. If we respect niceties of legal usage, we hardly say that law exists at all. It *subsists*. The print in which it is engrossed or voice in which it is spoken exists, but they are categorially different from the law. The words are merely symbols of the law.

Without question or consideration he cheerily presumes that the terms of law pass into flux, regardless of the intention of the lawmakers; that the law being words and these being more or less fluid, the law too is fluid even though unchanged in the books. Words and their ways, then, are legislators, as well as those who sit in legislative halls. Who can believe this? Whereabouts in the law, the Constitution, the oath and obligation to support the Constitution, is there any warrant for this fanciful doctrine of irrigating and washing away the content of the law?[16]

The law fixes a standard and marks a course, to stand until further notice. Like a pledge, a contract, a will, laws are controls, not mere drift on the current of the times. Why write them down? They would flow away even during the writing. Law that does not stand is patently not law, and only what was duly enacted stands, or is. Further, only what was meant or clearly implied by the terms at adoption, is law.[17] What that was can always be ascertained by following the canons of construction; or, if not, it is void—terms, propositions admitting of no definite reference are by definition meaningless.[18]

Nor does a court, at least if it is faithful to its oath to the Constitution, *mold* law. It decides issues *according* to law. That is no more molding the law than an umpire's decision of a close play is molding the rules of the game. All the molding is done by the legislator. Any other is a usurpation of his authority. But "mold" is a gratifying term, like "grow," "evolve," and others, foreign though they are to the *bona fide* judicial act. More exactly, it is a persuasive, sophistical term, calculated to gain admission for meanings not to be found in the law.

The growth metaphor inspires second-order lawyers (law pedagogues) like nothing else. Under its spell they can vicariously indulge themselves as both legislators and judges, as in this:

" . . . The judge who decides a series of such questions [as that of whether the power of Congress to regulate commerce involves power to regulate navigation] is participating in the decision of the larger question: 'What kind of government are we to have?' Under the old myth [*sic*], he was simply recording what kind of government the Constitution, explicated by technical reason, said we were to have. But with the old myth gone he is taking part in this great process of decision on the basis, in part, of his belief as to what kind of government it is best for us to have, in the light of what he takes to be our highest political conceptions and our best ideals . . . "[19]

But the commerce clause *itself* does or does not involve power to regulate navigation, without regard to judges' beliefs about what is best for us. We are not in tutelage to judges; and their beliefs about what is best for us, or this professorial outsider's surmises about such beliefs, besides being no part of law, are of no more account than anyone else's. Only *our* beliefs or such as have been duly legislated, are of any pertinency. Judges who substitute theirs are subverting the judicial office and usurping sovereign power. The supposition that they have to do that is on a level with the supposition that a private citizen, instead of obeying the law, must on occasion substitute for the law his idea of what is best for the state. If simultaneously another private citizen substitutes an antithetical idea and the two collide, will the court let them both off, reasoning, forsooth, that chaos is best for us? *Reductio ad absurdum*, professor.

He quotes Justice Holmes, who had a way of making sophistry seem respectable: "The very considerations which judges most rarely mention, and always with an apology, are the secret root from which the law draws all the juices of life. I mean, of course, considerations of what is expedient for the community concerned."[20]

The judge must offer apology? Nonsense. Honesty, propriety never need to apologize. But if he defaults in the performance of his duties, he needs to offer more—his resignation. To ordain "what is expedient for the community concerned" is wholly legislative. (The judge's part is perfectly fulfilled when he exactly, faithfully, ascertains and applies the law—therein is the life of the law, so far a judgeship is concerned.) Expediency here is a matter of policy, and is therefore debatable; of public policy, therefore it is legislative, not judicial.

The idea that the *judge* is ever to determine what is best for the state is repugnant to *law*. What is best is something for the state— the sovereign alone, through its voice the legislator—to determine officially, and in the law as it stands the sovereign has spoken.

The Constitution does not *grow*, except as amended. The Bible, Plato, Shakespeare do not grow. Anyone who might mistake himself or his conceits for them would be laughed to scorn. The Supreme Court does not grow the Constitution. The presumption that it does, and that the Constitution is a pliant substance put at the disposal of judges, is wholly subversive, for it means that the judges, who are bound to uphold it, are, rather, empowered to remake it. The question whether the judges can "mold" or "grow"—modify—the Constitution is never legitimately before a court.

By induced vagueness—induced not from the Constitution itself, which is in terms singularly clear—the "molders" create an atmosphere calculated to obfuscate and so to give the appearance of shapes and substances not there. To hear them, one would think that where the Constitution does not minutely particularize, the judges are commissioned to "mold" its terms as they choose. What would they have —a reduction of the Constitution to singular terms corresponding to the language of certain savages who scarcely comprehend general words and have a different word for each individual thing?[21] Presumably we ought then to have a different word for each one of each man's rights, for each one's tax, each arrest, each fine, on the assumption that, otherwise, the judges will have to legislate in each case. Those who wrote and ratified the Constitution were too enlightened for such petty possibilities to occupy them.[22] Madison, less anticipating any need to guard against such a turn than striving to con-

vince the public that the proposed Constitution virtually precluded
tyranny and irresponsibility of all sorts, emphasized the duty of
judges to *ascertain* the meaning of constitutional terms, which is the
very antithesis of the "molding" and "growing" artifices. Madison
also went to pains to satisfy the public that the judiciary would be
drawn from men of such qualifications as to insure the highest integrity; and it may be doubted whether the Constitution would have
been adopted if the people had had any inkling that the Supreme
Court was to follow the career of inconstancy and aggrandizement
that in time it has come to follow.[23] Hamilton, too, gave assurances
of the adequacy of the Constitution against what all feared most,
namely, tyranny.[24] Today, because of the Court's license with constitutional terms, imposing on them now this meaning, now that,
now the opposite, we live under judicial opportunism rather than
under law.

We can justly ascribe to John Marshall a large share of blame
for this disaster, in spite of great virtues implicit in his work under
other aspects. In presuming to declare the Supreme Court supralegislative, with power to veto Congress directly, he gave this as a
ground: "It is emphatically the province and duty of the judicial
department to say what the law is."[25] Now to say what the law
is, is but to say what the lawmakers have ordained. Since judges
are not the lawmakers, they can only say what the legislature or
the framers of the constitution have said it is.

Here "say" is, and by Marshall is exploited as, an ambiguous
word. An author says such and such: his findings, productions,
opinions. Afterwards an expositor of his work may say it over to us.
He, the expositor, is in no sense the originator. He is but the second
or servant of the originator and of us, and suffers discredit as soon
as he presumes to substitute himself for his principal. Now at the
bar the judge is but an expositor and executant, showing the law and
determining, under the bond of fact, reason, and oath, the application of the law to the case before him. When he says in good faith
what the law is, he is only resaying what the lawmakers have said,
ordained, legislated; for only that, constitutionally, is the law. A
judge's mere saying is no more the making of law than a biologist's
saying is the making of life.

Implicit in every act of Congress is a presumption of respect for
the Congressmen's oath to uphold the Constitution, and hence a
presumption that congressional acts are congressionally held to be
constitutional. Since nothing in the Constitution expressly empowers
the Court to overrule Congress, Marshall's Court could only presume

that it had inherent power to do it, and that is what is involved in his dictum that it is the judge's duty to say what the law is.[26] He was not content to say, by due process of construction, what the Constitution provided, implied, or allowed; he went on to decree what the law must (not) *be.* In doing this he put the judicial authority above that of Congress and so broke the balance of powers designed by the authors of the Constitution. He thus opened the way for the aggrandizement and usurpation that have brought the Supreme Court to the oligarchic position it occupies today, a position beneath which both Congress and President bow in awe.

Since "the law"—judocratic law—is now a patchwork of contradictions, practically anything passes. Take this bit of woolgathering, a contribution of Justice Holmes to our jurisprudence: "prophecies of what the courts will do in fact . . . are what I mean by the law."[27] What if the prophets differ? Will the law be now this, now the opposite, according to the prophecies? Yes, he might have said; for consider judicial reversals, especially the Supreme Court's reversals of itself. Such, then, according to this judge, is the law, to wit: a gamble on what behest, or conceit, or vagary shall next issue from the areopagitic summit, good but till their fitful honors shall change their minds. Where, Your Honor, is the Constitution now? Or would you say, with your professorial disciple, that we are only naive if we suppose that we have a government of constitutional law and not of willful men?

Let one of our contemporary judges speak on this—Supreme Court Justice Douglas: "A judge who is asked to construe or interpret the Constitution often rejects the gloss which his predecessors have put on it . . . For the gloss may, in his view, offend the spirit of the Constitution or do violence to it . . . [A judge] cannot do otherwise [than reject precedent] unless he lets men long dead and unaware of the problems of the age in which he lives do his thinking for him."[28]

Gloss? A gloss *in his view?* If the gloss altered the Constitution, of course it was illicit, violating Article V (the amendment article). If it was not that, not illicit, then presumably it was only an explication, a showing of the content of the Constitution, in which case the judge who afterwards rejected it was in fact rejecting the Constitution, sworn though he was to support it. And "his view"—does this mean his disposition, predisposition, politics, or such? If so he was duty-bound, by his oath, to divest himself of it on the bench. Or does it mean that in some way, occult shall we suppose, a man is helplessly bound by egoism? Then this judge must be a stranger to science, where objectivity, the antithesis of one's "views," is a universal requirement; a stranger likewise to scholarship, where the same standard rules.[29] And since these standards are not altogether different from standards of law, it is inescapable that this judge, however high his merits otherwise, is representing himself in these utterances as a stranger to law also. Compare: "Under the guise of interpreting the Constitution we must take care that we do not import into the discussion our own personal views of what would be wise, just and fitting rules of government to be adopted by a free people and confound them with constitutional limitations."[30] Thus the Supreme Court at a time (1908) when it was not yet so captivated with itself as to be unable to distinguish between its ego and the Constitution.

If the Court can change the Constitution by taking liberties with its language, so can Congress. Both Court and Congress are under the same bond: to support the Constitution. If while bound to support it the Court can yet change it, even reverse it, Congress, and we might add the President, can with as good authority do the same. In law, none of them can do this; in fact, no one can destroy and support a thing at once. Support, security of the Constitution presupposes the integrity of its terms. By changing these in any manner or degree from what they were as adopted, the Court undermines the whole, in violation of its trust and office.

In lawmaking do we provide for, allow, or even countenance the possibility that what we prescribe shall be satisfied by something else, even its antithesis? If we did, lawmaking would be futile, and law itself would be a nullity. Now just such a program is tacitly attributed to the authors of the Constitution by judocracy; or if not that, then ineptitude and failure. How else could the judocrat presume "reversals," for example, to be constitutionally justified? To justify himself, this pretender does not balk at misrepresenting and reversing the founders of the country.

Those who condone this, as if intent on or indifferent to nullification, find nothing discomfiting in it as yet, since the visible results so far happen to accord with their special interests. But one "reversal," like one lie, may induce another. Where will the nullificationists be when the incidence is on them? Once the Court's decision is "reversed," once its decision is *not* its decision, anything goes: you are sustained and not sustained and the whole rational foundation of things, in this case the Constitution, has collapsed.[31]

This inner breakdown may be concealed or be too deep-lying to draw the attention of many, but it is there, the hard logical consequence of the inconstancy of the Supreme Court and its partisans.

The law cannot both be and not be.[32] A judge cannot both make and unmake, sustain and reverse, a declaration of law, as one cannot both tell lies and be truthful. A "reversal" is like a breach of contract or a bankruptcy. A judge who knows his business and scrupulously adheres to it will no more "reverse" what is not his to reverse —the Constitution, the law of the land—than he will take what is not his. He is not so shallow as to suppose that his mere saying is the law, which can be made over or unmade by another mere saying from the bench; nor so obtuse as to surmise that the authors of the Constitution in charging him to decide *cases* under oath to uphold the Constitution, were delegating him power to alter the Constitution in the slightest respect; nor so vain or delirious as to mistake himself for the law—a perversity on a par with a tradesman's weighing his hand in weighing out the goods to the customer. Such a one will not be found dissembling terms and committing himself to anything so specious as the proposition of *Brown* v. *Board of Education* that for things to be equal, such as education facilities, they cannot be separate; or decreeing the outrageous humiliation, in that shattering decision, making white children *facilities* to Negroes; or doing anything so perverse as using one part of the Constitution (Amendment XIV) to give the appearance of widening another (Amendment I), thereby abridging a third (Amendment X). Without a certain jealousy for truth and without the judicial wherewithal to bring it to prevail over the arts of dissimulation, other qualities in a judge such as pass for great liberality, great zeal for rights, great resoluteness, are only meretricious appearances, beneath which a reality of half-truth, inconsistency, arbitrariness, and obstinacy may soon be discovered.

In every instance in which the Supreme Court "reverses" itself on a constitutional question, it not only pronounces the law of the land to be not the law of the land, it wantonly casts down the judicial apparatus itself.[33] Thereafter the Court is literally unfitted to perform the judicial office, just as a perjured witness or one mentally deranged is unfitted to testify under oath. The fact that it continues to function, producing more and more "reversals" and even going so far as to avow a necessity for them,[34] only shows that it is functioning like a *de facto* government which has seized control upon default of the legitimate government. Only the toleration of a public oblivious to the implications, plus the complacency of Congress and the President, allows the pretensions of the Court thereafter to stand.

It might be objected that reason does not hold such great sway: though it controls where the premises are conceded, it does not sup-

ply or control them; discretion, resolution, even caprice, all beyond
the dominion of reason, are sources of the premises; and in the judicial process even so personal a voice as conscience may play a part.[35]
Still, one man's conscience is not another man's law, and even less
is it the law of the land.

Judocracy thinks of "the judicial mind" as if it were esoteric, and
of decision processes as if they resisted rational accounting. But a
judge not capable of articulating the ground of his decision is hardly
qualified for the bench. He cannot show that law is the ground,
and while this does not preclude its being the ground, it also does
not preclude arbitrariness and caprice. Yet worse, he leaves it all
a mystery (to know that you confront arbitrariness or caprice is
something—enough to put you on guard—but to be left mystified is
complete frustration). Out of this star chamber of the judicial mind
"reversals" may issue with ease, for the secret, mysterious powers
that are in control may shift in any direction when the same question happens to come before the judge a second time. Justly, legitimately, the same question can hardly return: nothing would ever
be judicially settled if it could. But litigants know he has "reversed"
before, and so have reason to try him again. They know, too, that
if he doesn't "reverse" this time, there is still a chance that he will
"distinguish," making seem a difference between Tweedledum on
Monday and Tweedledum again on Tuesday.[36] Thus the Supreme
Court may be overwhelmed with a thousand or more cases in its
year of eight or nine months, and be hotly divided five to four
again and again.

Implicit in any of the Supreme Court's "reversals" on constitutional questions is a denial that only the states have power to change
the Constitution (since any such "reversal" presumes to change
some constitutional principle or meaning promulgated by the Court
itself, by decreeing its opposite). This presumption is now made
explicit in the Court's summary denial of a state's right to exercise
its sovereignty by *interposition*. By means of interposition the state
asserts authority to repel what it believes to be an encroachment on
the powers reserved to it in Amendment X of the Constitution; it
interposes its authority between Federal authority and the people
of that state. The interposition may take the form of legislation
intended to bar the enforcement of Federal laws which the state
considers violative of states' rights. It may tacitly appeal to the
amendment provisions of the Constitution by initiating an informal

referendum of the states, in which the interposing state waits on the others to act, hoping that more than a fourth of them will side with it. If they do this, it will show that the three-fourths majority necessary for constitutionality is now lacking and consequently, the interpositionist believes, that the Federal action is in fact constitutionally groundless.[37]

The interposition question has been raised with regard to school integration and has been adjudicated. In Louisiana, a statute renouncing the authority of the Supreme Court decision in *Brown* v. *Board of Education* and barring Federal enforcement of school integration was adopted. Very soon it was before a special Federal district court in New Orleans, and very soon voided. Concerning the state's presumed right to judge the Federal action, the court said:

" . . . The fact is that the Constitution itself established the Supreme Court of the United States as the final tribunal for constitutional adjudication. By definition, there can be no appeal from its decisions . . .

" . . . there is nothing in Article V that justifies the presumption that what has authoritatively been declared to be the law ceases to be the law while the amendment [contemplated in interposition] is pending, or that the non-ratification of an amendment alters the Constitution or any decisions rendered under it.

"The conclusion is clear that interposition is not a constitutional doctrine."[38]

The Supreme Court, on appeal, quickly and unanimously sustained the lower court, and interposition, seen through its eyes, was dead. Not so in the eyes of interpositionists. Frank Voelker, Jr., chairman of the Louisiana State Sovereignty Commission, had this to say: "Our interposition was not addressed to the Supreme Court, and it was even presumptuous for the Court to pass on it." He said also that the state was "still interposing . . . our interposition is addressed to the states; we hold that the states are the final referees."[39]

When a state resorts to the sovereign powers reserved to it in Amendment X, has any branch of the Federal Government the legal capacity to contravene its action? Who, if anyone, shall give commands to sovereignty? In the event of a conflict between a state and the Supreme Court concerning the state's powers, who shall decide? Pending the decision, what is the status of a claim, or decision, of either the state or the Court?

Answers to these questions might seem to reduce to one: that the states have no capacity against Federal judicial authority.[40] Such is the answer of the New Orleans court, sustained unquestioningly by the Supreme Court: that the Supreme Court is "the ultimate judge of constitutionality."

This means that the Supreme Court's jurisdiction is not limited to matters in the Constitution but extends beyond, indefinitely beyond, since any matter beyond, if brought to judgment, will, merely by being defended on the ground that it is beyond the Constitution, present a question of constitutionality and so pass within the Court's power.[41] Thus the powers reserved to the states in Amendment X can be swallowed up. Just by being acknowledged in the Constitution to be beyond the scope of the Constitution, those powers are brought within its scope! Nominalism, casuistry, never went so far; words, language, never served so perversely to undo what they stood for, let us hope.

The Federal Government possesses a circumscribed, shadow sovereignty. If a state demurs to any of its acts, and to block them resorts to its own constitutionally reserved powers, Federal might is at hand with every resource to put it down. If the case concerns integration, the nearest of all subjects to the Federal courts now, an injunction comes forth with consummate dispatch, and the old lament about the law's delays is no longer quite understandable. The proceeding is in fact little more than a formality, the Federal authority being both prosecutor and judge. In case, however, of any need, the artifices of judocracy are omnificent. Terms will be redefined, "transmissions" and "absorptions" made, "moldings" artfully performed, and "evolutions" cited (in *Brown*, the term "equal" in "equal protection of the laws" is simply extended, distended, so as to encompass reserved powers of the states—a means capable of drawing any such power into the might of the Federal colossus).[42] At times the judocratic spirit rides high, tempting the mighty to deliver a crushing blow. Then comes a "reversal."

Probably no inkling of any of this was in the minds of the founders of the Federal Government. Hamilton, in appealing for ratification of the Constitution, gave assurances such as the following:

" . . . The State governments, by their original constitutions, are invested with complete sovereignty. In what does our security consist against usurpation from that quarter? Doubtless in the manner of their formation, and in the dependence of those who are to administer them upon the people. If the proposed construction of the federal government be found, upon an impartial examination of it, to be such as to afford, to a proper extent, the same species of security, all apprehensions on the score of usurpation ought to be discarded.[43]

"If the federal government should overpass the just bounds of its authority and make a tyrannical use of its powers, the people, whose creature it is, must appeal to the standard they have formed, and take such measures to redress the injury done to the Constitution as the exigency may suggest and prudence justify.[44]

" . . . To avoid an arbitrary discretion in the courts, it is indispensable that they should be bound down by strict rules and precedents, which serve to define and point out their duty in every particular case that comes before them . . . "[45]

Though Hamilton was grievously mistaken in some of his anticipations,[46] still it was the reasonings and assurances of men like him and Madison that persuaded the states to ratify. The comparison between what was promised and what now exists is that between "the greatest document ever struck by the hand of man" and a broken, dishonored compact. What was contemplated, what was imperative to a motley of revolted colonies with nothing to stay them but their own resource, was a government first so competent and secondly so honestly administered that it would stand of itself. Without high integrity, in the judiciary of all departments, the government would not very long have been a government. Where Hamilton lays it down that the courts shall be bound by strict rules and precedent, he is only saying this in different words. Madison is, if anything, more explicit. Federal jurisdiction "extends to certain enumerated objects only, and leaves to the several States a residuary and inviolable sovereignty over all other objects;" and though in "controversies relating to the boundary between the two jurisdictions" the Supreme Court is to make the decision, still the decision "is to be impartially made, according to the rules of the Constitution; and all the usual and most effectual precautions are to be taken to secure this impartiality."[47] But for pledges like these, there would probably have been no Constitution.

There is a serious lacuna in the Constitution which might still work harm even if judocracy had never arisen. Obviously a state has some constitutional right of interposition—it would not be sovereign, a state, if powerless to defend itself. But the means of effectively exercising its right are lacking. Though one state by itself can command nothing nationally, still it is only as states by themselves that the whole number of them or a three-fourths majority of them can command. They are added, not compounded, when they vote; hence if one cannot act, none can, and the sovereignty of the states is virtually extinguished.

Materially, factually, interposition is capable of conclusively demonstrating unconstitutionality. In case of a "reversal" the Court is committed to the assumption that what was established as constitutional ground in the decision reversed is no longer that, and has been replaced by its opposite. Now this means a constitutional change, of extreme character, and since only the states, by a majority of three-fourths, can change the Constitution at all, it is eminently appropriate for them to declare themselves on what has occurred. And the question for each declarant is only: Have I duly ratified this change? The negatives of thirteen states will defeat it and so make the "reversal" groundless. Of course interposition would aim at thirteen negatives.

Notice that it is not a matter of amendment, and hence that interposition need not conform with the procedure prescribed in the Constitution for that. It is only a matter of fact: the Court, if not utterly despotic must in "reversals" assume it to be fact that the Constitution, as duly found and declared in the precedent case or cases, has now been duly changed. To this the states need only declare what is the fact, and thirteen having declared in the negative, the Court's assumption will be an impossibility. The Court cannot rest on the sophistry that unless there was an amendment the old way still stands, for its "reversal" tacitly negates the old way, whereas the negatives of thirteen states tacitly reaffirm it. If now the Court does not retract, if it does not recall and renounce its "reversal" decision, it convicts itself of falsification (founding the decision on falsity) and of judicial despotism in imposing such a decision. If it is argued that the Court, in a "reversal," need not assume a change in the Constitution, the consequence is even worse; for that will mean that the Court, even more despotically, has flouted the Constitution and its oath to support it.

All of this, stemming from the amendment provision of the Constitution, plus regard for pertinent fact, is evidence of an implicit protection of states' rights in that provision.[48] But as matters stand, it is only an inferential sort of protection. Suppose thirteen states interposed with a bold constitutional *No* to some "reversal" decision. All that would result, most probably, would be: Federal court injunctions against state authorities, under sanction of imprisonment. And yet the conclusiveness and pertinency of what had been shown would be indisputable. An election on a bond issue, for example, resulting in less than a prescribed ratio of votes for passage, is no more decisive than this, and a thinking, non-judocratic court could not fail to see it. There is one difference, though it is extrinsic. In the election we can vote: means are provided and the results are effective; but on interposition we, the states, it seems, cannot.[49] Why? Because the courts, with the illogicality so often characteristic of them, have held interposition invalid and the states, awed or indifferent, have not asserted and effectuated their right. A due legal recognition of the arithmetical fact that if more than one-fourth of the states reject a policy, it cannot have, and therefore does not have, the three-fourths majority required for incorporation in the Constitution, and so cannot be presumed to justify a constitutional decision, would suffice. Evidently the Supreme Court believes that a constitutional amendment is necessary to establish the proposition that a fraction exceeding one-fourth does not, cannot, leave a remainder of three-fourths.[50] Well!

"The Constitution," the Court has said, "has left the performance of many duties in our governmental scheme to depend on the fidelity of the executive and legislative action and, ultimately, on the vigilance of the people in exercising their political rights."[51] Indeed. And what of the performance of judicial duties? On what does the Constitution leave that to depend? Ostensibly on nothing but good behavior—the judiciary article of the Constitution lays no other distinct requirement; no test or answerability, nothing positive to guard against partiality, caprice, tyranny. It contemplates a judiciary detached and neutral—as neutral as a pair of balances— eminently enlightened, and possessed of probity in the highest degree. One attribute of this exalted magistracy is "a power . . . such as it [the judiciary] has never possessed in any other country."[52] As we noticed, the men who expounded the Constitution to the states in the critical time before its ratification, gave very particular accounts of what to expect. There was certainly a dependence of the judiciary, according to them, a dependence on high fidelity and juridical competence; and in the event of misprision, usurpation, violation of states' rights, the states should at their own discretion rise and throw off the imposture.

That is to say, the Constitution implied another source of vigilance: the states. In them was an implied power over everything done in the name of the Constitution, and for their own protection and that of the Constitution, vigilance was always necessary. The Supreme Court in *Colegrove* v. *Green* was therefore in very poor grace in calling on the country to watch others in the government though not calling on the country to watch the Court.

It is proverbial that the laws assist those who are vigilant, not those who sleep over their rights. But it is not proverbial, rather it is repugnant to justice and to probity of mind, that the country should have to keep up a vigil on the Supreme Court lest it take away the rights it is constitutionally bound to uphold. No states keep such a vigil, it is true. While they slept, the Supreme Court transformed the Constitution: stretched the terms to suit itself; reversed meanings altogether, and even affected to use the Constitution to put down any—interpositionists—who, having become vigilant, mildly heeded the counsel of its great exponents by initiating steps to insure fidelity to it. "As the people are the only legitimate fountain of power [under the Constitution, according to Jefferson], and it is from them that the constitutional charter . . . is derived, it seems strictly consonant to the republican theory, to recur to the same original authority, not only whenever it may be necessary to enlarge, diminish, or new-model the powers of the government, but also whenever any one of the departments may commit encroachments on the chartered authorities of the others . . . how are the encroachments of the stronger to be prevented, or the wrongs of the weaker to be redressed, without an appeal to the people themselves, who, as the grantors of the commission, can alone declare its true meaning, and enforce its observance?"[53]

It is no wonder that judocracy should be deaf to this, and quick to arrest any stirrings it may cause; for the like of it is the death of judocracy. It is the sovereign ringingly articulate, before the onset of its somnolence. The answers to all our questions—whether Federal authority can lawfully contravene state action in defense of state rights; who shall judge such a question; what shall be the status of Federal incursions or decisions meanwhile—all the answers lie here, sleeping, like the sovereign powers which have slept so long. They are not answers that judocracy, itself on trial, is competent to give, nor are they hidden from non-jurists (reason and a sense for fact are antecedent to and the final ground of legal answers, and are not confined to nor always best exemplified by the bar).

A controversy between a state and the Supreme Court over reserved powers of the state, is obviously not to be adjudicated by either of the two. A judiciary in the least sensitive to proprieties of law and justice or not blinded by judomania would not fail to see that in an issue of this kind it itself was on trial and could no more enjoin the proceedings against it than a criminal defendant can enjoin them against him, and could no more judge its own cause, as it presumed to do in the Louisiana instance, than the criminal can judge his. Obviously the reserved, sovereign power of the state is not subject to any Federal organ, including the Court (the only way this has been kept from view is by the judocratic tactics of encroachment, making it appear that all is within the Federal jurisdiction in any instant case). A conflict between the two must accordingly be judged by a third. With us, having no Crown, no sovereign but ourselves, that one is, as Jefferson observed, simply the people, which is to say, practically, the states jointly. Except for judocratic obfuscation, this would have declared itself at the first arisal of the question, for anything so obvious is eloquent of itself; but the obfuscation precluded or discouraged the formation and development of a technique of procedure by which the plaintiff state could bring its case. Consequently, interposition, the only recourse, is made to look like outlawry when in fact it is a sovereign voice speaking. It is not too much to say that if the Constitution had been insistently held before the eyes of the first judocrats, their future would have been so troubled that they must have desisted, and that bars and controls over them such as might almost be read out of the Constitution would have been established. Possibly a paper parliament of all the states, for the resolution of questions between any one of them and the Federal power, would have formed, and a route to it for appellant states would have been designated, which might now be as clearly marked as the route up to the Supreme Court.

In that case would it not have been something more than a paper parliament, namely, a second, supererogatory United States? A plausible conjecture is that it would not, for a very potent reason: the Supreme Court would have seen the handwriting on high and returned to the status so evidently determined for it in the Constitution and so clearly delineated by the *Federalist* expositors. In that event appeals to this impromptu parliament would not have been necessary many times, and if abused would have elicited measures for regulating them, too. The whole effect must have been to keep the Constitution unobscured, unaltered, and unobstructed and so to preclude the artifices of judocrats for substituting their will for it.

In words inspired by Jefferson: "the several states who formed that instrument [the Constitution], being sovereign and independent, have the unquestionable right to judge of the infraction [by Federal acts]; and . . . a nullification, by those sovereignties, of all unauthorized acts done under color of that instrument, is the rightful remedy."[54]

And in the words of Madison: "The states, then, being the parties to the constitutional compact, and in their sovereign capacity, it follows of necessity that there can be no tribunal, above their authority, to decide, in the last resort, whether the compact made by them be violated; and consequently, that, as the parties to it, they must themselves decide, in the last resort, such questions as may be of sufficient magnitude to require their interposition."[55]

Put beside the utterances of the Federal courts in the Louisiana interposition case, this must have been disturbing to any who took satisfaction in such utterances. It is idle to lean on the formality that the judges were acting in the judicial capacity and Jefferson not; for that presumes that coming from the bench a decision or opinion is endowed with indisputable authority, without more. Jefferson is denying that the authority presumed in such a case even exists.

Interposition is a form of sovereign self-defense. It exposes Federal aggrandizement to the world and elicits from the bench, as may be seen in the Louisiana instance, and from apologists for the bench as we have seen at some length in this book, those forced defenses that only betray the duplicity underlying. Besides this, interposition is an alarm and appeal sent out to the other states—one or two states standing alone against the Federal giant would be doomed. The appeal is a desperate call for a moral stay of a challenged Federal action pending a decision by the ultimate sovereign, the states, or people.

The lack of an express provision or convention for carrying an appeal to the shadow parliament of states is insignificant when we consider the powers left to the states in Amendment X. No Federal organ can legally judge these powers or presume to say what they will do when rallied or solicited by one of the states; hence none can presume to decide the outcome of an interposition appeal to them. The Supreme Court, Congress, the President all are outsiders here. Any encroachment by them on this domain is as much a violation of sovereignty as the like on Mexico or Canada would be. And to forbid or try to checkmate such an appeal differs very little from trying at Washington to block an appeal by one of the Mexican states or Canadian provinces to the others. The comparison may be carried farther. Consider the South, its history, its racial realities, and the shock of all the obliquities by which *Brown* v. *Board of Education* was thrust upon it. What difference is there between the South's lot now and the lot of the border states of Russia under the Russian yoke? In the integrationist fanfare a good deal is surmised about what the world will think of us if integration is obstructed here.[56] What would it think, I wonder, if truly apprised of this internal tyranny in the nation claiming first place as an exemplar of freedom? What would it think if informed that our cherished Constitution, our model to the world of liberty and security, can be turned inside out by a *court*, made to mean what the judges, by five votes and answerable to no one, wish it to mean? And what would the civilized world think of the Supreme Court doctrine that white school pupils are public *facilities* to Negroes?

When such a doctrine can be forced on anybody, barbarism holds sway. Argument, reason are in eclipse. The Supreme Court, by no showing of law, fact, or reason, but solely by the antithesis of each, is so easily the winner in its contest with the Constitution that the Constitution might as well have pleaded *nolo contendere*. Judocracy knows no law. Its words drip perfidy. A forthright mind, witnessing it in operation, is overcome and shrinks from it as from a noisome, odious spectacle.

<hr/>

[1] *Taylor* v. *Board of Education of New Rochelle*, 191 F. Supp. 181.

[2] *Ibid.*, p. 192.

[3] *Plessy* v. *Ferguson, loc. cit.*, p. 559.

[4] Even this is now questioned by Federal judges. A special bench of them in New Orleans went so far as to poll attorneys general of all the states on whether, under the equal-protection and due-process clauses, a state or subdivision is free to close down its public schools permanently. A singular question and singular judicial course, and the more so when considered alongside a simultaneous action of the United States Attorney General aimed at compelling Virginia to close all its public schools if one county, where they were closed, would not capitulate to integration and reopen them. It signifies that equal protection and due process, thanks to the tactics of judocracy, are now, with some, an enigma, capable of what you will.

Suppose the answer to the judges' question is No (as it was from some of the states). Then what of such particulars as: how many schools there must be, how many and what kinds of courses, how long a term, what educational standards? Who but the courts shall now decide such questions? What will the teachers say, if any are left who are willing to work under such a regime—or will the courts put them under injunction and hold them like captives? And where will the money come from? Will marshals or paratroopers be sent in to compel the legislature or city council to vote it, and the taxpayers to pay it?

If Washington can compel a state to have schools or any certain school, then the state is practically stripped of sovereignty and reduced to the level of a minion of the Federal Government. Why should it then act at all— why not close down, leaving all to Washington? Of course Washington is not prepared for that; and the extent to which it is not prepared is a measure of the extent to which the Supreme Court has overreached itself: of its aggrandizement and usurpation.

Suppose a community where there are only parochial schools; must it at the behest of Washington establish public schools and force a new kind of integration, namely, secular and religious? Will people be forbidden to send their children to private schools? Will these be obliged to close? Absurdity generates agsurdity: the mysterious transformation of equal protection and due process at the hands of judocracy produces this mockery of the Constitution and of the judicial office.

[5] Cp. ". . . no rule, whether of morality or of law, which contravenes an Act of Parliament, binds any Court throughout the realm." A.V. Dicey, *op. cit.*, p. 425.

[6] Edward S. Corwin, *Twilight of the Supreme Court*, pp. 114-115. Cp. below, n. 9.

[7] *Ibid.*, p. 117. [8] *Ibid.*, p. 86.

[9] What is termed "freedom of judicial decision" probably devolved the following inference, made not in jest but full academic seriousness: ". . . most so-called 'doubtful cases' could very evidently have been decided just the opposite way to which they were decided without the least infraction of the rules of logical discourse or the least attenuation of the principle of *stare decisis*." Corwin, *ibid.*, p. 114.

But are judges really given "freedom of judicial decision"? Who gave it? Not, assuredly, the givers of the Constitution, who were not prodigals, and not intent on contriving for judocracy, and who took care to bind the judges to uphold the Constitution, unconditionally. If the law and facts of a case are seen impartially they do not yield antithetical decisions as presumed here; they are or they are not thus and so, they logically entail or they do not logically entail such and such consequences.

Every choice, if such it is, of a premise in any controversial matter may legitimately be met with "Why?", to which it will never be an answer just to say "Because I choose." Arbitrariness, abuse, caprice are tolerable at no point in the process. What else will choice, substantive choice, be? Will it not be, in particular, a cryptic *ex post facto* law enacted then and there by the judge? Let him show his hand.

If he performs the judicial task of demonstrably ascertaining the answer to the question before him, the judge no more has to choose, to will, to favor than a teacher does in answering a pupil's question. The correct, true answer is not chosen, it is proved; which discredits such visionary conceptions as this: "The pre-existence of a body of legal rules does not eliminate discretion on the part of the judge whether he shall apply them . . . the complexity of the issues presented to him and the wealth of competing analogies frequently allow a judge to make his own constructive choice without resort to strict deduction from existing legal rules . . . The so-called reasoning may be no more than a judicial reflex, or an intuitive or emotional reaction." A. G. Guest, ed., *Oxford Essays in Jurisprudence*, London, Oxford University Press, 1961, pp. 177, 187. Justice Black thinks somewhat this way too. ". . . constitutional provisions do require courts to choose between competing policies, such as the Fourth Amendment which, by its terms, necessitates a judicial decision as to what is an 'unreasonable' search or seizure." *Rochin* v. *California, loc. cit.*, p. 176. But deciding a question according to law and fact is by no means a matter of choosing between "competing policies." Mr. Guest himself seems to demur and recant. He says, some lines farther on, ". . . the object of the legal process is decision, and there has to be a reasoned justification for the decision made." *Op. cit.*, p. 187.

Justice Holmes was another who at times maundered in these mists. He remarked, "You can give any conclusion a logical form." *Collected Legal Papers*, New York, Peter Smith, 1952, p. 181. Yes. But that does not give the argument logical *soundness*, which requires, further, that the premises be true; and judges cannot *give* the true, but must demonstrably ascertain it, down to the last detail.

[10] Charles L. Black, Jr., *op. cit.*, p. 31.

[11] *Ibid.*, p. 32. To say there is no law without men "to interpret and mold and apply" it is like saying there is no science but applied science. Interpreting law is

only showing it, apropos of cases; and lawfully, a judge can no more mold the law than he can mold the facts of a case.

12 *Ibid.,* p. 223.

13 Denying Marshall, he says "the judge's 'will' must sometimes play a part." *Ibid.,* p. 164.

14 1 *Comm.* 91.   15 *Op. cit.,* pp. 162, 163.

16 The whole concept of fluidity or plasticity in constitutional terms is inconsistent with law. The only terms in the Constitution are of course those written and ratified by the authorities who established it, and the only meanings are those they impressed or implied (obviously so, for no one means anything other than what *he* means). They are a tablet descended to us which only a counterfeiting could change. Of course diligent inquiry may discover contents unnoticed before, but only if they are there. It can add nothing.

The language of 1789 or 1868 is not redefined by changes in today's usage. The words are signs, those of the past pointing their way, ours pointing perhaps another. Not the words but what they point to is what controls. Judocrats and their apologists thrive by keeping this distinction from sight, a deception comparable to hiding a legacy from a legatee by making him think the past bequeaths nothing. "Due" today may have a different meaning from "due" yesterday, likewise "process" and "law," but all such meaning is beyond constitutional due process of law, not having been legally adopted. A law on the books is not one thing today, another tomorrow, one thing to this person, another to that, so nullifying equal protection. Language is not the law but only a register or album of it.

In a Louisiana Federal court proceeding challenging a state law under which the voters of one parish (county) had elected to abolish public schools, the presiding judge said, "in today's concept of due process of law, a child has a right to a public education, even though a state's constitution has no requirement for maintenance of such a public school system." Baton Rouge *State-Times,* April 14, 1961. *Today's* concept—is it the concept inscribed in the Fourteenth Amendment in 1868 or in the Fifth Amendment in 1791? Under that concept school segregation was not questioned. No change of it, no amendment to it, has been made in the Constitution. What then can "today's concept" of due process of law have to do with constitutional due process of law? Of course nothing—unless you will say that the Constitution sympathetically changes with changes in our concepts: that it is not a fixed, firm legal instrument but a conceptual fashionplate, which is to say not a constitution at all. The case in question is reported in 197 F. Supp. 649.

The Constitution is not water nor a drift on water; it is a governing course through waters. A written constitution is necessarily of that nature, since a writing is not self-amending. There are, however, cliches in juridical parlance which tacitly deny this, and color legal authorship and teaching. To "give meaning" or "give content" to a term is, for example, a supposed prerogative of judgeship. If this is strictly meant it is transparent fiction; if loosely meant it is a deception. To give either meaning or content would presume that the legislators had not done so and that the judges were empowered to substitute for them and really make the laws. That would be judocracy, or artless dictatorship. A *judge* no more gives content or meaning to the laws than an astronomer gives stars to the heavens. He sees and shows it, rather: takes it from them instead of giving it to them. If he gives anything it is only a linguistic expression, to us, not to them. The lawmakers and they alone, lawfully, give the content and meaning.

Constitutional fluidity, as the doctrine here might be called, is entirely foreign to the American constitutional conception. It is subversion in disguise. Remove the disguise and you find judolatry bearing gifts to judocracy.

[17] Professor Corwin speaks of "the inherent capacity of words to take on new meanings" and thinks it a "reasonable assumption" that the lawmaker has this in mind in lawmaking. *Twilight of the Supreme Court,* p. 113. Now can it be seriously thought that lawmakers resign themselves, and us, to so vague a government as that of next year's or the next decade's linguistic usage? *Who* does this and where are the proofs that he does? Imagine a candidate who committed himself to such a policy—how could he pledge any definite thing and how should we know what to expect of him? Quite the contrary; only his, our, usage now—only that usage is or can be legislated, since to legislate requires terms and meanings, and we have only such terms and meanings as we do have. In making a contract, what if one party, to vary Professor Corwin's example slightly, counted on "the inherent capacity" of minds to change, and offered that as a reason for taking it upon himself to alter the contract terms after a while; would any court sustain him, would anyone care to enter a contract with him, would he not be inherently incapable of making a contract? I am afraid a prospective lawmaker of like stamp would be inherently incapable if being elected.

[18] It is a consequence of this that if we rely on the Supreme Court decision in *Brown* v. *Board of Education,* as well may we reject that decision. For there the Court despaired, ostensibly, of finding the constitutional intent of equal protection in regard to education, yet at the same time declared that equal protection meant integration; which is the same as to say that the point, the law, is unascertainable, yet is ascertained; it is not, yet is. So we, if we rely on the decision, must withal reject its ground and therefore it, thanks to the Court's inconsistency. We must, like the Court, reverse ourselves, so to speak. Reversal unfounds and corrupts in all directions when made the general policy or "law."

"Thieves for their robbery have authority/When judges steal themselves." Shakespeare, *Measure for Measure,* II, 2.

[19] *Op. cit.,* p. 166. [20] *Ibid.,* p. 164.

[21] See, for example, Otto Jespersen, *Language,* London, George Allen & Unwin, 1922, p. 429. "If," says the Oxford philosopher Friedrich Waismann, "language was such that each and every word was peculiar and each colour word had a definite, clearly defined meaning, we should find that we could not use it. That is, we should come up against alternatives: 'Was it this colour or not?'—which we could not decide. I cannot get back to the impression I had then . . ." A. G. N. Flew, ed., *Logic and Language, Second Series,* Oxford, Basil Blackwell, 1953, p. 21.

The dean of law at Yale writes of judges as "lawmakers in applying the words and history of the Constitution to new situations." Eugene V. Rostow, *Sovereign Prerogative,* New Haven, Yale University Press, 1962, p. 131. This presumes that the legislator cannot see ahead or else that life and the world are so indeterminate that nothing can gauge them, and hence that many eventualities which judges have to handle are extra-legal. But then, being outside the law, such eventualities must not belong in the judges' lap; and if it is now said, perversely, that they really are not outside, then they are covered already and there is no need of making more law to cover them. The law a judge deals in is already made—all *law* is.

Would judge-made law stand? Would the judge who made it be bound to adhere to it? What would bind him? For if he can make law at all, can he not make it at will and so make a new one the next time? He could always *distinguish,* and hence need never admit that the question before him was the same as a previous one. Although this must be repugnant to even the crudest conception of law, it has a vogue among academic lawyers. It is little different from the "law of the case" doctrine. According to that, a judicial decision is not law itself but only evidence of the law, good for the instant case. The Supreme Court has said of decisions: "They are, at most, only evidence of what the laws are, and are not themselves laws. They are often re-examined, reversed, and qualified by the Courts themselves . . . " *Swift* v. *Tyson,* 16 Peters 1, 18 (1842). Any litigant, anyone who has experienced the law, must be astonished by this. To him the law was applied, by him it was borne, in him it was realized. To him it was a force taking away or sustaining property, liberty, life. The judges here must not have realized what they were saying.

The decision and its opposite, or reversal, could not both be evidence of law (they might be evidence of caprice, folly, or worse). As evidence, one of them would cancel the other. But which? Both being decisions, equally authentic, how could we tell which was to stand? Law thus evidenced would be law, yet not law. This is literal reduction to absurdity, carrying with it into absurdity the "law of the case" doctrine, if not also the "judge-made law" doctrine.

22 Courts *per se* are no more authorities on words than on philology or physics, and hence it would become them to turn for enlightenment to those who are authorities. From a very large body of learning which they would find, I pick one sentence concerning words and meaning: "If we know what a word designates, we know the conditions and applicability of the word; we know under what conditions we can apply the word to a given particular thing in the world and under what conditions we cannot." John Hospers, *Introduction to Philosophical Analysis,* New York, Prentice-Hall, 1953, p. 25.

It would be very presumptuous to say that the words in the Constitution were specious, cryptic, equivocal, or otherwise indeterminate at the adoption of the Constitution (even if they were, *bona fide* decisions at law could only treat them so and hence refuse to apply them—law is nothing if not univocal). What the designations were, is surely ascertainable through faithful application of the canons of construction.

23 *Federalist* 39.

24 *Federalist* 78. See also an article "Government by Judiciary," by L. B. Boudin in the *Political Science Quarterly,* vol, 26, pp. 238-270.

25 *Marbury* v. *Madison, loc. cit.,* p. 177. It is paradoxical, to say the least, that a court should judge itself, and something is grievously amiss when it either has to do so or wills to do so. If a judge must recuse himself when he has a connection with a party before his court, *a fortiori* must the court do so in the event that it itself is a party or virtually so. The anomaly of such a turn, the impropriety of a court's putting itself in a position where it passes judgment on itself, is a fair measure of the blunder that got the court into that position, the blunder, in this case, of presuming to pass judgment on a coordinate branch of the Government. If Congress overreaches itself, the Supreme

Court need not do so. And if this leaves things at loose ends or worse, the remedy is with the sovereign, the states or people.

Jefferson said on this topic, speaking of the executive branch as well as the legislative and judiciary: " . . . each of the three departments has equally the right to decide for itself what is its duty under the Constitution, without any regard to what the others may have decided for themselves under a similar question." Quoted in E. S. Corwin, *The Supreme Court Over the Constitution,* p. 70. Madison held the same view: "As the three branches of government are coordinate and equally bound to support the Constitution, each must in the exercise of its functions be guided by the text of the Constitution according to its own interpretation of it . . . " *Ibid.,* p. 7. And, "I beg to know, upon what principle it can be contended, that any one department draws from the Constitution greater powers than another, in making out the limits of the powers of the several departments . . . Nothing has yet been offered to invalidate the doctrine, that the meaning of the Constitution may as well be ascertained by the legislative as by the judicial authority." *Ibid.,* p. 50.

26 The idea that a court, in a system of government such as ours, has inherent power to invalidate an act of Congress is a contradiction in terms. It presumes legislative power (unmaking laws is either legislative, and hence contrary, in a court, to the first provision of the Constitution, or else it is destructive of the legislative power and hence destructive of the Constitution). The courts are instruments, effectors, of the law, not makers or unmakers of it. That a court *per se* should presume to make or unmake law is the same as an ambassador presuming to make or unmake government policy, or an executor presuming to make or unmake the will entrusted to him. That an English court should venture to overthrow an act of Parliament is, in England, I believe, incredible (see Dicey, *op. cit.,* p. 425)—a telling refutation of suppositions that a court has inherent power over the laws.

27 *Collected Legal Papers,* p. 173. Compare Justice Brewer: "The courts . . . make no laws, they establish no policy, they never enter into the domain of public action. They do not govern." Quoted in E. S. Corwin, *Twilight of the Supreme Court,* p. xxv. Said Chief Justice Waite: "Our [the Supreme Court's] province is to decide what the law is, not to declare what it should be . . . If the law is wrong, it ought to be changed, but the power for that is not with us." *Minor* v. *Happersett,* 21 Wallace 162, 178 (1875).

28 Quoted in Blaustein and Ferguson, *op. cit.,* p. 24.

29 Cp.: "Science . . . may be regarded as a minimal problem, consisting of the completest possible presentment of facts with the least possible expenditure of thought." Ernst Mach, *Science of Mechanics,* Thomas J. McCormack trans., 5th ed., LaSalle, Ill., Open Court Publishing Co., 1942, p. 587. "Scientific method, broadly speaking, consists of techniques and rules designed to make degrees of belief coincide as nearly as possible with degrees of credibility." Bertrand Russell, *Human Knowledge: Its Scope and Limits,* London, George Allen & Unwin, 1948, p. 414. "Historical understanding . . . demands that the historian be detached from himself and that he recognize the differences between himself and his fellow men." Raymond Aron in *Evidence and Inference,* Daniel Lerner ed., Chicago, Free Press of Glencoe, 1960, p. 26.

30 *Twining* v. *New Jersey, loc. cit.,* p. 106.

31 It cannot be maintained with any logicality that the reversal *per se* supersedes the reversed decision. It only contradicts it, and contradiction has no

sequential import—one contradictory is not before or after the other; if temporal at all, they are simultaneous, logically tenseless. Even if we take the later decision to be controlling, the Supreme Court cannot do so without usurping either the lawmaking power, in violation of Article I of the Constitution, or the amending power, in violation of Article V. If it is said that this is only formalistic and does not fully represent what has occurred; that the passage of time between the original decision and the reversal of it has materially altered the case; I answer, first, the law is the law through time, it is not washed away by the flow of events; secondly, the only repeal of a law is by legislative act and the only modification of the Constitution is by amendment; hence, as before, the Court is chargeable with usurping either congressional power or state power.

32 It is easy and even a commonplace for law to be mistaken for the sources of law. So distinguished a jurist as Holmes has, it seems, made this mistake on the first page of his *Common Law*. "The life of the law has not been logic," he says, "it has been experience. The felt necessities of the time, the prevalent moral and political theories, intuitions of public policy, avowed or unconscious, even the prejudices which judges share with their fellow-men, have had a good deal more to do than the syllogism in determining the rules by which man should be governed." Boston, Little, Brown & Co., 1923. But in fact it is not the life of the law that is before us in a miscellany like this, but the life of the people. The law is no doubt a fixation and register of these forces and more; but it and they are far from being the same, just as a law of nature is very different from the phenomena answering to it, or an epitaph very different from the dead. No matter what it is founded on, it, the law, stands until duly changed or repealed.

What Holmes brought out might, with a little more appropriateness, be called the life and death of the law. But the life, once the law is born, is of a different order, which is more like reason, logic, than it is like the flux of affairs that impressed him. The law lives—stands, is real—only as it is unaffected by this flux. It lives, applies, only as it articulates with reason. Ascertaining whether in a particular issue it does so articulate is, ironically for Holmes' dictum, a matter almost entirely of logic. His identification of logic with the syllogism was very amateurish, like identifying mathematics with long division. About the same time that he was doing this and declaring the inadequacy of the syllogism to the law, another, the prominent constitutional scholar Edward S. Corwin, wrote: "The judicial function is essentially a syllogistic one . . . " *Twilight of the Supreme Court*, p. 114.

33 As will be seen in ch. 11, a "reversal" of a constitutional decision cannot be redeemed on the ground of correcting previous judicial error; for the law of the land, which the Court has promulgated in the previous decision, cannot be judicial error. Nor can changed conditions or new information avail, for that would require that they first be enacted into law, which would mean judicial usurpation of the lawmaking function. Against such pretension of the judiciary stands also the following: If a law is made, it was not extant before, and the operation by which it is made, if it is a Federal law, can be performed only by Congress, or by the states jointly in case of making or amending the Constitution. If there was no such law before, the judges cannot be expounding *it*. Then what they are doing is indistinguishable from judicial usurpation; that is, despotism.

34 As in: "This case calls upon us to reconsider a precedent decision, as the Court throughout its history often has been required to do." *West Virginia Board of Education* v. *Barnette, loc. cit.,* p. 360. Put a little more plainly, but not distortively, this says the Court is "required" to consider whether the law of the land is not the law of the land. The Court is never required to embrace absurdity, which is what this is. Suppose the outcome is a "reversal," as it was here. Then everything done by the previous decision must be undone, else justice is travestied. But to do that will almost certainly be *ultra vires*—in some cases it would require resurrection of the dead. Further, no decision could ever be made or enforced without risk of discrimination and gross injustice; for the possibility of its "reversal" would always hover over it.

35 For example, Mr. Norman S. Marsh writes: "The judge in this broad sense [of having no "license to act in an arbitrary manner"] is bound by the law, and the fundamental assumptions of a free society underlying it, which he must interpret to the best of his abilities in the light of his own conscience." But he adds, concerning a proposal to the International Commission of Jurists at New Delhi in 1959: "The reference to the judge's abilities and conscience . . . was omitted in the Conclusions of the Committee on the Judiciary and the Legal Profession . . . presumably for fear that it might suggest an arbitrary and incalculable element in the judicial function." In A. G. Guest, *op. cit.,* p. 253.

36 Reversals have taken on the character of comedy when, as in a 1961 instance concerning use in court of illegally obtained evidence against a defendant, *Mapp* v. *Ohio,* 367 U. S. 643, the press takes note that this reversed a 1949 decision, which reversed one of 1914, and goes on to anticipate a reversal presently of the 1961 instance, merely on the presumption that one reversal justifies another. Baton Rouge *State-Times,* June 24, 1961.

And if precedent might be desired for cyclical or chain reversals, as these may fitly be called, it is readily found in several directions. From one of these comes the following example:

"Thus, we have this situation: in 1907, the Court expressly left the question [of free speech—whether it is protected in the states by the due-process clause of the Constitution] undecided; in 1920, it stated that it did not consider it or decide it, but simply conceded it for the purposes of the case; in 1922, it stated that the Federal Constitution 'imposes upon the States no obligation to confer upon those within their jurisdiction either the right of free speech or the right of silence.' Yet, in 1925, it stated that 'we may and do assume' that freedom of speech and of the press is one of the 'fundamental personal rights and liberties' protected by the due process clause. And hence, in 1925, the Court adopted as the law on this point, the dissenting opinions of Judge Harlan in 1907, and of Judge Brandeis in 1920." Charles Warren, in Association of American Law Schools, *op. cit.,* vol. 2, p. 260. The Court "adopted as the law"—*sic.* Perhaps this is only a slip of the pen, nevertheless, in its way it is a contribution to judocracy. Courts, being bound by the law, do not *adopt* it. They have no such option. They have the duty to uphold and apply *the* law given them. To this it might be replied that the law is a question—What is *the* law? Which invites the cynical answer, Try finding out from the Court's continual it-is, it-is-not argument with itself. What the Court duly found and pronounced to be the law the first time is what it is unless subsequently changed by the lawmaker; for otherwise the law is not the law, the Court is made ridiculous, and government is frustrated.

Radiated into academic halls, the motif of judicial inconstancy becomes solemnly farcical. One may read:

"It is probably true, as Charles Warren asserts, that when the word 'liberty' was included in the Fifth and Fourteenth Amendments it was intended to suggest no more than the old English idea of the right of a person to be free from physical restraint (arrest) without due process of law . . . But when one recalls that the whole concept of due process of law in the English tradition apparently applied only to *procedural* matters and that the application of this clause after 1890 to the *substantive* content of social and economic legislation represented a distinct addition to or growth in the original meaning, a similar expansion of the word 'liberty' seems entirely possible and proper.

"The attempt to persuade the Supreme Court to expand [*sic*] the meaning of the word 'liberty' developed much more slowly than the similar attempt to obtain protection for property and business against governmental regulation through an expansion of the word 'property' in the Fourteenth Amendment.

". . . it seems proper that a majority which finds its desires being frustrated through the exercise of judicial power should endeavor to exert pressure upon judges to see things its way." Robert K. Carr, *The Supreme Court and Judicial Review,* New York, Farrar & Rhinehart, 1942, pp. 178f, 292.

So the law, the Constitution, is wax in the Court's hands, to be made into what the judicial lobbyist, a creature of the judolatrous mind, can induce the Court to make it. Having taken a little liberty (with, ironically, liberty itself), let the judges take more, and more, till I and my side get what we want. A fit comparison of this base illegitimacy, this abject, unconscious degradation contemplated for our highest judgeships, comes to mind from an episode in the novel, *Tess of the d'Urbervilles,* by Thomas Hardy. The girl has an illegitimate baby, which is taken in by her family and grows to be so much liked by the girl's little brother that he appeals to her: "Have another one, Tess"!

[37] In *Kohl* v. *United States,* 91 U. S. 367, interposition was put on trial nearly a century ago, and held void.

[38] *Bush* v. *Orleans Parish School Board,* 188 F. Supp. 916, 925, 926. Evidently the courts misapprehend the interpositionist in saying that nonratification of an amendment would not alter the Constitution. Of course it wouldn't, nor need the interpositionist presume that it would. What it would do would be to show that a judicial assumption of such and such constitutional ground had been repudiated by the ultimate constitutional authority, the states, and hence that the resulting decision could not be, in reality, constitutional.

Formally, legally, this would probably amount to nothing; for what could a demi-amendment, one put in motion by extra-constitutional means, establish constitutionally? To be valid, to make any difference against a decision, it would have to pass through the prescribed amendment procedure, including initiation by two-thirds of the states or of Congress. But then it would be an amendment, not an interposition. To say that the questioned constitutional article stood until duly amended or repealed, and that a change of sentiment meanwhile on the part of thirteen states made no difference, would, though formally correct, be in fact only an artful dodge. *De jure,* interposition may be nothing, but *de facto* it is capable of showing that the *de jure* claim is now hollow and only needs to be put to trial to be invalidated.

Still, before any state, sovereign though it is, could raise its voice effectively, the two-thirds majority would have to whisper approval. Between the urge to speak and the occasion of being heard—though, mind you, it is sovereign states that would speak—there is a space over which the judges maintain an iron rule. The Constitution keeps the doors closed and the judges are un-approachable behind them. What they say, that, ostensibly, meretriciously, is the law: any meaning may be given to a constitutional term, any decision may be "reversed," the Supreme Court can stand the country on its consitutional head, and nothing can be done to stop it unless two-thirds of us rise and start an amendment action against it.

Back of the heaviness of the amendment design was the purpose of insuring stability in the new central government, lest it die like its predecessor under the Articles of Confederation. (*Federalist* 49) And now we have a judicial establishment which can freely unmake the law of the land, remake it, unmake it, indefinitely, even to farcicality. This, the ultimate of instability, procured with the help of a device to insure stability! The explanation? In one word, infidelity. The framers put utmost faith in the integrity and loyalty of the bench. The above is their, and our, reward.

[39] Baton Rouge *State-Times*, December 13 and 16, 1960.

[40] The New Orleans court said: "From the fact that the Supreme Court of the United States rather than any state authority is the ultimate judge of con-stitutionality, another consequence . . . results. It is that the jurisdiction of the lower federal courts and the correctness of their decisions on constitutional ques-tions cannot be reviewed by the state governments." *Loc. cit.*, p. 925. This is a patent *non sequitur*. From the premise that A has consummate, unchallengeable authority, it by no means follows that B, his subordinate, has it. Of course a state government, having no Federal jurisdiction, cannot review Federal judicial decisions. But this is not the point. Interposition purports to be an expression of state sovereignty, which sovereignty created the Federal establishment and retained power to limit it at will. Though the Supreme Court is the court of last resort on a question of Federal constitutionality, it still is not the ultimate determiner. The states, or people, are that. Madison observed: "However true . . . it may be, that the [Federal] judicial department is, in all questions sub-mitted to it by the forms of the Constitution, to decide in the last resort, this resort must necessarily be deemed the last in relation to the authorities of the other departments of the government; not in relation to the rights of the parties to the constitutional compact, from which the judicial, as well as the other departments, hold their delegated trusts." Jonathan Elliot, *op. cit.*, p. 549. Jeffer-son said: "[the states alone are] parties to the compact, and solely authorized to judge in the last resort of the powers exercised under it." *Works*, vol. 8, p. 471. We hear much today about respect for courts. Do the courts ever hear anything about respect for the power over them?

[41] Judicial power is above all parties, though in a limited sense. It is power under the Constitution, not over it. The states, having powers both over the Constitution and extrinsic to it (Article V, Amendment X), are ultimately over the Federal courts and, in all respects but those specified in the Constitution, are independent of them. The question now arises, Is the Federal judiciary to override the Constitution and engross powers which the Constitution knows only in the states? Here the conflict is not between the states and the Federal Government *per se*, but between the states and the Supreme Court. The states, in interposing their sovereignty, do nothing but what the Constitution, according

to its expositors in the *Federalist,* contemplated in the event of aggrandizement by any Federal branch (see above, p. 237).

It is out of the question to judge whether a state, acting in its sovereign capacity, is legally right or wrong, since there is no law over the sovereign. But in our dual system of state and federal government the question, Where are the boundaries, and is such and such act a sovereign act? is continually alive. When the Supreme Court takes the liberty of modifying constitutional terms this question may arise between the Court and the states. Who then shall judge? Certainly not one of the adversaries—not the Court, for example. The Constitution makes no explicit provision for resolving a controversy between a state and the Supreme Court; which must signify, first, that such an eventuality is left to the sovereign constitutional authority, the states, to provide for if need be, and secondly, that the authors of the Constituion had such confidence in the competence, integrity, and loyalty of the bench that they scarcely entertained the possibility of judicial defalcation and aggrandizement, under which we slavishly live.

42 Since 1871 any extension of Federal power into the sphere of powers reserved to the states is, aside from being obviously a violation of rights under Amendment X, a veto of the decision that year in *Collector v. Day,* 11 Wall., 113, expressly declaring their inviolability. The obviousness of the violation may in time become a shield against it and bring under scrutiny the chief devices used by judocracy to strip the states of their sovereign powers: the equal-protection and due-process-of-law clauses, transformed into master-keys for opening any lock in a state's entire reserve. It would be guesswork, however, to suppose that this critical inspection is likely to go far. Federal encroachment is not only obvious to the states, but is in a manner courted by them, for it carries money with it. Ease and security are dearer than rights, to a softened, indifferent society. A sign of the light esteem for states' rights today is seen in the coolness towards interposition.

43 *Federalist* 31. 44 *Federalist* 33. 45 *Federalist* 78.

46 For example, ". . . I am at a loss to discover what temptation the persons intrusted with the administration of the general government could ever feel to divest the States of the residuary authorities [powers not delegated to the general government]" (*Federalist* 17); ". . . there is greater probability of encroachment by the members [states] upon the federal head, than by the federal head upon the members" (*Federalist* 31); ". . . bills of right in the sense and to the extent in which they are contended for, are not only unnecessary in the proposed Constitution, but would even be dangerous" (*Federalist* 84).

47 *Federalist* 39.

48 Some, including Madison, have thought this illegitimate, but that is by no means shown. Either you have the required three-fourths majority or you do not, and if you do not, the amendment fails. Madison wrote: ". . . to establish a positive and permanent rule, giving such power to such a minority over such a majority, would overturn the first principle of free government, and in practice necessarily overturn the government itself." *North American Review,* vol. 31 (1830), p. 543. Voting down an amendment or any proposal requiring a three-fourths majority for adoption is by no means putting the majority at the mercy of the minority. Rather, it is but disproving a majority presumption, the truth of which is a necessary ground for the action or policy in question. The principle is virtually the same as that followed in scientific and learned investigations, in

which the investigator searches for "negative instances," which at once disprove a positive contention. And instead of overturning a government founded on constitutional principles, it would thwart policies and actions which ignore or defy the principles, and so would contribute to sustaining the government.

⁴⁹ It might be objected that enlisting 13 states against an amendment would be more like enlisting 13 votes against the bonds. Yes, provided there were only 26 qualified voters and, say, 51 per cent were necessary for passage. Or it might be said that the analogue of the 13 interposing states would have to be, say, 13 voters opposed to the bonds, who take it on themselves to declare their opposition and count on that to defeat the bonds without an election. To this the answer is that straw votes are sometimes taken, and may work that way.

⁵⁰ Apart from the logic of the case, there is an inequitableness about it, which an alert judiciary would long since have redressed or exposed for others to redress. The states have an indefinite range of sovereign powers, yet frustrated by the aggrandizement of the courts, they cannot exercise some of them unless, after a round-robin subscribed by two-thirds, they initiate and can gain adoption of an amendment specifying the right to exercise them. That is to say, the absolute, inviolable powers in Amendment X are made to depend on Article V of the Constitution. This is a contradiction in terms, such powers being of course wholly independent. In fact, application of Article V, the procedure of adopting an amendment, is itself dependent on the exercise of sovereign powers such as those reserved in Amendment X, since without that exercise no amendment could be voted. Deprivation of a right by naked power is unethical *per se,* being incompatible with the concept or institution of rights. Depriving a state in this manner is comparable to depriving a person of inalienable attributes, as his eyesight or hearing. In order to look around him or call his dog, must he first obtain permission of others present?

⁵¹ *Colegrove* v. *Green, loc. cit.,* p. 556.

⁵² Thomas M. Cooley, *op. cit.,* p. 41.

⁵³ In the *Federalist,* no. 49. That Jefferson had in mind not the prospect of conflicts between Federal and state power but between the three Federal branches is immaterial; for his location of sovereignty in the people and his recognition of their exclusive, ultimate authority to determine constitutional questions, applies equally and perhaps with him even more emphatically to conflicts between Federal and state powers.

⁵⁴ Elliot, *op. cit.,* p. 545.

⁵⁵ *Ibid.,* p. 548. The words of Madison here and of Jefferson in the passage just before accord very closely if not exactly with the stand of the governors of Mississippi and Alabama against Federal authority at the time integration was forced on their state universities, 1962-1963. If it is asked what had happened between the time Madison and Jefferson spoke and the time of the constitutional debacle preceding the scandalous occurrences at those universities, the answer may be fittingly indicated in one word: Judocracy.

⁵⁶ A candid regard for the realities would cool the zeal about this. What the integrationist press and Washington policy wish us to look like in foreign eyes is hardly identifiable with what we exhibit at home. Lately we have been solicitous, officially, of Africans and are growing so sensitive about it that a stranger might suppose we were trying to persuade ourselves as much as them. Who is deceived? "Insults, phone calls, and threats are almost our daily lot for the past two years in New York and Washington," and there are " 'constant

and painful' threats to the security and tranquillity of Negro diplomats in this country"—thus one of the Africans, Telli Dialli, of Guinea (Associated Press, July 6, 1961).

Perhaps it is the mortifying effect of such realities that motivates the Government's action in behalf of mass attacks on racial barriers in the South, as at Montgomery in 1961. Out of the shock tactics applied there, the following policy might be read: Strike where it is easiest, and likeliest to stir notoriety.—I wonder, are there symptoms of sadism in this?—If it had been desired to test the Montgomery segregation laws without instigating violence, of course that could easily have been done at any time. But it would not have been spectacular —and this was an occasion for contrived, petty martyrdom and for sensational Federal action as if to convince the world and make it forget the realities in New York, Washington, and elsewhere.

Spontaneous racial violence was rather frequent about that time in New York and Chicago, but Washington took no hand. "During the past week, nearly two dozen persons were attacked and beaten by gangs of Negro teen-agers" in a Chicago neighborhood where one, a Negro, was killed and another, white, was stabbed and left lying on a sidewalk (United Press International, July 18, 1961). In New York City 1,171 policemen were attacked, though not in racial clashes only, the first six months of 1961 (New York *Times*, August 21, 1961). Further:

"One apartment house alone has had thirty such incidents (rapes and 'muggings') this year. And similar complaints are heard far and wide.

"Now this is obviously intolerable in a supposedly civilized city . . . It is a crisis when people have to organize as vigilantes to protect life and property." New York *Herald Tribune*, September 12, 1962.

Official Washington is so carried away with the will to integrate that sometimes it strains the limits of civility, to say nothing of the now commonplace inroads on personal rights. Here, for instance, is the former Secretary of Labor, Arthur J. Goldberg, since elevated to a seat on the Supreme Court, lashing out at clubs that exclude Negroes, calling them "a miserable source of bigotry and prejudice" (Associated Press, April 29, 1961). He goes on to complain that Negroes are not invited into white homes. The idea is spread that since Washington is now more than half Negro, "a failure to provide an equal number of Negroes at cocktail parties and at official as well as private dinners is a form of 'discrimination'" (David Lawrence newspaper column, May 22, 1961). Attorney-General Kennedy goes farther, lambasting Boston for rejecting Irish and Catholics in the past, and contemporary Northern journalists for criticizing segregation in the South while they themselves segregate in their clubs—all of which he calls hypocrisy (United Press International, April 27, 1961). The Secretary of the Interior, Steward L. Udall, finds occasion to coerce the Washington professional football team into putting on a Negro player! (United Press International, June 14, 1961)

When nothing else succeeds, the integrationist is not above flouting the amenities and stigmatizing people he never saw, with the epithet "immoral" or the like. Secretary Goldberg, with apocalyptic gravity, had spoken of a "moral imperative" to integrate, and the judge in the New Rochelle school case presumed to castigate the school board on "moral" grounds. Some things the world, or a good part of it, instinctively abhors; for instance, lying, betrayal, calumniation. These, at any rate, we might agree to call immoral. Assuredly it is calumniation, hence immoral itself, to pronounce anyone, without enlightened consideration and because he does not feel as you do, immoral. "He who reflects on another man's want of breeding," it was remarked by Caesar, "shows he wants it as much himself." Plutarch, *Lives,* A. H. Clough trans., Boston, Little, Brown & Co., 5 vols., 1885, vol. 4, p. 274. "Wherein thou judgest another, thou condemnest thyself." St. Paul, *Romans,* 2:1. The distinctions between natural kinds, the aversion of one type or element to another, the keeping of distance, is of no more moral significance than the difference between tall and short, pretty and ugly.

All the make-believe and affected moralizing here come to nought before one simple datum of racial reality: the panic and flight of white people upon news that Negroes are moving into their neighborhood. Negroes themselves have been driven to a suicidal strategy by this. "Panic selling by white persons in an integrated section of the Lakeview community near Hempstead, New York, has led to a campaign by Negro residents to keep the area from becoming predominantly Negro" (Associated Press, June 20, 1961). The item goes on to say that the Negroes "run the risk of creating a segregated situation" and that the hope is to keep to the "present ratio of about eight white persons to each Negro" —something reminiscent of the ratio written into the Constitution, Article I, Section 2, for use in counting the population. In Baltimore a Negro lawyer, "having succeeded in crossing the housing barrier into an upper-middle-class white neighborhood . . . fears the settling of more Negroes on his street will lower the value of his own property and create a slum area" (*Johns Hopkins Magazine,* March, 1961, p. 11).

Integrationist writers uniformly betray and sometimes candidly admit incomprehension of some of the racial realities in a segregated community. One in the *New Yorker,* for example, was nonplussed over "just exactly what effect" the possible domination of white people in an Alabama community by a plurality of Negroes "would have on their daily lives" (June 10, 1961, p. 73). Perhaps it would have improved his comprehension to inform himself first on matters closer home; for instance, by reconnoitering the panic scene in Lakeview. It is doubtful, however, that anything short of miracle would have overcome his mystification at "the absence of menace from the atmosphere, and, more than that, the courtesy displayed in nearly all casual encounters between the races" in the Southern community (p. 66). His perplexity is rather like that of the foreigner in England, over many things, epitomized in his question about how the downy lawns and swards are produced, and the answer "Only a matter of planting four centuries ago and cultivating steadily." Only culture perceives culture.

The significance of the white and black ratios sometimes proposed for neighborhoods is worth consideration. Is it an admission of contentment with token integration or of a realization that that is all the Negro can expect? In either case it means that real integration, such as the New Rochelle judge with his idea of "social contact and interaction" contemplated, is an illusion. It means, to take the suggested Lakeview scale, that seven-eighths of the Negroes are to be doubly segregated—segregated first by the one-eighth who manage to cross the barrier and, secondly, by nature taking its course. Doubtless, intelligent and undeceived Negroes will feel the sting of this. Honest segregation must be more tolerable to an honest mind than pseudo integration.

Chapter 11

JUDICIAL PROBITY

Lawyers and judges are a fraternity with usages and dignities worthy of the highest respect. Over this fraternity, in the United States, is the lofty authority of the Supreme Court. It is a little like the Crown in England and commands a corresponding homage in the profession here. If a lawyer would criticize it, he is likely to suffer criticism himself for impropriety and although he may have instructive information to give, yet he may find the channels of publication closed to him.

Within the guild this is perfectly understandable. It is just as in the army and navy and clergy. Guild members must always conform with guild rules.

Guilds exist, however, only as means to ends, and their inner formalities may be but remotely related to the appointed ends, and of no concern at all to outsiders. A great deal of what has been said since 1954 against criticism of the Supreme Court flounders in confusion over the formalities of law or of the bar, on the one hand, and the concrete realities of the law and its incidence on the people on the other hand.

Respect for authority, judicial, political, clerical, or other, has no prestige over reason, fact, or truth. When such authority speaks on these, it, like everyone else, is subject to them. If it fails to respect this limitation, it proves itself arbitrary and provokes challenge. Some of the bar have been grievously disturbed by what they seem to regard as mutiny against the king, or Court. For example, Professor Charles Fairman of the Harvard Law School, writing on "The Attack on the Segregation Cases" (he seems apologetic for the word "attack," a rude word in the vocabulary of the robe), opens an article in the *Harvard Law Review* with these apprehensions: "The Supreme Court has run into a storm of protest, as severe as it has ever encountered. If the protests are unjust, then the protestants, however sincere, are doing enormous public harm. I believe that the attacks are unjust, that on the controverted matters the Court has been right, that it has acted with courage, and that it merits our confidence and support."[1]

The "enormous public harm" would be, presumably, a loss in the prestige of the Court, since there would surely be no substantial harm but on the contrary a substantial public benefit in bringing out and condemning errors in law, fact, or reason, or abuses of authority, on the Court's part if such have occurred. Possibly Professor Fairman means that the Court must not be challenged lest respect for law suffer. This would presume that the Court was the law or that it approximated infallibility or sanctity in its apprehension of the law. But the Court's recent career of reversing itself and more and more undermining public confidence is hardly in keeping with law, infallibility, or sanctity. And from what we have seen in this book of its handling of the school cases—a performance which, for appraisal of fact, respect for reason and law, and even correctness of reference and accuracy of statement, would do little credit to a law sophomore—from this it must be apparent that the unstinted support Professor Fairman solicits for the Court is hardly what the facts, seriously regarded, suggest. It is apparent that Mr. Fairman has not studiously considered the facts or that he so exalts the judicial office that he forgets what it is for. Where he is confident that "on the controverted matters the Court has been right," many others are confident that it has been wrong, Congress even going so far as to establish a sub-committee to keep watch on its actions (below, p. 319). Who is right or wrong, or what rightness and wrongness here consist of—such is not the question legally, but is rather a snare which hardly ever fails to catch those who confuse law and sentiment and who incline to substitute their own sentiment for the law. Here the only pertinent idea of right and wrong is the one embodied in the law. Were it otherwise, every man, in all his dealings regulated by law, would be subject to extra-legal and hence fortuitous, irresponsible, yet binding judgment.

As if speaking for the American bar in answer to criticisms of the segregation decisions and as if answering the "Declaration of Constitutional Principles" made by some ninety-six Southern Senators and Congressmen in the two houses of Congress on March 12, 1956, a group of approximately one hundred prominent lawyers, law professors, and law deans from all sections of the country came before the public on October 27, 1956 with a criticism of critics of the Court and an appeal for public respect for the Court.[2] The following are some passages from the Southern Declaration.

"We regard the decision of the Supreme Court in the school cases as a clear abuse of judicial power. It climaxes a trend in the Federal Judiciary undertaking to legislate, in derogation of the authority of Congress, and to encroach upon the reserved rights of the States and the people.

"The original Constitution does not mention education. Neither does the Fourteenth Amendment nor any other Amendment. The debates preceding the submission of the Fourteenth Amendment clearly show that there was no intent that it should affect the systems of education maintained by the States.

"The very Congress which proposed the Amendment subsequently provided for segregated schools in the District of Columbia.

"When the Amendment was adopted in 1868, there were 37 States of the Union. Every one of the 26 States that had any substantial racial differences among its people either approved the operation of segregated schools already in existence or subsequently established such schools by action of the same law-making body which considered the Fourteenth Amendment. . .

"In the case of *Plessy* v. *Ferguson* in 1896 the Supreme Court expressly declared that under the Fourteenth Amendment no person was denied any of his rights if the States provided separate but equal public facilities. This decision has been followed in many other cases. It is notable that the Supreme Court, speaking through Chief Justice Taft, a former President of the United States, unanimously declared in 1927 in *Lum* v. *Rice* that the 'separate but equal' principle is '. . . within the discretion of the State in regulating its public schools and does not conflict with the Fourteenth Amendment.'

"This interpretation, restated time and again, became a part of the life of the people of many of the States and confirmed their habits, customs, traditions and way of life. It is founded on elemental humanity and common sense, for parents should not be deprived by government of the right to direct the lives and education of their own children.

"Though there has been no constitutional amendment or Act of Congress changing this established legal principle almost a century old, the Supreme Court of the United States, with no legal basis for such action, undertook to exercise their naked judicial power and substituted their personal political and social ideas for the established law of the land . . .

"We reaffirm our reliance on the Constitution as the fundamental law of the land.

"We decry the Supreme Court's encroachments on rights reserved to the States and to the people, contrary to established law and to the Constitution.

"We commend the motives of those States which have declared the intention to resist forced integration by any lawful means . . .

"We pledge ourselves to use all lawful means to bring about a reversal of this decision which is contrary to the Constitution and to prevent the use of force in its implementation."[3]

While admitting that the Court is not above criticism, the hundred lawyers who rose to its defense protested against what they called abuse of it and reckless attacks on it. Of such they said: "To accuse the Court of usurping authority when it reviews legislative acts or of exercising 'naked power' is to jeopardize the very institution of judicial review."[4]

Reading this, one might suppose that people were abusing the Court just because it "reviewed legislative acts." That of course is not the case; and it illustrates how easily some, in disputing a question like segregation, may fall into the ways of sophistry. The like may be said of the next sentence, reading, "To appeal for 'resistance' to decisions of the Court 'by any lawful means' is to utter a self-contradiction, whose ambiguity can only be calculated to promote disrespect for our fundamental law." Here it is presumed that since the Constitution is the supreme law of the land and is ultimately applied through Supreme Court interpretations of it, lawful opposition to such interpretations must be a contradiction in terms. Were that so, a person could never lawfully oppose anything the Court says on the Constitution; and since the Court has often said opposite, contradictory things on it, reversing itself again and again, the country would be practically silenced and the constitutional rights of free speech, press, and assembly would be practically nullified. Likewise the constitutional provision for amendments would be burked or made superfluous. All this in consequence of this counsel, volunteered by the hundred lawyers. How far the lawyers have forgotten the laws! And how far short they have fallen of meeting the Southerners' argument. That argument called only for lawful resistance, which of course can be carried on in manifold ways, thanks to the manifoldness of the law (for which thanks to lawyers). And the example of Lincoln is still vivid, confounding them: "that burlesque upon judicial decisions [the Dred Scott decision] must be overruled and expunged from the books of authority."[5]

Further, if it is lawless to oppose a Supreme Court decision, as the distinguished counsel say here, then it was lawless for the appellants in the 1954 school cases to have opposed the Plessy decision of 1896 and the numerous other decisions upholding segregation. Thus counsel in convicting one party of lawlessness upholds lawlessness in the other. And this after arraigning Congressmen and Senators for illogicality!

Perhaps it is by like reasoning that they accuse their adversaries of "disrespect for our fundamental law" and go on to say "our concern

is for the tradition of law observance and respect for the judiciary . . ."
This intimates that those who disagree with the 1954 decisions, or
other decisions, and advocate opposing them by lawful means, are
without respect for the judiciary. We are to suppose, then, that Lincoln
lacked such respect and that the Thirteenth and Fourteenth Amendments, so far as due to his efforts, are a perpetuation, in the Constitution itself, of disrespect for the judiciary. This is confounded nonsense
and the hundred lawyers must either not have meant what they said
or not have comprehended what they said. Were they serious? Did
they really believe that a hundred Senators and Congressmen, among
them some of the most eminent, lacked respect for the judiciary just
because they felt outraged by one or two Court decisions?

Respect is not abjection. Neither is it a shield to hide misfeasance
in the respected. Nor is it to be confused with veneration. The essence
of respect seems to be deference to a right or dignity. Now the
peculiar right, or office, of a court of justice is to make binding legal
decisions, and in making them it commands unqualified respect. The
prerogative of deciding, the unique authority back of the deciding, is
the object of respect. But though a decision carries indisputable
authority in its sphere, miscarriages may have occurred in the process
by which it was reached. Where questions of fact or reason are concerned, the court has no special authority. There others may judge
with greater authority, and all with some authority—why else the
jury system? Since all, "we the people," are ultimately the source of
law, they may reject the court's decision by changing the law. In the
meantime they are free, and by the Bill of Rights secure, to criticize
the decision.

Do the one hundred themselves respect a decision drawn from a
piece of gibberish, such as "more explicit safeguard of prohibited unfairness"? Or the outrageous infraction of reason in the conceit,
"Separate educational facilities are inherently unequal"? Or the
odious implication that white pupils are educational *facilities*, publicly
coercible, to Negro pupils? Or the confusion, only incidental it is true
but certainly a mark of carelessness, between a Chinaman and a
schoolgirl? Are they in earnest with themselves in upholding this
recklessness or passing it by in silence, or is it possible they are so
possessed by curial devotion that they don't realize what they are
doing? (They say the Court treated the case "with the utmost deliberation"!) Are they respectful to their adversaries in maligning them
for standing against such patent abuse of our highest judicial office?
If Yes to all this, then are they qualified spokesmen for the bar?

They speak like royalists alleging *lèse majesté,* and to some may call to mind Francis Bacon's sage observation: "lawyers, being bound and subject to the decrees of the laws prevailing in their several countries . . . have not their judgment free, but write as in fetters."[6] But the Court is not just the crown of the American bar and is no more royal than the executive or legislative, including the Congressmen and Senators these men have maligned. Merit, constancy, trustworthiness are the only material grounds of the Court's prestige. A man can courteously conform with all the amenities and yet for good reason condemn a court decision. Error, irrationality, misfeasance are reprehensible everywhere, not excluding the courts.

Strictly, the Supreme Court, acting in its unique judicial capacity, cannot err. Supreme, it is above judicial correction and so above judicial error—what it decrees is *per se* the model of judicial correctness, not because the Court is supremely wise and perspicacious, but because its decisions are judicially final. The late Justice Jackson said: "The Supreme Court is not final because infallible, but infallible because final."[7] The infallibility, however, is only circumstantial, *ex officio*, residing in the prerogative of ultimate decision-making; for as soon as the principle of the decision is enunciated or found out (it must have a principle drawn from the law, otherwise it is arbitrary), it is open to question. Like any mortal the Court errs if it misjudges fact or reason, and then it is subject to correction, to check and balance, at the hands of the other branches of government. Only in the exercise of the discretion inherent in its office, only, that is, in the act of deciding the bearing of law upon law and facts, is it supreme, final, and therefore above error.

If it cannot err within these bounds, then *a fortiori* it cannot correct its error within such bounds. Thus we have *stare decisis*, and a decision once made stands permanently or until such time as the law it concerns has been repealed or modified. Accordingly, it is confounding for the Court to say, as it did in *Smith* v. *Allwright*, that "when convinced of former error, [it] has never felt constrained to follow precedent."[8] Law is undone, even made farcical, when the *yes* of the highest tribunal can, at the tribunal's option, be changed to *no*. It makes legal what was illegal, and illegal what was legal. This is to make and unmake law, putting the Court in the role of lawmaker and therefore in violation of the first article of the Constitution. It snuffs out the checks and balances.

One may reply that times change, new light is gained, facts are not what they were, and the Constitution must be adapted to the age. Who would deny that? For we are not slaves of the Constitution, though we live by it. In it is a provision, the amendment provision, Article V, allowing for all imaginable change and exactly defining the procedure. That, however, is not enough for some persons, such as the hundred protesting lawyers, who speak of an "evolving interpretation of the great constitutional clauses—commerce among the states, due process of law and equal protection of the laws" and who see in the 1954 school decisions "the culmination of a steady line of growth in the application of the concept of equal protection of the law."

But growth and evolution are no test, no criterion of law; they are neither constitutional nor unconstitutional; debt, crime, evil also grow and evolve. Letting down the constitutional bars is no guarantee of growth and evolution; as well may degeneration, subversion, dissolution result. What one party considers growth another may consider corruption. Where one relies on the constancy of constitutional terms, the other hopes to compromise them. Against both, the Constitution, regarding neither "growth" nor the opposite but rather its own preservation in accordance with the national will, leaves the way open for any change, provided only that it be made in the manner prescribed in the amendment article.

Since amendment is the only *constitutional* means of making a change, with what justification can it be supposed that judicially induced "growth" and "evolution" are legitimate means? Growth and evolution of what? Of language? Of judicial insight? Let us consider these.

Is it supposed that because the Constitution is embedded in language, a change in the meaning of the language is a change in it? This would be exceedingly superficial. The authors of the Constitution did not devise a futuristic language or artfully compound and obscure their meanings. Quite the contrary. The instrument they produced is not cryptically two, three, a half, or anything more or less than the selfsame, unique Constitution, and similarly for its parts down to each term in it. Posterity, though free to change any or all of it in the prescribed way, is given no license to take any part as meaning anything but what it meant when written; which is always approximately ascertainable by the traditional means of construction. A party to a contract would be outraged if informed by the other party that times having changed and the word "perform," for example, having changed too, he now was not bound to perform his part as originally intended— and we may suppose that the courts would be surprised also. A scholar would be repelled by the suggestion that the language of Shakespeare must be given the sense of the same words today. To be sure, the courts have to ascertain and declare meanings and in successive cases they may elicit more and more meaning from any disputed term. But this is not evolution or growth, not a transformation of the Constitution. It must come from the Constitution, not from the times. Otherwise it is not a construing but an amending.

Since there is no explicit statement of the meaning of "amendment" or "construction" in the Constitution, a Court so minded may virtually amend under the guise of construing. Thus it may transform the equal-protection clause into *identical* protection, and can expect "evolutionary" constructionists, if they are integrationists, to applaud. In this shadowy zone between construction and amendment it can operate with free rein, or what the Southern Declaration not inaccurately calls "naked power." The hundred lawyers objected to that term. Perhaps "star chamber" would have been more to their taste.

They remark that "in many of its most important provisions" the Constitution "speaks in general terms, as is fitting in a document intended, as John Marshall declared, 'to endure for ages to come'." But surely this does not mean that the framers, or Marshall either, meant the Court to expand, to narrow, reverse, or in any way alter those terms; and they trusted the judiciary to follow the terms as written— *they* are the only constitutional terms—leaving changes to the amending process. That a term in law is general (laws are by nature general) does not mean that it is a blank check made out to the courts. Generality is not vagueness. Every general term short of the *summum* of its kind is specific as well as general, standing as species to one next above it in the hierarchy of classification. In construing a general term we cannot use its generality as an excuse for reading into it anything not comprehended in its definition at the time it was indited. If we could, what would be the point of making covenants, for how would anyone know what he was committing himself to or what to expect from the other party?

The lawyers might have taken notice that Marshall also said: "Judicial power, as contradistinguished from the power of the laws, has no existence. Courts are the mere instruments of the law, and can will nothing. When they are said to exercise a discretion it is a mere legal discretion, a discretion to be exercised in discerning the course prescribed by law; and when that is discerned it is the duty of the court to follow it. Judicial power is never exercised for the purpose of giving effect to the will of the judges; always for the purpose of giving effect to the will of the Legislature, or, in other words, to the will of the law."[9]

The Supreme Court today tacitly renounces Marshall's statement that once a judicial determination of law has been made, it is the duty of judges to follow it; for *Plessy* v. *Ferguson* and other cases determined that *separate* was compatible with *equal*, racially, and now this is denied in the school decisions. One might dispute Marshall by pointing out that some things measure differently now; that in school, for example, more play and less work equate to the same credits as formerly. But "equal" has not been changed by this. It has not "grown" or "evolved" since 1896. Nothing can make it more equal or less equal. The law is the law, applicable to whatever facts answer to its terms.

Quite apart from Marshall's pronouncement that it is a court's duty to abide by its decisions, reversal of a decision on a constitutional question is repugnant to the Constitution. For the decision is nothing other than the Constitution at work, an effector, a tentacle, of it, and a reversal of the decision therefore nullifies or stultifies the Constitution. Supreme Court decisions conclusively declare the operation, the concrete reality, of the Constitution and the laws made under it, thus determining particularistically what, under Article VI, is the supreme law of the land. This the Court's nine can no more undo or amend than can a man in the street, since any change in it is then a change of law, and therefore a matter for Congress or the states. The judges are subject to the law they thus establish, quite as much as other men.

There is a supposition that where correction of past "error" of the Court would require a constitutional amendment rather than congressional action only, it is fitting for the Court to reverse itself. In *Smith* v. *Allwright* the majority, after declaring that when "convinced of former error" the Court "has never felt constrained to follow precedent," goes on to say: "In constitutional questions, where correction depends upon amendment and not upon legislative action this Court throughout its history has freely exercised its power to re-examine the basis of its constitutional decisions."[10]

Even judges can be naive. Here they forget that whatever "depends upon amendment" is out of their hands. And to forget that is to forget the Constitution, which in clearest terms vests in the states alone the power of amendment (Article V). They forget what they are bound by oath to support.

One of them, retired Justice Reed, remarks: "Occasionally other means than amendments are available to overcome constitutional decisions contrary to purposes desired by the people . . . The Court has avoided the impasse of unconstitutional decisions, explicitly or by implication. Such controversial areas of legislation as minimum wages and child labor . . . were thus in later years opened to federal legislation on re-examination in newly presented cases."[11] As if conscious of nothing untoward in reversals, and as if the Court were a superpolitical organ under mandate to intuit "purposes desired by the people" and to minister to them! Some of the people may intuit the authors of the Constitution turning in their graves.

The supposition that it is fitting for the Court to reverse itself—how can this easy regard for law and judicial authority be reconciled with the judicial finality, and therefore the fixity, implicit in decisions of a court of last resort? It was too much for Justice Roberts, who said, in dissenting from the majority in *Smith* v. *Allwright:* "The reason for my concern is that the instant decision, overruling that announced about nine years ago, tends to bring adjudications of this tribunal into the same class as a restricted railroad ticket, good for this day and train only. I have no assurance, in view of current decisions, that the opinion announced today may not shortly be repudiated and overruled by judges who deem they have new light on the subject. In the present term the court has overruled three cases."[12]

Justice Roberts adds, concerning the case nine years before (*Grovey* v. *Townsend*): "Not a fact differentiates that case from this except the names of the parties."[13] The decision in that case, which concerned voting in Texas primaries, was unanimous. Brandeis, Cardozo, Hughes, and Stone were on the Court at the time.

Joined by Justice Frankfurter, Justice Roberts said in *Mahnich* v. *Southern Steamship Company,* shortly before *Smith* v. *Allwright:*

"The evil resulting from overruling earlier considered decisions must be evident. In the present case, the court below naturally felt bound to follow and apply the law as clearly announced by this court. If litigants and lower federal courts are not to do so, the law becomes not a chart to govern conduct but a game of chance; instead of settling rights and liabilities it unsettles them. Counsel and parties will bring and prosecute actions in the teeth of the decisions that such actions are not maintainable on the not improbable chance that the asserted rule will be thrown overboard. Defendants will not know whether to litigate or to settle for they will have no assurance that a declared rule will be followed. But the more deplorable consequence will inevitably be that the administration of justice will fall into disrepute. Respect for tribunals must fall when the bar and the public come to understand that nothing that has been said in prior adjudication has force in a current controversy."[14]

With bitter irony he looked ahead and envisioned this:

". . . a custom of members of this court to make public announcement of a change of views and to indicate that they will change their votes on the same question when another case comes before the court.

This might, to some extent, obviate the predicament in which the lower courts, the bar, and the public find themselves."[15]

What more devastating verdict on a tribunal of justice! And it comes from no extremist but rather a moderate, joined by another moderate, Mr. Frankfurter. But alas, ten years later Mr. Frankfurter, like one fulfilling the Roberts prophecy, was with the rest in the most spectacular reversal of all, *Brown* v. *Board of Education*. And not long after that, a phalanx of lawyers and law professors is formed to defend this career of inconstancy, in the name of the Constitution, sobriety, and public well-being!

There are two weighty consequences of the judicial ultimacy of the Supreme Court's constitutional decisions (assuming the decisions are within the bounds of the Court's authority): (1) No one of them is more real, or authoritative, than another. (2) No one of them can void another.

None is more real or of higher authority than another because their ultimacy, being without degree, implies equality of them all. Consequently no one of them can nullify another. Reversals, therefore, cannot legitimately occur. When they do occur, which is often nowadays—Senator Stennis has cited 66 instances, 37 of them in the last 25 years[16]—it is proof of aberration, to say the least.

The later of two antithetical decisions might be thought to countervail the earlier. Why? Not for constitutional reasons, assuredly, since time is not a coefficient of the Constitution and counts no more for the second of two inconsistent constitutional decisions than for the first. Perhaps we incline to assume, by analogy with practices in some other spheres, that later orders (decisions) supersede earlier ones. Here, however, the case is quite different; it is not a case of successive volitions or actions, but of law; and inasmuch as Supreme Court decisions on constitutional issues declare the law with finality, the law today remains the same as that declared yesterday. A decision today will not, therefore, disturb the already declared law, unless some abuse has occurred.

Accordingly, there must have been abuse in either the Plessy or the Brown decision. In the former the principle is that racially separate facilities may be equal; in the latter it is that they cannot be equal. Now it is abuse in the ordinary sense to go against fact or reason in the exercise of judicial discretion. In previous chapters of this book it has been conclusively shown, I think, that the Court did this in the Brown case when it enunciated the proposition that separate educational facilities are inherently unequal. But there is a further sense in which it occurred in *Brown*. This is in reversal *per se*. As we have observed, the Court's constitutional decisions are the going law of the land, they are the Constitution in effect, integral in principle with it, and binding, as Marshall said, on the judges. Since the principle or law they enunciate can be lawfully changed only by constitutional change, and since reversal is such change to the utmost degree, the Court cannot, lawfully, reverse them. That is an encroachment on the sovereign power, a usurpation of the authority of the states, or the people.

Reversals—contradictory, incompatible decisions—leave litigants in an impossible position or in the position, at all events, of nullificationists. For which of the incompatible decisions holds? Of course the Court means that the later one holds. But that is logically impossible now, since the later one contradicts the earlier, and the earlier, being the effective law of the land, cannot be denied and must on the contrary be supported by the Court. The litigant who adheres to the earlier decision, if now he about-turns and adheres to the later, will be nullifying the law of the land, as will the adverse party.

The only escape seems to be to deny that the law heretofore declared by the Court was really the law. To which an utterance by former President Eisenhower may stand as a reply: "The people who have this deep emotional reaction on the other side [segregationists] were not acting over these past three generations in defiance of the law. They were acting in compliance with the law as interpreted by the Supreme Court of the United States under the decision of 1896."[17] To this we may add that to compel them to act the opposite way now will, lawfully, require that the law be changed accordingly. It has not been changed and the Court is powerless to change it.

If the law heretofore declared by the Court is not really the law, what reason is there for supposing that the latest declaration is really the law? If we cannot rely on the Court in a former instance, can we rely on it in the present one? A witness in court who contradicts himself is discredited. Are we to think that courts which contradict themselves are not discredited?

Once more it will perhaps be pleaded that now the Court has probed deeper and has gained new light. Let the judges, if they so please, transmit their light to the legislators, with admonishings perhaps. That is the limit of their proper, or constitutional capacity, and to exceed that limit is to infringe the legislative province, in violation of their oath to uphold the Constitution. Probing, moreover, can find in the Constitution only what is there to be found; and being found, it stands and must receive the submission of the Court. Thus what the Court found again and again, before the Brown case, is still there, binding on judges and all, until duly repealed or amended. Marshall observed of a constitution: "Its nature . . . requires, that only its great outlines should be marked, its important objects designated, and the minor ingredients which compose those objects be deduced from the nature of the objects themselves."[18] The deducings, or findings, cannot be one thing today and the opposite another day, since, axiomatically, an ingredient either is or is not in the Constitution. The Court having decided which, that ends it. In the judicial function there is a presumption of conclusiveness. Decisions have to be univocal, otherwise nothing is settled—and it is to reach settlements that litigants go to court. If thereafter the Court disturbs, reverses, a settlement or decision duly reached, it does so at the cost of subverting the law of the land and the probity of the Court.

Between the Court and the country a gulf exists. The Court on its side has assumed absolute power; for the power to substitute *yes* for *no* and *no* for *yes* at will, to be unanswerable for self-contradictions, to have your cake and eat it too, is absolute. On the other side, the country is, for the time, helpless. It is divided into irreconcilable factions, those who are favored by the Court's *yes* and those who are victims of its *no*. Though perhaps unawares, the *yes* party is as helpless as the *no's* since the Court can reverse it too, which, if we heed Justice Roberts' warning, we may expect it to do any day.

Let inner contradiction persist and somewhere a breakdown is inevitable. An outsider finds it difficult to comprehend the failure of judges and legal scholars to realize the existence of contradiction where constitutional decisions are reversed. The law of the land is not both the law and not the law—nothing but sheer logical self-destruction and unintelligibility is that. The Supreme Court can no more reverse itself on a constitutional issue than it can reverse the multiplication table. To do so it must say the law it has duly found and declared to be the law is not the law; which is the same as to say that ten is not ten. Its Constitution reversals in every instance exemplify defiance of reason. For their form is always: Yes but No, or No but Yes, violating one of the most elementary principles of reason. And none but the logically naive can give credence to the Court apologists' doctrine about evolution of terms. Like a deed or a contract, a law does not evolve; and *yes* does not evolve into *no*, though it may be degraded or corrupted as if it did.

On a logical question it is idle to dispute, like disputing a geometrical theorem or the addition of a column of figures. Not disputing but seeing is the thing. If we don't see that the seat of a disagreement happens to be bad reasoning, and still more if we don't see that it is reasoning at all but take it to be some clash of interests, there is no prospect of resolving the trouble. It is like the difference between law and facts. But the law is framed in reasoning, and so there is a further difference, that between law and logic. The conclusions of law and the steps leading to them depend on logic at almost every juncture.

C. S. Peirce remarked: "Few persons care to study logic, because everybody conceives himself to be proficient enough in the art of reasoning already. But I observe that this satisfaction is limited to one's own ratiocination, and does not extend to that of other men."[19] Lawyers today, like most other persons, are rarely educated in the discipline of logic or the refined analyses of philosophy. I doubt that any considerable number of American law schools require their matriculates to have completed successfully a thorough course in logic, let alone more advanced philosophical study. When questions arise in law which are really logical questions it is accordingly no great surprise that today's lawyers, law professors, and judges mistake them for something else. Thus "equal protection" is construed in a fashion so illogical that no two things of any description could be equal. Thus the duly established law of the land is freely ruled not to be the law of the land. Lawyers, law deans, and law professors take up the cudgels, when it is in no sense a matter which cudgeling can settle. Though one side beats down the other, that does not prove that no two distinct things can be equal or that the law of the land is not the law of the land. Reason does not battle and is not affected by madcaps who do. It goes right on governing and takes its toll of the unreasoning, in the form of perpetual conflict and insecurity. Not recognizing its sway, not seeing that it is invincible, the adversaries are perpetually at a loss and can only attribute their plight to viciousness in each other.

A capital example of logical *naïveté* at law is the reasoning by which courts hold that corporations are persons. Perhaps to nobody outside the bar would it occur that a corporation is a person in any but a figurative sense—a sense in which anything whatever can be personified, addressed, and conceived to act of its own will; such as Peace, Golf, Evil, Taxation, Trade. In personifying the corporation, the courts presume the Fourteenth Amendment to be applicable, in particular the equal-protection clause and the clause just before it, which forbids the states to "deprive any person of life, liberty, or property, without due process of law."

The reasoning is that inasmuch as "the property of a corporation is in fact the property of the corporators,"[20] and these are persons, therefore the corporation must be a person. More succinctly, it is reasoning from the fact that the possessors individually are persons to the conclusion that the aggregate of them is a person. Of course this assumes the general proposition that composite things have the same attributes as their components. If that were so, then since a regiment is composed of men, it must be a man; and since a man is made up of cells, ergo he is a cell; and you could go on and "prove" that he is a molecule or an atom and that the whole population of the earth, being composed of men, is an atom too. A sophomore who reasoned thus would fail his course and a practical man who did so would risk his life and belongings.[21]

It is no justification to say that the personality of a corporation is limited to its possession of property. What is possession, and how can it alone constitute personality? Ants and microbes possess property to a degree, but that hardly makes them persons. Paupers are propertyless but still are persons. So property is neither necessary nor sufficient to personality. Further, if a corporation is a person, then a large one is a large person and constitutionally we can no more restrain the peaceable assembly or affiliation of large ones than we can that of fat men. The First Amendment, which protects the right of persons to join, must therefore protect corporations in forming monopolies. This, we think today, is absurd; but it is an inescapable consequence of our courts' ascription of personality to corporations. Thanks to that, and particularly to the illogicality back of it, we are obliged to live the absurdity, though quite obviously nothing of the kind was necessary for protecting corporations' shareholders against deprival of their constitutional property rights.

Judicial probity is not constituted of simple honesty alone. It is more than immunity to the temptation of bribe-taking or of yielding to prejudice or partisanship. It requires powers of rational insight, trained, practiced, and informed, plus the poise and strength that come of a life ruled by them. So endowed, a judge, doubtless, need never falter; not so endowed, he is not fitted for the office.

The idea of a judge sympathetically aligned with partisan interests, one ruled by affinities, not by reason, is thoroughly repugnant to the idea of impartial justice; and the eagerness of his partisans to praise him in the name of justice is worthy of contempt. A judge who cannot divest himself of all inclination towards the cause before him and look upon it with the same calm neutrality as that of a scientist looking at microbes or at the stars is *eo ipso* disqualified for judicial office. The distinctive business of a judge is quite as clearcut as that of a chemist discerning the elements or of a geometrician divining theorems. He has nothing to win or lose. He can do nothing legitimately but expound and demonstrate. As the chemist and astronomer are bound by the material composition of the world, which they profess to discover and elucidate to us, so the judge is bound by the law. That a proposition is true, false, or probable, that a conclusion follows from established grounds or not, are the questions to be decided, and judicial affinities have no more to do with the decision of them than with the decision of whether an arithmetical answer is correct or whether a fever is due to a certain germ. Opinions and counter-opinions put forth by the Supreme Court justices today often read like polemics. You may say that polemics are fine when needed. Indeed; but the admission of such need, within the Supreme Court, is an admission of lack of probity in some sense. Lack of probity, to any degree, is lack of fitness for judicial office.

A conception of judicial office as an agonistic or missionary force is discernible in legal writing today. Judges are lined up on sides and writers take the part of bravos for them. While not unknown in fields of scholarship, this unabashed partisanship is, to say the least, unusual there. Scholarship is a mode of science, and science cares not for sides. Hot is no better or worse than cold to it. That such authors are sincere is not in question; but partisans of any shade may be sincere. Probity requires much more than sincerity.

A concealed illogicality runs through much of the writing here, especially that of integrationists. Professor Fairman writes: "Let us accept that the historical record supplies evidence of the most persuasive character that the Congress which submitted the fourteenth amendment never contemplated that the amendment would of its own force abolish segregation in public schools. Note, however, that it is another thing to claim that Congress contemplated that the amendment would not abolish segregation. There is an immense difference. The Founding Fathers in 1787 did not contemplate that Congress would forbid interstate movement of lottery tickets or stolen automobiles, that it would support agricultural prices or establish social security, or that it would enact thousands of other measures that now seem essential and beyond question."[22]

The like of this probably passes among law journal readers as a sensible, fair, even magnanimous representation. Let us see. Suppose with Professor Fairman that the authors of the Fourteenth

Amendment never contemplated [intended] that the Amendment would "of its own force" abolish public school segregation. Does that mean that it nevertheless might abolish it? If so, this would be because of something in the Amendment's "own force" not intended by the authors. But the authors intended only what they did intend; hence there is nothing else in the Amendment's "own force." And the only intent of law is the intent embodied in it by its makers, and its only force the force of the terms they give it. If this were not so, everyone could read his own intent into a law and deny the intent of the legislators. Law would not be law.

But Professor Fairman thinks that even though there was no intent to abolish segregation, still that did not exclude the possibility. Now this is quite incredible. It must mean either that the authors intended to include a possibility contrary to their intent, or else that, by some means, external forces could legitimately enter and reverse what was intended. In other words, (1) the authors did not intend what they did intend or (2) their intent could be superseded, even reversed, by others. Of course (1) is self-contradictory and hence impossible, while (2) would mean amending the Constitution unconstitutionally. The like of (2) is the door to judocracy. It is a subterranean passage by which forces other than those recognized in the Constitution make their way in and do their subversive work.

More pointedly, Professor Fairman is maintaining that in not intending something, though not declaring your rejection of it, you may thereby commit yourself to it. Or, what you do not expressly reject, though you implicitly adhere to its negative, you at the same time may embrace. Given that such and such is not the case, then it may be or is the case! Alas for logicality!

Or does he mean that Congress committed itself neither way? His term "contemplate," rather than "intent," might suggest that. But this will not do. Lawmakers do more than contemplate. They intend and prescribe, and only so far as they do, do they make law. Nor were Congress and the Amendment-ratifying states non-committal about segregation. Congress continued segregation in the Washington public schools for nearly a century and many of the segregation states did likewise.

There is a certain mysticism about writings like this. We are not to take the Constitution as a limited body of known or demonstrable guarantees and restraints which we alone can modify, extend, or curtail, but as an organ with a life of its own and capable of inverting, contradicting, and transforming itself, with the result that its *yes* becomes *no*. If we ask why it is to be so regarded, we may as well expect the answer to be correspondingly mystical, for nothing remotely suggestive of a warrant, either explicit or implicit, is found in the Constitution: nothing in any way suggesting that the Constitution is a Leviathan or Frankensteinian monster endowed with power to rise over us and order us into about-step. The Constitution is a body of resolutions which *we the people* have instituted. To speak of it as growing and evolving, independently of its authors, is like saying the Declaration of Independence or Gettysburg Address grows and evolves. But that way of speaking spreads enough cloud to keep the unwary from seeing, and carries an agreeably mystical spell which charms them into unwitting acquiescence, perhaps.

The habit of citing modern technological developments to show that our forebears in 1787 could have had no reference to them and that the Constitution has had to be cut to fit them, is rather specious. The defining idea, the genus or category, not how many differentiations of it might come about (since all such are subordinate to it), was the thing; and of course if you were going beyond the generic bounds, that was new territory, which you could not lawfully enter until such time as a constitutional amendment or other legislative action opened it to you.[23] In this process of interpreting and applying terms, you yourself might grow or change otherwise, but that was you, not the Constitution. The language of sophistry confuses the two things and artfully draws from the confusion the kind of result it wants.

Some months after the school decisions Mr. Alexander M. Bickel published in the *Harvard Law Review* an article entitled "The Original Understanding and the Segregation Decisions." Mr. Bickel, who was a research associate in the Harvard Law School and afterwards a law professor at Yale, had served as a law clerk to Associate Justice Frankfurter in 1952, when the segregation cases were first argued before the Supreme Court. In this article he says:

" . . . there is no evidence whatever showing that for its sponsors the civil rights formula [from which the Fourteenth Amendment took rise in Congress] had anything to do with unsegregated public schools; Wilson, its sponsor in the House, specifically disclaimed any such notion . . . Indeed, no specific purpose going beyond the coverage of the Civil Rights Act is suggested [concerning the first section of the Fourteenth Amendment]; rather an awareness on the part of these framers that it was *a constitution* they were writing, which led to a choice of language capable of growth.

"[The Supreme Court in 1954] could have deemed itself bound by the legislative history showing the immediate objectives to which

Section 1 of the Fourteenth Amendment was addressed, and rather clearly demonstrating that it was not expected in 1866 to apply to segregation. The Court would in that event also have repudiated much of the provision's 'line of growth.' . . . the record of history, properly understood, left the way open to, in fact invited, a decision based on the moral and material state of the nation in 1954, not 1866."[24]

A convenient paraphrase of this might run: It was not intended that school segregation be affected, but the framers purposely used supple language which could mean that; and although the Court in 1954 would have been justified in abiding by the framers' intent not to disturb segregation, yet in that event it would have stifled growth; and history justified and even invited the Court to put aside the intent of the framers and draw its decision from the spirit of 1954.

So we are to understand, nearly as in the Fairman argument above, that the framers intended not to touch segregation, yet willed and artfully contrived for its doom. Well, it is sometimes said that the Fourteenth Amendment was a conspiracy to shield corporations through getting them classed as persons, but the idea that it was devised, intended, to compass or allow what was *not* intended, that it was a virtual conspiracy against itself—this is too much. Again "growth" is the watchword. By now it has itself grown, into something like magic, able to transform or annul the past, replacing the law of 1868 with the mood of 1954, without boo to Congress or the states.

Perhaps Mr. Bickel learned this from his chief and the others of the Supreme Court. In any event it is sufficiently respected to be authoritatively cited by Professor Fairman. Both Fairman and Bickel end on a moral note. Thus Fairman: "It is the law's ancient truth that no man may be judge in his own case, and no race may justly maintain its sole competence to measure the equal protection to be accorded to fellow citizens. These simple verities are bound to prevail. It is futile to make war 'to keep the past upon its throne.' Once the Court's judgment is everywhere in the course of execution, difficult though that objective now appears, this country will gain the much-needed calm that comes from doing right, and the hurtful attack upon the Court will cease."[25]

Right, verities, and so forth—if as represented here and if legally pertinent to segregation, how is it that the Supreme Court and lower courts, as well as the lawmakers and the country, rejected them heretofore? Did virtue and ethics remain in legal oblivion till 1954? Readers may think of a simpler explanation—that somebody here is quite deluded. And even if not that, some will balk at the expression "doing right." This would be instructive. It would recall to us that the law is not gauged by this or that individual's conception of right, but is a due enactment of lawmakers, registering *their* or *their constituents'* conception of right; from which no court of justice can depart without betraying its trust, and which no professor of law can endeavor to transform casuistically without compromising his office.

So much dust is raised in attempts to make the law say or seem to say what on a straightforward reading it does not say, that if we turn away and consult such an authority as Justice Story, it is like suddenly entering a new atmosphere, fair and luminous.

"What is to become of constitutions of government," he asked, "if they are to rest, not upon the plain import of their words, but upon conjectural enlargements and restrictions, to suit the temporary passions and interests of the day? Let us never forget that our constitutions of government are solemn instruments, addressed to the common sense of the people, and designed to fix and perpetuate their rights and their liberties. They are not to be frittered away to please the demagogues of the day. They are not to be violated to gratify the ambition of political leaders. They are to speak in the same voice now and forever. They are of no man's private interpretation. They are ordained by the will of the people; and can be changed only by the sovereign command of the people."[26]

It would be illusory to suppose that even so forthright a declaration may not be taken differently by different parties. If you are a strict constructionist, Story is unchallengeable; if a loose constructionist, he was dead to the "line of growth" and would fossilize the Constitution. An extremist may go so far as to regard the Supreme Court as a political organ, not through degeneration or revolution but by destiny, if not original nature. Thus:

"It is my view that the Supreme Court inevitably acts in a political context, and that the greatest danger to the Court and from the Court comes when that fact is inadequately realized. Felix Frankfurter wrote in 1938 that we need a 'more continuous awareness of the role of the Court in the dynamic process of American society.' I agree with that and with Konefsky's conclusion that 'only by acknowledging that the Supreme Court is a political institution performing a political function can we hope to escape from naive notions as to the nature of our Constitution and to foster a more informed understanding of the Court's place in the American system of government'."[27]

But a constitution, a system of law, presupposes objectivity in the law; that is, a standard which is invariant, on which all can rely and to which all are subject. Without this, there is no legal security; and equality before the law, equal protection, or anything worthy to be called fairness, is out of the question. The integrity of the system and the guarantee of the rights under it presuppose the integrity of its terms, which is to say the terms bear the exact meaning their authors gave them: they gave no other meanings, and only they gave or lawfully could give them any meanings. Is this a fossilization? Then integrity, honesty, probity, all the virtues must be fossilizings, and in order not to fossilize, one must own to dissembling, infidelity, and the rest. This is the end—reduction to absurdity —to which the "evolving," "line-of-growth" concepts lead. No evolutionary formula or line of growth was written into the Constitution, and so none is there, although an ample means of change, left entirely to us, is there, in the amendment article. We, and we alone, are to employ it, in lines of growth, of contraction, or whatever direction we choose. Judges are no more authorized to employ it than the man in the street.[28]

Suppose the people could vote on the question of whether the Supreme Court is "a political institution performing a political function" or, as Marshall said, a "mere instrument of the law . . . never exercised for the purpose of giving effect to the will of the judges; always for the purpose of giving effect to . . . the will of the law." Perhaps no one will doubt what the outcome would be. Were it true that the Court is properly a political instrument, who could object to making it politically responsible by providing for periodical election of the judges? The fact that such a thing is repugnant to all parties goes far to show that the Court is not a political instrument, save by degradation, and that those who think it is have deluded themselves.

The Court today powerfully encourages the supposition that it is political, by overstepping such limits as those declared by Marshall. When in the Brown case it can cite no law to justify its decision, and turns outside to psychology and sociology for support, clearly it is erecting the tenets of those academic *arrivistes*, fluid and inconclusive as they are, into law.[29] Could Marshall speak, doubtless he would say the Court, in this, has substituted its will for that of the lawmakers, to its great discredit. Authors today look upon the Court's proceedings as if they were a spectacular feud, with Justices Black, Douglas, and two or three others habitually poised against the rest, and the losing side usually to be counted on for a refight after a time.[30]

Such is the way of judocracy. Contrast probity. To it everything in judocracy is repugnant. Probity sees and demonstrates and is governed thereby, never by the ego. Probity is sensitively aloof from all partisanship, liberal or conservative, from causes, from doctrinal right and wrong; and an undefiled judicature is probity at work. Without lack, probity has nothing to attain, it has only to be attained. Doubtless a judge, to attain it, must first conquer himself and thereafter must be perpetually on guard lest some betraying, egoistic, non-judicial motive break through. He is always doing others' business, fulfilling others' directions; the sovereign's, the legislator's, the law's. He is never, on the bench, his own, John Smith, but His Honor, a non-partisan tribune above self; else he fails. Exalted thus, he can never substitute himself to any degree for the law or the lawmaker. This utterly precludes "judicial lawmaking." It also lays upon the judge the responsibility of demonstrating, not as with some, merely declaiming, the decision he reaches. That some controversial tenet about the Bill of Rights, for instance, should be ordained to the country by judges is repugnant here; for if it is not demonstrably the law it is not at all law but only a question mark, as jurists realize who say that where there is room for reasonable doubt, judgment must be withheld. To demonstrate that it is the law will require the same objectivity that is required in scientific work; which will mean abandonment of partisan causes and submission to the duly ascertained facts of law. There are no judicial causes to be attained. So far as the judge is concerned, the law is all causes, already attained.

There is, it seems, even a technique for judicial duplicity concerning precedents. We find in Professor Herman Pritchett's *Roosevelt Court* the following directions:

"First, [the Court] may simply ignore the conflicting precedent in writing the decision in the current case . . .

"A second course . . . is to distinguish the precedent from the case at hand, or to qualify its doctrine. This process is usually not too great a strain on the capacities of a clever justice, for the facts of two cases are never identical . . .

"Finally, of course, a precedent which the Court finds it necessary to depart from may meet the fate of a short sharp shock on a big black block by being specifically overruled by name."[31]

Mr. Pritchett gives cases to illustrate, and a tabulation running to thirty-two such within the decade ending in 1946, with the comment: "There is general agreement that the law must grow, and an omelet cannot be made without breaking eggs."[32]

The metaphor is a fair enough example from the writing in this field; the analogy a fair sample, too. Not to linger over them, one might point out that if constitutional law is cookery, the cooks are not Supreme Court judges. They are the states. The judges are waiters.

But the kitchen is not the setting to show off the talents of the characters represented in this. Our pedagogical impresario needs a rogues' gallery for the purpose. He who will "simply ignore" his commitments is a miscreant, whom the world holds in utter contempt. He who dissimulates, pretending that two plus two today does not equal two plus two yesterday, is a universally recognized cheat.

These types in and over the law! Not a word of condemnation or sign of revulsion, no surprise, no notice of the perfidy nor hint of the moral or legal significance. But is it surprising that the acceptance and even prestige of what comes from these auspices should profoundly disturb persons of a different ethical outlook and standard?

It was the like of this, not in politics but in religion, that moved Jonathan Swift to write the famous satire, *A Tale of a Tub*. The parent of the Church wills to his three sons certain cloaks warranted good for life if given proper care. In time, tempted by vanities and ambitions, the three fall into disagreements. Again and again they refer to the will on disputed points, each always making out of it what he wants to until finally it becomes ineffective and is put aside and forgotten. The consequence is separation, disaffection, animosity, and strife: Catholicism versus Lutheranism versus Presbyterianism. Since the Supreme Court went outside the law to draw support for its school decision, and was not too particular about the probative character of what it chose, perhaps it would find rich possibilities in Swift's allegory, no matter about the consequences. Or if not the Court, then its aides and apologists.

Though dishonoring its decisions on occasion, the Court is not above justifying them by half-mystical means. We read of its "appeal to a 'higher law,' to a set of overarching principles of rightness neither articulated in any document nor capable of being defined in words, but which the Court has a duty nonetheless to discover."[33] Or in Justice Frankfurter's words, "many a decision of this Court rests on some inarticulate major premise and is none the worse for it."[34]

Why endeavor to discover inscrutable principles or perhaps any principles if they are to be compromised or repudiated at any time? "The day is long past," says Mr. Sanford H. Kadish, "if it ever existed, when the judicial function was regarded as narrowly confined to applying pure rules of law to judicially proven facts."[35] Of what use then, one may ask, would still purer rules or principles be?

Every constitutional decision employs constitutional elements. Unless these are cognized, they cannot be intelligibly employed, and if they are cognized they can be stated, or formulated as principles. Once stated, promulgated, they stand as the explicit law of the land. In any case arising, the question is then whether the applicable principle is one previously ascertained or one requiring to be ascertained; and if it is a case essentially similar to a previous case the principle already ascertained applies, inasmuch as that principle is the law of the land and therefore binding on the Court. The idea that cases differing by a shade are essentially different and so come into different constitutional categories, is wholly uninformed. The essence, not the accidents, governs. Were that not so, no two men could be treated each as a man, no number of dollar bills as each a dollar, and science, organized society, and law itself, as we know them, would be impossible.

Competent adjudication can say whether an instant case is like a previous one, or whether the question it presents is like the previous; just as competent medical diagnosis and competent authority in all manner of pursuits can determine the answers to corresponding questions. The Supreme Court, having ventured a little way into what it considers science, might profit by looking further, into the real thing. Let its panegyrists go forth in that direction too, breaking their habit of ruminating perpetually on one another's cud.

The enlightened lay world must be astonished to learn that what it has so long considered the certainty and sanctity of the Constitution is an illusion. That what was the law is not the law, though we have made no change; that the Constitution naturally varies with the judges, nothing previously decided being binding on them; that a technique of repudiation exists, involving palpably unethical choices; that the underlying thought and reasoning holds that there is no other course open (which is as much as to say that the Constitution contains the germ of its own corruption); that thus we are brought to a stage where integrity, probity, and justice under law are but illusory expectations of the naive—all of this must be an alarming discovery to the American citizen. Out of it came the school segregation decisions and the host of related decisions.

[1] Vol. 70, p. 83 (1956). The Court has known severe criticism in the past. Cf. Charles Warren, *The Supreme Court in United States History,* 3 vols., Boston, Little, Brown & Co., 1922, vol. 3, pp. 26ff.

[2] This was published the next day in the New York *Times,* and an appendix to it was distributed by Ernest Angell, Esq., of New York City. Persons whose memory goes back a generation may recall a very different expression from spokesmen of the bar, concerning respect for law and the Court, mentioned in Alpheus T. Mason's *Supreme Court from Taft to Warren,* p. 207: "In 1935 the Lawyers' Committee of the American Liberty League declared, in advance of a Supreme Court ruling, the Wagner Labor Relations Act 'unconstitutional,' and openly advised employers to ignore its provisions." So at one time of controversy the Supreme Court is defied and at another it is exalted, by lawyers, in the name of the law.

[3] *Congressional Record,* 84th Congress, 2nd sess., vol. 102, pt. 4, pp. 4515f.

[4] Cp. the Court itself on its power: "The only check upon our own exercise of power is our own sense of self-restraint." *United States* v. *Butler,* 297 U. S. 1, 78 (1935).

[5] *Collected Works,* Basler ed., vol. 2, p. 454.

[6] *Physical and Metaphysical Works of Lord Bacon,* ed. by Joseph Devey, London, George Bell & Sons, 1891, p. 347.

[7] *Brown v. Allen, loc. cit.,* p. 540.

[8] *Smith* v. *Allwright,* 321 U. S. 649, 665 (1943).

[9] *Osborn* v. *Bank of the United States, loc. cit.,* p. 866.

[10] *Loc. cit.,* p. 665. [11] *Loc. cit.,* p. 5. [12] *Loc. cit.,* p. 669.

[13] *Ibid.* [14] 321 U. S. 96, 112 (1944). [15] *Ibid.*

[16] *Congressional Record,* 85th Congress, 1st sess., vol. 103, pt. 2, p. 2144.

[17] *Congressional Record,* 84th Congress, 2d sess., vol. 102, pt. 5, p. 6892.

[18] *McCulloch* v. *Maryland,* 4 Wheaton 316, 407.

[19] Charles Hartshorne and Paul Weiss, eds., *Collected Papers of Charles Sanders Peirce,* 6 vols., Cambridge, Harvard University Press, 1931-35, vol. 5, p. 223. "Logic is a necessary preparation," Austin observes, for the education of a lawyer. *Op. cit.,* vol. 2, p. 1086.

[20] *Railroad Tax Cases,* 13 F. 722, 747 (1882). See also *Santa Clara County, California* v. *Southern Pacific Railroad,* 118 U. S. 394, 396 (1886). A philosophically enlightened account of the corporation concept will be found in H. L. A. Hart's *Definition and Theory in Jurisprudence,* Oxford, Clarendon Press, 1953.

We find the Supreme Court today, in *Beauharnais* v. *Illinois,* making the same kind of logical error. There it said, in an opinion by Justice Frankfurter, "if an utterance directed at an individual may be the object of criminal sanctions, we cannot deny to a State power to punish the same utterance directed at a defined group . . . " *Loc. cit.,* p. 258. This presupposes that what holds of an individual holds of any group or class of which he is a member. Then if the individual is a thief, so is the class of thieves a thief; if he weighs 150 pounds, so does the class. And, incredible nonsense that it is, once exposed, this "reasoning" was probably the chief determiner of the decision, a decision against a Chicago appellant convicted for distributing handbills calling on white people to resist "Negro aggressions and infiltrations into all white neighborhoods" and warning of "rapes, robberies, knives, guns and marijuana of the Negro" (*ibid.,* p. 276). Four of the justices—Black, Douglas, Jackson, and Reed—dissented.

Former Justice Roberts observes: "The great mass of constitutional litigation arising under the Fourteenth Amendment has fallen under the due process clause. A fair reading of the clause would seem to indicate that the word 'person' as used in that clause refers to natural persons. The first sentence of the section speaks of all persons born or naturalized. The first clause of the second sentence refers to citizens of the United States. The due process and equal protection clauses each refer to any person, and the former protects the life, liberty, or property of such person. A corporation is not born or naturalized and is not a citizen of the United States. A corporation has only in a metaphorical sense a life of which it might be deprived." *The Court and the Constitution*, Cambridge, Harvard University Press, 1951, p. 68. One might add that, having only a metaphorical life, the corporation would be only a metaphorical person and citizen, as it is commonly thought to be; but then its property would be only metaphorical too, and deprivation thereof likewise only metaphorical. In short, if it is a person, it is not a natural person but only a fictitious one and its property only make-believe; and if it is not a person, its property is not covered by the Fourteenth Amendment. Either way, *it* is not entitled to the personal protection secured by the Amendment, and the courts in granting that protection must be said to have erred radically. Of course the corporators are individually entitled to protection.

[21] Such "reasoning" is nevertheless fairly often the reliance of the Supreme Court (and determines the fate of litigants before it). For example: the Court said in *Yick Wo* v. *Hopkins, loc. cit.*, p. 369, and again in *Missouri ex rel. Gaines* v. *Canada*, 305 U. S. 337, 350, that the equal protection of the laws is "a pledge of the protection of equal laws." Well! Is the income tax law of a state then equal to the divorce law or to the speed law? Since there is no substantive or factual ground for this remarkable transmutation of terms, we must suppose it to have an axiomatic ground. Results such as these will follow: "the equal liability to taxes" will mean "the liability to equal taxes," "the crying need of faith" will mean "the need of crying faith," and "the easy way of virtue" will equal "the way of easy virtue." Mathematically, the results of such an axiom would be stunning: a/bc would equal b/ac, meaning, for example, that 1/2x3 equals 2/1x3, or 1/6 equals 4/6 and hence 1 equals 4! How precarious the foundation of justice in the Supreme Court!

Another example: A covenant was made by landowners not to sell to Negroes or Mongolians. That the owners had a right to make such a covenant was admitted by the Supreme Court, but when the state (Missouri) acted to uphold this right, the Court forbid, saying the state was denying equal protection. This presumes that in upholding a person's right to perform an act, the state itself is performing the act—presumes that defending a right is exercising that right. So palpable an error would mean failure for our lowly sophomore in the study of reasoning. What you have a legal right to do, the state must of course protect you in doing, otherwise the right is null. So here (*Shelley* v. *Kraemer*, 334 U.S. 1) the Supreme Court was extinguishing an admitted right, though it has no more jurisdiction over rights than it has over the sky. Such aberration, such travesty of reasoning, such naive ineptitude and irresponsibility —on this collapsing foundation reposes the system of justice in the United States.

[22] *Loc. cit.*, p. 86.

[23] Cp.: "Constitutional provisions do not change, but their operation extends to new matters as the modes of business and the habits of life of the people vary with each succeeding generation. The law of the common carrier is the same

today as when transportation on land was by coach and wagons, and on water by canal boat and sailing vessel, yet in its actual operation it touches and regulates transportation by modes then unknown, the railroad train and the steamship." *In re Debs, Petitioner,* 158 U.S. 564, 591.

24 Vol. 69, pp. 56, 63, 64-65.

25 *Loc. cit.,* p. 94. After Professor Fairman's sanguine prediction, the following reports of actualities must be disturbing:

"Today, the Federal troops are gone [from Little Rock]; only a handful of Federalized National Guardsmen patrols the high school. But there is left a sort if sickness in Little Rock.

"It is a sickness that has various origins: atavistic fears; the confusion of a community that was not really prepared to change its way of life; the fear of a militant pressure group that has become the prime action agency in the city.

" . . . The incidents and the war of nerves have now produced a sort of paralysis in leadership." New York *Times Magazine,* March 10, 1958, pp. 11, **76.**

"They are afraid to say so in public, but many of the North's big-city mayors groan in private that their biggest and most worrisome problem is the crime rate among Negroes.

"In 1,551 U. S. cities, according to the FBI tally for 1956, Negroes, making up 10 per cent of the U. S. population, accounted for about 30 per cent of all arrests, and 60 per cent of the arrests for crimes involving violence or threat of bodily harm—murder, non-negligent manslaughter, rape, robbery, and aggravated assault. In one city after another, the figures—where they are not hidden or suppressed by politicians—reveal a shocking pattern . . .

"Unlike the Caucasian immigrant of an earlier day, a Negro can scarcely ever hope, even in the North, that the white society will really accept him on his human merits." *Time,* April 21, 1958, p. 16. See below, p. 316.

26 Quoted in William D. Guthrie, *Lectures on the Fourteenth Amendment,* Boston, Little, Brown & Co., 1898, p. 39.

27 C. Herman Pritchett, quoted in Ruth Locke Roettinger, *The Supreme Court and State Police Power,* Washington, Public Affairs Press, 1957, p. 230.

28 "The Constitution," said the eminent James Iredell, of North Carolina, in the debates preceding ratification, "can be altered with as much regularity, and as little confusion, as any act of Assembly; not, indeed, quite so easily, which would be extremely impolitic; but it is a most happy circumstance, that there is a remedy in the system itself for its own fallibility, so that alterations can without difficulty be made, agreeable to the general sense of the people." Jonathan Elliot, *op. cit.,* vol. 4, p. **177.** Iredell was afterwards appointed to the Supreme Court by President Washington, and served with distinction.

29 Citation of the psycho-sociological writings was not mere judicial notice, since what they contain is by no means common, admitted knowledge. On the contrary, much of it is hearsay, much admittedly uncertain, and most if not all of it controversial. That it was used probatively by the Court when the appellees had had no opportunity to cross-examine the authors or to make rebuttal, hence in violation of the most elementary idea of justice, is something the country must not have realized; for such an enormity could hardly have passed without causing public remonstrance, as occurred in Georgia (the Legislature there called for impeachment of the participating justices).

30 Some years ago Professor Arthur M. Schlesinger, Jr. wrote: "The Black-Douglas group believes that the Supreme Court can play an affirmative role

in promoting the social welfare; the Frankfurter-Jackson group advocates a policy of judicial self-restraint. One group is more concerned with the employment of the judicial power for their own conception of the social good; the other with expanding the range of allowable judgment for legislatures, even if it means upholding conclusions they privately condemn. One group regards the Court as an instrument to achieve desired social results; the second as an instrument to permit the other branches of government to achieve the results the people want for better or worse. In brief, the Black-Douglas wing appears to be more concerned with settling particular cases in accordance with their own social preconceptions; the Frankfurter-Jackson wing with preserving the judiciary in its established but limited place in the American system." Quoted in Samuel J. Konefsky, *Legacy of Holmes and Brandeis,* New York, Macmillan Company, 1956, p. 289n.

Mr. Konefsky speaks of the Court itself "changing its own prior meanings of the Constitution" and gives the following corroboration from Felix Frankfurter's *Mr. Justice Holmes:* "His [Holmes'] influence was powerful in arresting the tide which reached its crest in the *Lochner* case. There followed a period of judicial recession, of greater tolerance towards the exercise of legislative discretion. Between 1908 and the World War, the Court allowed legislation to prevail which in various aspects curbed freedom of enterprise and withdrew phases of industrial relations from the area of individual bargaining. In the period between Muller v. Oregon, in 1908, and Bunting v. Oregon, in 1917, Mr. Justice Holmes' views prevailed. But those who had assumed a permanent change in the Court's outlook were to be disappointed . . . Change in the Court's personnel, and pressure of post-war economic and social views soon reflected themselves in decisions." *Ibid.,* pp. 108-109.

31 Pp. 54, 55, 56. This work was published by the Macmillan Company in 1948. Professor Pritchett, who is a contemporary author of prominence in this sphere, ridicules what he calls "label thinking," which, he informs us, "starts off with the assumption that certain kinds of restrictions are unconstitutional and limits the judicial task to determining whether the restriction in the instant case fits into one of the proscribed categories." He says that such thinking "unfits a justice to make distinctions based on matters of degree . . . leads a judge into a world of abstractions in which the facts of a particular case are unimportant . . . encourages a justice to apply to a statute legal rather than empirical tests . . . " *Civil Liberties and the Vinson Court,* Chicago, University of Chicago Press, 1954, p. 249. Consider the last, "legal rather than empirical tests." It means that we are not to look to the law for governance, but to the judge—his appraisals, prognostications, idealities. Since these vary among judges, uncertainty and instability would quickly result, not to speak of unequal protection. And supposing that it is a *judge's* business to test a law, what test is there for him to apply but a legal one? One not legal? That would be the betrayal of everything—law, constitution, oath, trust. Moreover, judicial respect for the sovereign authority, or people, and for their representatives, the legislature, precludes judicial encroachment upon them. They, not the judge, determine legal needs and provide for them.

Consider also the proposition that without a free rein the judicial mind cannot "make distinctions based on matters of degree." Here the question, if there is one, is only a question of how far the legal prescriptions are to go, and that, too, is a legislative not a judicial question. It has been recognized since Aristotle that the lawgiver cannot prescribe down to the last syllable, since not all variations within some categories can be foretold. But here, in the contentions of this author, it is not a matter of inadequate categories or legislative prescriptions, but just the opposite: the idea that the judge shall not be bound by legislative prescriptions, but shall be free to make his own. Now this is not law, it is judocracy. Contrast the observation by Professor H. L. A. Hart: "how to classify particulars . . . is the heart of a judicial decision" (71 *Harvard Law Review* 593, 610); and of course classifying particulars is allocating them to categories, and it is the business of the lawmaker, not the judge, to establish the categories and the rights or sanctions appertaining to them. To suppose that a judge cannot "make distinctions based on matters of degree" without being independent of such categories, is fanciful. Matters of degree are nothing till we know what sort of matters, and that categorizes them at once. It comes down to a question—pseudo question—of who shall legislate, who shall write the law and hence the categories, the legislator or the judge. And of course the office of legislating is exclusively the legislator's. Judocracy confuses the judicial and legislative offices, either from lack of comprehension or from motives of subversion. Cf. ch. 8, n. 10.

The idea that a judge cannot think, reason, judge, without free rein, is totally mistaken. The acutest, clearest, most rigorous thinking, in fields outside of law, goes on under definitions and rules of the most precise description; and before judocracy got in its work such thinking was found in the law. The whole apparatus of government, in a constitutional system, is under reins, reins too loosely held today, in our case, to save the system from judocratic corruption. It is no injustice to say that one, perhaps the chief, reason for this corruption is lack of rigorous, reflective thinking and consequent lack of comprehension of the offices of government. Nor is it an exaggeration to say that minds disciplined in critical, philosophical study must be astonished to see what passes for understanding today in "political science" as well as a great deal of law.

[32] *Ibid.*, p. 57.

[33] Sanford H. Kadish, 66 *Yale Law Journal* 319, 325.

[34] *Niemotko* v. *Maryland*, 340 U. S. 268, 285.

[35] 66 *Yale Law Journal*, 319, 359.

CHAPTER 12

CONSCIENCE v. CONSCIENCE

Mr. A.: "The thought of race-mixing is unutterably sickening to me. It is simply against the blood. I seem literally to feel antibodies forming. If you think this is prejudice or conventionality or anything but inmost nature, you cannot know the truth. It is idle, I mean foreign to the subject, to tell me that after all, people are people or that we are one nation or that white and colored mingle in streets and stores, so why not in schools and domiciles and in general. Thieves, cutthroats, and vermin also move in public; but I don't take that as a reason for joining them. Argument is beside the point—you wouldn't argue with nausea, I suppose? Everything has its place. The world is wide enough to accommodate white and black among their own kind. Forcing them together is contrary to nature—certainly my nature."

Mr. B.: "I try to keep an open mind. Reason and reflection can see where passion is blind. Nothing else that I know can assure justice and confidence. Nothing else can satisfy the mind, or at least my mind; and no problem is solved as long as doubt or mental reservation remains. If you compromise reason or put it off, it will not let you rest. If you are not a rational-minded person, you cannot understand the other side and you must live under a constant cloud. Reason is neither white nor black, but above both. If I take sides without its sanction, I am like a child and am not really qualified to decide."

Mr. C.: "It is an ethical matter. I will not take advantage of my fellowman, nor oppress, humble, or cruelly use anyone. Who am I to judge another's rights? As a human being, one of my species, I recognize all others as of the same status as I. My rights are no more than theirs. Not just on Sunday or in principle, but under all like circumstances. Or, if I don't live up to this, I can only say I have failed, and then I am humbled before my own conscience."

At bay, the naked spirit stands as a natural wonder, like fire or adamant. It speaks and we are silent.

Beyond conviction, it is the ultimate ground of conviction. It sustained the martyrs and motivated the reformers and was the source of the Bill of Rights. It is discernible in the utterances of the three types of mind speaking here.

This invincible spirit is as much as anything else the source and limit of law and law courts. To enjoin it is not within the power of courts. If they nevertheless venture to do such a thing deviously, under color of law, they undermine their own authority and the authority of law.

If blue and green dim each other to sickliness, how can a perceptive mind deny it or vow not to see it? Or in the event of finding certain lights and contexts in which they become tolerant of each other, with what reason does anyone suppose that this cancels the normal differences between them, or that such differences are only imaginary? Black and white being at opposite poles, what leads people to dissemble or deny it? Not respect for facts and not unfettered reason, the qualities explicit in the testimonies of Mr. A and Mr. B, for such qualities are uncompromising before facts. Is it the quality apparent in Mr. C, that of benevolence?

Let us suppose that it is. Benevolence may be an aid to seeing, or it may be an obstruction through inclining us to see what is not, or not to see what is. Of course no amount of factual knowledge or of reason is a substitute for it. But neither is it an unfailing substitute for either of them. Though it gratifies the heart and softens the harsh and otherwise overwhelming lot of many, benevolence is not truth, wisdom, or justice. Nor is it uniform—what looks like callousness on one view may be benevolence on another.

On account of benevolence, let us suppose, or of dispositions very much like it, the Negro is to be accorded a new status. The will of C is in that case going to override that of A and possibly that of B. Black, with its unique qualities, is not to be black in the future, or is not to be recognized as such; nor white, white. They are to be artificially integrated.

Can benevolence go so far? Granted that it is the inspiration, how can it know that integration will satisfy? More than benevolence is evidently at work. What more? Perhaps it is the realization that the Negro cannot surmount the natural, historical barriers between him and the white. Perhaps it is the belief that the barriers are not natural but legal and conventional and can be overcome by legislation, including "judge-made" law, and moral persuasion. Perhaps it is a political awakening and ambition on the part of the Negro, or solicitation of him by white office-seekers; or perhaps it is visionary zeal.

There is abundant reason to think that the dispositions of A are destined to be sacrificed in the integration process. What if A resists?

To suppose that he will not is taking a very short view of human nature. It is frequently said in accounts of what is already happening that white people are *fleeing* to escape integration—leaving their homes, selling out, migrating.

In the 1957 congressional hearings on civil rights there is this item quoted from a Chicago witness: "The minute the Negroes move into a white block or move into a white school, the first year it is mixed up a little bit, the second year the whites move out and give it to them."[1]

Representative James C. Davis, chairman of a subcommittee which investigated racial integration in the public schools of Washington, testified that "introduction of Negroes into a white school does not turn it into an integrated school; it turns it into a Negro school within the course of a few years, just as fast as the white people can make arrangements to uproot themselves from the community and re-establish themselves over in Virginia or Maryland."[2]

A contemporary article in the *Saturday Evening Post*, by John Bartlow Martin, said: "About 30 per cent of Baltimore's people are Negroes. As they spread from the center of town, block by block, white people move out. . . . [In Baltimore, Washington, Louisville, St. Louis, and Kansas City] whites are fleeing to the suburbs, so more and more schools may become all-Negro. . . The same thing is happening in Northern cities. In New York, 29½ per cent of Negro pupils are attending schools that are predominantly Negro. In Chicago, Negro leaders have estimated that 90 per cent of Negro elementary pupils are in all-Negro schools."[3]

A Chicago Negro newspaper editor, Lee Blackwell, observed that "when whites move from an area into which Negroes are moving they only add to the problem of the Negro. Instead, people should attempt to live together, to interchange cultures."[4]

The spectacle of masses of people routed by other people and fleeing from them—what is this but a pogrom? Some persons today minimize race, and yet this spectacle shows a race driving a race before it with a peculiar weapon: its own mere presence. And it is made sardonic by the fact that the Negro's desire is not to drive the white out but to get close to him; made pathetic, too, by the Negro's unawareness that although it is not his will to perpetrate pogroms, his nature is doing so. The fugitive whites are so many Mr. A's.

How strange to them must be the Negro editor's proposition (which could be duplicated from white editors) that they should stay back and "interchange cultures" with the Negroes! But it is not difficult, perhaps, to comprehend the presumptuousness of such a proposition—

a great deal of doctrine has been in the air to the effect that race is nothing, that prejudice is everything, that race-mixing is natural and only restrained by the deadweight of unreasoning custom, that it is a function of education, religion, and government to encourage it. If we look into the grounds of this doctrine or the devices by which it is propagated, we find very little to its credit. On the contrary there is evidence strongly antithetical to it, as we have seen.

It is a delicate if not unspeakable thing to judge a fellow mortal's person, ancestry, country, or race in his presence or to his humiliation. But then in quite another sense it is a delicate thing not to consider such matters, and requires a sufferance which in some circumstances becomes odious. The facts bespoken by A are not annulled by the points of view of B or C, unless in the willing mind of B or C. But the presumption of integration propagandists, or their purpose, disregards this. They seem to take for granted that what they do not see or object to is not there or is not objectionable. This vanity, as much as anything else, makes and perpetuates racial disharmony.

It sets one force against others, the C's against the A's, for example, when if undisturbed these would find their natural relation and the ordinances suitable for maintaining it. In its zeal it refuses to stop at measures for redressing clear wrongs and shortcomings. It drives on, intent on curbing or extinguishing the opposition—the A party as it happens. This is nature insidiously fighting nature, and it signalizes failure in government; for government, the art of political harmony, has failed when blood differences break into conflict under its jurisdiction, and the more so when one race aggressively sets itself to integrate with another, against the other's will but with the government's powerful aid.

Is it an illusion to find that Negro and white are indigenously different, different even to the point of repugnancy? Some deny, in theory, that there is this difference. But the flight of the white from Negro contact is a fact extremely embarrassing to such a theory. There is strong evidence, some of it noticed in previous chapters, of primordial aversion to the Negro. The evidence cited by the Supreme Court as support for its 1954 school-integration decision, if it points to anything conclusive, points to that aversion; which in turn points logically not to integration but the opposite.

There is a radical difference between correction of wrongs and aggrandizement of rights. Equality of rights does not involve a right of persons, factions, or races to intrude in the sphere of others, nor does it take away the others' right of rejection. Equality here is a political, not a racial right—racially it is void of significance. It does not entitle colored people to status of any kind with white people, and vice versa. Nothing in it bears one way or the other on ambitions of the Negro for amalgamation. All this is too obvious not to be realized by the enlightened; who, if they overlook it, have perhaps been carried away by racial militancy or perhaps by the desperate realization of racial incompatibility and the temptation to try ulterior steps. The rights are one thing, the ambitions another. By confusing them, whether from misconception or deliberate intention, the protagonists of integration keep race tension alive.

Free association means not mere coexistence or compresence. It involves assent. Now an individual is under no law so far as his assent to association is concerned. He may be put under compulsion, but that does not insure assent: it would be like compelling him to like army rations or a cross-eyed female. Of course he may come to like them, but also he may not. It is strictly for him to determine. He has the only vote, subject to no law and no man, a suffrage far exceeding in authority the suffrage he exercises at the polls.

Integrationists would override this authority. Or they would expect it to vanish obligingly. Their own authority, *their* right of assent, remains entire, and is even reinforced by ambition. They themselves are to be free to choose, others not; for to choose is also to reject, and others are not to have that right. Association is choosing and reciprocally being chosen, between which there is a great difference, finely illustrated by history: the difference between highly civilized states in which the autonomies and dignities of individuals and types are respected, and undifferentiated masses in which nobody is anybody.

Perhaps the integrationist press is mindful, not heedless, of this when it publishes opportune photographs of white and black side by side, as if to say, "See, there is really no difference." But look farther, beyond the chance pictorial juxtaposition of white and black school pupils or ball players. There is the familiar aversion of white to black; mollified in some instances by complexities of experience, but in others intensified. It establishes an invisible but controlling inequality. Nothing in Negro experience, to judge from the intensity with which Negroes are striving for white company, resembles it. Integration puts the Negro with the white at no cost of this kind to the Negro, but with various degrees of disgust and revulsion as the cost to the white. Therein is the inequality, and there, incredibly, is the integrationist case. For the Negro now can say that if he cannot have the white's company, cannot with the support of the law defy nature, he is made to feel inferior, which means unequal protection; and the Supreme Court is there to bring him relief. The white can only say he is made to feel, for example, nauseated; and the Court has no relief for him. The poor, the unfortunate, the lowly of all kinds feel inferior; and the Court is silent to them. On the other hand, the Negro's inferiority sense, or what the Court pleases to ascribe to him as inferiority sense, brings him the very sky, putting him in a special, privileged category. He need not see or sense himself as others see and sense him.

One kind of feeling, personal inferiority, thus prevails at law over another, personal aversion. We are to understand that the Constitution sanctions this, in the equal-protection clause. But equal protection knows nothing of feelings. It is only the uniform, even reach of the governmental hand to its beneficiaries. Feelings are neither constitutional nor unconstitutional, lawful nor unlawful. The opposition between feelings of the types exemplified by Mr. A, Mr. B, and Mr. C is therefore without legal significance. Yet it was feeling, of inferiority, that turned the Brown decision.

It is also feeling that supports the decision, one might say, the feeling of fairness and benevolence; B and C against A. Even though the equal-protection right means nothing with respect to feelings, the whole affair of *Brown* is one of feeling, and in the name of equal protection. The feelings were in the air, so to speak, and the decision only registered them. The conscience of the country, manifested in them, is the real authority behind *Brown*.

An editor, a Senator, or pastor may profess to know this, by moral insight, and may be convinced that integration is a moral matter, above the law.[5] His conscience and what he takes to be the conscience of others, he conceives to be a voice from above, superior to the law and Constitution. He is then able to say that regardless of constitutional considerations, there is a higher law justifying integration. He takes this "higher law" to be morally binding on everyone. The A party, who feel as profoundly as he, but on the opposite side, are thus morally reduced to submission, in his philosophy.

But no one's conscience is a higher law to others, for no conscience is above another. How could it be? It is unique, wholly inward, and inalienable. To others it is even inaccessible. Autonomous, it excludes the dictates of every other conscience. No one's conscience is heard by another. In total solitude, a world to itself, it can give no orders and erect no standard, in the name of morals or anything else. The attempt to do so is the extreme offense against conscience. When an integrationist alliance of Jewish, Catholic, and Protestant clergy took form in 1963 and called for integration on moral grounds, a Florida Baptist convention of a hundred churches reacted by opposing integration, likewise on moral grounds.[6] Neither could speak with any authority over the other.

Because of the autonomy of conscience in everyone, the only tolerable relation of conscience to conscience is that of lord to lord. All being peers, none can have hegemony. Yet the most characteristic mark of conscience where anything such as religion, politics, or race is concerned, is the zeal to reform and rule. It forgets itself, is soon half beside itself in the determination to subjugate others, and incurs the risk of being subjugated itself. This is the annihilation of the authority and sanctity of conscience.

When it is said that there is a higher, moral law known by conscience, and when persons disappointed by the actual, enacted laws claim this as authority for their purposes, they seem to assume divine election of themselves as lawgivers. Or if not that, they assume the position of superiors in some other respect, such as insight or character. And conscience is the light by which they do this. Their position is expressible thus: Conscience is not equal to conscience, and the time comes when one conscience is justly impelled to override others.

Their contention is ruined by a fatal mistake: No conscience is above another, as no equal is above another. Admit a scale and the whole autonomy and inner authority of conscience vanishes. Obviously individuals do scale in many ways, some in multiples of the others; but that has no pertinence here. Conscience is not the individual himself, but a complex of compunctions uniquely his. The uniqueness cannot be measured or held in question, for like the individual himself, it is all or nothing, in every instance. Anyone who professes authority over it in the name of his own conscience or of visions of "higher law," must be under a delusion.

To resort to claims of such authority is not entirely different from resorting to arms, since it forcibly exceeds law to gain ends outside of law. To call this authority higher law is a contradiction in terms, since it has no legal status at all. To sanctify it with the title "moral," when it has no moral status at all, is a contradiction of that too. Nothing is moral that is not socially instituted, as nothing is legal that is not duly legislated. It may be desired, idealized, beneficial, and more, to some; but until established in the social system it has no moral status. Beyond the system there may be sublime realities, open to exalted minds, but they have no *moral* authority. Invoking "higher law" is not a case of attaining to these; high-mindedness or intellectual love of God, for example, is hardly attained that way. And in any event, invoking "higher law" for the purpose of over-riding the real law is strictly anti-moral, since it denies the authority and integrity of the moral system or society against which it is invoked.

Where conscience is widely at odds with conscience the moral and political system is disintegrating. The racial integration movement points in that direction. Possibly the movement generates tolerances where they might not have existed otherwise, but certainly it brings out hitherto subdued aversions and antipathies. It attempts to gain by coercion what is not coercible—a person cannot be compelled to like, welcome, or be at ease with another person, since all such attitudes are the antithesis of compulsion; nor can he be compelled to pretend to himself that his perception and sensibilities are unreal.[7] All of this is an engineered falsity. Though the falsity may not be identified openly, the sense of it is profound and is probably a powerful motive in the silent element of the opposition to integration. The silence of this element, like the volubility of others, may be mistaken by integrationists for stark prejudice or ill will or obstinacy. From this to the conviction that segregation is immoral is a short step for integrationists.

What if integrationists were wholly free of prejudice and obstinacy themselves, and tried to see all the facts? That would mean seeing themselves as others see them, the others including three and four-year-old children who shrink from Negroes, as well as adults who sacrifice their homes and flee at the news of Negroes moving near. Candor, integrity will not disown or disguise the facts, or maintain that primordial nature is nothing, or be deceived into thinking that racial realities are annulled by legal forms or by moralizing. Nor will it hear to taking the dictates of one party's conscience, without more, over the dictates of the other's.

If the integrationist is willing to put his case on grounds such as these, he has kept it a secret. To him, black is not black, nor is white white. There are no real lines of inclusion or exclusion, only bias, prejudice, pretense, bigotry. Consequently there are no real barriers, let alone sanctities, surrounding race and its institutions. All doors ought to be open.

Is this true? That is, waiving the question of whether his factual statements are tenable, we ask whether his doctrinal statement that all doors ought to be open can be maintained. But that is the same as asking whether that statement is or can be true. Now there is no conclusive way of determining what, if anything, *ought* to be, and here the integrationist is putting his case on the presumption that there is such a way. So he is practically relinquishing the case in stating it—what admits of no proof cannot establish anything in argument. His *ought* is almost certainly his own conscience, heard in

a slightly different key; and his conscience has no authority over
anyone else's. To say that all racial doors ought to be open is then
of no more probative force than to say that none ought to be open.

The capacity of conscience to determine questions of race is clearly
quite limited. We may pertinently ask whether conscience is not misleading and even obstructive when it becomes so dominant a force as it
is in the segregation controversy. For how can a controversy be resolved
by means which entitle and impel each party to maintain his stand
irreconcilably? That stand is idiosyncratic, leaving nothing to media-
tion, hence nothing to draw either party towards the other.

"Obey thy conscience, yes; but first be sure it is not an ass." It is
worse than an ass if it leads anyone to suppose that a metamorphosis
or apocalypse has come over nature, proving racial lines to be illusory
and stamping as prejudice and bigotry the belief that they ever were
real. It is worse still, to the point of perversity, if it induces the sentiment that we ought not to think of black as black and white as white:
that we ought not to admit the obvious or what has been proven by
the most decisive means, if it seems repugnant to conscience.

Here emerges the substance of the integrationist case: denial of the
world, so far as it bears against integration, and with this denial a
claim to transcendental authority for integration. Because of constitutional equality before the law, because of court decisions trans-
lating this into equality before people, and because, it is reasoned,
people *ought*, accordingly, to acknowledge no racial barriers, integrationists are tempted to claim higher-law justification for their stand.
Or it may be put: What ought to be is beyond question; equality of
people before one another ought to be the rule and the fact; racial
lines ought therefore to be erased. That they are not erased, that
integration is deferred, obstructed, and prevented is then declared
repugnant to higher law and to its monitor, conscience.

There is such a thing as proving too much—so much that nothing
remains but it. When integration transfers its case beyond the realm
of fact, going so far as to see nothing at all where a great part of the
world sees mountains and thickets, it leaves behind it the source and
scene of all the troubles and the possibility, whatever that may be,
of resolving them. For a while the fascination of its vision sustains
it. But presently the facts of existence obtrude themselves anew and
the dream is at an end. The higher law was so remote that it ruled
scarcely at all here below.

The "higher law" and its evangel, conscience, prove nothing concerning integration. Everyone — Mr. A, Mr. B, Mr. C, Governor
Wallace — can equally claim them as indisputable justification for

their course, with results utterly frustrating all around. The trouble is that only legislation can make law, and the law it makes is not higher; and if a law is higher, it is not *the* law. The spell of conscience is not law nor a proof of law.

Conscience, if it is not an ass, does not make pretensions to dominate the world. It sees that its dictates have no more authority over others than theirs have over it. In the early days of the country this was realized with great vividness and made into a pillar of the Constitution in the name of religious freedom: "Congress shall make no law respecting an establishment of religion . . ." In this may be seen a model to all who are tempted to impose their sentiments on others, under whatever pretension: As Congress is without capacity to make laws concerning religion, so the conscience of one party is without capacity to give directions to that of another. Alliances and conciliations are the most that can reasonably be expected between them, and these presuppose either natural affinity or some condition of mutual dependence, without which it is everyone for himself.

Where, it may be asked, is the Negro in this conflict of conscience? What of his conscience? The question seems not to have been asked, though a great deal has been said on the subject of indignity and humiliation of the Negro. In any event his case is no parallel to the white man's. He rests on the "right"—"constitutional right"—to put himself upon the white, but it is rare or unheard of for the white to claim the correlative "right." What type of *conscience* would it be, in either white or Negro, that would claim such a "right"? Would it not be, rather, a perversion of conscience? And yet perversion of rights at law may inspire all manner of other perversions; as when a court rules that Negroes have a constitutional right, under the equal protection guarantee, to *contact* and *interaction* with white people.[8] This, if true, or rather if tolerated, since it obviously could not be proved true, is the end of the world of the Constitution. Just ahead lies the desert of SCUR. There no questions of conscience, and no conscience to ask them, are to be anticipated.

On a matter of conscience simply, the majority does not rule. Practically, politically, the majority does rule, but not over conscience. The solicitude for minority rights, the toleration of the legislative filibuster, and occasional recognition of "the unwritten law" imply a legal regard for realities not amenable to legal forms. Of these peculiar realities, conscience is a vivid example. Though it may be either gratified or outraged by a law, it can hardly be governed by it. Consequently a majority vote for integration could not be expected to control a sentiment so profound and conscientious as that of the South even against token integration. Behind the forced submission it would bring would be an unspeakable revulsion against those responsible for it.

The wisdom of the fathers of the Constitution did not falter here. Though having no immediate reason to expect such a thing as a war of conscience against conscience, with the Government on one side, they provided, indirectly at least, against the possibility. In the Constitution, said Madison, "liberty of conscience" is "completely exempted from all authority whatever of the United States."[9] But this, like every other exemption or provision of the Constitution, depended on adherence to its terms, and the terms represented a limited federation of inviolate sovereignties (states). Under judocracy both the terms and the sovereignties have been tortured and put in subjection.

In international comity there is an instructive parallel. However small or impotent a country may be, it is sovereign, and there are no degrees of sovereignty, Switzerland, for example, having in that respect equal status with its neighbors, France and Germany. So with the states of the United States with respect to one another, and so with the conscience of Mr. A. with respect to Mr. B. and Mr. C. It is all or nothing, unanimity or separation. Coercion as an alternative is martyrdom. If the North imposes its will on the South by forcing Negro on white, it will be martyrizing the conscience of a people possessing "the priceless heritage of the finest blood in the World."[10]

---

[1] *Hearings before Subcommittee No. 5 of the Committee on the Judiciary, House of Representatives, Eighty-fifth Congress, First Session*, p. 1047.

[2] *Ibid.*, p. 1141. [3] July 13, 1957, pp. 33, 58.

[4] Associated Press, August 24, 1957. The proposal to "interchange cultures" invites attention to the status of Negro culture. Professor Arnold J. Toynbee, who distinguishes some twenty-one civilizations identifiable by race, observes, "when we classify mankind by colour, the only one of the primary races, given by this classification, which has not made a creative contribution to any of our twenty-one civilizations is the Black Race." *Study of History*, unabridged ed., vol. 1., p. 233.

[5] Congressman Celler, chairman of the House Committee on the Judiciary and of the Subcommittee on Civil Rights, says that now a state is "morally told" by the Supreme Court to integrate the schools. *Hearings*, p. 999. It would be illuminating, no doubt, to know the rationale of law and that of morals presumed to support this proposition.

[6] Associated Press, July 19, 1963.

[7] E. A. Westermarck, reiterating Kant, observes, "feelings which naturally differ infinitely in degree cannot form a uniform standard of good and evil, nor

has anyone a right to form judgments for others by his own feelings." *Ethical Relativity,* New York, Harcourt, Brace & Co., 1932, p. 37.

[8] Above, p. 220.

[9] Jonathan B. Elliot, *op. cit.,* vol. 4., p. 576.

[10] Arnold J. Toynbee, *Study of History,* unabridged ed., vol. 1, p. 219.

Chapter 13

THE TEMPER OF THE SOUTH

Without experience one cannot judge experience. Without experience of the palpable actualities of life within Negro masses and their effect on neighboring white people, no one is qualified to judge of Negro-white problems. Insulated idealism is no qualification. It is no more competent here than in war or disaster.

To judge regardless, is not only incompetent; it is presumptuous and it is unethical. A good deal of Northern opinion of the South concerning the Negro, and reflections of this opinion in Congress and the Supreme Court, deserves all these epithets. A physician does not diagnose or prescribe for a case he has not seen. He does not know fully its type or whether it departs from familiar types. A scrupulous judge or critic does not render judgments without full and fair hearings. On a matter of the complexity of the South's attitude concerning the Negro a full and fair hearing requires qualifications obviously not possessed by just anyone who ventures to write or to pass judicial opinion.

It is out of the question to deal understandingly with the temper of the South concerning the Negro by following external presuppositions and formulae. What if these prove to be only expressions of a contrary temper, arising from a different life and history? Such are no more pertinent than our notions respecting the internal affairs of France or South Africa. There is in the South a manifold of experience, conviction, and loyalty which, concerning the Negro question, is fixed and probably final. It is in no way hostile, cruel, or indifferent, of itself, towards the Negro. It is white fully aware of black, and categorically marking and maintaining their distinction.

Three centuries made this, plus long preparation before in the Old World. The Civil War did not alter it—fighting is of little efficacy against such a thing. The Supreme Court's segregation decisions have not altered it. They have intensified it.

The North is a complete contrast to this solid unison. A multitudinous, stirring miscellany, a perpetual flux of elements from everywhere, it knows no lines comparable to the South's. Black and white are different, obviously; but in the great concourse of all, and with the black a rarity, there is only passing notice. Other differences, as between Jew and gentile, Oriental and Western, English-speaking and non-English-speaking, stand out almost as prominently.

Here are reflected two histories: the white South, a homogeneous people whose situation generated unanimity and rigidity on the matter of race; the heterogeneous North, where the view of race corresponds also to the North's situation and experience of race. As the South's national character and conditions produced one result, the North's, far different, produced another. Immigration did not come south after the Civil War, but sprinkled and here and there glutted the North with all elements. We are even now two peoples. A Southerner today as in generations past is very likely to find himself more easy and at home in England than in the North.

When a Northerner criticizes the South concerning race (the same probably goes for other topics of his criticism), it is a good chance he is only expressing predispositions and policies characteristic of his own situation. There the status of one population element is scarcely different from that of another, socially or morally, in the vast miscellany. It is like the frontier, where few distinctions are made except in the size of one's stake, and one asks no questions about his neighbor lest his own status fall under question. Rank and tradition have made hardly a mark beyond what is liable to obliteration with a turn in business or a new expressway. Historical antecedents terminated at the shore. To minds thus conditioned the thought of a different order close at hand, like the South's, is not likely to be agreeable, and since restraint is not a product of backgrounds like theirs, it takes little provocation for them to arraign, denounce, and condemn.

Two rather different peoples and histories, two grand outcomes of the course of nature, one of them now presuming to overthrow the other because of its dissimilarity (!), though, to be sure, formulating reasons to the purpose; which reasons transform the dissimilarity into a wrong—the wrong of maintaining racial lines. But that is not a *wrong*, in itself. For it to be such, it must breach some covenant or some generally admitted humane principle. There is no covenant, unless we might consider the Constitution such a thing. But the Constitution from the first and also from the time of the Fourteenth Amendment was no prohibition upon segregation, and it is that now only because of what we have seen to be, irrefragably, a subversion of it by the Supreme Court. Then as for segregation being a violation of humane principle, while that is arguable, far more than arguability is necessary before we have a principle of the generality and applicability this would require. It is very doubtful that anything short of general revulsion will give such a principle—a general revulsion against segregation. But there is no such. While many people at a distance may feel it unfair, the like is not the case among those who live closest to the Negro, whether in the South or the North, in America or elsewhere. So it cannot be said that there is a general revulsion against segregation. Quite the contrary; there is a profound revulsion in the white against Negro contact, as Lincoln was candid to recognize. Further, it is only fair to observe that segregation in the South is of course mutual. White people seclude themselves as punctiliously as they exclude the Negro, and the same is generally the Negro practice as well. So it cannot reasonably be maintained that there is a humane general principle making segregation *per se* wrong. The North in presuming to abolish segregation in the South is therefore without that as a ground. It can only justify itself by the aforesaid vice of subversion of the Constitution or else by force. In alleging wrongs on the part of the South, the North would be in a better position if it would first clear itself of these two. Subversion of the Constitution is a corruption of law and justice, beyond question. Resort to force to sustain such a corruption only compounds and multiplies the viciousness.

Has the North seriously thought of what it is about? Literally, desegregation by force would be the constitutional undoing of the South, the disjoining of a system engrained with segregation for three centuries. This break-up would be only a beginning. It would throw upon the South the conditions that segregation was lawfully instituted to prevent: the noisomeness of massive contact, the intolerable prospect of Negro domination in some localities, the disconcertion of morale and endeavor. Such insufferable conditions gave birth to the Ku Klux Klan in Reconstruction times and at length so turned the Northern Congress that it put a stop to them. Who would gain by a repetition of this? What would happen to the stability and security of government, business, work, education, and life at large? Are Northern minds so possessed as to think that sending in the Army is the answer? Sending in the Army is a confession, and an advertisement to the world, of national failure. Suppose it wins a victory— blasts the community, mows down the people. What will that prove? Only that America is, literally, not civilized, that its cherished Consitution is a makeshift, that law has collapsed at the foundation. All of this for the sake of gratifying the North's obsession about something it knows only in the abstract, though the abstract of it, by contrast with the actualities the South has to bear, is of no more moment than the abstract of Utopia.

By contrast with this, the South cares not to impose its way on the North. Nor does it indulge in invidious comparisons — in the Southern press, for example, there are no lurid exhibits of the worst things to be discovered in the North, no fabrications by roving agents in search of sensations, no noticeable policy or disposition to retaliate in kind for what the Northern press makes a fairly regular business at the cost of the South.[1] To the Northern public accustomed to such fare, this probably means there are no grounds for retaliation, nothing to expose or to regard with condescension. To others, in the South, in Canada, and in Europe, such complacency may call to mind the old lament about not seeing ourselves as others see us. The cultivated mind everywhere disdains the spirit of censoriousness.

There are men who do not choose to impugn or injure those with whom they disagree; whose nature is devoid of the motive to dominate and the urge to show off their qualities; who are superior to the vice of vituperation; in whom reserve and even silence are more eloquent than bombast in others. In a word, gentlemen. In the South, despite great losses and many handicaps, owing to the race blight and the North's aggrandizement stemming from it during and since the Civil War, this elite spirit survives.

The tone and tradition of cultivated English life gave the South its aristocratic distinction in the formative years. Some today, for example the historian T. J. Wertenbaker, take pains to make us aware that Virginians were not titled, nor Carolinians, and it is a stock observation that not all owned slaves or lived in mansions. This is like saying that not all Englishmen are dukes or earls. Yet the aristocracy set the tone, which carried throughout the region as the population expanded and spread to new lands; giving the dignity, politeness, and becoming manners distinctive of Southern life. The underdog strata did not exemplify all these qualities, doubtless. But they respected them, and do today. I venture that none of them would say to the Queen of England, "We have a daughter who is just like you. People are always saying she could be your twin sister." This, according to the Associated Press, did occur at a garden party at Buckingham Palace, given for Americans attending the American Bar Association's meeting in London in 1957.[2]

In Dr. Wertenbaker's *The Old South—the Founding of American Civilization* there are many evidences of the Southern manner of life in the colonial age.

"We are introduced into the daily life of a wealthy Virginia planter in the closing years of the colonial period by the pages of the *Journal* of Philip Vickers Fithian, the Princeton graduate employed as tutor by Colonel Robert Carter, of Nomini Hall, in Westmoreland County. We see the Colonel practicing on the flute or the piano, or studying thorough bass, or reading philosophy, or conversing learnedly of eclipses, telescopes and the planets. We follow Fithian himself as he strolls in the formal garden, or browses in the very extensive library, or plays the violin in a family musicale, or looks over the latest London newspapers, or wonders at a case of mathematical instruments which has just arrived from England, or expresses his admiration for the beauty and dignity of Nomini Hall itself. It is a fascinating picture of refined, leisurely, cultured life, in which neither the business of managing a great plantation nor an occasional ball or marriage festival interrupts for long the customary school work, music, interesting conversation, the reading of the classics, law, philosophy and English literature.

" . . . But nothing can be farther from the truth than the belief that the gay life absorbed all the leisure moments of the typical wealthy planter. There were many, like Jefferson, who enjoyed a quiet moment with Cicero or Horace, many who delighted in an evening devoted to music, many who preferred Shakespeare to the fox hunt, many who turned enthusiastically to architecture, landscape gardening, art and philosophy. But they devoted themselves to these things in the spirit of the cultured gentleman, not as professionals, not as productive artists or scholars. They kept abreast of the best literature of their time, but they were not themselves poets or essayists or novelists; they built beautiful residences, but they were not professional architects; they were acquainted with theology, but they did not enter into theological disputes. In statecraft and political theory alone did they forsake the role of the amateur and become creators, and in these fields their accomplishment was truly amazing."[3]

An article, "Art in the Early South," in the *South Atlantic Quarterly*, by Mary H. Flournoy, gives more particulars. The first musical society in America (1762) was the St. Cecelia of Charleston, and in Charleston also the first concerts (1732) were performed.[4] Opera was first established in New Orleans. The first American composer to win recognition in Europe was the Louisianian, Louis Mereon Gottschalk.[5] In Virginia the first theatrical performance was given (1665) and the first theater established (Williamsburg, 1716).[6] At Williamsburg also was "the earliest patronage of sculpture in America."[7] Josiah Quincy, of Massachusetts, "was so struck with the architectural beauty of Charleston that he said he 'found there what he never expected to find in America;'" and Henry James "believed that the high, complicated, inflated spire of St. Michael's Church, in Charleston, 'produced the impression of grace and form as nothing else in America.'"[8] The first state universities, the first law school, and the first college for women were in the South. Thomas Jefferson's library, exceeding 6,000 volumes, was "the most remarkable private collection then to be found in America." It was purchased by Congress and became the nucleus of the Library of Congress. A century before the Revolution, William Byrd had given thirty-nine free libraries to Virginia.[9]

Jay B. Hubbell, in his book *The South in American Literature—1607-1900*, observes that at the University of Virginia, William and Mary, and South Carolina College (which became the University of South Carolina) "the work in history, law, economics, and political science was probably more thorough" than that elsewhere in the country.[10] Speaking of the visit of La Rochefoucauld to Virginia in 1796, he recalls that he "found the common people perhaps more ignorant than elsewhere, but he added: 'In spite of the Virginian love for dissipation, the taste for reading is commoner there among men of the first class than in any other part of America.'"[11] Thackeray and other upper-class English visitors, in spite of slavery, "often felt more at home" in the South than in the North.[12] William Ellery Channing wrote: "I believe I have praised the Virginians before, in my letters, for their hospitality. I blush for my own people, when I compare the selfish prudence of a Yankee with the generous confidence of a Virginian. Here is one single trait which attaches me to the people I live with more than all the virtues of New England. They *love money* less than we do. They are more disinterested. Their patriotism is not tied to their purse-strings. Could I only take from the Virginians their *sensuality* and their *slaves*, I should think them the greatest people in the world."[13]

These are qualities that do not come from nothing or persist by accident. They were elements of what Arnold Toynbee has styled the South's "priceless heritage of the finest blood in the World."[14] Today as two centuries ago they are incommensurable with dollars-and-cents standards and statistical indices. The "solid South," the Southern genre, which is still something of an enigma to the North, and now and then is fictitiously "analyzed" by strangers from there, reflects them. A common supposition is that race is the explanation; that it produced and sustains the solidarity that puzzles so many. This is like explaining the English character as something evolved from England's attitude towards the Irish. The Negro was little

more than an accident initially, in the South. Had he never been
brought here, plantation life, a magnification of English country life,
would have differed little, except in scale, from the life it was. The
temper of the South is what it is, with or without Negroes. One might
more plausibly trace it to differences with the North: the differences
between a homogeneous, aristocratically imbued people and a melting
pot of all kinds. Whereas in the melting pot anything goes, theoretically, outside the melting pot that is not so. It is the difference between many and one, flux and fixity, international and national
The South is more a nation than the Union.

To the South the prospect of race mixing is correspondingly more
repugnant. It means destruction of racial autonomy and of the associated institutions. It means unspeakable violation of sensibilities
hitherto always respected by law and custom. It means the reversal
of history "with all deliberate speed;" reversal of a history in which,
with unquestioned sanction of the Constitution and laws, the status
of black and white was naturally determined and was confirmed and
reconfirmed with hardly an exception during three deliberate centuries.
This reversal means betrayal of the whole past by a court entrusted
to uphold the legal model and essence of the past, the Constitution.
In such betrayal there is special cause for dismay and disaffection.
That the highest court of justice in the land should do this destroys
confidence in the court and drives people to align it against the Constitution. It makes enemies of friends and brings on a cold civil war.

To some the Court betrayal is more odious and is more poignantly
felt than the prospect of integration. They know that integration will
hardly affect them, since abundance of means, which is theirs in one
form or another, can always insure the color bar, south, north, in
Africa, everywhere. But nothing can compensate for the betrayal.
It is a breaking of faith, a corruption of blood.

To others integration will be little more than nominal, touching
them too lightly for notice. It is only an idea. Disputing it leaves
them indifferent.

Those who contemplate the inescapable realities, regardless of
whether they themselves must experience them, who are not far
away but on the scene and familiar with it, are certain to react otherwise. They are the great majority of the South, who shrink from
the thought of integration. Words, arguments fall dead on them and
even arouse suspicion. You do not argue about repugnancies.

So far as the North sees this, it must know there can be no coercing this spirit, this ultimatum of human nature. So far as it does
not see it, it misses the heart of the case, and cannot interfere with-

out committing outrage. At this plane civility forbids compulsion and demands restraint and respect instead. Thus it is that the aged, the sick, the bereaved, women, infants, the cleric, the eminent, all have their titles and honor, without arguments or proofs. Similarly, and in a sense equally, whole peoples, and the individuals constituting them, have in a civil society corresponding rights and dignities. The whole case for racial separation lies here. At whatever stage, the objection to integration comes back to this intuitive, primordial aversion.

No free agent is personally answerable at law to another. No Negro *per se* has personal rights over a white person, or vice versa. But when a Negro sues to put himself with white people, he is claiming a personal right over them: the right to join them, to enter their lives, to override their natural and legal right of withdrawal.

This has nothing to do with equal protection, just as a tramp's claim to reception in a rich man's parlor has no such implication. Or if it does, then the most elemental rights of persons are nothing and the Constitution, by which they are secured, is nothing. Equal protection is bounded by these, not superior to them, else there is nothing for it to protect.

Nor is it necessary that Negroes have access to whites in order to secure themselves against indignity. The poor do not have to intrude on the rich to avoid indignity or injustice. In the past the Supreme Court has elucidated the point, saying:

" . . . The argument [of the Negro plaintiff, Plessy] necessarily assumes . . . that equal rights cannot be secured to the negro except by an enforced commingling of the two races. We cannot accept this proposition. If the two races are to meet upon terms of social equality, it must be the result of natural affinities, a mutual appreciation of each other's merits and a voluntary consent of individuals. As was said by the Court of Appeals of New York in *People* v. *Gallagher*, 93 N. Y. 438, 448, 'this end can neither be accomplished nor promoted by laws which conflict with the general sentiment of the community upon which they are designed to operate . . . ' Legislation is powerless to eradicate racial instincts or to abolish distinctions based upon physical differences, and the attempt to do so can only result in accentuating the difficulties of the present situation."[15]

Perhaps the North today believes that it has a fairer perception of the Negro than the South has, and rests on that belief in trying to impose its will on the South. Would it, if that were so, try to force white with Negro? Is not the attempt itself evidence of some lack of perception? The revulsion in the white is too strong and too widely met, in the South and over the world, to warrant any other supposition short of willfulness or vengefulness on the part of the North. A fair comprehension of facts and a fair disposition for dealing with them does not lead to attempts to deny nature and history —attempts to deny the facts. Lincoln, a man of acute perception and high probity, faced the facts and freely declared himself: "Physical difference" between white and Negro "will probably forever forbid their living together upon the footing of perfect equality."[16]

Sympathy, which the North has given the Negro with great generosity, is not the same thing as perception, especially when at a distance. Beyond a point, it may only obstruct or distort perception. The sympathizer, especially if far from the scene, thinks of humanity wronged, of the weak and helpless under cruel oppressors, which so offends him that indignation and fury may blind him to the realities. That the object of his sympathy is not humanity in abstraction but men and women with qualities such as provoke intuitive rejection in the neighboring white, is not likely to occur to him. Sympathy has become partisanship and prejudice in him.

Oppression, too, of an ineffable character, sickening to the sensibilities and, if not thrown off, a source of constant distraction and tension, is the lot of the white party. Though it is the prime if not entire reason for the South's adamant position, one who had never been on the scene long enough to comprehend would probably not suspect it. The integrationist press does not hint of it. A frequent theme of the press is toleration, liberality, good will. Indeed? A unilateral toleration and so forth, extending only to the Negro side? Yet a cool, informed regard, liberal, tolerant, or what you will, can hardly fail to see that the South deserves high credit, higher perhaps than any other part of the world, for the extent of racial harmony it has achieved; for surely racial differences make and perpetuate the greatest differences between peoples, and in collision bring out the worst that is in them. That collisions were kept down and a fair degree of toleration was maintained in spite of lamentable exceptions, is a tribute to both white and Negro.

The late United States Senator William E. Borah, who was unsurpassed in the Senate for the liberality, force, and sympathetic understanding of his views, paid tribute to the South for this achievement. He said in an address in the Senate on January 7, 1938:

" . . . I shall contend that the southern people have met the race problem and dealt with it with greater patience, greater tolerance, greater intelligence, and greater success than any people in recorded history, dealing with a problem of similar nature . . .

"I know of no finer sense of duty than that displayed by the South in the help it gives the Negro in bettering his condition as to property, as to economic strength, and as to education . . .

"It is true, as is contended here, that at times he has suffered from mob violence in the South, but it is equally true that he has suffered from race riots in the North. But in all things which make for the advancement of the race as a race, the North has no advantage over the South in the story of the advancement of the Negro. We have shown no greater patience, no greater tolerance, no greater ability to deal with this race than have our brothers in the South."[17]

Whatever the attainment, whatever the merits implicit in it, it does not excuse—nothing excuses—cruelty or violation of rights. Consider, however, the provocations. White people with the history and circumstances of the South are sensitive to them beyond the surmises of people under other conditions. Threats, assault, rape, murder of the white at the hands of the Negro in the South are correspondingly different. Eliminate them and the harsh treatment of the Negro dies out. Toleration and accord develop. Perhaps far-away critics forget or have never known that the atrocities committed on Negroes in the South are commonly results of Negro crimes and personal advances against the white and that these have a heightened and horrifying offensiveness to the white.

It is only willfulness to ignore the facts, and injustice and intolerance to condemn without comprehending the facts. One may reply that people ought not to let themselves be at the mercy of such facts, and that as citizens they ought not to shun other citizens of a different color. Now this itself is very presumptuous—it is what, in others, the integrationist press calls bias, intolerance, bigotry. A man cannot dictate to his peers in this way. If he persists, he only betrays motives of willfulness and coerciveness, and these are wholly foreign to the concept, *ought*. Over a white woman's unspeakable dread of the Negro male, over intuitive revulsion, there is no *ought*, unless it is that such horrors ought not to be.

Sensibility is not bigoted or fanatical, nor is it ethical or unethical —moral or immoral predicates do not pertain to it. It is dull or fine, gross or delicate, rich or poor, or something between. Under staid conditions it forms into types, by which peoples and civilizations are often distinguished. Without appreciation of this, one is in no position to judge others.

Upon the whole, the North lacks that appreciation as far as the South is concerned. Individuals there may have it, but they are seldom heard. The idea propagated in the press and politics, and even in the pulpit, is that the South has a peculiar, malicious attitude towards the Negro. There is certainly a general attitude in the South towards the Negro, but the idea that it is malicious has little foundation. Natural aversion is not malice. Consider the showings by Professor Brittin;[18] consider the strife in localities in the North as Negroes become more numerous; consider the reactions of white South Africa to the Negroes there, of the French in Africa to them, and of the English to black immigrants. Recognition of immiscibility and face-to-face incompatibilities, and the institution of civil means for securing respect for them, is not malice and not unethical. The North's persistence in believing the contrary, instead of ascertaining and respecting the untoward facts, is hardly what we should expect of an ethical preceptor.

It is not so much the South's temper as the North's, or the militant integrationist North's, that agitates the country. The South intends no blow, no harm, nothing at all, to the North. It is convinced, according to all signs, that the expression of so much hostile sentiment in the Northern press and other media is not reliably representative of Northern attitudes, and that it is not fully sincere. The most frequently heard Southern interpretation is that this thunder is only political, meant to rally Negro votes. But it must be more than that. How else account for the numerous resolutions of churchmen, for example, calling for integration? Perhaps some in the South dismiss these as only political in a broader sense—eclesiastico-political. Such an enormity, however, as the demand of two high members of the Presbyterian hierarchy for the use of "troops and tanks if necessary"[19] to enforce integration in Southern schools is far more than either politics or ecclesiasticism. Troops and tanks are so far from being means to education or to bona fide integration that reasonable minds must have been aghast at the proposal. So was another Presbyterian authority, the Rev. Philip Howerton, moderator of the Southern Presbyterian Church, who replied that the use of force "can accomplish nothing but chaos."[20]

An old canard represents the South as a land of race prejudice and fiery tempers. In fact the temper of Southern people, contrasted to that of Northern integrationists today, seems reserved; and against the abolitionist temper of a century ago, no Southerners, probably nobody anywhere, could expect to win laurels. Racial aversion is not prejudice. Conceivably it may sometimes be only feigned, but again it is so deeply felt that it is literally unspeakable. Critics of the South's racial stand must have no comprehension of this, though it is the nerve of all the trouble. Have they investigated? Have they tried to put themselves in the Southerner's place?

Not all of the Northern press is, shall I say, biased—"biased" is what it commonly calls anything racial from the South. The *Christian Science Monitor,* of Boston, which I believe has been more honored than any other newspaper in the country for integrity and high tone, sympathetically observes: "It is only fair to note that . . . the South labors under extra difficulties. In that section millions of kindly, intelligent Americans are convinced that both races can progress better if a degree of separation is maintained. Most of the South's critics would very likely find themselves taking this same position if they lived under the same conditions. Usually transplanted Northerners become most ardent segregationists."[21]

It would be a great gain for both North and South if the will to see and understand could prevail—not that the South's feeling towards the Negro would be changed, but the North would come to see that what it had envisioned hitherto was far wide of the mark; that the South's stand was not one of enmity towards the Negro; that it had a fully comprehensible etiology; and that it is not to be suppressed by fiat, whether judicial or legislative.[22]

In this process of self-enlightenment perhaps a few other discoveries would come out. Despite good will and considerable indulgence towards the North apart from the segregation complex, there is still in the South a quality which the rather free Northern manner continually irritates. An elite spirit and tradition does not advertise itself and does not belie itself by discourtesies to anyone. Nor does it fail to perceive discourtesies at the hands of others, who, however, mistake its silence and reserve for an admission of the faults they may allege. Take the practice of Northern journalists who come "down" and, apparently assuming that a running survey is sufficient to discover everything, hasten to make known the existence of sloth, squalor, degeneracy, diffidence, to the dismay, no doubt, of readers back home; not realizing, doubtless, that strangers who only scan things this way can say the like about much of, for example, France and Italy, not excluding Paris; and not suspecting that the real character and culture are behind the scenes, out of their sight. How much of these exhibits is of Negro life the reader may not be told, now that the Northern press has ceased to distinguish white from Negro.[23]

Occasionally someone in the South, some independent small town editor for example, breaks under the strain and speaks out in self-defense. But it is a rare thing indeed for anyone to reply in kind.

To a discerning mind it must be apparent that the disparity here, the self-restraint on the Southern side, the vituperative intemperance on the other, is eloquent of much that cannot be measured by impressionistic sketches of Negro quarters and of lowly white ne'er-do-wells. The poise of a mind and manner bred in an old, elite tradition is proof against the slurs of *parvenu* detractors.

Sometimes these slurs take a very odd turn, fixing on language. In the rural South, among the very poor, a linguistic fusion of a kind has occurred, giving a miscellany of what seem to be Negroid pronunciations. Negroes say "Ah" for "I," "doe" for "door," and the like. The peasant whites say something between "Ah" and "I," but hardly "doe." Other white people, still under the influence of cultivated British diction, characteristically soften both the "i" and the "r." Since any softening is in sharp contrast to the language of those who, such as the touring journalists, speak a sharp "I-ee," "dah-rr," and the like, it is no wonder they think they hear more extreme forms than they do. Or perhaps the explanation is not in the hearing so much as in the ill-tuned rendering they give it in print. I have read somewhere that Sir Arthur J. Balfour, the learned Prime Minister, thought Virginia speech, especially in such features as its softening of the vowels after hard "c" and "g," the most elegant of all spoken English. Naturally a person's language tells much, being his very expression. So it is no slight matter for persons who speak virtually a foreign language to misrepresent and disparage the language of the South, a language which in its distinctive exemplifications is not simply soft but is imbued with the artless complaisance of an elite heritage. If almost no one in the South chooses to reply to the slurs on Southern language, it is less because there is nothing to say than because the natural reticence of the elite spirit is unmoved by effrontery.

It is deeply moved, however, by falsity and betrayal. President Eisenhower and Attorney-General Rogers gave deep offense by utterances which spoke of disrespect for law and of disloyalty to the country and its traditions through resistance to integration in the South's schools. The President said, after the Supreme Court's hurried reversal of the Federal district court decision granting Little Rock two and a half years for desegregation, "I hope that all of us may live up to our traditional and proud boast that ours is a government of laws."[24] This and much else said by others then and since then intimates that segregationists, if not the South generally, lack respect for law. It takes no account of the Supreme Court's own denial of the law of the land (law repeatedly sustained by the Court and by congressional acts). It disregards the extraordinary means by which the Court did this—its presumptions in violation of valid reasoning, its disregard of facts pertinent, its dozen other obliquities noticed in the foregoing, all combining into the manifestly false proposition, "Separate educational facilities are inherently unequal." Whoever supports the school decisions supports, even though unwittingly and with motives of generosity, this defiance of law, not to speak of the falsity underlying.[25]

In a vague way some integrationists have all along spoken of difficulties ahead for integration. What difficulties? Those, we may be sure, which we have seen in these pages, originating in and always returning to the primordial aversion of the white man for the Negro. But there is now little prospect that the fundamental facts will be recognized and public policy be made to conform with them. What if, in the determination to have compulsory integration, it becomes necessary to put bayonets over the South? Is that for the common good? What will the civilized world think of it? What must thoughtful and scrupulous minds think of it now, in anticipation? What, too, will be thought of the perfidy behind it all—the Supreme Court's renunciation of fact, reason, and the law of the land?

We have noticed that integrationists often invoke moral sanctions and try to apply them coercively to the South. What now of the morality of first deceiving oneself and then perpetrating the deception upon others—what of accusing others of defying the law when the "law" the accuser stands on is itself a demonstrable defiance of law? This, assuredly, is monumental falsity. There is a principle of law that no man shall profit by his own iniquity or take advantage by his own wrong.[26] Resting on the demonstrable falsity underlying *Brown* v. *Board of Education,* integrationists who accuse the South of iniquity are violating this principle. They go further and make believe that supporting the school decision—supporting the fruit of falsity—is a virtue, even connecting it with "higher moral law." But an ethical mind, surely, must know it travels under false pretenses if it accuses others of disrespect for law while itself defending judicial defiance of law; and must feel compunctions against hypocrisy if it pretends that no legal, no judicial miscarriage has occurred, or that that is immaterial and the only thing that matters is the Court's decision.

It is no defense that the integrationist of this type is uninformed —ignorance is a strange ground on which to found moral condemnation. It is no defense that he is morally inspired—his adversaries, too, may be morally inspired. Without enlightenment, without comprehension, no one is qualified to moralize to others; and with an educated man's portion of these, one is disinclined to such a pretension anyhow, knowing the ultimate moral autonomy of everyone. Nor will the educated, on reflection, be likely to commit the common integrationist blunder of mistaking their private moral sentiments for law.

Instead of presuming to condemn the South for so much, suppose the North turned its attention to itself. I will not be tempted to say what it might discover, but would ask, Why should it force its sentiments, or its indifference to what others find intolerable, upon a people so different in history and temper from itself? There is such a thing as internal, intranational aggression, and probably nowhere in the world is it more in evidence now than here. With it goes the misrepresentation and self-deception familiar in international aggression. The North, in all this, is acting towards the South in a fashion similar to that of Russia towards its victims.

There is a clearly indicated and in some ways sweet to contemplate answer to all the questions now agitating North and South: Separation. Let the South go in peace. Let the North show its good faith by consenting.

Almost certainly the South would rather be out of the Union than be driven to integration. So the North, if it would not be an oppressor, must make a choice of: (1) consenting to separation; (2) instituting some thorough plan for resettling integrationist Negroes out of the South; (3) amending the Constitution so as to strike down the Court's school decisions and at the same time provide competent means for securing equal protection. For the South, any of these courses would be an advance.

The alternative is an indefinite period of attrition; inevitable outbreaks of violence; fresh retaliatory dragonnades, after the example of Little Rock; strife, sorrow, disunion, with an illuminating lesson to the world on the subject of aggression and tyranny within America, and disillusion of nations concerning our leadership and fitness for leadership.

Far simpler would it be, as matters stand now, for the separation to occur. The prospect of irreconcilability, compulsion, guerrilla action, and all the fruits, is little less than terrifying. Nature is not going to give—not soon, if ever: the primordial aversion, with its inured consequences of three centuries, is hardly amenable to court decrees against it. The North is unwilling to learn, if we may judge by the utterances of its mouthpieces: it is firmly set in the belief that "prejudice," "discrimination," malice, obstinacy account for the

South's stand. Its representatives in Washington, notably such as Senators Douglas and Javits, continually work for repressive and punitive measures. For a long time the South has endured this. Now it is acutely conscious of a betrayal, betrayal of the Constitution, and what that means to it the victim.

Why then hold out? If the North is sincere, why should it not welcome the separation? And on the other hand, if the North is worthy to prevail, can it afford to resort to tyranny? Enlightened men worthy to govern do not force their sentiments on others. They do not violate or rudely disregard the sentiments of the others.

Separation, to be sure, is not talked in the South. Only with deep misgivings would the idea be entertained at present. But to suppose that the present calm will continue when the now foreseeable reign of force and terror draws near, would be to dream. The prospect of a complete change, notwithstanding deep devotion to the United States and its Constitution, to both of which the South contributed a very fair share, would be hard to resist. Prospective settlers here a century and more ago looked on the New World as paradise by contrast to the world of hardship and oppression they had known. The South will look to itself as all of that, a sweet land needing only to be free. It takes little imagination to see that within one or two generations such a land and people might flourish beyond anything dreamt of in its present semi-subjugated state.

For a century now race has been a pall over the South. The only endurable course was the one that was taken. As time passed and destiny became more apparent, people realized that the Negro could not be perpetually denied. A painful dilemma arose: Either maintain the system of privation, with the persistent necessity of cultivating a blindness towards it lest it become an obsession, or else capitulate in some degree to amalgamation. The latter being utterly revolting, the first alternative was assumed. Segregation is objectionable to the white man indeed. He does not *want* to bar out other men or to harm or humiliate them. It is simply that, of two evils, integration and segregation, he finds segregation the lesser. Not he alone, but an accident of history, putting people so different as white and Negro side by side, must take the blame. To suppose that such an accident can be overcome by coercing the white victim to submit to a revolting inversion of nature, is manifest folly. Artfulness, seemingly unknown to integrationists, is needed for anything savoring of that, artfulness in the form of a willing repression of antipathies, the cultivation of forbearing and generous sentiments, and the gradual institution of means for making secure the results. Ironically, it was chiefly in the South that advances of this kind were made; made not in disregard of the racial realities, but out of humane consideratoin, with the high-minded purpose of palliating the realities, not denying them.

It is unnatural and unworthy that minds should be preoccupied with such a matter as race. That race should become a pall, causing a whole people to shrink before it and impelling them to maintain rigid barriers against it for their own peace of mind, is a veritable curse. That the North, uninformed and militantly unwilling to be informed, should deceive itself into thinking that ill will on the part of the South is the whole explanation, and aggressively resolve to force its will on the South, is an intensification of the curse, which now recoils on the North, blinding it to the tyranny of its own course. Instead of looking deliberately at the realities and striving for an accord with them, the North, or its more outspoken element, acts as if nothing untoward, nothing but Southern obstinacy, stood in the way, and vehemently denounces the South with charges of race-hate, bigotry, moral profligacy, and defiance of law. All of this for, one might say, nothing. For the South generally has done nothing but what the world, including the North, under comparable conditions has done: it has only withdrawn and sheltered itself naturally, instinctively, from contact repugnant to it. Blind to this fact, carried away by visionary interpretations and presumptions, the North convicts itself of the very thing it accuses the South of: violation of moral principle. For it is a violation of moral principle, at least in the Anglo-American tradition, to indict and condemn without fair warrant.

Thus race corrupts even its patron and benefactor. It induces him, at a distance, to suppose there are no race differences, and to make up a vocabulary—"racist," "hate-monger," "bigot"—of derision for those who know better. It leads him to ignore the obvious falsity of the Supreme Court decision, which, like any other obvious falsity, men of probity can only repudiate and deplore. Then it tempts him to bring up *ad hoc* justifications, such as the allegation that because you demur to a patently subversive court decision and resolve to exhaust all legal means for deferring its application, you are lawless; and that your example is an invitation to others to take to violence. One thing is certain: this subversion of reason, judgment, and integrity is unrelated to anything likely to placate the country with regard to race.

It is idle to blame the South. Blame nature, blame mankind. Better yet, blame nothing, but instead consider the facts. Integrationists urge this, I know, but only to a point. They mean, consider the facts that must be overcome to enforce integration. Thus Professor Paul A. Freund of the Harvard Law School calls for "reason, good will, and practical sense"—but as means for "devising ways of complying with school desegregation."[27] Reason, good will, and practical sense, not thus restricted to partisan purposes but turned freely upon the facts, would show what is all too familiar to those who have lived with them: a sensitive people doomed to the toleration not just of disagreeable neighbors but of utterly foreign, antithetical nature, of poignant repugnancy before which it shrinks as one species before another; yet impelled by fellow-creature motives to be sympathetic and indulgent. Confronted by this, what may reason, good will, and practical sense be expected to enjoin? Not, assuredly the outraging of our inmost nature—reason, good will, and practical sense do not defy nature. Then not integration.

Rather, what is indicated is some possible accord, such as a plan of mutual, enlightened regard and security. It is contrary to reason and practical sense to talk coercion, artful or otherwise. It is a betrayal of good will to try to enlist it on the side of such error. Some may be passive to integration, others may adventurously encourage it. Let them. But let them not force it on the rest.

---

[1] In one of its sallies against the South the sensationalist magazine, *Life,* aimed at the old city of Mobile and found in the vicinity a Negro area, where it pictured an old man with a cluster of children walking along a sandy-looking road. "Like all but one road in town," it said, "this is not paved . . ." (September 10, 1956) As this, to anyone who had ever been there, was a plain misstatement, I inquired to see just how far wrong it was, and received from Mayor Joseph N. Langan the information that in Mobile there were 444 miles of paved streets at that time and that with the completion of work then in progress every street in the city, except some in lately annexed territory, would be paved. Not to my surprise, he made no reference to the scandalous magazine. Mobile is a dream-like old town, noted for its flowery lawns and grand houses, especially along Government Street. If a magazine finds it its business to appraise a city's streets, it can hardly omit such a one as this, one among the country's most distinctive; and if it makes believe that such do not exist and squalor prevails, as the magazine did in this instance, of course it discredits itself. Gross misrepresentation of America, so often charged against the Russian press, is found right here at home.

[2] Associated Press, August 1, 1957. When Queen Elizabeth and Prince Philip visited Chicago some years ago there were such greetings as "Hey, Queen" and "Hi, Liz" from "the yelling people." *Time,* July 20, 1959, p. 47. The forbearance this must have cost the English would not have been unappreciated in the South.

On receiving a passport an American traveler during General Eisenhower's presidency received also, from the President, a letter in which this sentence appeared: "As you travel abroad, the respect you show for foreign laws and customs, your courteous regard for other ways of life, and your speech and manner help to mold the reputation of our country." Perhaps the woman so naively familiar with the English Queen had not read or would not have comprehended this. More is the pity, for the likes of her are doubtless the reason for such a letter, one which I am sure had to be written, yet which hardly misses being an example itself of what it discountenances. To say, "Do not be disrespectful or discourteous, do not speak rudely or show bad manners," which is what the letter says under a faint disguise, is lamentably presumptuous. I doubt that it and the reasons for it are much more provocative to people of other countries than to those of the South.

[3] New York, Charles Scribner's Sons, 1942, pp. 40f.

[4] Vol. 29, p. 403.   [5] P. 404.   [6] P. 407.   [7] P. 411.   [8] P. 413.   [9] P. 417.

[10] Durham, Duke University Press, 1954, p. 178.   [11] P. 94.   [12] P. 193.

[13] P. 205. Professor Wertenbaker remarks of "the warm welcome accorded the English theater in the South, the bitter opposition of Philadelphia, the complete ban laid down by New England . . ." On literary tastes he comments: "The Annapolis gentlemen, taking their reading rather lightly, steeped themselves in fiction and drama, shied off from works on theology, and searched Cicero and Horace chiefly for quotations for witty sallies; the Bostonian, wincing under the warnings of the clergy that fiction was a harmful mental dissipation, read his Fielding or his Richardson with a guilty conscience, to be atoned for only by more copious doses of theology or books on piety; the Virginian read the classics to round out his education as a gentleman and Coke and Locke to equip himself for a place in the colonial government, salving his conscience with Bishop Tillotson's works or perhaps *The Whole Duty of Man.*" *The Golden Age of Colonial Culture,* New York, New York University Press, 1942, pp. 151, 153.

The contrast went much beyond literary interests. Item: When Jefferson invited European professors to the faculty of the University of Virginia at its founding, he was sharply criticized in the North on suspicion of disloyalty. Cf. Philip Alexander Bruce: *History of the University of Virginia,* 1819-1919, 5 vols., New York, Macmillan Company, 1920-22, vol. 2, pp. 1ff.

[14] Not that Professor Toynbee affirms this himself; he gathers it from controversial anthropological sources. *Study of History,* unabridged ed., vol. 1, p. 219.

[15] *Plessy* v. *Ferguson, loc. cit.,* p. 551.   [16] Above, p. 110.

[17] *Congressional Record,* 75th Congress, 3d sess., vol. 83, pt. 1, pp. 138, 139, 140.

[18] Below, pp. 324 ff.

[19] Rev. Eugene Carson Blake, Stated Clerk, and Rev. Theophilus M. Taylor, Moderator, of the United Presbyterian Church in the United States of America. New York *Times,* September 11, 1958.

[20] New York *Times,* September 12, 1958.   [21] September 11, 1957.

[22] The shallowness and one-sidedness characteristic of much of the American press, especially where race is concerned, is an obstacle to seeing and understanding. A reader who had nothing from which to form judgments of what happened at Little Rock, except the ugly versions transmitted by the domestic press, must be rather non-plussed on reading such an account as the following, by the Japanese novelist Ashihei Hino:

"I visited Little Rock with a preconception mixed with dread. I had thought it was a fearsome place of bigotry where poor Negroes were ruthlessly persecuted by whites.

"I found out quickly my preconception was completely wrong. It was a quiet, beautiful city . . . Whites and colored people were living together in harmony.

"Facilities for the Negroes were as good as those in New York, Boston and Chicago I had seen earlier.

"Now I know it is wrong to consider the Little Rock school incident as a peak of the Negro problem. It is indeed far more complex and deeprooted."—Associated Press, Tokyo, November 26, 1958.

23 In New York City there is or was a Commission on Intergroup Relations, created by a 1958 law prohibiting "discrimination" in the lease or sale of houses and apartments. One of the early acts of this Commission was a request to newspapers to reject advertisements which used the term "inter-racial," the Commission having found, according to the New York *Times,* September 22, 1958, that the term had come to mean "for Negroes only." Fourteen newspapers in the city and on Long Island, among them the *Wall Street Journal,* agreed to reject the advertisements. The *Times* made no mention of any objection by anyone—no objection to curtailing the freedom of publication and no objection to withholding useful and lawful information from readers. Since the press is usually quick to defend its constitutional freedom, this episode may be taken as a signal example of the power of race sentiment over constitutional rights, in New York at least.

24 New York *Times,* September 13, 1958.

25 One writer, Eugene V. Rostow, dean of law at Yale, speaks of "the creativity of the judicial process." *The Supreme Court and the Quest for Law,* New York, Macmillan Company, 1960, p. xvii. How, now, would he like to be subjected to trial under a law non-existent before and "created" *ad hoc* by the judge? What if the creative judge were a surrealist or abstract expressionist and created a law so *avant-garde* that the dean could not tell where he stood under it, or whether he stood anywhere? Conceivably he would have, on regaining his senses, a deeper appreciation of the first provision of the United States Constitution, vesting all lawmaking power in Congress.

26 "*Ex dolo malo non oritur actio.* No court will lend its aid to a man who founds his cause of action upon an immoral or an illegal act." *Sullivan* v. *Horgan,* 17 R. I. 109, 20 A. 232. " . . . no right can accrue from an act in itself unlawful," *Talbot* v. *Seeman,* 1 Cranch 1, 28. Cf. Benjamin N. Cardozo, *The Nature of the Judicial Process,* p. 41.

27 New York *Times,* November 13, 1958.

CHAPTER 14

RESULTS AND PROSPECTS

The overthrow of the school-segregation laws filled many minds with flushed expectations, but the years since have been years of disillusion. Nearly a decade after *Brown* there was in some states no integration and in others it amounted to no more than a faint gesture. Rancor, friction, and violence have occurred both in the South and elsewhere, and conspicuously in New York and Washington. Where the Negro-white population ratio is low the results have been fairly peaceable. Where it is high, that is, in the South, some states have enacted pupil-assignment laws, laws for withdrawing funds from desegregating schools, or laws for subsidizing tuition in private schools; and a few contemplate and have prepared for the last resort, the abolition of public schools.

Early attempts in New York City to integrate schools by exchanging white and Negro pupils at a distance and transferring teachers, generated extreme animosity. This has now become a fixed policy and practice, though under continual criticism and opposition; and by 1963 the proportion of schools in New York City having 90 per cent or more non-white pupils was increasing.[1] An account in the New York *Times* on March 3, 1957 told of "segregation practices" there and in Buffalo and a half dozen other cities, and of "friction found in school districts throughout the state," and quoted the State Commissioner of Education as saying: "We are greatly worried at the increase in the number and intensity of the interracial problems. Some of the school superintendents do not know how to handle the new issues that are arising." This was six months after the New York City police and the Board of Education had joined "to make the classrooms safe for both students and teachers." The Police Commissioner initiated this undertaking "in the hope of ending such 'shocking' classroom incidents as assaults on teachers and students, rape, coercion, extortion and oppression."[2]

The New York conditions at that time were paralleled in the schools in Washington, according to testimony brought out in a congressional investigation there. School principals and teachers testified of: fights, sex assaults, obscenity, a tenfold increase in pregnancies, property destruction, arson, extortion, necessity of calling the police to establish

314

order in the schools, and so on. White principals and teachers were now in the minority at the elementary level. One high school principal found that even though Negro pupils came from families economically and occupationally comparable to those of the whites, they lagged scholastically.[3]

At large, it would be difficult to say whether real integration in contrast to token integration has gained in the intervening years. In numbers, or ostensibly, there have been gains, but in some places "resegregation" has occurred, with the flight of white residents from neighborhoods exposed to Negroes. Five years after the ordeal in Little Rock, desegregation there had brought only 68 Negro pupils into schools with whites.[4] In North Carolina, which was to set the pace in the South, the Advisory Committee of the Civil Rights Commission complained that by 1961 only 226 Negro pupils—fewer than one-tenth of one per cent of them—had been desegregated and that Negroes were suffering "severe discrimination" in nearly all walks of life.[5]

The numerical gain may have been overmatched by the great intensification of rancor, division, and violence through 1963. In the North, with its laws against racial "discrimination" in employment, there was "seething unrest" owing to " 'gentlemen's agreements' or naked prejudice" against employing Negroes and to the fact that "the laws don't work," according to an article in the New York *Times Magazine*.[6] In this article it is also said, a few sentences before, that "horror runs through all white economic levels in the North at the idea of having a Negro family move into the neighborhood."[7] A statement attributed to an officer of the National Association for the Advancement of Colored People runs: "Being black should be no more significant than being a redhead, or being stout or tall or short."[8]

Here is naively dramatized the whole affair of integration. First, horror on the part of the white; secondly, accusation of prejudice; thirdly, supposition that racial consciousness ought not to exist. To an attentive mind the first contains the whole story: what strikes horror into people needs no supplementation of prejudice or of unethicality to explain their shrinking from it and their formation of habits and policies for insuring avoidance of it in the future; and in substance that is all there is to segregation. To an integrationist mind, on the other hand, never suspecting its own prejudice, there is nothing to see but prejudice and iniquity, and nothing to conclude but that others are violating a moral obligation. But it would be a strange, perverse conception of moral obligation to say that one is morally bound not to shrink from horror. Is it immoral for three-year-old white children to do so—to react as they do to Negro children (cf. p. 111) or for Indians to do the like (cf. p. 112)? Since these reactions are natural, ingenuous, not maliciously inspired, it is no more justifiable to condemn them than it would be to condemn fire because it burns or water because it drowns. Adapted to the spontaneous, unpremeditated terms of childhood, the idea that being a Negro is no more than being red-headed or stout, tall or short, is about the same as the idea that being medicine is no different from being cake or candy or ice cream.

The elemental reality immediately apparent in this is apparent also in reactions at the high school age. The following was reported from the first integrated high school in Little Rock: "After six months in the school, [the Negro pupils] seem as effectively isolated or ostracized as though they were in a hostile land where no one spoke their language. In the student cafeteria on the mezzanine, they sit at a small table that the white students have in effect reserved for them. No white ever sits with them."[9]

Five years after this the same publication, constantly alert for anything indicative of integration's progress, found the scene little changed:

"In some classes, several Negroes bunch together, apparently out of choice. In others, a single Negro sits next to a white. But at the 'social' level in the cafeteria, the isolation is complete. Negroes have their 'own' table. Some tried to sit with whites at the beginning of school and were rebuffed—the whites moved away. They have not crossed over since.

" . . . It will take more than legal desegregation to break up traditional behavior patterns."[10]

It is a thesis of many apologists for integration that the Negro scholastic lag, which is commonly taken to be about two years, is due to inferior living standards and to inferior Negro schools.[11] Though it seems impossible to tell about this with assurance, on account of the great number of elements probably involved and the lack of scientific means of determining their operation, we have seen that a study of it in Nashville, on a scale and with a degree of thoroughness probably unsurpassed, did not confirm it. The New York *Times* on September 23, 1956 reported Negro pupils as much as four years behind white pupils in a Kentucky educational achievement test, and categorically declared, "Because the Negro schools have generally been poorer than the white ones, the Negro children have not so adequate an education." Shortly afterwards (October 7, 1956) the same newspaper said of Louisville, where integration had been introduced with little show of disorder, that "in the first grade the gap is already visible. By the fifth grade it has grown to a year and one-half in educational standards, and by the eighth to two years."

In Dallas the results of a series of nationally standardized tests to determine the aptitude of pupils were published by the Board of Education in November, 1955, showing: 26 per cent of Negro pupils in the first grade, and 69 per cent of the white, were at or above the national average. The aptitude index (national normal, 100) for second grade pupils was: Negro 84, white 99; fourth grade, Negro 82, white 105; sixth grade, Negro 80, white 101.

A lawsuit to force integration in the New Orleans public schools evoked testimony that integration would "create a health menace and lower educational standards." Eight physicians, including the president of the Louisiana Board of Health, predicted that it would cause a spread of venereal disease. A psychiatrist said it would be "psychiatrically traumatizing to the children of both races." The New Orleans school superintendent stated that Negro pupils were from 1.5 to 3.4 grades behind the white.[12]

There appeared in the *Bulletin* of the American Association of University Professors[13] a complaint by a contributor from Tuskegee Institute that Southern colleges and universities that now admitted Negro students for the first time had instituted double standards of grading for their sake. This, he said, was a concession on account of deficiencies in their preparation for college—something, he intimated, which happened at Northern universities also. He objected to it, calling it discrimination against white students.

As time passed and the legal machinery accelerated integration or the prospects of it, the outcry against the Supreme Court grew, and other decisions by it and by lower Federal courts drew opposition.

In Louisiana an association of school principals reproached a Federal district judge for what it considered precipitate action in a segregation case and said: "It is the concern of this group that by continued harassment of our school officials, brought about by outside agitators and Federal litigation, that our better talent will be driven from the educational field."[14] The governor of Florida, "upset, bewildered and confused by mounting racial tensions," expressed himself in these words: "It is folly for anyone to expect judicial dictations to compel social adjustment. The hearts and minds of people are not changed by the mere declaration of a principle."[15] A county commissioners' association in Georgia declared: "We do not recognize that tyranny in any form, including judicial tyranny, is in keeping with our fundamental democratic concepts and with principles of our Christian religion."[16]

A joint committee of Congress (Senate-House Printing Committee) voted to defy a Federal district court order forbidding the printing of a booklet entitled *A Handbook for Americans*. The chairman, Senator Hayden of Arizona, publicly announced that the committee had instructed the printer "to proceed with the printing and publication, and to disregard as unconstitutional the processes of any court. If a court can enjoin Congress from issuing a report, it will be only a matter of time before our remarks on the floor of the Senate or the House of Representatives would be subject to judicial review and a complete breakdown of the constitutional principle of separation of powers would ensue."[17]

A member of the Supreme Court of Alabama, James J. Mayfield, "accused the U. S. Supreme Court of 'twisting the Federal Constitution so as to arrive at its infamous integration decision . . . I have sworn to uphold the Constitution of the sovereign state of Alabama, and when I can no longer carry forth my oath of office to maintain segregation in Alabama, I shall resign'."[18]

The Supreme Court of Georgia, standing on the reserved rights of states in the Tenth Amendment, unanimously refused to reconsider a murder case remanded by the United States Supreme Court for reconsideration, saying: "This court bows to the Supreme Court on all Federal questions of law, but we will not supinely surrender sovereign powers of this State." The question concerned a motion for a new trial. In their refusal to reconsider, the judges said that the Supreme Court "apparently concluded . . . that this court should reverse the trial court because discretion was not exercised in the way the Supreme Court would have exercised it."[19]

The National Conference of Chief Justices, which is composed of the chief justices of all the states and territories, showed deep concern, according to the New York *Times*,[20] over "encroachments by one branch of government upon the powers of other branches," and passed a resolution at its 1956 meeting to "'reassert and reaffirm the essentiality and vitality' of the principle of separation of powers and to 'commend to the legislative and judicial branches of our governments strict adherence to its implications and requirements'." Chief Justice Livingston of the Alabama Supreme Court stated in an address after the 1957 meeting of these judges that they were "united in condemning recent decisions of the U. S. Supreme Court."[21] A year afterwards even sharper criticisms of the Court came from the Conference.[22]

Congress itself, through a subcommittee of the House Judiciary Committee, instituted in 1957 an inquiry into recent decisions of the Court.

Sir Paul Vinogradoff, the eminent jurisconsult, observed that "sooner or later we come to a point where law is obeyed not on account of material compulsion, but for other reasons—in consequence of reasonable acceptance, or instinctive conformity, or habit, or absence of organized resistance. If it were not so, how could commonwealths and legal systems exist?"[23]

United States Attorney General Herbert Brownell, Jr. in an address to the National Bar Association, September 2, 1955, stated: "Without active interest and the support of all the citizens, and particularly the lawyers, laws are often unenforced, forgotten, and rights thereunder lost . . . A law is not self-executing. There must be a means of obtaining compliance with its provisions and there must be wholehearted support and cooperation on the part of all our citizens . . ."[24]

If these authorities are correct, it is easy to see why school integration had got nowhere in some states, years after it was decreed, and why resistance to it remains strong in others that have it. Nor is it surprising to read that in the capitals of Alabama and Florida, bus segregation was still the practice, despite the invalidation of laws requiring it by the Supreme Court.[25]

That a law should be "forgotten" and so become a dead letter, that without public support it cannot stand, is instructive. To a studious mind it may signify: law is not always majestic, nor even always real; attempts to enforce it when it is not the will of the people are misconceived, tending to generate disrespect for all law; imposition or perpetuation of it in those circumstances is a sign of political irresponsibility or of disunion in the land. All of this is witnessed now in states where segregation has been an institution with the sanction of custom and law for two or three centuries.

What formerly was the legal as well as historical fact is now officially annulled by the Supreme Court's action, and the opposite is decreed. Now this is not just the "invalidation" of a law, inasmuch as the segregation laws had been repeatedly sustained by the Supreme Court; it is the invalidation of a validation, or sequence of validations. One consequence is that a man can now be summarily ordered by a Federal court to do thus and so, and failing, be summarily ordered to jail.[26]

Some persons appeal to what they term higher law, or moral law; for example, the spectacular magazine, *Life*, which says "The Court's position on segregation . . . is supported by its own reasoning plus the ultimate sanction of all our laws: it accords with that higher moral law on which our founding philosophy is based."[27] What, now? Morality talked up in this peerless fleshpot? If patriotism is the last refuge of a scoundrel, supercilious moralism must be not far behind. The New York *Times,* which often calls segregation a bias, considered it "shameful" that a congressional investigation of the effects of school integration in Washington should take place (though not considering it bias to think that way), and had the following to say about segregation: " . . . the whole problem ceases to be a physical one and becomes a moral one. It involves some deep ethical and religious concepts."[28]

It is a perpetual puzzle that newspapers and mass magazines should presume to lecture the public on moral subjects, owing so much, themselves, to immoral ones (crime, corruption, vulgarity, which they vicariously dispense to the public at a profit). Unquestionably, the ethics of journalism is manifest in the conduct of journalism; and frequently this conduct is such as to stultify the anonymous sermons it preaches and to cause thoughtful readers to suspect a double, hence unethical, standard.

What are the moral principles that are violated by segregation, not just according to unaccredited journalistic tribunes, but in the minds of thoughtful, independent men?

Is it a higher moral law that in a free country a person should submit continually to revulsion and unnatural coercion of his sensibilities? Not as penance and not in the name of charitableness, humility, or the like, but for the sake of extorted advantages to others? Or that he should sacrifice the natural prerogative of persons to be aloof from other persons? Is it a higher law that one species of man, profoundly alien and unwelcome to another, should yet be entitled to put itself with the other?

Or is it that we should do unto others as we would that they do unto us? But this will sustain segregation perfectly, since the white *would* be segregated, as he *would* himself segregate. Is it that we should act so that we could will that the maxim of our action become universal law? Again the white will answer that he would and does will that—that everywhere, given the Negro-white differences, there be no forced mingling.

If higher law applies, we must be given a demonstration of it, lest illusion and conflict about it prevail. But if it is demonstrated, then it is not higher, in the sense of transcendental; rather it is here and now, intelligible and not mysterious, public not secret. If on the other hand it is not demonstrated, it cannot be called law, either higher or other. Those who resort to it are then open to the suspicion of having no case and of having either no comprehension of their lack or no scruple against misrepresenting it.[29]

Government, justice, the commonwealth are not of this mythical description. Law is not, or not for long, an ethic of visionaries. Except with tyrants it is a covenanted policy in which a working balance of interests is struck and maintained. If there are irreconcilable conflicts of interest, then either subjugation of one to another or else a standoff, a live-and-let-live truce, becomes inevitable. The latter is natural segregation. Having experienced both it and the former, the American Negro wants them ended and is led to think that a legal formality such as the Supreme Court decision against school segregation will do it.

This presumes that you can write off history and nature by edict. It is like ordering causes to have no effects. How far it can go and how licentious it can become in regard to historical fact is indicated in the bowdlerizing of Stephen Foster's songs about the Negro by radio broadcasting companies, which have no scruple against changing Foster's words (just as they have none against turning famous music and verse into vulgar advertisements). They will not brook "darky," "mammy," and "massa," for example, and they take the liberty of making substitutes, which a Negro Congressman defends on the ground that Foster's words "tend to degrade."[30] On the contrary, the words aptly and sympathetically represented their subject, in the station he occupied. If it is objectionable to keep alive cherished songs of the past, it must also be objectionable to preserve many writings of a kindred nature, and we should purge libraries[31] of *Uncle Remus, The Nigger of the Narcissus, Nigger Heaven, Prancing Nigger,* G. W. Cable, Roark Bradford, Octavus Roy Cohen, and so on, and see what can be done to doctor the Bible so as to give the sons of Ham another color; and since it is now unlawful in some jurisdictions to record a person's race (not because of white objections, to be sure), perhaps it will be wrong presently to designate a person in any manner black or colored or to publish a photograph showing non-white complexion.[32] We criticize Russia and other countries for communism and tyranny but do not notice that in presuming to obliterate natural distinctions we are following the communist line. If there is a difference between them and us in this respect, it is that we are voluntarily communizing ourselves, whereas they had communism more or less forced on them.

The distinctions between black and white, such as the Supreme Court's citations vividly show, remain unaffected by argument, court decree, ethical or political principle. Segregation is not a matter of principle. What principle? There is no principle obliging men to deny the facts of existence, though there are advantages to be gained by recognizing these and sometimes amending them where we can. One such advantage is mutual understanding and respect of peoples. It is very doubtful that Negro leaders have much to their credit here, though the same cannot be said of plain, unindoctrinated Negroes who in the South at least comprehend and respect the white disposition. Since segregation arises from racial differences, whatever there is to be done to soften it or make it respectable must accord with such differences and not go upon the fanciful supposition that a legal form can abolish them. The law is one thing, the facts are another.

What is called the race problem is chiefly political in the strict sense of that term, not social or psychological; a problem, that is, of peoples, one race or racial faction against another. By themselves in their own lands and communities, segregated by geography, history, or custom, races are no problem. In the extreme cases of black enslaved by white, then emancipated, then growing ambitious to amalgamate, everything is changed. Does it please the white to amalgamate? If so, so be it, as far at least as nature and politics are concerned. If not, then by the same token will political barriers, not to speak of private ones, be erected to prevent it. This means more or less rigid segregation, with frustration of the Negro ambition; out of which arises the race problem as we have it in the United States. It is of little point for social investigators to come in and draw up tables of comparative statistics, for it is now not a matter of exhibiting or proving anything sociologically, but a matter of political will and action. The Negro ambition and the white resistance to it generate perpetual political trouble.

Ignoring the primordial fact of white repugnance and resorting to coercion is the opposite of a solution—it is the generation of more and harder problems. What goes in Minnesota, with a twentieth of the Negro population of Mississippi, cannot be presumed to be the thing for Mississippi, nor vice versa. This is not because Mississippians willfully refuse to have it so, but because race facts and race experiences in Mississippi, inured through the better part of two centuries, are a reality far surpassing Minnesota's in magnitude and complexity. One might retort that this would not be so if Mississippi would change her ways. That, however, disregards or underestimates the *vera causa*, the primordial racial aversion, something which is not extinguished at will. It also disregards history, which is not merely the past but, in this case, the past determining the present. In the South the race problem is a complex of this primordial aversion and customs, institutions, and laws arising from it.

To suppose that the difference between North and South concerning race is one of ideals is uninformed, to say the least. At close range the Southern stand can be seen to rest on bare, massive racial fact, which does not take ideal form easily. At a distance, that of Minnesota or Massachusetts, for example, the whole affair becomes ideal or theoretic; and it would not be far wrong to say that idealism on this subject is proportional to the distance. No doubt the South would be glad to exchange its racial realities for the North's racial ideals, and I believe the legislature of Mississippi has undertaken to initiate action to the purpose by calling on Congress to appropriate money to encourage Negro migration, and an Alabama Congressman has introduced such a bill;[33] but apparently Congress, since it has not complied, is disposed to let the North retain the ideals and Mississippi and Alabama retain the realities. The North-South difference seems to be less a difference between ideals *per se* than between ideals at a distance and experience first hand.

Professor Myrdal quotes a Milwaukee manufacturer as saying, "Negroes here should be in the South. They should never have come to Milwaukee, for by so doing they have created a social problem for the city."[34] Myrdal found that in Minneapolis a young Negro trained to be a mechanic had trouble finding a job, not, it was said, because employers were prejudiced but because some of their customers were. He adds that the like is to be met in "any similar Northern city," and, "the white North definitely became more prejudiced when hundreds of thousands of crude Southern Negroes moved in."[35] A Negro pastor of a white church in Old Mystic, Connecticut, concluded after a visit to South Carolina that Negroes were better off occupationally there than in Connecticut.[36] The publisher of a Negro newspaper (Newark, N. J. *Telegram*), after a year or more of studying racial relations in the South, expressed himself to the effect that the Negro's lot was better there—"Right now the southern Negro is in a better spot educationally, politically, and economically than the Negroes any place else in the world."[37] The well known Mississippi editor, Hodding Carter, a man noted for the liberality and forcefulness of his opinions, has said: "Over the past ten years I have had occasion to visit all but two of our forty-eight states. In each of them I have made a habit of asking all manner of white persons whether they would welcome a Negro influx even if it added less than the national 1 in 10 ratio to their overall population. Not one person in a hundred has told me he would . . . Despite the great contributions that thousands of Negroes have made to the national welfare, and despite the good citizenship of many more thousands, the relative record of the Negro as a citizen in the areas of his greatest concentrations, North or South, is not such as to make him welcome elsewhere."[38]

Consider the perennial flux of bills in Congress aimed against the South by persons from a distance. For what reason? Fundamentally for not acquiescing in contacts and conditions naturally repugnant, of which the ultimate, in some settings a fairly constant menace, is the rape of white women by Negroes.

Now rape in New York City, if noticed (a news report on crime in one police precinct in Harlem casually mentions thirty-four rapes in six months),[39] may get a man as much as twenty years in prison, I believe, as against the death penalty in the South. New York, not because it is openly unfair, I am sure, but because its mold and complexion and resulting disposition are quite different, looks upon the Southern system with suspicion and challenge. It looks with the eyes of New York, projecting the cosmopolitan disposition, cosmopolitan not in the flattering sense but in the sense of multitude, all and sundry, upon what it sees, and wonders why all does not conform with that disposition. Other places likewise project themselves into what they see. What is this but provincialism all around, the same as that of the traveler who speaks only his own language and wonders why others don't speak it too? There is an instructive difference, however, between the metropolitan provincialism and that of the South, concerning race. Whereas the former, to judge by its public expressions, would impose its racial attitude on the South (and on England, France, and South Africa), the converse is not the case. The South has long been content to let others alone. Today, letting others alone is a capital virtue. In race matters it is probably the chief virtue. It never brings to anyone that nowadays frequent and poignantly enlightening invitation, "Go home, --!"

Some months after the Supreme Court's Brown decision there appeared an article in the *Antioch Review* (Winter, 1954-55) by Norman A. Brittin describing the race scene and integration prospect in Alabama, especially in the vicinity of Auburn, where Mr. Brittin, "a transplanted Yankee, a New Yorker by birth," in the editor's words, was a professor of sociology in the Alabama Polytechnic Institute, now Auburn University. Professor Brittin had lived in Alabama six years. Parts of his article follow.

"With all good will toward the Negro, a white parent in Alabama must look with concern on the prospect of nonsegregated schools. In view of the low standards of education, morals, and home environment among so large a number of Negroes, it seems to him entirely defensible—perhaps even mandatory—to throw up safeguards for culture. It seems to him—and I agree—that this is so important a matter and so reasonable a desire that all responsible persons, regardless of locality or race, must recognize it and respect it."[40]

"Of course the problem of nonsegregation in public schools is more acute in the South because there are so many more Negroes in the South than in the other regions of the country. According to 1950 census reports, there was approximately one Negro pupil to every three white pupils 5-13 years old in the sixteen Southern states; in the rest of the country, approximately one Negro pupil to every twenty white pupils. Many localities have higher or lower proportions than these; but one-third of the counties of Alabama have from 40 to 84.4 per cent Negro population. Successfully to amalgamate the races in the schools of Lee County, where I live, would be difficult enough because Lee County is 40.2 per cent nonwhite. But in Macon County, home of Tuskegee Institute, where the population is 84.4 per cent nonwhite, what would nonsegregation mean? Macon County had in 1950 798 white children 5-14 years old. They were outnumbered nearly seven to one by Negro children of the same ages —of whom there were 5,237. There were 93 white six-year-olds, 553 Negro. The white people of Macon County can look upon nonsegregation in their schools as nothing but cultural disaster.

"The Yale sociologist Maurice Davie asserts that Negroes now lag about a generation behind the whites in education. Since this is so (and the lag may be even greater in the Deep South), Southern white parents feel that they would be foolhardy indeed to permit any wholesale amalgamation of the races in their schools. It is no wonder that they will do anything—zoning, gerrymandering of school districts, even legally abolishing the public schools—in order to preserve segregation."[41]

"The people of New York City are probably in the best position to appreciate what nonsegregation would do to education in Alabama. It would be like moving into the slums, or like bringing hordes of children from the slums into the schools of the finest neighborhoods. For most Alabama Negroes live in crowded huts and shanties, they are ignorant, they are dirty, they are frequently drunken and immoral, their reading matter is trashy or nonexistent, their speech is an ungrammatical *patois*. We may instantly acknowledge that they are often kind and lovable, that many of them work hard, and that they deserve respect. But such acknowledgment is beside the point. From these homes come the Negro students; from these homes come many of the Negro teachers. So nonsegregation would mean that the schools could not maintain decent educational standards because of the tremendous numbers of Negro pupils who come from substandard homes.

"I trust that no one will think me merely priggish because I emphasize home conditions. I am no more priggish than are all the whites in the North who resist the movement of Negroes into restricted residential districts and who sell out and move away as soon as Negroes begin to dwell in homes even near white neighborhoods.

"Southerners who are inclined to be tolerant speak of the Negro as amoral, not immoral. It may not matter greatly that the motherly-looking Negro woman walking by the courthouse jets a great splash of tobacco juice on the sidewalk, and an illegitimate baby now and then may not pose a serious threat to the morals of the community; but girls who are sexually experienced by the age of twelve create a school problem uncommon in most white schools, and the fact that most Negro families are started casually with no father in evidence goes to show the correctness of those who assert that the Alabama Negro is not civilized in the sense that the whites are. Some authorities estimate that there is ten times as much illegitimacy among Negroes as among whites. By and large, the Negro of the Deep South still does not recognize, perhaps does not understand, the moral standards of the white community.

"The homicide rate of the South for 1952 was nearly four times that of the rest of the nation. It was so high because of the huge number of Negro homicides: the Negro homicide rate runs to more than five times that of whites in the South."[42]

" . . . if 1,000 Negro pupils were to be amalgamated suddenly with 800 white pupils, the result would be an educational chaos; and if the 1,000 were spaced over sixteen years, the result would be, though not so appalling, a lowering of the present quality of education."[43]

"If nonsegregation in the schools of the South seems to the Negroes to be worth having, they must make up their minds, regardless of court decisions, to earn it through intelligence and character. Obviously the Negroes would gain eventually by being only gradually admitted to mixed schools; for the few admitted each year would come out with an education superior to that which they would have received if they had entered along with a horde of ill-qualified Negro pupils. Obviously also the white people of the Deep South, regardless of court decisions, will never permit any abrupt and wholesale de-segregation in their schools."[44]

It is engaging to think what might have been the Supreme Court's decision had evidence of this kind come under consideration, and difficult to see how, if such evidence was not considered, the Court could venture to declare the psycho-educational principles of *Brown* and give them the status of law;[45] for the Court held without exception and on the authority of such assumed principles that white pupils must be mixed with colored, "with all deliberate speed." That is as much as to say that the Constitution requires white people to set their children back some years educationally, as well as subject them to ignominy and possible demoralization by degrading them to Negro standards.

Though the Court admitted no exception, it rested on a ground which admits all manner of exception and which the Court implicitly acknowledges as admitting such. There is a passage in the Brown opinion reading: "To separate them [children in grade and high schools] from others of similar age and qualifications solely because of their race generates a feeling of inferiority . . . [which] has a detrimental effect upon the colored children . . . [because it] affects the motivation of a child to learn."[46] Notice that it speaks of children racially different but of similar age and qualifications, not of others. What if in a given case they are not of similar qualifications though of the same age? Since the Court's premise is expressly limited to those of similar qualifications, we may assume, as before, that others are not covered and so are not subject to integration. Then most of the country, if the general assumption of Negro retardation is admitted (it is included in the psychological testimony on which the Court relies—above, p. 123), must be exempted from integration requirements. If it were found, as in Louisville, that even in the first grade there was a disparity in qualifications, then, if the Court were consistent, it would have to exempt that grade, and *a fortiori* the grades following.

At all events the ground on which the Court stands—equal qualifications at equal ages—is one on which anti-integration communities, as we have observed, might also stand, should they choose to litigate the question further. Unless the Court renounced it, these holdouts could hardly be denied, and integration would be a dead letter with them. And if the Court did renounce it, then its 1954 school decisions would collapse into groundless, arbitrary dictates.

328 THE SOUTH AND SEGREGATION

Add to this the Court's doctrine that separate schools are inherently unequal and therefore a violation of the equal-protection guarantee; then all must be integrated regardless. So the older pupil must be put with the younger in many an instance, or the qualified with the unqualified. And yet the stated ground, limited as it is to pupils of equal age and qualifications, precludes that. Confusion upon confusion.

There is a saving possibility, though what chance it might have now can only be guessed. The Court says that the meaning of "equal" in "equal protection of the laws" was left undetermined by the authors of the Fourteenth Amendment, as far as public education was concerned, and proceeds to fix a meaning, namely, identical protection, or integration. Suppose now that Congress, with its constitutionally vested power to enforce the provisions of the Amendment, should directly exercise this power with respect to education. Having repeatedly rejected integration, it would have to fix its own meaning, without which there would be nothing to enforce and no enforcement standards. The whole question of unequal qualifications of Negro and white pupils must arise, and it is hardly likely that Congress would legislate any standard that would require white pupils to be set back to Negro levels. Then equality, we may presume, would have to be understood comparatively, perhaps more as equity than as a rigid balance.

In fact that is the case already. The act of Congress of August 30, 1890 (26 Stat. 417) providing for endowment of colleges of agriculture and mechanic arts, commonly called land-grant colleges today and including many state universities, incorporates the following: "no money shall be paid out under this act to any State or Territory for the support and maintenance of a college where a distinction of race or color is made in the admission of students, but the establishment and maintenance of such colleges separately for white and colored students shall be held to be a compliance with the provisions of this act if the funds received in such State or Territory be equitably divided as hereinafter set forth."

The school-lunch act of 1946 includes a segregation provision: "If a state maintains separate schools for minority and for majority races, no funds made available pursuant to this chapter shall be paid or disbursed to it unless a just and equitable distribution is made within the state for the benefit of such minority races, of funds paid to it under this chapter." 42 U.S.C.A. 1760.

This exemplifies the congressional conception of equal protection in education.[47] Even if the Court were to "find" it "invalid," Congress presumably would still have the constitutional authority to determine, by appropriate legislation, what the states had to do to satisfy the equal-protection requirement. Even if equal protection did mean integration, enforcement of it would still be, constitutionally, a matter for Congress to determine. A parallel, among many, was the Eighteenth (Prohibition) Amendment, to enforce which the Volstead Act was passed by Congress.[48]

It taxes reason to see how the Court can any longer countenance the now manifest errors embedded in the stated grounds of the Brown decision. Without compunction the Court corrects what it pronounces to be errors of its predecessors. Will it now correct its own? If not, a continuation, even intensification, of the discord already produced is foreseeable, possibly with a breakdown of state services in jurisdictions where integration is so repugnant that people would rather forego such services altogether. Where such a thing happens government has failed, and to that extent ceased to exist. The President and the Army can meet violence with violence but how can they meet "No, thank you"?

It is all too evident that the prime reliance of integration extremists both in and out of Congress has been military force. Even military force, however, is incompetent against the ultimate will of the people, which is the ultimate law. Force may produce civil war, but that itself proves the error of it, if not the ineptitude and viciousness of those employing it.

If our authorities do not want civil dissolution and military tyranny, they can have peace, provided they are willing to heed the terms. These are the same terms the country has stood on all along until the 1954 reversal; the same that were instituted at the adoption of the Constitution, at the adoption of the Fourteenth Amendment, and through the long line of judicial decisions specifying and applying the provisions of the Constitution to race matters. They literally constitute our system in that regard. To reinstate them will of course require recall of the school-segregation decisions and of the numerous corollary decisions. By that the Supreme Court would clear itself of the obliquity of those decisions and prepare the way for the revival of its prestige.

To Negroes possessed of judgment and personal respectability, this would mean little if any loss. Judgment and personal respectability, regardless of who possesses them, inform a person of his station and its duties, and inhibit pretensions to what is not his own. The aim of forcing his way into elements where he is not welcome is a degrading compromise of personal dignity. The supposition that you have to force yourself on others in order to be yourself—a mute testimonial of Negro "demonstrators" in street processions day after day in 1963—is foreign to personal integrity and dignity. It is foreign also to the good sense of the plain Negro, who probably realizes that integration beyond the token, putative form is not for today, in the South at any rate. Such a one knows, however, that it is possible to advance, that through peaceful endeavor, through cultural evolution, the barriers can be diminished. Barriers of many kinds surround everyone. Let Negroes in the meantime do their utmost to insure the equality the uncorrupted law entitles them to: bona fide, factual, constitutional equality, instead of the make-believe with which the Supreme Court has deluded so many. In this endeavor they could expect strong sympathy and support from the South.

If fact and reason are not to be denied, then segregation in some form is not to be denied. It is but the recognition of natural differences and the adoption of ordinances corresponding. If Negroes who are segregated feel umbrage, that is perhaps no more than the feeling of women that, as they sometimes say, this is a man's world; and in some cases the Negro's complaint may be less a sign of deprivation than it is a stratagem for illicitly transcending the limits created by natural differences between Negro and white. To deny the differences is to deny plain facts. To decree measures which disregard them, as the Supreme Court has done, is to instigate strife; so obviously that the judges can hardly complain if suspected of doing it designedly or else thoughtlessly.

If tranquillity is the end (as it is in the Constitution) racial matters, like others of a personal kind, must be left to find their natural level and relation. They are of a different gender from economic, technical, and legal matters; they are psychological and historical—psychologically they far outweigh the inferiority matter cited by the Court. If that psychological item justified the Court's decision, these others more than justify recall of the decision.

For races to find and secure their natural, relative positions presupposes freedom and mutual respect. To find the optimum relationship of races presupposes not bayonets but good will, candor, understanding, and programs of action. Coercion, either by law or by arms, is the death of all these and a guarantee of their opposites; as well as a powerful sign of malfeasance or incompetence in those responsible.

To conclude that good will and understanding will resolve integration-segregation questions completely, would be rather fanciful. The most that can be reasonably expected, through them, is toleration. Toleration, however, is something mutual, which means: to each his natural due; each in his place. That is the same as (a) segregation where ethnic differences are extreme and the people are very sensitive to them, and (b) integration where these are not the conditions and the people are consequently indifferent to their ethnic past or future. Between the types in (a) the difference is so great that toleration, if it exists, obviously indicates, or is, segregation of each from the other.

Good will is not a blessing of everyone. Contrary to the supposition of popular moralizers, it is not subject to command. It is nature transcending nature, and that, like the grace of God, transcends our formulae. Moreover, and most ironically, what Mr. A considers good will in himself Mr. B may consider ill will or indifference. And even good will is inhibited and at length sinks into abeyance when the sensibilities are persistently offended. To expect white to admit black just through good will is an abrogation of both good will and understanding.

Understanding is even less favoring than good will. What is it but clear, comprehensive, articulate regard? It neither gilds nor veils the realities, but sets them out exactly. It does not abolish dislike and disgust; it discovers and delineates them. Its pitiless light is certain to disillusion the integrationist, for it will show the white side as well as the black, and the white side is simply, primordially, repugnance.[49] Further, it will show that integration either designs to override the white reality and deny the Negro reality or else is only a polemic in default or defiance, itself, of understanding. Yet further, understanding of so palpable a matter as race is much likelier to come of long, close-range experience than of idealization at a distance. Senator Borah must have been mindful of this when he deferred to the South on the race question, saying it had dealt with it more patiently, more understandingly, and more successfully than had any other power in history.

[1] New York *Times Magazine,* June 30, 1963, p. 24.

[2] New York *World-Telegram,* October 10, 1956.

[3] See the *Report* of the Subcommittee to Investigate Public School Standards and Conditions, and Juvenile Delinquency in the District of Columbia, House of Representatives, 84th Congress, 2d sess., 1957, especially pp. 24-46. Five years afterwards Washington still had racial violence, attributed to integration. The Director of its Department of Corrections was lamenting "the increase in aggravated assaults on Washington streets" and tracing them to "Negro hos-

tility towards whites," which he said "stems from the new-found freedom of Negro youths resulting from sociological changes that were inaugurated by Supreme Court desegregation decisions." Washington *Evening Star*, March 16, 1962.

The violence seems to have increased in scope and intensity until climaxed by a race riot at a high school football game on Thanksgiving Day, 1962. An elaborate interracial-committee investigation ensued, concluding with a massive *Report to the Superintendent of Schools,* from which the following excerpts are taken:

"Integration is a most complicated undertaking. It is not accomplished simply by opening classroom doors. It is not brought about by a paper decision to recognize the rights of fellow citizens. It is not achieved by an emotional urge that follows the prodding of the heart rather than the leadership of the head. We do a grave disservice to boys and girls of both races when we direct them to integrate and thrust them into indiscriminate mingling without the thorough preparation which is a mandate for success in any undertaking . . . " Letter of Transmittal of the Chairman, p. 3.

"Testimony before the full committee developed an awareness of administrative lack of control over hoodlum elements in the school system and a deteriorating condition in mass audience events outside of the school buildings. Violence, assaults, disrespect of teachers are acts of an undesirable element of students. An atmosphere of 'permissiveness' has discouraged the personnel of many schools and caused a city-wide lessening of discipline standards. Fear rages through many school buildings which have become tramping grounds for outside influences, including thugs, hoodlums, and persons of the lowest character. The school administration has difficulty in coping with this situation. The morale of many teachers has suffered and the percentage of resignations and transfers has increased . . . " P. 17.

A glimpse of the character of Negro education now accomplished in the Washington schools under the rule of integration is given in this: "Some . . . graduate from high school without acquiring the ability to read and write and later meet rejection when they apply for jobs . . . P. 22.

How, we may wonder, could the schools *graduate* illiterates? What is their conception of education? What do they mean by certifying completion of high school by pupils who in fact must not have qualified as completing the work of even the first or second grade? Under such a "system" is it very strange that lawlessness and violence should rack the Washington schools?

[4] Associated Press, November 30, 1962.   [5] New York *Times,* April 7, 1963.

[6] June 30, 1963, p. 13.   [7] *Ibid.*   [8] *Ibid.,* p. 24.

[9] New York *Times Magazine,* March 23, 1958, p. 88.   [10] June 2, 1963, p. 57.

[11] With doctrinal integrationists it is practically an article of faith that educational, intellectual, and moral differences between Negro and white are due to social and economic disadvantages of the Negro. So valiant is this conviction that any challenge of it can be expected to draw an outcry from sympathetic social scientists, whose "science," it seems, deserts them, leaving them hardly distinguishable from ordinary partisans. Dr. Frank C. J. McGurk, a psychologist at Lehigh University, carried out a test of high school seniors in schools in New Jersey and Pennsylvania, designed to show whether the socioeconomic hypothesis, as it may be termed, holds up. The test consisted of two sets of questions "defined as non-cultural and cultural according to the pooled judgments of 78 school teachers, psychologists and sociologists." It was administered

to 213 white and 213 Negro pupils of the same age and of two socioeconomic levels, one high the other low, determined by their scores on a standard test of this (Sims Record Card). The results were a showing of white superiority, which was more pronounced at the higher level than at the lower. " . . . as the socioeconomic status of the Negro increases, racial differences in test score increase—they do not decrease." *Journal of Abnormal and Social Psychology,* vol. 48, p. 450. Moreover, the high-status Negroes surpassed the low-status ones not so much on cultural questions as on non-cultural questions. *Journal of Applied Psychology,* vol. 37, p. 276. In fine, an increase in the Negro socioeconomic status was not paralleled by an increase in Negro attainment compared to white attainment, nor, so far as cultural test results were concerned, was it paralleled by a corresponding superiority to low-status Negroes. The socioeconomic hypothesis was, so far, confuted.

Accounts of Dr. McGurk's study were published in 1953 and subsequently, and included one in which he inferred that Negro educational capacity is inferior to the white (*U. S. News and World Report,* September 21, 1956). Soon he was pilloried and threatened. Speaking at a meeting of the American Psychological Association in 1959, he told of attempts to have him dismissed from his position (he was then at Villanova University; the attempts failed), and remarked that intimidation had gone so far that some investigators would not testify now on social issues. New York *Times,* September 8, 1959. Challenged in the *Harvard Educational Review,* he replied there with citations of results reached by other psychologists and: "For the inclusive period of 1937 to 1950, not one study appeared in the literature which showed that the mean test score of Negroes equalled or exceeded the mean test score of the group of whites with which the Negroes were compared . . . The test scores of Negroes and whites are in the same relationship now as they were in 1918. The various differences in socioeconomic environments of the Negroes, between 1918 and 1950, have not altered the Negro-white test score relationship." Vol. 29, pp. 55, 58.

Convictions (Fixations? Doctrines?), such as the one connected with the socioeconomic hypothesis, can be a handicap in scientific work. Scientifically, objectively, they are prejudices. What have they to do with facts and relations of facts? Zeal for ascertaining the facts and the relations between them is in no way dependent on conviction or doctrine, but rather on openness of mind and capacity to find out. Huxley was convinced, J. Arthur Thomson likewise, that the Negro is destined, anthropologically, to inferiority. These convictions, those of integrationists to the contrary, those of the Soviet partisan biologist Lysenko, and all such, regardless of which side they are on, fall together. In natural science, nothing is absolute; nothing is more than a probable hypothesis. But the degree of probability, which is the guide of enlightened policy and action, is determined by the accuracy, impartiality, and comprehensiveness of the findings of fact, with which neither integration nor segregation has anything to do.

12 Baton Rouge *State-Times,* December 12, 1955.

13 Vol. 41 (1955) pp. 347ff.   14 Baton Rouge *State-Times,* January 28, 1957.

15 International News Service, January 9, 1957.

16 International News Service, November 15, 1956.

17 Associated Press, May 4, 1956.   18 Associated Press, March 28, 1956.

19 211 Ga. 763; 88 S.E. 2d 376.   20 August 28, 1956.

21 Associated Press, July 19, 1957.

[22] Associated Press, August 21, 1958. The chief justices of the state supreme courts of Georgia, Maryland, Massachusetts, Michigan, Minnesota, New Hampshire, Oregon, South Carolina, Texas, and Wisconsin, constituting a committee of the Conference, had the following to say in their report to the Conference:

"It seems strange that under a constitutional doctrine which requires all others to recognize the Supreme Court's rulings on constitutional questions as binding adjudications of the meaning and application of the Constitution, the Court itself has so frequently overturned its own decisions thereon, after the lapse of periods varying from one to ninety-five years . . .

"It has long been an American boast that we have a government of laws, not of men. We believe that any studying of recent decisions of the Supreme Court will raise at least considerable doubt as to the validity of that boast."

[23] *Op. cit.,* p. 52.

[24] Press release September 2, 1955. Cp. Justice Holmes: "The first requirement of a sound body of law is, that it should correspond with the actual feelings and demands of the community, whether right or wrong." *The Common Law,* Boston, Little, Brown & Co., 1923, p. 41. Justice Stone: " . . . sober second thought of the community . . . is the firm base on which all law must ultimately rest." 50 *Harvard Law Review* 4, 25. Abraham Lincoln: "With public sentiment, nothing can fail; without it, nothing can succeed." Samuel Bannister Harding, *Select Orations Illustrating American Political History,* New York, Macmillan Company, 1909, p. 338. Illinois Supreme Court: ". . . all of the verdicts represent nothing but a refusal by juries to enforce a law which they do not personally approve or which is distasteful to them." *People ex rel. Scott Bibb* v. *Mayor and Common Council of Alton,* 175 Ill. 615, a case of a Negro parent to compel admission of his children to white schools, tried and retried seven times by juries, through nine years. See also Chicago Commission on Race Relations, *The Negro in Chicago,* University of Chicago Press, 1922, p. 237.

[25] United Press, April 11, 1957.

[26] All this is difficult if not impossible to reconcile with the Constitution where it provides: "The trial of all crimes, except in cases of impeachment, shall be by jury . . . " Art. III, Sec. 2, (3); and: "No person shall be held to answer for a capital, or otherwise infamous crime, unless on a presentment or indictment of a grand jury, except in cases arising in the land or naval forces, or in the militia, when in actual service in time of war or public danger . . . " Art. V. "It is an error," the eminent constitutionalist Charles Warren has observed, "to speak of the [Supreme] Court as enforcing its decrees. It delivers its judgments and issues its mandate and other judicial process, and there its judicial powers end. In case of disobedience by the loser in the suit, the responsibility for ultimate enforcement lies elsewhere than on the Court."—*Supreme Court and Sovereign States,* Princeton, Princeton University Press, 1924, p. 77.

[27] May 28, 1956, p. 47.   [28] December 30, 1956.

[29] Cp. p. 287. Often the appeal of the frustrated partisan to "higher law" or "natural rights" is clouded with mysticism or inarticulateness and strongly suggests the disingenuous. Of such law and rights the following from an address by the late Margaret Macdonald, who ranked with the most eminent thinkers of her time, seems, by contrast, apocalyptic: "The statements of the Law of Nature are not statements of the laws of nature, not even of the laws of an 'ideal' nature. For nature provides no standards or ideals. All that exists, exists

at the same level or is of the same logical type. There are not, by nature, prize roses, works of art, oppressed or unoppressed citizens. Standards are determined by human choice, not set by nature independently of men." Aristotelian Society, *Proceedings,* New Series, London, Harrison, vol. 47, p. 238.

A contributor the the *Northwestern Law Review* surmises that "general acceptance of the moral basis of the principle of desegregation is as important to its implementation as legal sanctions available for its enforcement," and goes on to say: "Ultimately the conscience of the South will make itself heard to the good of both races. The brotherhood of man is on the march. Human dignity, with God's help, will not be denied." (Vol. 52, pp. 301, 319) Grandiloquence is not a gauge of morality, and would not be noticed here except that it is fairly characteristic of integrationist talk on that subject. The Department of Justice in a brief to the Supreme Court arguing for integration (*Brief for the United States on the Further Argument of the Questions of Relief,* October term, 1954, p. 6), was not content to rest on legal grounds, remarking that desegregation is "a fundamental human right, supported by considerations of morality as well as law;" and a previous brief from that source (*Brief for the United States as* amicus curiae, 1952, p. 31) urged desegregation as a means to "conserve and fortify the moral as well as the material sources of its [the free world's] strength." In such writing "moral" is always a question-begging term and often it is scarcely more than a transparent disguise of dogmatism. In the South segregation is eminently moral if by "moral" is meant customary, traditional, socially approved, or the like. If the meaning is not that, but rather an ideality; not what is instituted and lived, but something idealized apart from practical life, which is probably the case in instances like these, then of course it is restricted to those who happen to incline to it, and has no sanction over others. A's ideals need not be B's. If A is surreptitiously or tyrannously intent on forcing them on B, his ideological equal, is that itself "moral"? To associate such a purpose with God and brotherhood is hardly piety, one would think.

30 United Press, July 23, 24, 1957.

31 So indeed we should, according to the National Association for the Advancement of Colored People. In the town of Torrington, Conn. that racial organ attempted to have not only *Br'er Rabbit* but also Poe's *Gold Bug,* among others, eliminated from school readings. Associated Press, December 21, 1960. It lodged a like objection against Mark Twain's *Huckleberry Finn* in San Francisco. United Press International, May 19, 1962. New York City banned this famous story from its schools some time before, which led the *Christian Science Monitor* to query, "Are we to rewrite history, like the Soviets, and deny that the American Negro, however remarkably, has risen from primitive cultures in Africa?" September 14, 1957.

One might observe that if such authors as Mark Twain and Poe must go, so too, presumably, must Lincoln the Great Emancipator, since he often said "nigger" ("Negro" was unknown then, "negro" sufficing, as it did even in Supreme Court diction until a decade or so ago). On one occasion he spoke as follows: "Judge Douglas deduces, or draws out, from my speech [at Springfield] this tendency of mine to set the states at war with one another, to make all the institutions uniform, and set the niggers and white people to marry together . . . There is no danger that the people of Kentucky will shoulder their muskets, and, with a young nigger stuck on every bayonet, march into Illinois and force them upon us." Samuel Bannister Harding, *op. cit.,* pp. 333, 338.

[32] This is indeed the case already, in employment, rentals, education, one or more, in New York City, San Francisco, and a score or more states. In New York and Massachusetts it is contrary to law, as interpreted by administrative agencies, for school authorities to require a photograph of a prospective teacher. One may wonder whether it is unlawful for the authorities to look at her in the flesh, since so much more is discovered that way than through photographs. To forbid a photograph means that the employer is not free to regard visible personal qualities, let the consequences be what they may to himself, to other employees, or to the business. He is not to deal as a person with persons but as a computer with statistics, or a robot with robots. SCUR has little satrapies, we see, over the land.

[33] H. R. 4672, 1957, by Representative George W. Andrews.

[34] *Op. cit.*, p. 385. [35] *Ibid.*, pp. 662, 1292-1293.

[36] Associated Press, June 6, 1957.

[37] Quoted in *Hearings,* Subcommittee No. 5, Committee on the Judiciary, House of Representatives, 85th Congress, 1st. sess., p. 1136.

[38] *Virginia Quarterly Review,* vol. 33, p. 167.

[39] New York *Times,* July 16, 1959.

[40] P. 389.   [41] P. 393.   [42] Pp. 393-394.   [43] P. 395.   [44] P. 396.

[45] As a matter of fact the question was not really tried in the lower [Kansas] court. Only one side was presented with any fullness—that of Brown *et al.* The state made scarcely more than a perfunctory case. When the Supreme Court took evidence, so to speak, in the writings it cited (above, ch. 6), it took only what it considered favorable to the appellants (integrationists). So in reply to those who say that school segregation had never really been submitted to judicial trial before *Brown,* it may justly be said that it was not tried then. Only one side was justly set out or, by the Supreme Court, justly sought out.

[46] *Loc. cit.,* p. 494.

[47] The like congressional conception is also evident in the Hospital Survey and Construction Act, Title VI, Section 612, 60 Stat. 1043, known as the Hill-Burton Act, adopted in 1946: "The State plan shall provide for adequate hospital facilities for the people residing in a State, without discrimination on account of race, creed, or color . . . but an exception shall be made in cases where separate hospital facilities are provided for separate population groups, if the plan makes equitable provision on the basis of need for facilities and services of like quality for each such group." In 1963 Congress defeated an amendment which would have outlawed segregation in hospitals under this Act.

Still further evidence that segregation accords with official American policy may be seen in the adherence of the United States to the Geneva Convention of July 27, 1929, Relative to the Treatment of Prisoners of War, providing: "Belligerents shall, so far as possible, avoid assembling in a single camp prisoners of different races or nationalities." Title III, Section II, Article 9, U. S. Department of State, Treaty Series No. 846. It is noteworthy, however, that integration now prevails in the armed services of the United States; but also noteworthy that General Mark Clark, who commanded the only Negro infantry division in the late war, a division which he appraised as the poorest of ten comprised in the Fifth Army, has said: "I must reiterate that it would be a grave error now for the Army to attempt the indiscriminate mixing of white and Negro soldiers." *Calculated Risk,* New York, Harper and Brothers, 1950, p. 415.

A pamphlet by Clarence O. Amonette entitled *The Segregation Cases: Ipse Dixit Decisions,* published by the author at Berkeley, Calif. gives much information on the historical disposition of Congress towards segregation.

[48] Amidst criticism of the South today for not desegregating its schools, and charges of lawlessness and denial of rights, it is piquant to notice the following not very complimentary remarks about Northern nullification of the Constitution a generation ago:

"In my opinion nothing has delayed effective enforcement of the 18th Amendment more than disregard of the law by men and women in high position, and people holding public office who have only opposed the law and talked in a loud voice about 'something good' they had just bought from their own private bootlegger.

"In New York State open opposition to and disregard of the law by the head of our state government and a recent representative at Washington has made it appear to the general public that the law was wrong and not to be obeyed." D. M. Hazelton, U. S. Commissioner, in W. C. Durant, editor and publisher, *Law Observance,* New York, 1929, p. 284.

A parallel to this might have been noticed in Northern communities at the time of the "reverse freedom rides" in 1962. In Concord, N.H. (pop. 29,200), for example, the prospect that thirty-five Negroes were coming was enough to cause public agitation. "A consensus of Concord residents questioned," said the Concord *Monitor* of July 2, "revealed hate, suspicion and anger directed . . . primarily against the Negroes themselves . . . Most persons expressed themselves differently, but . . . seemed to agree with a service station attendant who thought the Negroes 'ought to be shoved back on the bus and sent back where they belong.' " An editorial in the paper July 7 sagely observed: "Most in this community have casually favored equal rights for black or white. But the prospect that our sincerity in this might be tested has shown us how superficial our pretensions have been and how different are our instincts."

[49] To say, "But there are white people, too, who are repugnant," is beside the mark; for it is not disputed that anyone can reject them—how they *are* rejected! Yet though you can do this to them, merely on the ground of your displeasure, or indeed on unstated grounds, you must not do it to Negroes. If people are left free, Negroes will find their natural place, like others, which may mean that some will be admitted where now they are not admitted. Integrationists want to force this, not seeing or not caring that it is a denial of nature and the death of freedom.

INDEX